Keywords of
Nineteenth-Century Art

For D.P.A.

Keywords of Nineteenth-Century Art

Christine Lindey

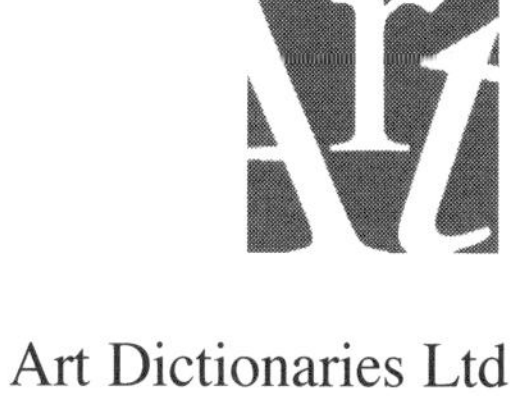

Art Dictionaries Ltd

First published in 2006 by Art Dictionaries Ltd,
81G Pembroke Road, Bristol BS8 3EA

© Christine Lindey

ISBN–10 0 9532609 33 (hardback)
ISBN–10 0 9532609 17 (softback)
ISBN–13 978-0-9532609-3-5
ISBN–13 978-0-9532609-1-1

British Library Cataloguing in Publication Data
A catalogue record for this book is available from The British Library

Designed by Stephen Morris Communications, smc@freeuk.com
and printed by MPG Books Ltd., Bodmin, Cornwall

Contents

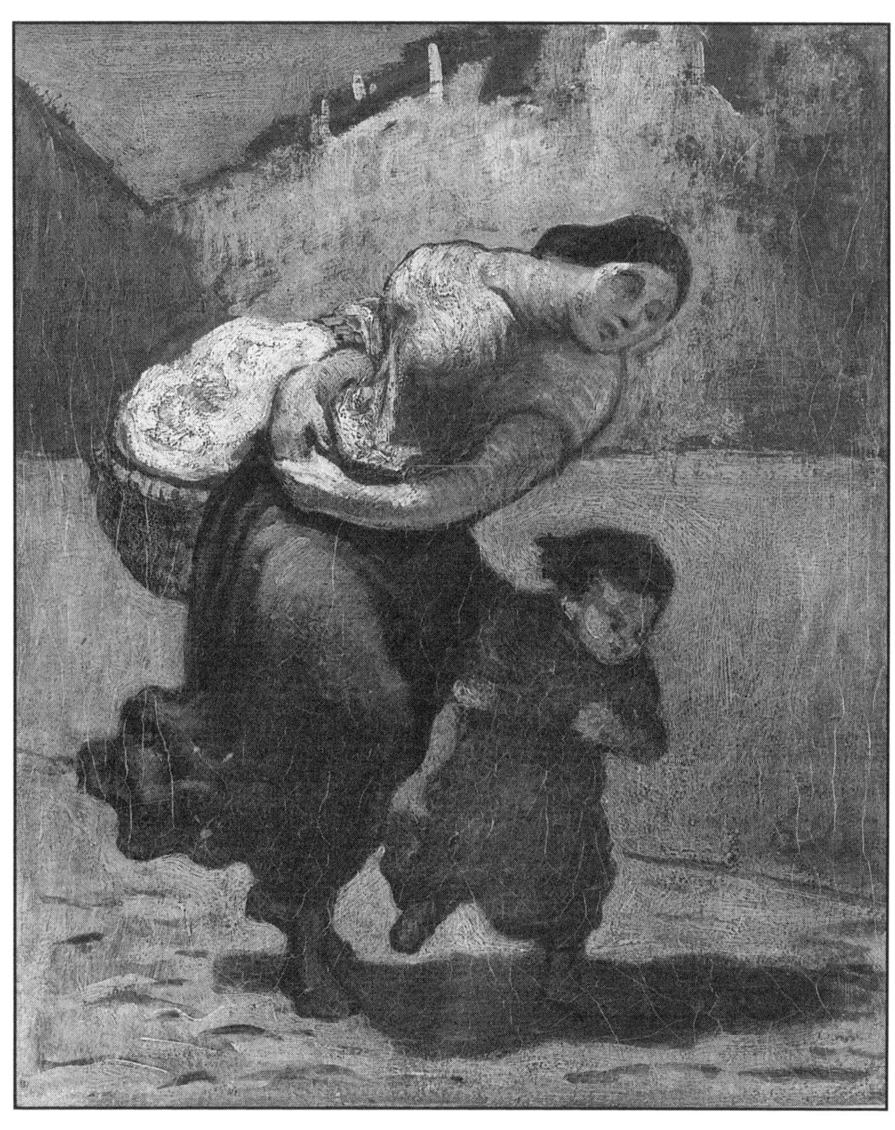

The Burden, Honoré Daumier, oil on canvas
[National Gallery in Prague]

Acknowledgements

If Carol Mann had not encouraged me to resume writing, this book would truly not have been written. I would also like to thank my family and friends, especially Bob Duncan, Leo Galbraith, Diana Lloyd, Lynn MacRitchie, June Redfern and the late Martin Owler for having a faith in my abilities that far outstrips my own.
To Daniel Ahern a special thank you.

I much appreciate the support and stimulation given by my students and colleagues at West Herts College, the London College of Communication, University of the Arts (formerly the London College of Printing, London Institute) and Birkbeck College, University of London. The librarians in these institutions as well as at the National Art Library, London and at the London Library were very helpful. Finally I would like to thank my editor Kathleen McLauchlan for her tact and good humour.

Christine Lindey, October 2005.

Introduction

THIS BOOK OFFERS AN INTRODUCTION TO THE THEORY AND PRACTICE OF FINE ART in the nineteenth century (c.1800-1900) via a discussion of fifty key terms. These are selected to explain the social structures and institutions, the aesthetic concepts, the subject matter and the formal means which conditioned artists' works and professional lives. The book thus avoids the hackneyed definition of major movements or artists' groups, preferring to discuss these through diverse attitudes to each keyword; for example, the differing attitudes of the Romantic, Barbizon, and Symbolist artists and their publics to exhibitions, landscape, drawing and the antique.

Each essay is organised chronologically to explore the changing meanings and/or status of the terms within a shifting socio-historical and aesthetic context. They are built around copious contemporary quotations, which are primarily selected from the journals, letters, lectures and critical writings of art students, artists, artist/teachers and artist/critics. These are augmented with the views of influential writers and thinkers. Existing anthologies of such texts have provided me with an invaluable resource, especially the following: Charles Harrison and Paul Wood, *Art in Theory, 1815-1900: An Anthology of Changing Ideas*; Craig Harrison, *The Essence of Art: Victorian Advice in the Practice of Painting*; Joshua C. Taylor, *Nineteenth Century Theories of Art*; Lorenz Eitner, *Neoclassicism and Romanticism, 1750-1850: Sources and Documents*; Herschel B. Chipp, *Theories of Modern Art, a Source Book by Artists and Critics*; Elizabeth Gilmore Holt, *The Triumph of Art for the Public, The Emerging Role of Exhibitions and Critics*, and by the same author, *From the Classicists to the Impressionists, Art and Architecture in the 19th Century*. For these I am profoundly grateful. The notes provide brief references to the original sources of selected texts (titles and summary dates), but for further details the reader will need to refer to the relevant book.

The quotations are drawn from a wide range of sources but the writings of a few individuals such as Stendhal and Van Gogh are frequently quoted. Chosen to exemplify particular historical, geographical, socio-political and aesthetic tendencies, these provide familiar pivotal figures to help guide the reader through a highly populated and fast changing art world. The views of anonymous or named contemporary journalist-critics such as Paul de Saint-Victor are very occasionally cited to elucidate matters of taste but the main intention is to provide an understanding of nineteenth-century art from the point of view of those who had personal experience of the creative process.

A range of European and North American art is discussed but the emphasis is on French and, to a lesser degree, British art. These were the two dominant world powers politically, economically and culturally. France was particularly influential within the visual arts because strong state support created the institutions which provided the theoretical, educational and formal models which were emulated by much of the rest of the developed world.

Academic art and the views of its conservative champions are considered alongside the work and opinions of avant-garde artists to convey the major aesthetic debates and public tastes of the century. The struggles of women artists to overcome social and professional exclusions are discussed in relation to the prevailing male-dominated norms. Regrettably, the mass-produced visual art of the age (posters, photographs, illustrations etc.) has been omitted due to lack of space. The focus is on painting rather than sculpture because this was the main area of critical and public interest in its own day.

The book aims to avoid obscure jargon. French words have been translated as far as possible but have been kept in the original language for those specialised terms which have no adequate English equivalent (e.g. *mise en trait*). The information can be accessed in a flexible manner. Associated ideas are appended to each term guiding the reader towards further, multiple readings without imposing an overly didactic format, so that the book may provide quick reference, a rich source of quotations as well as an overall insight into the major preoccupations of nineteenth-century art and artists.

Academy

IN STUDIO PARLANCE AN 'ACADEMY' CAME TO MEAN a type of highly finished, idealised DRAWING from the naked model. This was an exercise that art students had to master if they were to be accepted into the educational establishments supervised by the various national academies of art. The wider application of the word was to the art institutions, usually modelled on France's Académie des Beaux-Arts (Academy of Fine Arts), which existed throughout Europe, its colonies and ex-colonies. These powerful bodies provoked successive generations of students and artists into rebellion, frustrated as they were by the tyranny which academies exercised over the education and careers of artists through their control of public commissions, awards and public exhibitions – the means by which reputations were made or broken. David ended a speech to the National Convention in 1793 with an attack on academies and their members:

> **If there is someone among you, citizens, who must still be convinced of the absolute necessity of destroying wholesale all the Academies, those last refuges of aristocracy, then let him give me his attention... Let me demonstrate, to begin with, what damage the Academies do to art itself, how far they are from fulfilling the purpose which they have set themselves. Let me unmask the party spirit which guides them, the vile jealousies of their members, the cruel methods which they use to stifle nascent talent, and the monkish revenge which they wreak on the persecuted student to whom, by mischance, nature has given a talent which removes him from their tyrannical domination... In the name of humanity, in the name of justice for those who love art, and, above all, in the name of your love of youth: let us destroy, let us annihilate those sinister Academies. They must not be allowed to exist in the reign of liberty.[1]**

In 1814 the German Nazarene Friedrich Overbeck wrote of an artists' petition to Prince Metternich:

> **This petition...demonstrates that the academies have operated in a manner not advantageous but, rather, detrimental to the advancement of art, and it urges the German princes to reappropriate for the production of artworks the large sums of money that are so uselessly squandered on the academies.[2]**

Later on in the nineteenth century Renoir confided his thoughts to his notebook:

> **They ought to have cheaply-priced inns in luxuriant surroundings for those in the decorative arts. I say inns; but, if you wish, schools minus teachers. I don't want my pupils to be polished up any more than I want my garden to be tidied up.**
>
> **Young people should learn to see things for themselves.[3]**

At the root of opposition expressed by innovators like Renoir were the aesthetic values of France's Académie des Beaux-Arts: its emphasis on maintaining high intellectual values; its adherence to rigid hierarchies of subject matter, with HISTORY PAINTING at the pinnacle; its valuing of drawing and FINISH over colour and spontaneity.

The idea that art could be discussed and taught as an intellectual discipline akin to literature dates back to sixteenth-century Italy, where it was taken up by institutions like the Accademia di San Luca in Rome. Established in 1593, this is the oldest surviving academy. However, it was France's Academy, founded in Paris in 1648 (with a branch in Rome from 1666), which was the most influential.

This institution underwent significant structural changes between its foundation and the nineteenth century, though its underlying principles remained relatively constant. In 1793, during the revolutionary period, it was abolished. The cultural life of the Republic was entrusted to the Institut Français, an institution made up of a body of intellectuals and artists who would serve in an honorary capacity. Its aesthetic mission was to bring the purity of Greek and Roman art and morals to the new French Republic. In 1803 the fine arts section, dominated by David, was granted independent status, and it retained strong powers over the ÉCOLE DES BEAUX-ARTS in Paris, its provincial counterparts and the Académie de France (French Academy) in Rome.

With the Restoration in 1815 the Academy's role was formally defined: although it still had no active teaching role, it appointed the professors in both the Paris and Rome schools (and in practice these tended to be members of the Academy); it supervised state awards, including the all-important PRIX DE ROME, it organised the Salons and acted as the consultant to the government in matters of art. It was to retain these controls over artists' careers through much of the century, although it was no longer all-powerful by its closing decades. Hence the passions, often negative, which it aroused. In 1816 the fine arts section was renamed the Académie des Beaux-Arts, and from then on the terms Institut and Académie were often used interchangeably to refer to the same institution.

The Romantics' belief in innate GENIUS led to their almost universal distrust of the idea that art could be codified or taught. Most of them were impatient with the repression of emotion engendered by the academies. However, early in the century Géricault's critique focused on the Academy's stifling of genius by its over-nurturing of the young. Why, he wondered, was there such a dearth of talent, when modern France provided opportunities for study unmatched by ancient Athens and Rome? He concluded that these very facilities and awards attracted people into the profession who would not otherwise have bothered. The efforts of a well-intentioned government to nurture talent was in fact misguided, since for the young to follow identical paths of study for years on end was inimical to the development of that originality which Géricault saw as essential to genius:

> **…although obstacles and difficulties frighten mediocre men, they are the necessary food of genius… The Academy, alas, does too much: it extinguishes the sparks of this sacred fire, it smothers it, not granting nature the time to allow it to catch. A fire must be nurtured, yet the Academy throws on too much fuel.**[4]

Géricault's notion that formulistic teaching led to mediocrity epitomised the outlook of the Romantic movement:

> **Like a swarm of maggots, crawling from a rotting cheese, a countless mob of artists crawls from the Academies. In these… reigns a despotism which permits only what can be seen every day to enter the students' brains. Mindless drawing after plaster casts and models goes on for years; the goal is not truth to nature but an abstract aesthetic mannerism which kills all character… Such empty busywork is aptly named academic.**[5]

These views, expressed by the Tyrolese painter Joseph Anton Koch, were echoed by Eugène

Delacroix when he set about listing terms and definitions to be included in his unrealised dictionary of art: '...*Academies*. What Voltaire says of them, that they have never produced the greatest men.'[6] In his journals he was frequently dismissive of any school's ability to teach much. He cited the Carracci, whose sixteenth-century schools were seen to have been the first academies, as offering dry teachings which could not fail but engender tasteless and shallow works far too concerned with copying than with listening to the artist's own inspiration and passions. This Romantic stress on the individual (male) genius was bound to conflict with the social and universal ideal established by David's Republicanism. Yet Delacroix, like Corot, was elected to the Academy – albeit belatedly. He was thus well placed to point out the corruption and chicaneries inherent within such an institution, which were so conducive to mediocrity:

> **Yesterday, we elected that insipid Signol to the Institute. Meissonier got as many as sixteen votes, and thus the only people left to compete with him were Signol and that antiquated old Hesse, both of them representatives, or offspring, of the *École*. But shuddering at the idea of seeing an original talent enter the Academy, these two groups joined forces to destroy him. This was done at the price of Signol's election.[7]**

Similar institutions were established from the mid-eighteenth century in Europe and its colonies, the first in the Americas being that in Mexico in 1785. Most shared values similar to those of France's Académie des Beaux-Arts, although there were differences. For example, in 1768 the Royal Academy in England was founded by artists rather than by the state, though it depended on aristocratic patronage and continued to do so throughout the nineteenth century. In contrast, the American painter Samuel F.B. Morse, founder and first president of the National Academy of Design in New York (established in 1825), set out an alternative set of ideals. He insisted that it should be run by artists for artists, and was contemptuous of the notion of patronage in its Old World sense of dependence on aristocratic protection. He equated the independence of the artist with the independence of the individual within a Republic, as opposed to the servility of the individual within an aristocratic state:

> **...the artists of the National Academy have some sense of character to be deadened, some pride of profession to be humbled, some aspirings after excellence in art to be brought down, some of the independent spirit of their country to lose, before they can be bent to the purposes of such an anti-republican institution.[8]**

Not all innovators were hostile to the academies. Constable, for example, who had been taught at the Royal Academy and won associate membership in 1819, felt slighted that the honour of full membership was delayed until 1829, as his friend Leslie recalled:

> **That this distinction should not have been conferred on him at a much earlier period of his life is a proof that the progress of an original style of art, in the estimation even of artists, is very slow. Much as he was pleased at the attainment of this honour, he could not help saying, 'it has been delayed until I am solitary, and cannot impart it' ...[9]**

Even Delacroix was ambivalent – critical of the Academy yet aware of the professional clout which membership brought: 'This election is none the worse for being long delayed: the difficulty I had in winning it increases its value for me.'[10] He felt that his progressive views could now have some influence, as although he had not been made a professor at the École des Beaux-Arts he would be a member of the Salon jury: 'I like to think that I may be of some use there, for I shall find hardly anyone to share my views, and it will be most necessary not to be ill.'[11]

During the bourgeois reigns of Louis-Philippe (1830-48) and the Emperor Napoleon III (1852-70), members of the Academy tended to dilute the severe Neo-classicism insisted on by Davidian academic theory. A policy of neutralising opposition by gradual and limited absorption had begun. Hence in 1855, for the Fine Arts section of the Exposition Universelle in Paris, Ingres, Delacroix, Vernet and Decamps were chosen as the leading exponents of 'the major styles' which coexisted in France, and were each given a retrospective. Courbet was one of the few major artists who consistently eschewed the professional advantages which the Academy offered. Having refused to study within the École des Beaux-Arts as a young man, he had continued to assert his artistic freedom. To his horror he was named Chevalier of the Legion of Honour in 1870 by the new Republican government. He wrote to the Minister of Arts, refusing the award:

> **I am fifty years old and I have always lived in freedom. Let me end my life as a free man. When I am dead, they must be able to say of me, 'That one never belonged to any church, to any institution, to any academy, and above all to any regime except the regime of liberty.'**[12]

The following year during the Paris Commune, as President of the Artists' Committee, Courbet abolished the Academy. But the Commune was soon crushed and with it such policies.

The process of neutralising opposition by assimilation of the least controversial aspects of new tendencies was continued during the Third Republic, when there were plans to ask Millet and Moreau to help in decorating the Panthéon, while Manet, Carolus-Duran and others were to decorate the Trocadéro.

A similar softening of aesthetic dogma occurred elsewhere during the last decades of the century. In Russia, for example, the painter Ilya Repin pointed out the changes in a letter to Diaghilev:

> **There is a big difference between the Academy of one hundred years ago and our present Academy. Back in the old days it suppressed individuality, now it encourages it. But it was always supreme in its understanding of the form of art because that was what it always studied – it was a conservatory for the study of form.**[13]

Yet for those who were excluded the century was one of continuing attempts to be accepted by the official academies. In England women could not win membership of the Royal Academy throughout the century despite its having had two women as founder-members in 1768. On several occasions women were proposed. Elizabeth Thompson was nominated and rejected three times (1879-1881): first, because of the Academy's definition of members in its founding charter as 'men of fair moral character,' and second, because 'the letter of the law as given in Article 1 of the Instrument does not provide for the election of women as members.'[14] Not till the 1920s was the first woman elected an associate member.

From the late 1840s women artists battled to study at the Royal Academy Schools, where they were only allowed to attend public lectures. Returning from one of these, Anna Mary Howitt expressed her regrets to the painter Barbara Bodichon:

> **Did I tell you I went one night to hear Leslie. [sic] Lecture at the Royal Academy. Oh!**

how terribly did I long to be a man so as to paint there. When I saw the first room all the students' easels standing about – lots of canvasses and easels against the walls,…a perfect atmosphere of inspiration, and then passed on into the second room hung around with the Academicians' inaugural pictures, one seemed to be stepping into a freer, larger, and more earnest artistic world – a world, alas! which one's womanhood debars one from enjoying – Oh I felt quite sick at heart.[15]

In 1859 a group of 38 progressive women petitioned each of the forty Royal Academicians to accept women students to its school. Pointing out that there were now more women artists compared to their rarity at the time of the Academy's foundation, the petition continued: '…it thus becomes of the greatest importance that they should have the best means of study placed within their reach.'[16] The exclusion of women from the proper study of drawing in all its branches left them at a disadvantage:

It is generally acknowledged that study from the Antique and from Nature, under the direction of qualified masters, forms the best education for the artist; this education is given in the Royal Academy to young men, and it is given gratuitously. The difficulty and expense of obtaining good instruction oblige many women artists to enter upon their profession without adequate preparatory study.[17]

This petition was rejected on the grounds that it would mean setting up a separate life class. However, one of the petitioners, Laura Herford, applied to the school in 1860 with a drawing which she initialled rather than giving her Christian name. She was accepted before her sex was discovered by an embarrassed administration and in July 1860 she was the first woman to enrol. In 1863 women were barred from the Academy's school. Feminist outcries led this rule to be revoked in 1867. Yet the Royal Academy continued to find obstacles. Only a few women were allowed entry and they were excluded from the all-important life drawing classes on the grounds of propriety. After many years of petitioning women were finally given their own life classes there in 1893, albeit with a partially draped model, by which time access to such classes elsewhere had become more widely available.

The situation in France was no better. Either through custom or through regulations there were no women students at the École des Beaux-Arts until 1897; nor were there any women on the Salon jury until 1898. There were no women members of the Académie des Beaux-Arts during the nineteenth century, and they were also absent from the organising committees of the Exposition Universelle and other important decision-making bodies.

In Germany a few exceptions were made for well-connected daughters, often of famous artists. For example, in 1814 Caroline Luise Seidler, grand-daughter of an impoverished Prussian aristocrat, was financed by the Archduke August to study at the Munich Academy for one year. She reminisced:

How happy was I in the event! Now could I liberate myself from oppressive, indeed overwhelming domestic circumstances; the beginning of an independent existence had been placed in my hands. An artist's life of freedom beckoned to me with all its magic; with its troubles, but with its rewarding, delightful undertakings as well. [18]

But officially the doors to all German academies remained closed to women until 1914. Similar situations existed elsewhere in Europe, although honorary membership was occasionally granted in exceptional cases. Rosa Bonheur, for example, was accorded this award by several academies, including those of Amsterdam (1854), Milan (1862) and Lisbon (1890). In the USA policies were more progressive. For example, the National Academy of Design in New York offered separate life classes for women in the last decades of the century. The Pennsylvania Academy of the Fine Arts accepted women into the life class from 1868, yet Thomas Eakins lost his teaching job there when he removed the loincloth from the male model in a mixed gender class in 1886.

Alternatives did exist and most bourgeois women until the last decades of the century were privately educated either with private tutors or in fee-paying schools of art for women. But all too often these were not highly regarded by the profession, which considered them to be little else than training for art as an accomplishment. In the last two decades of the century women flocked to the private *ateliers*, such as the Académie Julian in Paris, which offered serious art education to both sexes. Although such establishments sometimes called themselves academies they had no links with the prestigious state-supported institutions. Exceptionally, Germany had three state-subsidised art schools for women: in Berlin (founded 1867), in Munich (founded 1882) and in Karlsruhe (founded 1885). In England in the latter part of the century regional schools of art were founded and some, such as the Glasgow School of Art, had relatively egalitarian outlooks. In London the Slade School of Art was founded in 1871 as an independent art school, and its progressive policies gave women access to the life class and to some mixed-gender tuition. The painter/critic Charlotte Weeks enthused: 'Here for the first time in England, indeed in Europe, a public Fine Art School was thrown open to male and female students on precisely the same terms, and giving to both sexes fair and equal opportunities.'[19]

For working-class and petit-bourgeois boys and girls there were schools devoted to training artisans for the so-called lesser decorative and industrial arts, which offered basic drawing but no access to life drawing or to the theories and aesthetics of high art. These included the École Royale de Dessin et de Mathématiques in Paris, founded during the reign of Louis XV to train craftsmen, and the national network of Schools of Design in England, founded in the 1830s to raise standards of manufacture. A parliamentary enquiry into art education during the 1860s identified the South Kensington School of Art as having a major role in general art training: it enabled men and women to become teachers and encouraged knowledge of 'elementary drawing among the humbler classes, the mechanical classes.'[20] In 1863 special funding was granted 'in respect of students who are artisans, or who are engaged in some industrial occupation, or are preparing to be so, or who are teachers or governesses, or are preparing to become so.'[21]

It was often suggested that the decorative arts were most suited to middle-class women, since they had not the intellect or ambition for high art. For example, in a lecture delivered in 1864, Ruskin suggested that women could imitate but not innovate:

> **We cannot consider how education may fit them (women) for any widely extending duty, until we are agreed what is their true constant duty...the woman's power is for rule, not for battle, – and her intellect is not for invention or creation, but for sweet ordering, arrangement, and decision.**[22]

In France Louvrier de Lajolais (director of the École Nationale des Arts Décoratifs) argued that it would be dangerous to admit women to the École des Beaux-Arts, since the majority of them 'who would have modestly but usefully gained from an education, suitable to the industrial arts, would not be able to resist the provocative seduction of believing themselves to be called to high destinies.'[23]

It is easy to find artists' statements which denigrate academies as bastions of conservatism. Yet for a multitude of jobbing artists the academies were the cocoons which allowed them to make a living for the best part of the century. In 1860 the Royal Academy's annual report stated: 'Most artists practising and exhibiting in the present day have been students in the Royal Academy...at present full three fourths of the Members of the Academy have been trained in these schools.'[24]

The painter Odilon Redon expressed loathing of the Academy, yet acknowledged its importance:

> **I may now confide to you, after having thought over my abilities and strength during my entire life, that I was moved to go to the Academy by a sincere desire to take my place in the sequence of other painters, being a student as they had been, and awaiting approval and justice from others. I did not take into account the type of art which would move me, nor my own temperament.**[25]

By the closing decades of the century the influence of the academies was waning under pressure from a widening of art education and the growth of the commercial art market. Nevertheless, particularly in France, the close links between the Academy and the state continued to be of importance for obtaining teaching posts, public commissions and sales.

See: ANTIQUE, *ATELIER*, DRAWING, ÉCOLE DES BEAUX-ARTS, EXHIBITION, HISTORY PAINTING

[1] *Discours sur la Nécessité de supprimer les Académies*, Convention Nationale, séance du 8 Août 1793, in Eitner, I, pp. 116-7

[2] Letter to Wilhelm Sutter, Sept 1 1814, in Taylor, p. 166

[3] Renoir, p. 217

[4] Undated notebook, first published 1842, in Harrison and Wood, p. 26

[5] J.A. Koch, *Moderne Kunstchronik*, c.1798-1820, first published 1834, in Eitner, I, p. 119

[6] Journal entry, 11 Jan 1857, in Delacroix, 1995, p. 352

[7] *Ibid*, 25 Nov 1861, pp. 436-7

[8] An 'examination' of a published address by J. Trumbull, first published 1834, Harrison and Wood, pp. 270-1

[9] C.R. Leslie, *Memoirs of the Life of John Constable*, 1845, London, pp. 146-7

[10] Letter to Pérignon, 21 Jan 1857, in Delacroix, 1971, p. 340

[11] *Ibid*

[12] 23 June 1870, in Courbet, p. 379

[13] Late 1890s, Harrison and Wood, p. 924

[14] Royal Academy Election Book, in Cherry, p. 65

[15] c.1848, *ibid*, p. 56

[16] *Athenaeum*, 30 April 1859, in Cherry, *ibid*, p. 224

[17] *Ibid*, p. 224

[18] C.L. Seidler, *Erinnerungen und Leben*, Berlin, 1874, in Greer, p. 305

[19] 'Women at Work: the Slade girls', *Magazine of Art*, 1883, in Cherry, *op. cit.*, p. 58

[20] Minutes, 28 April 1864, Parliamentary Papers, in Orr, p. 193

[21] Minutes, 17 March 1863, Parliamentary Papers, *ibid*, p. 193

[22] J. Ruskin, *Sesame and Lilies*, in Orr, *op. cit.*, pp. 190-1

[23] Report, Conseil Supérieur des Beaux-Arts, 18 March 1891, in Sauer, p. 18

[24] Cherry, *op. cit.*, p. 56

[25] O. Redon, *À soi-même: journal, 1867-1915*, in Holt, 1986, p. 491

Anatomy

THE NINETEENTH-CENTURY ART ACADEMIES CONTINUED THE EIGHTEENTH-CENTURY practice of considering anatomy, alongside DRAWING from the ANTIQUE and drawing from the living model, to be an essential part of an artist's education. Academic theory viewed the human figure to be the main vehicle for conveying ideas and emotions, so it was vital that artists – history painters above all – understood its full potential.

The English painter Benjamin Robert Haydon devoted his life to promoting the grandness of HISTORY PAINTING to an unconvinced English public. In a lecture in 1835 he explained the academic norm: '...the human figure is the basis of all drawing.'[1] This was due to man's physical and mental supremacy over all other creatures. In turn anatomy was the basis of drawing. It was Haydon's experience of dissecting a lion as well as a human being which had shown him both these truths:

> **Man, being the principal vehicle of conveying ideas by his features and form; the *first* thing to ascertain is the immediate causes of his motion as a being directed by his will; the next, the great characteristic distinction of him as man,...and the last, which of these causes of motion are excited by any particular passion or intention.**[2]

Although it was not known how the intentions of the will were reflected by the body, it was possible to observe it and it was the artist's duty to represent it:

> **The bones are the foundation of the form, and the muscles and the tendons the means by which he moves them, as his passions or intentions excite him.**

> **Each particular passion will excite a given number of these means, and none more or less than are requisite; the rest will remain unexcited...**

> **When the mind is thoroughly informed of the means *beneath* the skin, the eye instantly comprehends the *hint* above it; and when any passion is wanted to be expressed, the means and their consequences (if the artist be deeply qualified) will be as complete in form, and as true in effect, as nature, and the idea represented will be doubly effectual by the perfection of the means of representation.**[3]

Some art students dissected human and animal corpses, and attendance at anatomy lectures was considered essential. There they had to learn to name all the bones, muscles and tendons, sometimes studying alongside medical students. They also worked from the skeletons, casts and *écorchés* (flayed figures) which were standard fixtures in most art schools as well as from books and prints of detailed anatomical drawings. These latter were of particular importance to women students who until the later decades of the century were mostly excluded from anatomy classes. The animal painter Rosa Bonheur told her official biographer of her early years:

> **I studied myology, osteology, and physiology of all kinds of beasts. That was good preparation for the dissections I'd do later on, when the love of art made me start hanging around slaughterhouses. I pored over anatomy books taking tons of notes and even making outlines to help me remember things.**[4]

Only as a successful artist did she get special police permission to wear men's clothes, enabling her to work in the blood-soaked environment of the abattoirs.

When the American Neo-classical sculptor Harriet Hosmer was refused admission to an anatomy class in Boston, she arranged to be taught anatomy by a doctor at the Medical College of St. Louis. This was one of the rare American institutions which permitted women to study anatomy or any other aspect of the human body, though attitudes to women in America were generally more enlightened than they were in Europe. In England, possibly the first women-only anatomy class was advertised in the *Art Journal* in 1868. In France as late as 1880, Marie Bashkirtseff (writing under the pseudonym of Pauline Orell) protested at the obstacles faced by women: not only were they excluded from free state education at the École des Beaux-Arts, but they could not go to the lectures in anatomy, perspective, aesthetics etc., '...which men can attend even if they do not belong to the school.'[5]

In an unusually open-minded decision Penn Medical University in Philadelphia allowed women to study anatomy for the first time in 1860. The lectures there formed part of the program of the city's ACADEMY of the Fine Arts, which was equally progressive in permitting its women students to attend. Eliza Haldeman, Mary Cassatt's fellow student, jokingly advised her father upon his health:

> **Ain't I learning physiology? I just wish I could tell you all the hard Latin words I know, the names of the foramins fosses fissures fibers and functions, but I will astonish you with these when I come home.**[6]

In 1876 Thomas Eakins, their erstwhile fellow student, was appointed to teach painting and anatomy in the same academy. He was unusual in that he personally presided over his students' dissections. Admitting to a journalist that such work was unpopular ('I don't know of anyone who doesn't dislike it...It is dirty enough work at the best'), he justified its importance in terms of the Realist's concern for unadulterated accuracy:

> **...we are considerably concerned about learning how to paint. For anatomy as such, we care nothing whatever. To draw the human figure it is necessary to know as much as possible about it, about its structure and its movements, its bones and muscles, how they are made, and how they act.... no one dissects to quicken his eye for, or his delight in, beauty. He dissects simply to increase his knowledge of how beautiful objects are put together to the end that he may be able to imitate them.**[7]

Such was the continuing respect accorded to the study of anatomy that even the anti-academic Camille Pissarro advised his son of its importance: '...go to the academy and seriously devote yourself to drawing the nude. To draw the figure, you have to know anatomy.'[8] Van Gogh, who was largely self-taught by copying from books of anatomy and drawing manuals, grumbled about them to his brother Theo – though he accepted their usefulness:

> **I am still working on Bargue's Cours de dessin....The models are outstanding. Meanwhile I am reading one book on anatomy & another on perspective which Mr. Tersteeg also sent me. These studies are demanding & sometimes the books are extremely tedious, but I think all the same that it's doing me good to study them.**[9]

In 1896, when the ÉCOLE DES BEAUX-ARTS finally (and still grudgingly) admitted women students, rules of social decorum led it to stipulate that the men and women study the human body, including anatomy, in separate classes. Full of excitement at this rare opportunity to study the discipline, Paula Modersohn-Becker wrote home to her parents in Germany:

> **I hope to learn many things, particularly as there is a marvellous course in anatomy, free at the École des beaux-arts, which will add to my insufficient knowledge of anatomy. The knee was explained to us in such a brilliant way with the help of exercises and illustrations. Nowhere else are we offered this, we young women.**[10]

See: ACADEMY, DRAWING, ÉCOLE DES BEAUX-ARTS, NUDE, TRUTH

[1] B.R. Haydon, Lectures on Painting and Design, 1844, in Harrison and Wood, p. 232

[2] *Ibid*, p. 233

[3] *Ibid*, p. 234

[4] Klumpke, pp. 120-1

[5] La Citoyenne, 20th Feb 1880, in Sauer, p. 8

[6] 4 Feb 1860, in Mathews, p. 24

[7] *Scribner's Monthly*, XVIII, Sept 1879, in Harrison and Wood, p. 650

[8] Pissarro, p. 52

[9] 24 Sept 1880, in Van Gogh, 1996, pp. 76-7

[10] 11 Jan 1900, in Sauer, p. 28

Antique

IT COULD BE ARGUED THAT FEW NINETEENTH-CENTURY ARTISTS WERE FREE of the influence of the antique. Throughout the entire century artists as diverse as David, Millet, Bouguereau, Carpeaux and Seurat were formed by it. Part of the *raison d'être* of the PRIX DE ROME was to provide the most talented students with the opportunity to study the antique at first hand; well-heeled gentlemen embarked upon the Grand Tour in order to have their taste developed by exposure to its beneficial influence, and poorer art students from San Francisco to St Petersburg drew endlessly from the plaster casts of approved antiquities displayed by any self-respecting ACADEMY. Furthermore, the major museums boasted collections of original works, laboriously brought back by mules and sailing ships from the ruins of ancient Greece and the Roman Empire. Works such as the *Venus de Milo* (Louvre, Paris), the *Laocoön* (Vatican Museum, Rome), or the frieze and pediment of the Parthenon (British Museum, London) became part of a common visual currency.

Although the word antique tended to be reserved for such sculptures it might also be used interchangeably with 'ancients', although this latter term tended to include the broader field of classical poets such as Homer, as well as High Renaissance artists such as Raphael and

Michelangelo, who were seen as having re-energised the Greco-Roman classical tradition. Hence Ingres's declaration in 1818:

> **In matters of art, I am what I have always been. Age and reflection have, I hope, confirmed my taste, without diminishing its ardour. I still worship Raphael, his century, the ancients, and above all the divine Greeks.**[1]

Ingres's ideas were formed first in David's studio, where an entrance requirement was that students be literate in Latin so that they could read the classics, and then at the French Academy in Rome. Delécluze, another of David's students around the turn of the eighteenth and nineteenth centuries, recalled one of his master's pronouncements:

> **I want to make *pure Greek* work; I nourish my eyes on antique statues, I intend to even imitate a few. The Greeks had no scruples about reproducing a pre-existing composition, a movement or a type... They were right to believe that the idea in the arts lies more in the way in which it is rendered, in which it is expressed, than in the idea itself. To give the perfect appearance and form to one's idea is to be an artist.**[2]

For David antiquity – in particular Republican Rome – was also a source of powerful political and moral ideals. In contrast, Ingres's depoliticised vision of the antique was largely based upon Winckelmann's concept of art as the provider of an unblemished ideal, which found its purest embodiment in the white marble of ancient Greek sculpture. If the artist's job was to improve upon nature, an education steeped in the understanding of classical art would equip him/her to do so when confronted by the living model.

Although such ideals continued to hold sway during the waning years of Neo-classicism, they were to come under frequent attack throughout the century, as writers and artists called for greater MODERNITY and realism. These demands, which were initiated by the Romantics, inevitably involved an attack on the supremacy of the antique, as in Stendhal's 1824 Salon:

> **The battle lines have already been drawn. The *Journal des Débats* are going to be Classical, and swear only by David, crying out that *any painted figure must be a copy of a statue*, and that spectators should admire this, even if it bores them rigid. *Le Constitutionnel*, by contrast, has come out with some beautiful, slightly vague phrases, no doubt a sign of the times; but at least it has decided to defend a few new ideas. It has had the audacity to proclaim that art should take a step forward, even after David, and that there is more to painting than simply reproducing a large quantity of beautifully drawn muscles.**[3]

Yet the classical tradition had an enduring power. When Victor Hugo outlined Romanticism's modern spirit, identifying the grotesque as the defining characteristic of the new art, he did so in terms of justifying a move away from the canons of classicism:

> **...the modern spirit is born out of this fecund union of the categories of the grotesque and the sublime: a spirit complex, and infinitely varied in its manifestations, inexhaustible in its creativity, totally opposed to the uniform simplicity of the genius of the Ancients.**[4]

Similarly, despite his fierce espousal of the 'moderns' for his subject matter, the highest praise Delacroix could find for the local population in his travels to Tangier was that they resembled the 'ancients':

Imagine, my friend, what it is to see lying in the sun, walking about the streets, cobbling shoes, figures like Roman consuls, like Cato or Brutus, not even lacking that disdainful look which those rulers of the world must have worn; these people possess only a single blanket in which they walk about, sleep or are buried, and they look as satisfied as Cicero must have been in his curule chair... There's nothing finer in classical art.[5]

Yet he understood that the true danger from the Classicists was not so much their admiration for the antique, as their ossification of its principles:

I have Romans and Greeks on my doorstep: it makes me laugh heartily at David's Greeks, apart, of course, from his sublime skill as a painter. I know now what they were really like; their marbles tell the exact truth, but one has to know how to interpret them, and they are mere hieroglyphs to our wretched modern artists. If painting schools persist in setting Priam's family and the Atrides as subjects to the nurslings of the Muses, I am convinced, and you will agree with me, that they would gain far more from being shipped off as cabin boys on the first boat bound for the Barbary coast than from spending any more time wearing out the classic soil of Rome.[6]

Moreover, despite their tendency to admire the 'moderns', in that they took their subject matter from writers such as Shakespeare and Byron and looked at the Venetian painters and Rubens, many of the Romantics – including Delacroix – continued to respect the ancients as artists:

Raphael is halting and graceful: the Antique is full of the unaffected grace we see in nature. Nothing is disturbing, nothing regrettable, nothing missing, nothing superfluous. Modern artists can show no examples of an art like this.[7]

The traditionalists continued to wield major influence, partly due to their entrenched positions within the academies. In France, Ingres never compromised in his belief that the modern spirit of independence was harmful to the arts, a view expressed in his notebooks between c.1820 and 1848:

Homer was the first to reveal through poetry the beauties of nature... He...established the beautiful through precepts and through immortal examples... Later on, in the great modern periods, men of genius did over what had been done before them...

It is error then; error to believe that health for art resides in absolute independence; to believe that our natural disposition runs the risk of being stifled by the discipline of the ancients; that the classic doctrines impede or arrest the flight of the intelligence. Quite the contrary: they favour its development, they render its strength more certain and fructify its aspirations; they are a help and not a hindrance... What do you mean, what is it you come to preach to me with your pleadings in favour of the 'new'? Outside of nature there is no such thing as the new...; outside of art, as it was understood and practised by the ancients, ...there can be nothing but caprice and aimless wandering.[8]

Countless artists stressed the importance of the ancients in their education. For example, the British painter William Frith recalled his teacher Sass taking students to see the Raphael Cartoons, which were then in Hampton Court Palace, where he would deliver a lecture:

He always made us remove our hats on entering the room, and then in solemn tones, as if he were at church, he would expatiate on the wonders before him.[9]

Until the last quarter of the century classical art was of particular importance for women artists who were struggling to find an adequate art education. Finding the doors of the official academies closed to them, they were free to work from the antiquities to be found in the new museums of art – albeit under the restriction of being chaperoned, as Rosa Bonheur recalled:

...after my father died, my only teachers were the artists in the Louvre and good Nature herself. Memories of those artists combined for me with nature's teachings.

That's why I would happen to think about the Parthenon friezes while in a crowd of horse dealers trying out their beasts.[10]

Bonheur was unusual in that her progressively minded father had agreed to her working in the Louvre unchaperoned. For the Morisot sisters, born into the haute bourgeoisie, this was out of the question, yet they too began their serious studies from classical art in the Louvre. When their private art teacher Guichard realised that they intended to go beyond 'minor drawing room accomplishments,' he advised their mother that they must apply for permission to work in the Louvre: 'I shall give them lessons from the masters.'[11]

Guichard's lessons began in 1858. Yet after two years, sensitive to the changing outlooks of the times, Morisot felt a compelling desire to work from NATURE and asked to be taught by Corot. In the 1850s and 1860s the Realists and Naturalists followed the Romantics in seeking to evade the stranglehold of the antique by turning directly to the observation of nature. One of Monet's early experiments in naturalism (a drawing of a studio model) brought reproaches from his teacher, Charles Gleyre:

...it is too much in the character of the model – you have before you a short thickset man, you paint him short and thickset – he has enormous feet, you render them as they are. All that is very ugly. I want you to remember, young man, that when one draws a figure, one should always think of the antique.[12]

The battle was by no means over. In his defence of Manet in his 1867 Salon, Émile Zola still had to justify his criticism of the antique:'Circumstances have elected that the Classical Greek should be regarded as the standard of beauty, so that all works of art created by mankind have ever since been judged on their greater or lesser resemblance to Greek works of art.' After pointing out that this doctrine ignores the fact that for two thousand years the world and its various societies have been constantly changing and producing different artists, he scoffs at the doggedness with which this ideal is still clung to:

...but what of that! The 'absolute' of beauty is there, unchangeable, dominating the centuries. All life, all passions, all that creative energy which has enjoyed itself and suffered for two thousand years is miserably crushed under this idea.[13]

The influence of the antique carried on within art education and in academic and official art until the end of the century and beyond. Furthermore, as figures by Courbet, Millet and Rodin show, it lay so deep within the early modernists' psyches that they often continued to follow its proportions, compositional devices and poses even while believing that they were breaking from it. Odilon Redon perceptively realised that even the landscapes of the Barbizon painter, Camille Corot, retained the sentiment of the classical in their essential purity:

We shall always credit him with that rare quality, harmony of line, the last glow of

antiquity. While others, so-called *néo-grecs*, full of archaeology, have taken from the antique nothing but a heavy baggage of meaningless furniture, costumes and accessories,...he managed to revive its penetrating grace, through the superior force of his temperament.[14]

Such was the power of the antique that it also influenced artists by default. For example, Courbet felt he had to challenge classical ideals, and the *Bathers* of 1853 was envisaged in part as a critique of the antique, albeit closer to it than he realised. The naturalism initiated by Manet and the Impressionists can also be seen in relation to the long debate about the idealised, antique NUDE. Pissarro warned his son against blind acceptance of traditional rules:

I can see no harm in drawing the nude, the figure, if you are permeated with the idea of not following Legros in the field of Greek theory, and are resolved not to seek formulas, not to be influenced by *apt pupils*, not to *fix proportions in advance*, in a word if you can learn to see for yourself and to draw without relying on a ready made system.[15]

The academies clung to the importance of the antique. In the mid 1880s, during the short period of formal art education which he endured, Van Gogh struggled with the demands of an irritable drawing master at the Antwerp Academy. In one of his letters to Theo, he complained about the probable response to his latest work, a drawing from a plaster cast of a famous Roman sculpture:

I finished just yesterday the drawing which I made for the competition of the evening class. It is the figure of Germanicus which you know. Well, I am sure I shall come out bottom, because all the drawings of the others are utterly alike, and mine is absolutely different. But that drawing which they will think the best, I have seen how it was done. I was sitting just behind it and it is correct, it is whatever you like, but it is *dead*, and that is what all the drawings are which I saw.[16]

As late as 1879 Eakins was considered daringly adventurous in stressing the importance of direct, unidealised studies from the model, unmediated by reference to the Antique. An anonymous journalist reported a discussion with him:

The Greeks did not study the antique: the 'Theseus' and 'Ilyssus', and the draped figures in the Parthenon pediment were modelled from life, undoubtedly. And nature is just as varied and just as beautiful in our day as she was in the time of Phidias...Practically, copying Phidias endlessly dulls and deadens a student's impulse and observation. He gets to fancying that all nature is run on the Greek mould; that he must arrange his model in certain classical attitudes, and paint its individuality out of it; he becomes prejudiced, and his work rigid and formal. The beginner can at the very outset get more from the living model.[17]

As Van Gogh's letter shows, by the closing two decades of the century, the tradition was largely discredited among modernists. Far less steeped in the classics than their forbears, artists and public were increasingly used to naturalism and preoccupied by modernity. Yet it is worth recalling that Rodin, who died in 1917, left his valuable collection of ancient art to the French nation. Moreover, in the early years of the twentieth century the modernist Matisse, himself educated in the *ATELIERS* of Gérôme and Moreau at the ÉCOLE DES BEAUX-ARTS during the 1890s, would advise his own students to study the antique:

...antique sculpture, above all, will help you to render the fullness of form. Straight away I see this torso as a single and unique form, as an entity. In the antique all parts are considered equally. From this springs unity and tranquility of the mind.[18]

See: ACADEMY, *ATELIER*, BEAUTY, ÉCOLE DES BEAUX-ARTS, NUDE, NATURE

[1] Delaborde, pp. 93-4

[2] Delécluze, p. 62

[3] 'Salon de 1824', *Journal de Paris*, 29 Aug 1824, in Harrison and Wood, pp. 30-1

[4] Preface to *Cromwell*, Paris, 1827, Harrison and Wood, p. 46

[5] Letter to J.B. Pierret, 29 Feb 1832, in Delacroix, 1971, pp. 187-8

[6] Letter to A. Jal, 4 June 1832, *ibid*, pp. 193-4

[7] Journal entry, 23 Feb 1858, in Delacroix, 1995, p. 403

[8] Ingres's notes and observations were collected and published by H. Delaborde, *op. cit.* The translation here is from Harrison and Wood, pp. 184-5

[9] N. Wallis, ed., *A Victorian Canvas: the Memoirs of W.P. Frith, RA*, 1957, p. 35

[10] Klumpke, p. 148

[11] Morisot, p. 19

[12] Rewald, pp. 70-1

[13] 'Une nouvelle manière en peinture: Edouard Manet', *L'Artiste: Revue du XIXe siècle*, 1867, in Harrison and Wood, pp. 557-8

[14] 'Salon de 1868', *La Gironde*, 19 May 1868, in Lemaire, p. 229

[15] 4 June 1883, in Pissarro, p. 52

[16] Jan 1886, in Van Gogh, 1963, p. 257

[17] 'The Art Schools of Philadelphia', *Scribner's Monthly*, XVIII, Sept 1879, in Harrison and Wood, pp. 648-9

[18] H. Matisse, 'Notes de Sarah Stein', 1908, in Matisse, p. 64

Atelier

IN FRANCE THE *ATELIER* FORMED AN ESSENTIAL PART OF THE ARTIST'S LENGTHY EDUCATION. It was often the first place to which an aspiring artist would go to be taught DRAWING as a means of gaining entry to the ÉCOLE DES BEAUX-ARTS. Having been accepted by that institution students still continued to attend private *ateliers* to practise drawing, to learn painting (which the École did not teach until 1863) and to prepare for the École's frequent competitions, the plum being the PRIX DE ROME. Masters who were also members of the ACADEMY tended to favour their own pupils in judging competitions. Rivalry between the *ateliers* was fierce and the masters would bask in the glory of their students' successes.

On entering a studio young artists learned elementary drawing. This entailed copying parts of the human body, at first from engravings and then from plaster casts of Greco-Roman sculptures. Only after they had mastered these skills were students allowed to draw from the live MODEL. Then came compositional study in the form of pencil and oil sketches. Finally they learned painting, mostly by copying in the Louvre. The teaching varied from the careless to the severe, with the master appearing perhaps once or twice a week to make corrections and pronouncements. Balze recalled that Ingres 'used to correct our drawings with his thumbnail, so surely and with such force that he often cut right through the paper, thus combining theory and practice.'[1]

In the early years of the century the tone had been set by the studio of David, with his stress on the importance of drawing and erudition as the twin bases of HISTORY PAINTING. He insisted that his students learned Latin and in general demanded a high standard of intellectual rigour. On his midday visits all the students would listen with respect as he pronounced general principles in relation to the first work he saw. His progressive outlook led him to accept women students (as did Regnault), though they were taught separately.

The influence wielded by the private studios was such that despite the formal organisation of teaching at the École des Beaux-Arts, it was primarily in the studios that the aesthetic and technical baton was handed on from master to pupil, as in the Renaissance workshops. For example, one of the Prix de Rome students from David's studio was Ingres. He in turn taught Henri Lehmann, who ran the studio where the young Seurat learned to draw. This was a sequence of masters and students which spanned the century. Furthermore the studios themselves tended to be handed on or taken over by ex-students or close colleagues, preserving their traditions: thus David's *atelier* was taken over by Gros, who was succeeded by Delaroche, who passed on the studio to Gleyre.

Once an artist established his name – through a major Salon success and/or membership of the Academy – he might open a private studio. This was a mark of status and also a steady source of income. Ingres, who achieved Salon success and Academy membership in 1824, soon opened a studio that attracted numerous pupils, including Amaury-Duval, Lehmann, Flandrin and Chassériau. In the following decade Drölling (a pupil of David and winner of the Prix de Rome) opened his busy studio in the same year that he was elected to the Academy in 1833. These academic *ateliers*, closely associated with the École des Beaux-Arts, were the most prestigious. During the July Monarchy, the leading studio was that of Delaroche, who taught such prominent artists as Couture, Millet, Daubigny, Monticelli, Gérôme and many Prix de Rome winners. Gérôme went on to establish his own highly successful studio (1864-1903), which had a name for highly precise drawing, so carrying on the academic tradition until the end of the century.

The studios, which averaged about 45 students, were hierarchical in their social organisation. At the top was the master, who was called the *patron*. Below him were the *compagnons* (senior painting students), who often assisted the *patron* with his own works and who also earned money by providing provincial churches etc with copies of old masters made in the Louvre. The daily life of the studio was managed by one of the students, the *massier*, so called because he was in charge of the *masse*, the studio finances. At the bottom were the *rapins* (novices). Usually all the students worked in only one room, though Delaroche's *atelier* had two. There was no fixed time span within which a student would remain at any particular level. Rivalries were intense, favouritism was common and all worked in the knowledge that victory in the Prix de Rome was extremely unlikely. Hence the students endured the rigidities and cruelties of the Renaissance studio without its benefit of a secure future career.

By the mid-nineteenth century the rigidity of this teaching system was increasingly being questioned. Redon, who as a student in Gérôme's *atelier* had a nervous breakdown and never enrolled at the École des Beaux-Arts, wrote of his time there with some bitterness: 'He so obviously tried to inculcate in me his own way of seeing and either to make me his disciple or disgust me with art altogether.'[2] From around this period many students remained with their master only until they had learned their trade, after which they opted out of the academic rat race, moving on to independent *ateliers* headed by non-academicians like Gleyre or Couture or to independent industrial art schools.

Couture opened his studio after having a major Salon success in 1847 with *Romans of the Decadence*. Hugely popular, it provided an alternative for students who wished to eschew the academic system, yet who wanted an academic teaching programme. Among its alumni were Puvis de Chavannes, William Morris Hunt and Manet, this last being one of the few students with whom the master clashed. Couture emphasised spontaneity, freshness of colour and the importance of the sketch, his maxim being: 'Give three minutes to looking at a thing and one to painting it.'[3] Even so, Couture's approach to teaching was dogmatic and his *atelier* came under attack from some quarters by the early 1860s. Antonin Proust recalled his days there alongside Manet:

> **Couture's *atelier* consisted of twenty-five to thirty students. As in all studios, each student paid a monthly subscription to study from the model, man or woman. Couture came to visit us twice a week; he glanced at our studies with a distracted eye, ordered a 'break', rolled himself a cigarette, told some stories about his master Gros, and then took himself off.**[4]

Couture closed his studio in 1861, after which he recorded his ideas on the teaching of art in the influential *Conversations on Art Methods*, published in 1867. Having sought the seclusion of a country village, he subsequently relented and took a few, mostly American, private students including Eliza Haldeman and Mary Cassatt.

In 1861 radical students asked Courbet to set up a Realist studio, and in December he complied, justifying the move in an open letter published in the *Courrier du Dimanche*:

> **I cannot...presume to open a school, to educate students, to teach this or that part of the artistic tradition. I can only explain to artists (who would be my associates and not my students) the method whereby, in my view, one becomes a painter – the one that I myself used from the beginning in order to become one – while leaving it to everyone [to choose] his entirely individual direction, the complete freedom of his own expression in the application of that method. To that purpose, the development of a group *atelier*, recalling the fruitful collaborations of the Renaissance *ateliers*, can certainly be useful.**[5]

The studio lasted only a few months. Courbet found it too time consuming and the landlord complained about the students' unruly behaviour and the studio's slovenly upkeep. In the interests of realism Courbet supplemented the human models with horses, oxen and deer, not very practical or hygienic given the studio's crowded premises in central Paris. As an ox lolled on hay surrounded by the students and their easels Courbet stalked up and down the room expounding his ideas on art. According to some, it was a chamber for political debate, yet the mere fact of the existence of a studio with no formal teaching was such a novelty that it was much discussed.

During the first half of the century there were limited opportunities for women students, apart from private drawing masters or private schools mostly aimed at teaching accomplishment art to upper-class men and women. There were a few exceptions. When David allowed women students into his *atelier* in the Louvre, he was reprimanded for impropriety by the arts minister, even though he kept the women separated from the men. Fired by revolutionary egalitarianism, David defended his position. By 1813 there were three serious *ateliers* in Paris where women could draw from the naked model, run by David, Regnault and Guérin. In 1850s London, Leigh's art school offered separate life classes for women, and was run along the lines of a Paris *atelier*. Sophia Beale studied there in the late 1850s and recalled 'the wondrous 'High Art' pictures all over the house... As to instruction we did very much what we liked with little correction and much talk and theory.' [6]

Petit bourgeois and working-class women were directed towards the free state schools for the decorative and industrial arts, where they could learn a useful trade. In 1849 Rosa Bonheur and her sister Juliette took over the directorship of the Drawing School for Girls, which had been run by their father. Yet overall the teaching on offer was over-priced and inferior to that available to men, as Marie Bashkirtseff complained in 1890:

> **We have municipal drawing schools which are adequate for those destined for industry but none for a truly artistic outlook, or else two or three fashionable *ateliers* where rich young ladies amuse themselves with a little painting.**

> **But what we need, is the possibility of working as men do without having to perform amazing feats to get what men simply get.** [7]

For those who could afford it, the only way of bypassing the official system was to seek private tuition from a major artist, often the head of a successful *atelier*. Cassatt studied in this way with Gérôme and Couture. By the latter part of the century many artists saw this as a lucrative source of income, opening *ateliers* (with life classes) exclusively for women. Often they provided inferior teaching at inflated prices, sometimes double the fees charged to male students. There were a few which were serious, for example that opened in Boston in the 1860s by William Morris Hunt, an ex-student of Couture, which was modelled on the Parisian *ateliers*.

Gleyre's independent *atelier* (1843-63), which was favoured by free spirits including Renoir, Bazille, Sisley and Whistler, was remarkably open in its *mores*. Despite his academic approach to drawing, Gleyre daringly allowed mixed-gender teaching even in the life class, but this was highly unusual. Another exceptional case was the Académie Julian, an independent – and highly prestigious – *atelier* opened in 1868. It employed many well-known artists from the École des Beaux-Arts, including Bouguereau, Chapu and Gervais, and so kept stringent academic standards. Its ex-students frequently won Salon medals, and Marie Bashkirtseff was full of praise: 'the last Salons have shown that women, so disdained, make valiant students and firmly carry high the flag of the free school, the Atelier Julian [sic] which has opened its doors to them.' [8] In fact, the Académie Julian stopped offering mixed-gender teaching in 1879, and by 1889 it had become so successful that it opened three new studios for women only – where it charged inflated rates. Yet its rigorous teaching standards and liberal atmosphere made a productive combination: its alumni included Sérusier (who was *massier* there), Bonnard, Denis, Vuillard, Matisse, Corinth, Cassatt and Robert Henri. Henri recalled his experiences there in the late 1880s:

> **...as I knew it, [it]...was a great cabaret with singing and huge practical jokes and, as such, was a wonder... It was a factory, too, where thousands of drawings were turned out.**
>
> **It is true, too, that among the great numbers of students there were those who searched each other out and formed little groups which met independently of the school, and with art as a central interest, talked and developed ideas about everything under the sun.**[9]

For many, the experience was a disappointment. Raffaëlli recalled his grim years in Gérôme's *atelier*:

> **Not once in this gathering of men called to be artists did I hear art discussed or serious ideas. Nothing but crude and stupid joking all the time, nothing but filth.**[10]

From the 1860s the rigidity of the academic road to success began to break down. Many artists, including Courbet, Pissarro, Cézanne and Monet, chose to attend only the more relaxed organisations. These included the Académie Suisse, established in 1815 by an ex-model of David's, which was cheap and where little more than a model, a stove for warmth and the camaraderie of fellow students were provided.

Whatever its weaknesses, the city's art education system had a world reputation for excellence, and the practice of private teaching in studios set up by professional artists was emulated abroad. Moreover, male and female artists from Europe and America flocked to the Parisian studios: Cassatt, Haldeman, Henri and Eakins, for example, all started their training at the Pennsylvania Academy before going on to Paris. Eakins studied with Gérôme, from whom Cassatt also took private lessons. Eliza Haldeman, a friend of Cassatt's, wrote to her father:

> **I have commenced taking drawing lessons from Mr. Schuchelle [sic], that is, one of the young ladies at the Academy and myself go to his Studio once a week, and have him criticise the drawings we made that week, almost all the Pupils at the Academy take lessons in this way. As for painting, I don't think I shall commence it at all this winter. They generally study from the Antique two winters before commencing, and one of the young gentlemen studied two and half years here, and then went to Paris to finish, when he got there they put him to copying for a year before they allowed him to commence painting...**[11]

Despite the many horror stories of humiliations and cruelties and the sheer mediocrity of the teaching or lack of it provided by the *ateliers*, many artists acknowledged a debt to their masters. Renoir and Bazille, for example praised Gleyre's atelier. Matisse, having experienced a series of mind-numbingly poor teachers, gratefully recalled Moreau's studio at the École des Beaux-Arts, which he entered in 1895:

> **What a charming teacher he was. He, at least, was capable of enthusiasm... Moreau**

knew how to discriminate and showed us who were the greatest painters, whereas Bouguereau convinced us that we should admire Jules Romain... In fact it's there that I learned to draw. [12]

See: ACADEMY, DRAWING, ÉCOLE DES BEAUX-ARTS, MODEL, NUDE, *RAPIN*

[1] R. Balze, *Ingres et son école*, 1880, in Lethève, p. 20

[2] O. Redon, *À soi-même*, 1922, *ibid*

[3] Boime, p. 74

[4] Edouard Manet, *Souvenirs*, 1913, in Courthion, p. 39

[5] Courbet, pp. 204-5

[6] S.S. Beale, *Recollections of a Spinster Aunt*, 1908, in Cherry, 1993, pp. 59-60

[7] *La Citoyenne*, 20 Feb 1880, in Sauer, pp. 7-8

[8] *Ibid*, p. 8

[9] R. Henri, *The Art Spirit*, 1923, in Chipp, p. 103

[10] Lethève, p. 19

[11] 4 Feb 1860, in Mathews, p. 24

[12] Matisse, pp. 80-1

Avant-garde

THE TERM AVANT-GARDE (OR VANGUARD) WAS A MILITARY TERM meaning a detachment which went ahead of the main force to engage the enemy in initial skirmishes. It was first used in relation to art by Saint-Simon in 1825 and its meaning has been fluid and contested ever since. Used as a noun it denoted a social group of artists, while as an adjective it referred to their work and ideas. But the demarcation between the social and critical realm was often hazy. It was intertwined with bohemianism and modernism. Broadly speaking it identified artists who challenged the mainstream by being independent, experimental, innovatory, non-conformist and controversial. The avant-garde artist was a rebellious outsider who made the art of tomorrow today.

The avant-garde raised crucial questions about the problematic function of art and the social position of artists in the newly industrialised capitalist society. Gauguin raged: 'What a strange and mad public it is that exacts from the painter the utmost originality and then only accepts him when he is like the others!'[1] In the twentieth century avant-garde art won a new identity as the mainstream of western art, and retrospectively defined its nineteenth-century ancestry in its own 'art for art's sake' image. Given its later importance it may be surprising to learn how rarely the term avant-garde was actually used in the nineteenth century, when the words 'independent', 'intransigent' and 'Impressionist' were more frequently employed.

Avant-garde art was originally understood to have a political function. When Henri de Saint-Simon, an early French Socialist, first used the term in relation to art, he contrasted the social role of the scientist and the artist and concluded that artists must form a vanguard to spread the ideas of social progress:

The Savant...respects only rigorous reasoning and positive results, and considers the Artist

a somewhat wild spirit... We Artists...attach no great value to the work of the Savants... Let us unite. To achieve our one single goal, a separate task will fall to each of us.

We, the artists, will serve as the avant-garde: for amongst all the arms at our disposal, the power of the Arts is the swiftest and most expeditious. When we wish to spread new ideas amongst men... We aim for the heart and imagination, and hence our effect is the most vivid and the most decisive.[2]

Writing this in the last year of his life, during the stifling political climate of the July Monarchy, Saint-Simon was looking towards a Socialist future as an alternative to capitalism. His text went on to anticipate political change: 'If today our role seems limited or of secondary importance, it is for a simple reason: the Arts at present lack those elements most essential to their success – a common impulse and a general scheme.'[3]

The roots of avant-garde art lay in the Romantics' preoccupation with GENIUS, originality and individual freedom. The artist was viewed as a leader, an extraordinary being who was made so by having to draw upon his or her own inner resources. The breakdown of aristocratic patronage caused by the political and industrial revolutions of the late eighteenth century and beyond led to a search for a new role for art and artists. The anonymous market place thirsted for novelty, but within the boundaries of established aesthetics and conventional social and moral outlooks. Superhuman and contradictory demands were made of artists. They were expected both to be sensitive to the demands of the market place and to be geniuses who disdained merely material matters and concerned themselves solely with the elevated planes of originality and philosophical truths.

Most artists conformed, but those who questioned the prevalent cultural and social norms were consciously at odds with society. The bohemian was born. Calling the bourgeoisie philistine, the Romantics claimed the right to personal as well as artistic freedom. They lived wild and free, cross-dressed, cohabited, practised free love, dressed eccentrically, and generally delighted in opposing established authority in their social behaviour. The term bohemian referred to travelling people whose original home was thought to have been Bohemia. Rebellious artists and intellectuals of the early nineteenth century identified themselves with these rootless outsiders, often in a spirit of youthful high jinks. Balzac summed it up:'The Bohême consists of young people, who are still unknown, but who will be famous one day.'[4] Once famous they often rejoined the bourgeoisie from which most had come in the first place. Not all bohemians were avant-garde, and vice versa, yet many were.

The idea of an artistic avant-garde emerged when cultural and political radicalism converged. Karl Marx in 1848 used the term to describe the intellectuals who would lay the foundation for future revolutionary action. In 1845, when dissatisfaction with social and political conditions was leading to the 1848 European revolutions, the Fourierist Socialist Désiré Laverdant wrote:

Art, the expression of society, manifests, in its highest soaring, the most advanced social tendencies: it is the forerunner and the revealer. Therefore to know whether art worthily fulfils its proper mission as initiator, whether the artist is truly of the avant-garde, one must know where Humanity is going, know what the destiny of the human race is.[5]

During the 1840s there was a shift from theory to practice in bohemian circles whose antibourgeois stance was Realist, though this did not necessarily entail direct political action. For

Courbet, involvement in politics during the Socialist revolution of June 1848 meant adopting an intellectual stance, as he explained to his family from Paris:

I don't fight for two reasons. First, because I do not believe in wars fought with guns and cannon, and because it runs counter to my principles. For ten years now I have been waging a war of the intellect. It would be inconsistent of me to act otherwise.[6]

During the Second Republic (1848-51) he exhibited works including *After Dinner at Ornans* (1849), *The Stonebreakers* (1850) and *The Burial at Ornans* (1850). Realist and Socialist in content, they directly challenged bourgeois aesthetics and social *mores* in their subject matter and in their formal means. To *épater le bourgeois* in art was a political act, intended to shock the middle classes out of their complacency. Courbet linked his political beliefs to his bohemianism:

Yes, dear friend, even in our so civilised society, I must lead the life of a savage. I must break free from its very governments. The people have my sympathy. I must turn to them directly, I must get my knowledge from them, and they must provide me with a living. Therefore I have just embarked on the great wandering and independent life of the bohemian.[7]

Courbet typified the second-generation bohemian, committed to radical political action, for whom the struggle with the bourgeoisie was a necessity, rather than a high-spirited game. This was partly a matter of questioning and opposing rules of social propriety as well as those of academic art. Courbet's exuberant bohemian way of life left Boudin with a hangover:

...it was monstrously noisy. Heads whirled feverishly, reason tottered. Courbet proclaimed his creed, needless to say in a totally unintelligible manner... We sang, shouted and bellowed for so long that dawn found us with our glasses still in our hands. On our way home we made a din in the streets, it was all most undignified... This morning our heads felt dull.[8]

Louis-Napoléon's *coup d'état* of 1851 crushed the Second Republic and dashed the hopes of the radical left. From this point the link between avant-garde art and radical politics began to loosen. Baudelaire retreated from his earlier belief in the political function of art, and instead saw its role as consolatory. Courbet continued to take a Socialist stance in his public life, but his works became more private or elusive in content. In the 1860s Manet took on the mantle of leader of the avant-garde, and while some of his works, such as *The Execution of the Emperor Maximilian* (1867) did challenge the political and social status quo, they did so in a barbed or oblique manner which reflected the trapped position in which the avant-garde found itself under the Second Empire.

In the third quarter of the century to be avant-garde was to be committed to Realism and Naturalism. Manet's and the Impressionists' exploration of new formal means led to works that called on the viewer to concentrate more on their formal qualities – the how as opposed to the what:

The Intransigents' object was to transcribe their immediate perceptions on to their canvas without any interpretation. They considered any pictorial explanation as a capitulation.[9]

Nevertheless the commitment to individualism and originality, inherited from Romanticism, survived, shared by apolitical artists such as Renoir and Morisot and politically engaged colleagues like Courbet and Pissarro. For the Realists and Naturalists this meant TRUTH to the individual artist's originality of perception. Late in life Cézanne advised the young Emile Bernard: 'Your need to find a moral, an intellectual point of support in works,...will surely lead you, in front of nature, to sense your own means of expression.'[10] While William Morris Hunt, Millet's student, would later tell his own students: 'Everyone must express something as it looks to him... A few people dare to express themselves, and how interesting they are!'[11]

The artist's authentic response to the motif thus became crucial. Rawness, or a lack of polite finish, became a badge of courage for the avant-garde. Of Manet's works at the 1869 Salon, Berthe Morisot wrote:

> **His paintings, as they always do, produce the impression of a wild or even a somewhat unripe fruit. I do not in the least dislike them.**[12]

The term avant-garde had acquired such strong associations with political radicalism that few artists or critics used it during the 1860s and 1870s, the exception being Theodore Duret in *Critique d'avant-garde* (1876). In this case however, the term avant-garde only served Duret as a title for a book of essays, none of which discussed it. Yet it was during this period that the artistic avant-garde, as identified by the twentieth century, truly matured. As an old man Renoir recalled the determination of the young painters whom he met in Gleyre's studio in 1862 to 'set fire to the *pompiers*.' His son Jean wrote:

> **Everything conspired to influence him to follow the Intransigents: his love of life, his need to enjoy all the perceptions registered by his senses, as well as the talent of his comrades. The 'official school', only imitations of imitations of the old masters, was dead. Renoir and his friends were very much alive, and it was to them that the duty of revitalising French painting fell.**[13]

This stance placed Renoir and his friends at odds with the public and the official art world, which either mocked or rejected their works. Manet remained ambivalent in his attitude, yet produced work which knowingly broke established rules. When *Olympia* (1865) caused a scandal at the Salon he complained to Baudelaire. The critic's reply summed up the inevitable alienation of the avant-garde artist from bourgeois society:

> **I must do my best to demonstrate to you your own value. What you ask for is truly stupid. *People are making fun of you; pleasantries* set you on edge; no one does you justice, etc., etc. Do you think that you're the first to be placed in this position? Have you more genius than Chateaubriand and Wagner? And did people make fun of them? They did not die of it. And so as not to make you feel too proud of yourself, I shall add that these men were exemplary, each in his own genre, and in a world which was very rich, while you, *you are only the first in the decrepitude of your art*.**[14]

Even for artists from the *haute bourgeoisie* who had private incomes, such as Manet, Degas and Morisot, the critical approval which sales implied was important. For most artists the choice lay between poverty and conformity. Courbet wrote to his family:

> **...there is nothing more difficult in the world than to create art, especially when nobody understands it. The women want portraits without shading, the men want to dress in their Sunday best. There is no way around it, if you have to earn money with stuff like that you would be better off turning a wheel, at least you would not have to give up your**

convictions.[15]

The avant-garde and their defenders argued that freedom from institutionalised control would bring artistic freedom. Seizing control of its relationship with the public, it organised its own EXHIBITIONS. Yet in doing so it further challenged authority and set itself outside the mainstream. Courbet had set the precedent in 1855, provocatively placing his own exhibition the *Pavilion du Realisme* in the grounds of the Paris Exposition Universelle that housed the official Salon. Manet followed suit in 1867 while the Impressionists went further and organised eight group exhibitions of their own from 1874 to 1886.

This 'independence' proved to be elusive: market forces took on a regulatory role when the state moved away. By the last quarter of the century various artist-controlled independent exhibition societies existed, yet the avant-garde became ever more alienated from the public. Among this third generation of bohemians were the self-destructive pariahs who truly lived a life of misery, for example Toulouse-Lautrec, Gauguin, Van Gogh and perhaps above all the poet Rimbaud, who had foreseen as early as 1871 that the avant-garde artist's role would be to explore extremes of experience, to become an accursed 'criminal' in order to become a 'seer'.

So alienated had they become from society that many avant-garde artists sought escape from the urban centres which offered a modicum of critical and financial support. Hence Cézanne became the hero of the Symbolists partly because he was a recluse; they saw him as the disinterested, authentic outsider. To Emile Bernard, one of his young admirers, he wrote:

> **With a small temperament one can be very much of a painter... It is sufficient to have a sense of art – and this is without doubt the horror of the bourgeois, this sense. Therefore institutions, pensions, honours can only be made for cretins, humbugs and rascals.**[16]

This was partly, of course, because Cézanne had private means. Gauguin, who did not, escaped to Pont-Aven and Tahiti but sporadically returned to Paris to mingle with the Symbolist poets and critics whose support he courted. By the 1880s the avant-garde had a sophisticated following. A trend which the *haute bourgeoisie* had sought to crush politically and culturally in the mid-nineteenth century was becoming a canon of taste for this same social group. Gauguin astutely realised that the avant-garde was now in danger of becoming institutionalised:

> **In art there are only two types of people: revolutionaries and plagiarists. And in the end, doesn't the revolutionary's work become official, once the State takes it over?**[17]

Critical accolades in small magazines such as *La Revue Blanche* now rested partly on the degree to which an artist's works were incomprehensible. Gauguin self-consciously portrayed himself as the accursed rebel and prided himself on the unintelligibility of his work:

> **I have done the self-portrait which Vincent asked for. I believe it is one of my best things: absolutely incomprehensible (for example) it is so abstract. Head of a bandit in the foreground, a Jean Valjean (Les Miserables) personifying also a disreputable Impressionist painter, shackled always to this world... The Impressionist is pure, still unsullied by the putrid kiss of the École des Beaux-Arts.**[18]

Unable to engage directly either politically or culturally with society, the avant-garde had turned in on itself. By the end of the century it was associated with the trend of 'art for art's sake'. Perhaps from self-defensive bravado, some artists struck arrogant, elitist poses, disdaining the general public and scoffing at any notion of a social function for art. Whistler was one such: at the end of his notorious 'Ten O'Clock Lecture' of 1885, he personified art as woman, 'a cruel jade', who would only accept artists for her lovers:

> **...and in their intimacy they revel, he and she, in this knowledge; and he knows the happiness untasted by other mortal [sic].**
>
> **She is proud of her comrade, and promises that in after-years, others shall pass that way, and understand.**
>
> **So in all time does this superb one cast about for the man worthy her love – and Art seeks the Artist alone.**[19]

There was some opposition to this view. The Socialist-anarchist Signac argued that by virtue of being experimental, art was in itself politically interventionist, regardless of the artist's intentions:

> **This can easily be seen in the works that the Impressionists sent to the Exposition des Indépendants. By their new technique, which runs counter to the standard rules, they showed the futility of unchanging procedures. By their picturesque studies of working-class housing of Saint-Ouen and Montrouge, sordid and overwhelmingly real...they have contributed their witness to the great social process which pits the workers against Capital.**[20]

In contrast, Leo Tolstoy opposed avant-garde art on the grounds that its inaccessibility was elitist and that this prevented it from having a useful social function. Referring to his visits to 'Symbolist', 'Impressionist' and 'Neo-Impressionist' exhibitions in Paris in 1894 he concluded that art had become increasingly exclusive:

> **As soon as ever the art of the upper classes separated itself from universal art a conviction arose that art may be art and yet be incomprehensible to the masses...**
>
> **The assertion that art may be good art and at the same time incomprehensible to a great number of people, is extremely unjust, and its consequences are ruinous to art itself... Perverted art may not please the majority of men, but good art always pleases everyone.**[21]

For women it was difficult enough to join the rear-garde let alone the avant-garde. In the first place, their struggle was for professional acceptance – how could they rebel against an art establishment that excluded them? Secondly, the price paid for scandalous social behaviour was far higher than for men. Thirdly, it was socially unacceptable for bourgeois women to go to the male preserves of public cafés and brasseries where the avant-garde met, and unlikely that they would be welcome if they did so. Yet there were exceptions. Because of her fame, the traditional painter Rosa Bonheur was able to defy bourgeois conventions with bohemian abandon by publicly cross-dressing and openly living with another woman: 'I am a painter, I have earned my living honestly. My private life is nobody's concern.'[22]

Cassatt and Morisot, both from the *haute bourgeoisie*, were not bohemians but were staunchly avant-garde, both in their works and as loyal participants in the Impressionist exhibitions. In her old age Cassatt refused to serve on a selection jury, explaining:

> **That is entirely against my principles, I would never be able to forgive myself if through my means any picture were refused... I abominate the system and I think entire liberty**

the only way.[23]

In contrast, Renoir (making fun of his master's Swiss accent) recalled the scandalously bohemian attitude of a young woman student in Gleyre's *ATELIER*:

> **Old Gleyre sensed that the wind of revolt was rising in his school. He caught the freckled English girl putting a touch of vermilion on the nipples of the figure she was painting. Gleyre's face turned a bright red.**
>
> **'Id's intecend [sic]'**
>
> **'I am for free love and Courbet,' retorted the young lady.**[24]

Yet not only did the shy, conventional Gleyre allow women students to work from the naked model, he also permitted them to do so in mixed company as early as the 1860s.

It is easy to forget that the majority of nineteenth-century artists were rear-guard and that without them the avant-garde could not exist. But the situation was never clear cut. Some artists were bohemian but not avant-garde and *vice versa*, some were politically and socially conformist but avant-garde in their works, some changed as their lives progressed. In a society where the social position of the artist was equivocal, which cast the artist as pet entertainer and consoler, the birth of the avant-garde was inevitable. As the politicised mid-century avant-garde had realised, it was dependent on the bourgeoisie it so despised, and from which the majority of artists originated. Without it there would be no force against which to rebel. But the bourgeoisie was so powerful culturally and politically that it diffused the avant-garde's radical interventions by assimilating them.

The alienated *fin de siècle* avant-garde was the one inherited in the twentieth century by the capitalist west, which defined its official art according to its own canons. From Puccini's *La Bohême* (1896) to the New York studios of the 1950s romanticised myths about the avant-garde and its bohemianism captivated the young. It has been savaged by late twentieth-century art historians on the grounds of being sexist and elitist. Yet without Courbet's bravado, Morisot's daring, Manet's deceptive complexity, or Van Gogh's sincerity, would we know what it was like to have been alive at that time?

See: ACADEMY, EXHIBITION, GENIUS, MODERNITY, SENSATION, TEMPERAMENT

[1] Letter to Bibesco, July 1901, in Protter, p. 155

[2] *Opinions litteraires, philosophiques et industrielles*, 1825, in Harrison and Wood, pp. 39-41

[3] *Ibid*, p. 41

[4] H. de Balzac, *Un prince de la Bohême*, in Hauser, IV, p. 181

[5] *De la mission de l'art et du rôle des artistes*, 1845, in Meecham and Sheldon, p. 18

[6] 26 June 1848, in Courbet, p. 81

[7] Letter to Mr and Mrs Francis Wey, 31 July 1850, in Courbet, pp. 98-9

[8] Journal, 1859, in T.J. Clark, 1988, p. 52

[9] Renoir, p. 100

[10] 23 Dec 1904, in Cézanne, pp. 309-10

[11] In Hunt, p. 14

[12] In Morisot, p. 36

[13] In Renoir, p. 101

[14] Letter, 11 May 1865, in T.J. Clark, 1985, p. 82

[15] 10 Jan 1846, in Courbet, pp. 58-9

[16] 25 July 1904, in Cézanne, p. 306

[17] In Kuspit, p. 11

[18] Letter to Emile Schuffenecker, 8 Oct 1888, in Chipp, p. 67

[19] In Whistler, 1967, p. 157

[20] *La Révolte*, 1891, in Harrison and Wood, p. 797

[21] *What is art?*, 1898, in Harrison and Wood, pp. 818-19

[22] In Greer, p. 58

[23] Letter to Mr Morris, 29 Aug 1904, in Mathews, p. 294

[24] In Renoir, p. 100

Beauty

'THE BEAUTIFUL IN ART IS TRUTH BATHED IN THE IMPRESSION we have received from nature.'[1]

With these remarks Corot neatly linked together beauty, TRUTH and NATURE, the three major threads within nineteenth-century aesthetics. What seems endearing from our vantage point is the period's faith in the co-dependence of art and beauty. Most agreed that the artist should create beauty; it was its definition which changed according to temporal and cultural contexts. An American such as Thomas Cole, impatient with ties to a Europe that seemed inaccessible, found beauty in his local LANDSCAPE, the untamed nature of which would probably have shocked Corot, used as he was to the cultivated lands of the Roman campagna and the Barbizon region. Yet both artists linked beauty in art to nature. By the mid century, the two concepts were being questioned both in terms of their definition and their co-dependence. By the end of the century the beauty of evil was born.

When the century opened the ideas of Winckelmann and David were still current. Writing in the *Journal de France* to publicise the studio exhibition of his *Intervention of the Sabines* in 1800, David summarised his aesthetic:

> **Beauty of style, noble characterisation, truth of expression, tense and correct draughtsmanship, large, simple and natural effect, true colour, profound erudition in the portrayal of countenances and costumes, sure and deeply-felt execution: these are the principal qualities which strike one in this beautiful work.**[2]

In the pamphlet which accompanied the public exhibition of this painting, David clearly identified antiquity as the main canon of beauty:

> **Antiquity has not ceased to be the great school of modern painters, the source from which they draw the beauties of their art. We seek to imitate the ancient artists, in the genius of their conceptions, the purity of their design, the expressiveness of their features, and the grace of their forms.**[3]

Despite numerous attacks upon it, the classical ideal of beauty was maintained in the academies and in the works of major, officially accepted artists such as Ingres and Poynter throughout the century, so that alternative definitions were mostly made in relation to its stated criteria. These went back to eighteenth-century ideals of the 'true style', which later became known as Neo-classicism. Selecting from nature under the judicious guidance of the works of the masters (i.e. the antique and painters of the High Renaissance), the artist created a timeless, immutable, harmonious, beauty which appealed to humanity's finer aspirations. Ingres noted:

> **The Greeks have so excelled in sculpture, architecture, poetry, in all that they have touched, that the word greek [sic] has become synonymous with the word beautiful. Only they managed to be absolutely true, absolutely beautiful, because they saw, they recognised and they rendered... we are Gallic, we are barbaric, and it is only by making ourselves become closer to the Greeks, only through them, only by proceeding like them that we can earn the right to be called artists.[4]**

In France, Classicism was vigorously defended by Victor Cousin, the arch-priest of the sensible, *juste-milieu* art favoured by Louis-Philippe's regime. For him the beautiful equated the true, the good and the ideal. A supporter of Ingres, he was committed to the perfection of nature by art to create a cerebral, non-vulgar, higher world where mundaneness, irregularity and shabbiness have been left to the everyday world. Not surprisingly he aligned this stance with that of art for art's sake:

> **The arts are called the fine arts, because their sole object is to produce the disinterested emotion of beauty, without regard to the utility either of the spectator or the artist.[5]**

Cousin's *Lectures on the True, the Beautiful and the Good* were delivered at the Sorbonne from 1817 and published in 1836. They were then reissued in France and Britain in 1854, by which time they were seen as conservative and anti-realist by the progressives. While this classical definition of beauty remained resilient within academic art throughout the century many of the innovations stemmed from attacks upon it.

The Romantics presented the first serious challenge, when they asserted the importance of feeling as the source of all in art. Friedrich, arguably the most important of the German Romantic landscape painters of the early nineteenth century, was critical of the Nazarenes' dependence on earlier art, stressing the importance of truth to self for the artist:

> **If you want to know what beauty is, ask those who theorise about aesthetics. It may be useful to you at the coffee table, but not before the easel. There you need to feel what is beautiful.[6]**

Secondly, the Romantics disputed the Classicists' adherence to the timeless by frequent calls to create an art of their own times. In turn, Victor Hugo pointed out that the art and culture of the modern day was distinguished by the grotesque, which was everything which the classical lacked and that it was this very contrast with the beautiful which made modern portrayals of beauty even more beautiful than the bland, uncontrasted idealisations of the classical artists. He went on to identify the grotesque as the counterpart of the sublime and saw this contrast as vital to the new definition of beauty:

> **One form of the sublime contrasted with another is barely the sublime at all, for one needs a certain period of respite from everything, even from beauty. The grotesque, on the other hand, by its nature, marks a sort of pause, and forms a point of comparison refreshing and sharpening our faculties, from which we can rise up towards the beautiful. The salamander increases the beauty of the ondine, as the hobgoblin renders the sylph ever more ethereal.[7]**

In his diary Delacroix grappled with such ideas, debating whether perfection could be sacrificed to the desire to arouse emotions:

> **I adore Rubens, Michelangelo, etc... the fault of Racine lay in his very perfection. He is not considered beautiful because he is actually too beautiful. Perfect beauty implies perfect simplicity, a quality that at first sight does not arouse the emotions which we feel before gigantic works, objects whose very disproportion constitutes an element of beauty. Are works of this kind, whether in nature or art, actually more beautiful? Assuredly not, but they are capable of making a deeper impression.[8]**

This definition of the idea allowed him to discover the fierce beauty of a lion hunt or of terrifying Byronic tragedies.

It was Baudelaire's profound veneration for Delacroix's works which fired much of his influential art criticism. Pondering upon the continuing validity of Romanticism in his Salon of 1846 (which took the form of a book), he dwelled upon the movement's greater involvement with the realities of the present and defined its art as the most recent and up-to-date form of beauty. In his last chapter, entitled 'On the Heroism of Modern Life', the poet returned to the definition of MODERNITY. This time dispensing with the corollary of Romanticism, he made his prophetic redefinition of beauty, as modern and made up of the ephemeral as well as of the permanent, so seeing off the Classicists' adherence to the immutable as well as their deference to the ancients:

> **Before trying to distinguish the epic side of modern life, and before bringing examples to prove that our age is no less fertile in sublime themes than past ages, we may assert that since all centuries and all peoples have had their own form of beauty, so inevitably we have ours. That is in the order of things.**
>
> **All forms of beauty, like all possible phenomena, contain an element of the eternal and an element of the transitory – of the absolute and of the particular. Absolute and eternal beauty does not exist, or rather it is only an abstraction skimmed from the general surface of different beauties. The particular element in each manifestation comes from the emotions: and just as we have our own particular emotions, so we have our own beauty.[9]**

Although it would be another two decades before Manet and the Impressionists pursued the full implications of Baudelaire's celebration of the heroism of modern life, by the mid-century innovators as diverse as Courbet and the Barbizon artists in France and Constable, Ruskin and the Pre-Raphaelite Brotherhood in England did resituate beauty in the everyday and even in the mundane. Moreover, they became resistant to the notion of any form of idealisation or selection from nature. Courbet's self-conscious 'Letter to Young Artists', which was published in the *Courrier du Dimanche* in 1861, included the following statement:

> **Beauty is in nature, and occurs in reality under the most varied aspects. As soon as one finds it, it belongs to art, or rather to the artist who can see it. As soon as beauty is real and visible, it carries its artistic expression within itself. But the artist has no right to amplify that expression. He cannot touch it without running the risk of altering its nature and consequently, of weakening it. Beauty provided by nature is superior to all artistic conventions. Beauty, like truth, is relative to the times in which one lives and to the individual capable of understanding it. The expression of beauty is in direct relation to the power of perception acquired by the artist.[10]**

While Ruskin in *Modern Painters* wrote:

It is only by the habit of representing faithfully all things, that we can truly learn what is beautiful, and what is not. The ugliest objects contain some elements of beauty; and in all it is an element peculiar to themselves, which cannot be separated from their ugliness, but must either be enjoyed together with it or not at all. The more a painter accepts nature as he finds it, the more unexpected beauty he discovers in what he at first despised; but once let him arrogate the right of rejection, and he will gradually contract his circle of enjoyment, until what he supposed to be nobleness of selection ends in narrowness of perception.[11]

As artifice became more suspect, beauty was discovered in the artless naivety of the primitives: for the British in the works of Italian Renaissance artists before Raphael and for the French Realists in the *Images d'Épinal* (popular woodcuts).[12] In France, the commitment to the democratic ideal shared by progressive circles linked such attitudes to egalitarian political outlooks. When Champfleury praised Courbet's *Burial at Ornans* (1849) by comparing it with *Images d'Épinal* he was making a radical statement in terms of aesthetics and of politics, since these prints were produced by and for the common people, and had hitherto been denigrated as unsubtle and crude:

The effect is the same because the execution is so simple. Masterly art bears the same accent as naive art. The appearance is striking, as in a painting by an old master. The simplicity of the black dress achieves the grandeur of the red-robed parliaments painted by Largillière. The modern bourgeoisie stands before us in its ridiculousness, its ugliness and its beauty.[13]

With commitment to accuracy, truth to context became vital, as did the questioning of hierarchies of beautiful subjects. Millet wrote:

The whole of nature's arsenal has been at the disposal of men of might, and their genius has made them employ, not what we may think the most beautiful things, but the most suitable. Has not everything in creation its own place and hour? Who would venture to say that a potato is inferior to a pomegranate?[14]

He felt that it was impossible to define absolute beauty. In 1863 he repeated similar ideas and concluded that 'the beautiful is the suitable.'[15] Beauty had become more personal, more mutable and more localised in terms of space and time, as the seeking after universal, unchanging rules began to appear too rigid and hierarchical in the more democratic and individualistic world of the second half of the century.

By the 1860s the beauty which the Realists had found in the humble was increasingly associated with images of the harsh realities of peasant life, and to a lesser degree with depictions of the urban poor. At the same time, sentimentalised and idealised portrayals of rural life by artists such as Jules Breton and later by Bouguereau were being absorbed into academic art. For innovators such as Manet and Degas, Baudelaire's definition of the beauty of modern life had now taken on a crucial meaning. Re-examined and developed in a long essay on *The Painter of Modern Life* (written in 1859 and published in 1863), his concept of contemporary beauty as enjoyed by the urban *flâneur* was utterly divorced from any bucolic association. The well manicured hands of a Manet dandy replaced the calloused thumbs of a Millet peasant. It was Manet and the Impressionists who truly encapsulated Baudelaire's definition of beauty as made up of the ephemeral and of the eternal. Manet told Antonin Proust that beauty was always changing, so that '…one doesn't just paint a landscape or a marine or figure study but the impressions of a moment in time.'[16]

Furthermore, the Impressionists' concern with capturing the ephemerality of modern life led to a greater emphasis on the beauty of execution, rather than of subject matter. Hence the increasing importance of the surface of the works, touch, brush marks and colour. As Pissarro exclaimed: 'Everything is beautiful, the whole secret lies in knowing how to interpret.'[17]

Such attitudes were to culminate in two divergent tendencies, both of which challenged Naturalism, a tame version of which had become acceptable to many western exhibition juries, critics and patrons by the 1880s. Until the end of the century most critics and writers, whatever their artistic credo, agreed that the artist should seek to create beauty, yet works such as Munch's *The Scream* (1893) were intended to prove otherwise. The concern with expressing states of mind via formal means led to the deliberate distortion of the visible world in a manner which accepted ugliness as a means of conveying meaning. Still a young student in 1881, Toulouse-Lautrec understood the importance of expressive exaggeration, prophetically explaining his aims to his friend Devismes:

I have tried to draw realistically and not ideally. It may be a defect, for I have no mercy on warts, and I like to adorn them with stray hairs, to make them bigger and more shiny. I don't know if you can control your pen, but when my pencil starts to go I have to give it its head, or crash! dead stop.[18]

Van Gogh would self-consciously refer to important new projects as 'ugly'. At the beginning of August 1888 he wrote to his brother Theo about the *Night Café* (1888):

…the painting is one of the ugliest I have done. It is similar to the Potato Eaters and yet different. I have tried to depict man's terrible passions with red and green.[19]

Returning to this theme a few weeks later, he showed that he was fully aware of the degree of distortion which his commitment to expressiveness required:

But what would Mr Tersteeg say about this picture, a man who, faced with a Sisley, Sisley mind you, the most unassuming and sensitive of the impressionists, said '…I can't help thinking that the artist who painted this was a bit tipsy.' Faced with my picture he'd say it was a raging case of delirium tremens.[20]

However, such works also engendered a reappraisal of the concept of beauty by some members of the AVANT-GARDE who now valued such 'ugliness' on aesthetic grounds. Maurice Denis explained the influence of Gauguin on his circle of students:

Thus, without ever having sought beauty in the classic sense, he soon had us engrossed in it. He wanted above all to convey character, to express the 'inner thought', even in ugliness. He was still an Impressionist, but he claimed to read the book 'wherein are written the eternal laws of Beauty'… And we extracted a law, instructive principles, and a method from his contradictions.[21]

In 1890 Albert Aurier's unstinting praise of Van Gogh's expressionist symbolism led him to accept that:

In all his works the execution is vigorous, exalted, brutal, intense. His frenzied, powerful,

often clumsy and somewhat heavy drawing exaggerates character, simplifies, and vaults masterfully and victoriously beyond detail to achieve a magisterial synthesis and a grand style – sometimes but not always.[22]

The same period witnessed the development of a cult of beauty, born of the British Aesthetic movement, in which looking at art became a sort of mystical, quasi-religious experience. As with Classicism, the role of art was to transport the viewer into rarefied realms which lay outside the petty strife and imperfections of mere daily life. In 1888, in his 'Ten O'Clock Lecture', Whistler firmly equated art with beauty and in so doing elevated the discipline by capitalising the word and giving it a feminine gender. He rejected claims to a false moralising dimension:

> **Alas! ladies and gentlemen, Art has been much maligned. She has naught in common with such practices. She is a goddess of dainty thought – reticent of habit, abjuring all obstructiveness, purposing in no way to better others. She is, withal, selfishly occupied with her own perfection only – having no desire to teach – seeking and finding the beautiful in all conditions and in all times.[23]**

Hence, the manifesto of the Salon de la Rose + Croix in Paris was committed to beauty, which was defined in terms of its opposition to realism and its commitment to 'ideality': 'You have to create BEAUTY to get into the Salon de la Rose + Croix.' [24]

The rules of this Salon set out the following guidelines:

> **1. The Order of the *Rose + Croix du Temple* is now enlarged to encompass the Rose + *Croix esthétique* in order to restore the cult of the IDEAL in all its splendour, with TRADITION as its base and BEAUTY as its means.**
> **2. The Salon of the Rose + Croix wants to ruin realism, reform Latin taste and create a school of idealist art.[25]**

In this sense the classical ideal of beauty resurfaced in Symbolism. Thus the start of the period offered the pallid enticements of Girodet's homo-erotic *Sleep of Endymion* (1791), while the *fin de siècle* featured souls whispering in the woods and glades of works by Serusier, Puvis de Chavannes and Beardsley. However, these later artists had absorbed a commitment to modernist formalisation which would have disturbed Girodet. Moreover in the intervening decades the claims for the beauties of untempered Realism were equally powerful, and some would argue, ultimately more characteristic of the century.

See: MODERNITY, NATURE, NUDE, PICTURESQUE, SUBLIME, TRUTH

[1] Corot, Notebook, c1855, in Caillier, I, p. 89

[2] In Holt, 1986, p. 14

[3] The picture of the Sabines, exhibited to the public at the National Place of the Sciences and the Arts, Hall of the former Academy of Arts by The Citizen DAVID, member of the National Institute, Paris, Year VIII, 1800, *ibid*, p. 4

[4] *Notes et pensées*, c1820-48, in Delaborde, p. 140

[5] *Lectures on the True, the Beautiful and the Good*, IX, in Harrison and Wood, p. 195

[6] 'Observations on Viewing a Collection of Paintings Largely by Living or Recently Deceased Artists', c1830, in Harrison and Wood, p. 51

[7] V. Hugo, Preface to *Cromwell*, 1827, in Harrison and Wood, p. 47

[8] 7 Sept 1854, in Delacroix, 1995, pp. 269-70

[9] Baudelaire, 1965, p. 117

[10] Courbet, p. 204

[11] *Modern Painters*, III, 1856, in K. Clark, 1964, p. 148

[12] These were cheap prints, usually woodcuts, produced by untrained or semi-trained artists in a non-illusionistic, often naïve style.

[13] *Grandes figures d'hier et d'aujourd'hui*, 1861, in Taylor, p. 337

[14] See Cartwright, p. 385

[15] Letter to Pelloquet, 2 June 1863, in Cartwright, p. 242

[16] A. Proust, *Edouard Manet: souvenirs*, 1913, in Shennan, p. 212

[17] Letter to Lucien Pissarro, 26 July 1893, in Pissarro, p. 212

[18] See Frey, p. 121

[19] Van Gogh, 1996, p. 396

[20] 9 Sept 1888, *ibid*, p. 399

[21] 'Définition du néo-traditionnisme', *Art et Critique*, 1890, in Chipp, p. 102

[22] See Dorra, p. 225

[23] Whistler, p. 136

[24] J. 'Sâr' Péladan, 'Manifesto and Rules of the Salon de la Rose + Croix', *Le Figaro*, 2 Sept 1891, in Harrison and Wood, p. 1056

[25] *Ibid*, p. 1057

Chiaroscuro

THE ITALIAN TERM CHIAROSCURO MEANS LITERALLY *CLAIR-OBSCUR* (LIGHT-DARK) although the Italian term was most frequently used. It describes the variations from dark to light in an image and was so closely linked with qualities of TONE, values, shading and modelling that it is not always possible to make sharp distinctions between them. Indeed, in his nine-volume *Traité complet de la peinture* (Complete Treatise on Painting) of 1829 Paillot de Montabert grouped all terms which relate to luminous qualities under *clair-obscur* (EFFECT, shading, modelling, aerial perspective). Generally speaking, chiaroscuro was of greatest importance during the earlier part of the century, after which the concept of tone began to dominate, although chiaroscuro continued to be taught and practised by academic painters until the century's end.

According to the academies one of the two primary functions of chiaroscuro was to create harmonious effects by distributing the lights and shadows in the overall organisation of the composition. The use of chiaroscuro was of particular importance in the days prior to widespread colour reproductions, when black and white engravings dominated the art prints market and other forms of printed imagery. Hence Paillot de Montabert stated:

> **It is chiefly to combinations of light and dark that effect owes its energy, sweetness and charm: this is shown by prints, which achieve a strong effect despite their lack of colour. Colour of course produces an effect of its own, but it is optically subordinate to those obtained by masses of light and dark half-lights and half-darks.**[1]

For both the Romantics and the Classicists chiaroscuro, whether this be in large swathes of LANDSCAPE or the shadowy edges of the smile on the lips of a Goddess, was – like COLOUR – associated with the individual vision of the artist.

The second function of chiaroscuro was to create illusions of solidity and space on a flat surface. With the scientist's objectivity Chevreul made this clear in his influential book, *De la loi du contraste simultané des couleurs (The Principles of Harmony and Contrast of Colours and their Applications to the Arts*, 1839):

> **It is, then, by the vivacity of White or coloured light, by the enfeebling of light by means of Black, that the painter manages, with the aid of a plane image, to attain all the illusion of an object in relief. The art of producing this effect by the distribution of light and shade constitutes essentially what is termed the art of *Chiaroscuro*.[2]**

Yet Chevreul also pointed out that the same result could be achieved with colour as well as in monochrome. Partly under the influence of his colour theories, independents from Boudin and Corot onwards dispensed totally with chiaroscuro in favour of a flatter spatial organisation and used colour as tone. Deep spatial recession and sharp modelling of individual objects would henceforth be associated with the old masters and the works of academic painters.

At the end of the century some Symbolists rediscovered the potential of chiaroscuro as a means of creating mood and mystery. In diary entries for 1880 Redon launched into a complex discussion of the use of tone (valeurs) by painters like Corot and Millet, before concluding that chiaroscuro was what enabled artists to convey thought:

> **I don't believe that...thought as such, has much to gain from this determination to take into consideration things that happen outside us. The only way that life can be expressed is through chiaroscuro. Those who think enjoy walking in the shadows.[3]**

See: EFFECT, *PLEIN-AIR*, TONE

[1] *Traité complet de la peinture*, 1829, in Boime, p. 29

[2] In Holt, 1986, pp. 338-9

[3] O. Redon, *A soi-même: journal (1867-1915): notes sur la vie, l'art et les artistes*, 1922, in Harrison and Wood, p. 852

Colour

WHEN DELACROIX ASSERTED IN HIS DIARY THAT 'COLOUR GIVES THE SEMBLANCE OF LIFE' he was repeating an idea which can be traced back to Plutarch in the second century A.D.[1] As can the idea of opposing colour to drawing: 'colour is more stimulating than line drawing because it is life-like and creates an illusion.'[2] The debate about the relative importance of colour and drawing had surfaced intermittently thereafter: it had, for example, dominated the arguments between the *Poussinists* and the *Rubénists* after the founding of France's Académie des Beaux-Arts in the seventeenth century. The Neo-classicists' marginalisation of colour, combined with the nineteenth century's taste for confrontational ideologies, ensured the debate's revival, particularly during the first half of the century.

In one of his studio critiques in the late 1790s David told Georges, one of his students:

> **That's what it is to like German music, you prefer harmony to melody and you do the same in painting: you put drawing after colour. Well, my friend, that's putting the cart before the horse.[3]**

Although in the spirit of freedom, he did add: 'But never mind, do as you feel, copy as you see.'[4]

The academic view in the nineteenth century remained close to that of Wincklemann, the Neo-classical theoretician who had argued that colour's embodiment of sensuality barred it from a major claim to beauty, which consisted 'not in colour, but in shape.'[5] Colour was a gift of nature, a manifestation of genius, hence unlike drawing it was unteachable and therefore uncontrollable. There was also a moral dimension: colour was characterised as a seductive whore while drawing was the chaste Madonna. Another of David's students, Ingres, was to uphold this stance until his death in 1867. With supreme disdain he noted: 'drawing comprises everything, except tint.'[6] Colour was a frivolous distraction from the elevated concerns of art: 'colour adds adornment to painting; but it is only the tiring woman, because all she does is make the true perfections of art more amiable.' Furthermore colour departed from the spiritual purity established by the ancients: 'No over ardent colour; it is antihistorical...the *historical tone* leaves the spirit peaceful. No more ambition in this than in anything else.'[7] For similar reasons, even the rebellious visionary William Blake defended contour against the 'blots and blurs' of colourists in a public address of 1810: 'A Jockey that is anything of a Jockey will never buy a Horse by the Colour & a Man who has got any brains will never buy a Picture by the Colour.'[8]

The debate was gendered. Colour was feminine: sensual but untrustworthy, it appealed directly to the emotions, and its charms could distract artists and viewers from the masculine purity of cerebral and spiritual values, the true realm of art. In the late 1860s Charles Blanc's influential exposition of the academic outlook stated:

> **Here we recognise the power of colour, and that its role is to tell us what agitates the heart, while drawing shows us what passes in the mind, a new proof of what we affirmed at the beginning of this work, that drawing is the masculine side of art, colour the feminine.**[9]

Blanc praised the expressive potential of colour and Delacroix's use of it in this way, yet he warned of its dangers:

> **...colourists can charm us... But the taste for colour, when it predominates absolutely, costs many *sacrifices*; often it turns the mind from its course, changes the sentiment, swallows up the thought.**[10]

The Romantics agreed that colour appealed directly to the emotions, but since they placed these at the centre of their concerns, for them it reigned supreme. Secondly, scientific enquiries into optics in the late eighteenth century had led to a reassessment of the place of colour in teaching art. Turner, in his course of six lectures delivered at the Royal Academy Schools between 1811 and 1828, devoted one to colour in which he argued that it was a legitimate area of study. However, since the final effect could not be predicted he agreed with the academic view that colour was the product of individual genius:

> **The science of art and her combinations (is) colouring, not colour. And here we are left by theory, and where we ought to be left, for the working of genius or the exercise of talent.**[11]

In France the battle was led by Delacroix who acknowledged the importance of Classicism yet pioneered a re-evaluation of colour in his works and in his writings which were to influence independent artists throughout the rest of the century:

Painters who are not colourists practise illumination, not painting. Unless you are deliberately setting out to do a monochrome or camaïeu painting in the proper sense of the word, you must consider colour as one of the most essential factors, together with chiaroscuro, proportion and perspective.[12]

He realised that colour was not only the expression of the artist's individual inner life, as others including Goethe had previously pointed out, but that its importance also lay in its ability to stimulate the spectator's imagination. In his 'Notes for a Dictionary of the Fine Arts' he returned to the subject:

Colour. **On its superiority or, if you prefer, its exquisiteness as regards the effect on the imagination.**[13]

Baudelaire, who hero-worshipped Delacroix, defined Romanticism in his 1846 Salon review as modernity, which he then characterised: 'To say the word Romanticism is to say modern art – that is, intimacy, spirituality, colour, aspiration towards the infinite.'[14] Devoting an entire section to colour, he lionised the autonomous, inner life of the artist and linked it to the expressive potential of colour:

Style and feeling in colour come from choice, and choice comes from temperament.

Colours can be gay and playful, playful and sad, rich and playful, gay, rich and sad, commonplace and original.

Thus Veronese's colour is tranquil and gay. Delacroix's colour is often plaintive.[15]

Perhaps Baudelaire's greatest insight was to develop the idea of synaesthesia, which he had discovered in the writings of the German poet and composer Hoffmann, a passage from whose *Kreisleriana* he quoted:

It is not only dreams, or in that mild delirium which precedes sleep, but it is even awakened when I hear music – that perception of an analogy and an intimate connection between colours, sounds and perfumes... The smell of red and brown marigolds above all produces a magical effect on my being. It makes me fall into a deep reverie, in which I seem to hear the solemn, deep tones of the oboe in the distance.[16]

For Baudelaire, such correspondences between colours, smells and sounds evoked a sense of euphoria. Of all aspects of visual phenomena, it was colour which was so eloquent that it had the power to alter the spectator's state of mind.

Although it would be several decades before the full implications of Baudelaire's ideas directly influenced artists, colour began to move centre-stage from the 1850s onwards. The English Pre-Raphaelite Brotherhood, influenced by the earlier German Nazarenes, sought to arrive at the spiritual and formal purity of the early Italian Renaissance. Sometimes working outdoors, without CHIAROSCURO on a white ground, they produced brilliantly coloured works such as Millais's *Ophelia* (1851) or Ford Madox Brown's *Pretty Baa Lambs* (1851-9). However, their commitment to detailed accuracy led them to produce works that still depended on traditional pictorial devices: colour remained subservient to its descriptive role within meticulous illusions of surface textures and deep spatial recessions.

The mid-century preoccupation with scientific objectivity encouraged a lively interest in the optical and chromatic colour theories of Goethe, Maxwell, Humbert de Superville, Rood and Chevreul. Moreover, the prioritising of colour by Turner, Constable, Delacroix and others led to empirical discoveries from close observation that were avidly studied by the next generation of independent artists. Delacroix had noted in his journal: '*Reflections. Every reflection contains green, and the edge of every shadow contains violet.*'[17] In works as early as the *Bark of Dante and Virgil* (1822) his use of complementary colours to mutually heighten the brilliancy of the water droplets challenged the greying EFFECT of the academician's half tones. In the late 1860s Blanc, whose ideas on colour were advanced despite his academic outlook, would perpetuate the studio anecdote about Delacroix setting out for the Louvre to see how Rubens managed to make his yellows sing. The artist had ordered a cab, which in those days were frequently painted yellow:

> **About to step into it, Delacroix stopped short, observing to his great surprise that the yellow of the carriage produced violet in the shadows. He dismissed the coachman, entered his studio full of emotion, and applied at once the law he had just discovered.**[18]

These discoveries came to fruition in the works of Manet and the Impressionists who first used colour which sang of its own accord, devoid of chiaroscuro. Already Manet's teacher Couture had advised:

> **As much as possible, use your colours pure, without mixing; if it is absolutely necessary to employ several colours to obtain exactly what you need, never go beyond three; if you increase this number, you introduce into your picture a bad element.**[19]

Manet's desire to grasp the momentary led him to work directly, quickly suppressing half tones. Colour and tone were merged and used in broad masses, and no attempt was made to create illusions of texture, so that colour lay on the surface of the canvas, unmasked. One of the recurring themes in contemporary criticism was amazement at the lightness of his palette.

For the Impressionists colour became a passion. Monet would tell Clemenceau:

> **Gradation of [colour] is the obsession, the joy, the torment of my days. To such a point that one day, finding myself at the death-bed of a woman who had been, and still was very dear to me, while I was fixing my gaze on her tragic temple, I caught myself in the act of automatically seeking the succession of appropriate gradations of colour which death was imposing on her immobile face. There were blue, yellow and grey tones – how can I put it? That was the point I had reached.**[20]

Working on a white or pale ground the Impressionists juxtaposed colour to retain the brilliancy of natural light, allowing the visible dabs of colour to unify and so flatten the picture surface, as the poet Félix Fénéon pointed out:

> **From the beginning, the Impressionist painters...had seen objects as interdependent, without chromatic autonomy, sharing luminous characteristics with their neighbours. Traditional painting had considered objects as ideally isolated...**

> **These reactions of colours, these sudden perceptions of complementaries, this Japanese vision could not be expressed by tenebrous sauces concocted on the palette. The painters therefore made separate notations, allowing colours to affect each other, vibrate from abrupt contact, and recombine at a distance... Sun was at last captured in their canvases.**[21]

Artists no longer mixed their colours; this was left to the response of the spectator's eye, so fulfilling Delacroix's prophecy. It could be argued that herein lay an equalising of the relations between viewer and creator. Moreover the means of production, in which pigment itself was central, were laid bare for all to witness.

On a more prosaic note, industrial and commercial inventions also contributed to change. At the end of the eighteenth century the innovation of cakes of ready-mixed pigment made water-colour painting from the motif a practical proposition. The collapsible metal tube was patented in England in 1841 and the screw cap was first produced by the French manufacturer Lefranc in 1859. By the 1860s ready-mixed oil colours in tubes became cheaply available. From the mid-century onwards innovations in the chemical industries brought the synthetic production of new colours such as cadmium yellow, cobalt violet and ultramarine. Working with oil paint *en PLEIN-AIR* became easier (though the practice went back to the eighteenth century) and artists benefitted from the availability of vivid, premixed pigments. Renoir would tell his son:

Paints in tubes, being easy to carry, allowed us to work from Nature, and Nature alone. Without paint in tubes, there would have been no Cézanne, no Monet, no Sisley or Pissarro, nothing of what the journalists were later to call Impressionism.[22]

The influence of the Impressionists prompted an upsurge in Naturalist art across the western world during the last two decades of the century. At the same time, their empirical discoveries were systematised by Seurat. His scientific use of the laws of simultaneous contrast, using small dots or dashes of juxtaposed, unmixed colour on a white ground, permitted him to return to the temperate tranquility of the studio while retaining the luminosity of colour seen in bright daylight. Seurat's technique – variously termed divisionist, pointillist, or Neo-Impressionist – was soon practised by others in France, Italy, the Low Countries and Scandinavia, albeit often informed by differing aesthetic intentions. Seurat was not given to leaving written testimonies. In one rare exception, a letter in which he explained his innovations, he was careful to differentiate technique from aesthetics, so making it clear that his use of colour (as well as other formal means) was intended as a means of expressing mood:

Esthetic:
Art is harmony. Harmony is the analogy of contrary elements and the analogy of similar elements of *tone, colour and line,* **considered according to their dominants and under the influence of light, in gay, calm, or sad combinations.**
The contraries are:
For tone, one more clear (luminous) for one more dark:
For colour, the complementaries, that is to say a certain red opposed to its complementary, etc. (red-green, orange-blue, yellow-violet).[23]

Seurat then identified gaiety of colour as the 'warm dominant', calmness of colour as 'an equality between warm and cold' and sadness of colour as 'cold dominant'.[24] His own intentions were thus closer to the Symbolists than to the scientific objectivity of the Impressionists.

In contrast Camille Pissarro, who enthusiastically adopted the method between the years 1883 and 1887, was more interested in its potential as a systematic means of using colour to achieve calmer, more harmonious and luminous works that were nevertheless as naturalistic as his previous Impressionist paintings. In 1887 he compared his divisionist work with the 'incomprehensible fantasy' of a Monet landscape, with its 'absolutely incoherent blobs of white mixed with Veronese greens and yellows [in which]…the drawing is completely lost': 'My *Eragny* has more calm, and you can see in this painting the advantage of unmixed colours and clear and solid draftsmanship.'[25] However, the limitations of the coloured dot began to preoccupy him. He finally rejected the rigidity of divisionist theory because of its inability to allow for the immediacy of response to SENSATION in front of the motif:

How can one combine the purity and simplicity of the dot with the fullness, suppleness, liberty, spontaneity and freshness of sensation postulated by our impressionist [sic] art?... for the dot is meagre, lacking in body, diaphanous, more monotonous than simple.[26]

Artists at the end of the century were gripped by a desire to convey the unseen and induce states of Baudelairian reverie and escape; this manifested itself in terms of expressive, non-naturalistic colour, at the expense of tone, line and chiaroscuro. David would have found such art incomprehensible. Gauguin foresaw that despite their innovations the Impressionists would become 'the officials of tomorrow' because of their continuing subservice to depicting NATURE:

[They] study colour, exclusively, insofar as the decorative effect, but without freedom, retaining the shackles of verisimilitude. For them the dream landscape, created from many different entities, does not exist.[27]

Using accurate colours to record the transience of visual phenomena resulted in lifeless and untruthful paintings. What the artist must do is create equivalents in pure colour, since the role of colour lay in its suggestive and enigmatic, rather than its descriptive qualities. It was, in short, Symbolist:

Colour, being itself enigmatic in the sensations which it gives us, can logically be employed only enigmatically. One does not use colour to draw but always to give the musical sensations which flow from itself, from its own nature, from its mysterious and enigmatic interior force.[28]

His erstwhile friend Van Gogh had reached similar conclusions, albeit with a greater commitment to working from nature. He did, however, try working from imagination, as he explained in a letter to his brother Theo in August 1888:

For instead of trying to reproduce exactly what I see before me, I make more arbitrary use of colour to express myself more forcefully...

I should like to paint the portrait of an artist friend who dreams great dreams,...I will paint him as he is, as faithfully as I can – to begin with. But that is not the end of the picture. To finish it, I shall be an obstinate colourist. I shall exaggerate the fairness of the hair, arrive at tones of orange, chrome, pale yellow. Behind the head – instead of painting the ordinary wall of the shabby apartment, I shall paint infinity. I shall do a simple background of the richest, most intense blue that I can contrive, and by this simple combination...I shall obtain a mysterious effect, like a star in the deep blue sky.[29]

That same month he painted the *Night Café* (1888), of which he wrote:

I have tried to express the idea that the café is a place where one can destroy oneself, go mad or commit a crime. In short, I have tried, by contrasting soft pink with blood-red and wine-red, soft Louis XV-green and Veronese green with yellow-greens and harsh blue-greens, all this in an atmosphere of an infernal furnace in pale sulphur, to express the powers of darkness in a common tavern.[30]

Max Nordau, one of the most influential journalists of his day, attacked the *fin-de-siècle* innovators partly in terms of their 'hysterical' and degenerate use of bright colours. Yet Munch, whose work was at the forefront of late nineteenth-century art scandals, was concerned with conveying the subjectivity of experience. He justified his distortion of local colour, in order to favour the expressive properties of raw, often unmixed pigment dragged in swathes across the canvas. He expressed his frustration at public incomprehension in his diary:

> **They do not understand...that a tree can be red or blue – that a face can be blue or green... They cannot get it into their heads that these paintings are made in all earnestness – in pain – and that they are the product of sleepless nights... Because in these images the painter gives what is most valuable to him – he gives his soul – his sorrow – his joy – he gives his own heart's blood.[31]**

Nevertheless throughout the century the majority of artists still used colour primarily for its descriptive properties in terms of representational, local colour. Only in modernist works at the end of the century did it soar in expressive expanses, making direct appeals to the spectator's soul.

See: DRAWING, NATURE, *PLEIN-AIR*, TOUCH

[1] 23 Feb 1852, in Delacroix, 1995, p. 160

[2] Plutarch, *Moralia*, in Barasch, p. 360

[3] In Delécluze, p. 60

[4] *Ibid*

[5] J.J. Winckelmann, *Geschichte der Kunst des Altertums*, 1763, in Barasch, p. 121

[6] See Delaborde, p. 123

[7] *Ibid*, pp. 132, 133. A tiring woman was one who dressed a queen

[8] See Eitner, I, p. 157

[9] *Grammaire des arts du dessin*, 1867, in Harrison and Wood, p. 619

[10] *Ibid*, p. 624

[11] In Harrison and Wood, p. 112

[12] Journal entry, 23 Feb 1852, in Delacroix, 1995, p. 160

[13] 25 Jan 1857, *ibid*, p. 378

[14] *Salon de 1846*, in Baudelaire, 1965, p. 47

[15] *Ibid*, pp. 50-1

[16] *Ibid*, p. 51

[17] 13 Jan 1857, in Delacroix, 1995, p. 355

[18] C. Blanc, *Grammaire des arts du dessin*, 1867, in Harrison and Wood, p. 621

[19] T. Couture, *Méthodes et entretiens d'atelier*, 1867, in Harrison and Wood, p. 616

[20] In Clemenceau, p. 19

[21] 'Les Impressionistes en 1886' *La Vogue*, 1886, in Taylor, p. 480

[22] Renoir, p. 73

[23] 28 Aug 1890, in Taylor, pp. 541-2

[24] *Ibid*

[25] Letter 9 Jan 1887, in Pissarro, p. 91

[26] 6 Sept 1888, *ibid*, p. 132

[27] *Divers choses*, 1896-8, in Chipp, p. 65

28 *Ibid*, p. 66

29 1 Aug 1888, in Van Gogh, 1996, pp. 390-1

30 9 Sept 1888, *ibid*, p. 399

31 2 Jan 1891, in Harrison and Wood, pp. 1042-3

Composition

SO CLOSELY WERE COMPOSITION AND THE OIL SKETCH (*ESQUISSE*) interlinked that the two terms became synonymous in nineteenth-century terminology. Although the oil sketch had occasionally been taught at the French Académie des Beaux-Arts since the seventeenth century, it did not become an autonomous element within the curriculum until the nineteenth. Delécluze recalled that his master David had initiated a monthly contest to stimulate his students 'to practise composition.'[1] This appears to have sowed the seeds for what became one of the major innovations within nineteenth-century French academic teaching. From 1817, a preliminary trial for the PRIX DE ROME took the form of an oil sketch, and the importance of the prize within the French academic system ensured that regular composition contests were enshrined within the *ATELIER* system.

Composition was understood to embody the summation of an artist's expression of the idea. It was thus the freest aspect of a student's education since academic theory held that composition, like colour, was the result of genius and so could not be taught. A wide range of artists and critics with otherwise conflicting views agreed on these two interrelated points. Early in the century the British Neo-classical sculptor John Flaxman told the students of the Royal Academy Schools: 'Expression distinguishes the species of action in the whole and in all the parts...it is the very soul of composition.'[2] The German Romantic Caspar David Friedrich wrote:

> **...it is a complete misunderstanding of what can be termed higher art when young painters form into groups in order to practise so-called composition (*Komponieren*). The ability to express one's feelings and responses through shape and colour is something which can neither be learnt nor acquired through mere dexterity of the hand.[3]**

Slightly later in the century, responding to reading David Sutter's *Philosophie des Beaux Arts appliquée à la peinture* (1858), the Realist Millet commented in his notebook:

> **The art of painting consists in expressing the appearance of bodies. This is not the end of art, but the means, the language which one uses in order to express one's thoughts. What we call *composition* is the art of transmitting these thoughts to other people. For that reason one can prescribe a rule to no one.[4]**

Nevertheless, particularly during the first half of the century, a set of criteria were mostly adhered to, not least due to a profound respect for Classical and Renaissance values. Symmetry, unity, harmony, clarity and variety were highly prized, in varying orders of priority. Moreover, the old masters were frequently cited as exemplars. Ingres noted:

> **I went with Paulin to see the *Stanze* (1814). Never have I found Raphael to be so beautiful... His Disputation and above all his Mass at Bolsena... What portraits in this one! and, in the other one, what beautiful and noble symmetry! a symmetry which he has almost**

always used, which gives his compositions such grandness, such majesty.[5]

The essential preoccupation was how best to convey meaning and/or narrative. Flaxman pointed out:

> **First, a poet speaks by words.**
>
> **The painter, and sculptor by action.**
>
> **Action singly, or in series – the subject of composition being comprised in the arts of design; thus the story of Laocoön is told by the agony of the father and sons, inextricably wound about in the folds of the serpent.**[6]

Thus, he argued, the mood of the subject conditions the composition: 'The parts will be more simple and rectilinear in repose, more angular in violent action.'[7]

Over half a century later Edward Poynter, the Paris-trained British apologist for Classicism, advised his students on composing the Old Testament subject of Jacob wrestling with the angel. He pointed out that an award would go to the 'sketch that tells the story best, and presents the most agreeable form of composition.'[8] This would be achieved by dwelling upon the meaning of the narrative, choosing its most original aspect in terms of suitability to the 'legendary nature of the story'.[9]

A reliance on geometric forms was frequent. Early in the century, in his lectures at the Royal Academy, Flaxman advised:

> **The general forms of masses in composition... are the pyramid-erect, inverted, or lateral, the circle, and the oval; they may be radiated, and the whole will have a flame-like undulation in effect, from the ever-varying succession of curves in the outline and action of the human figure.**[10]

During the last quarter of the century, Edward Armitage would entitle his eleventh lecture for the same institution *On the Composition of Decorative and Historical Pictures*, and tell his students:

> **This pyramidical theory of composition has been much quizzed and laughed at, but that is because the old-fashioned dilettanti who advocated it wanted to apply it universally. Now it is quite clearly unsuitable for subjects of action, or for filling with figures low long panels; but for altar pieces, or for pictures which are destined for central places, it is at once the most natural and the most effective method.**[11]

The overall organisation of CHIAROSCURO was understood to be vital, and Poussin's practice of making up a maquette with small clay figures within a box, so that the distribution of light within a composition could be worked out, was commonly advised and followed. When Géricault was preparing his *Raft of the Medusa* (1819), he actually had a model of a raft built, to which clay figures were added. Ingres reminded himself to 'make…a model room in the manner of Poussin: indispensable for achieving effects.'[12]

Similarly, Armitage reminisced to his students about his own early experiences in Delaroche's atelier, which he joined in 1837:

> **In my early days in Paris, when pictures were painted, and not single figures for the market, almost every young artist had his little puppet-show, into which he was continually peeping during the progress of his work.**[13]

During the first half of the century Classicists, Romantics and *juste-milieu* painters shared many of the above attitudes, while contesting the importance of overall EFFECT and the linking together of different passages within a composition. Predictably Ingres continued to adhere to the values of Classicism:

...the ancients separated all the objects in their paintings. It is a principle which they all more or less followed and which has been particularly criticised by the moderns because they have imposed the absolute opposite principle, that of linking everything.[14]

To condemn such concern for simplicity was madness because, he went on 'This rule of spacing out objects in painting and bas-reliefs came from the desire to express beauty fully and to show it in the development of lines.'[15]

In contrast Delacroix, following the example of his mentor Géricault, organised his canvasses in terms of establishing an overall effect based on dynamic contrasts of mass, light and colour, often based upon his early discoveries. In 1824 he noted in his journal: 'My picture is beginning to develop a rhythm, a powerful spiral movement.'[16] He argued that a gradual building up of detail did not make for great works; it was the overall effect which most mattered: 'The interest given to each separate object is lost in the general confusion, and an execution that seemed precise and suitable becomes dryness itself because of the total absence of sacrifices.'[17] Rather than dwelling upon comprehensively accurate description, selective 'sacrifices' allowed for greater dramatisation of the subject and helped to communicate its essential meaning.

The *juste-milieu* artists attempted to steer a middle way. In a series of lectures delivered at the Sorbonne from 1817, their champion Victor Cousin defined composition in terms of variety and unity:

True unity, is unity of expression, and variety is made only to spread over the entire work the idea or the single sentiment that it should express. It is useless to remark, that between composition thus defined, and what is often called composition, as the symmetry and arrangement of parts according to artificial rules, there is an abyss. True composition is nothing else than the most powerful means of expression.[18]

By the mid-century artists and critics were questioning Renaissance approaches to composition. Millet voiced his defiance of convention:

I have often met people who say with assurance, 'You must at least allow that there are certain rules of composition'... But since I have long felt that composition is only the means of telling others our thoughts in the clearest and most forcible way possible, and since I am convinced that ideas will of themselves find out the best means of expression, you may judge of my embarrassment![19]

A major cause of critical disquiet about Courbet's *Burial at Ornans* (1849) stemmed from his renunciation of a classical grouping of figures in favour of an egalitarian, frieze-like arrangement, within a shallow space, reminiscent of *Images d' Epinal* (popular woodcuts). In the early 1860s Manet was similarly accused. The Realists' and Impressionists' belief that a spontaneous response to the motif was inherently valuable entailed a suspicion of formulaic attitudes to painting – composition included. *Naïveté* of response was more highly prized than clever manipulation of forms: what became vital was an obsessive search for the motif. From l'Estaque Cézanne wrote to Zola: 'I am still busy painting. – I have here some beautiful views, but they do not quite make *motifs*.'[20] Moreover, the sketch aesthetic also implied a suspicion of artifice. Mallarmé proudly proclaimed:

> **Then composition (to borrow once more the slang of the studio) must play a considerable part in the aesthetics of a master of the Impressionists? No; certainly not; as a rule the grouping of modern persons does not suggest it, and for this reason our painter is pleased to dispense with it, and at the same time to avoid both affectation and style.[21]**

Furthermore the proliferation of photographic images, with their cropped figures, odd viewpoints, non-symmetrical groupings of figures or LANDSCAPE motifs, opened artists' eyes to the informal or even chaotic composition of motifs in the visible world. Duranty was quick to understand this new way of seeing:

> **...a figure, either in a room or on the street, it is not always in a straight line with two parallel objects or at an equal distance from them. It is confined on one side more than on the other by space. In a word, it is never at the centre of the canvas or the centre of the scene. It is not shown whole, but often appears cut off at the knee or mid-torso, or cropped lengthwise. At other times the eye takes it in from up close, at its full height, and relegates to perspectival diminution others in a street crowd.[22]**

A further impetus to innovation came from the discovery of Japanese prints in the early 1860s, in which flat space, asymmetry and the importance of large 'blank' areas created compositions which eschewed European traditions.

By the closing decades of the century, part of the AVANT-GARDE, notably those influenced by Cézanne, would be preoccupied by the problem of creating an equivalent for, rather than a representation of, the motif. Ironically, geometric values, which had been of such importance to Flaxman, once more came to the fore. In a frequently-quoted passage from a letter written two years before his death, Cézanne told the young Emile Bernard just how to organise a painting:

> **...treat nature by means of the cylinder, the sphere, the cone, everything brought into proper perspective so that that each side of an object or a plane is directed towards a central point. Lines parallel to the horizon give breadth, whether it is a section of nature or, if you prefer, of the show which the *Pater Omnipotens Aeterne Deus* spreads out before our eyes. Lines perpendicular to this horizon give depth.[23]**

For Gauguin and the Symbolists, the composition of line, colour and form became carriers of meaning in themselves. When explaining his *Manao Tupapau (The Spirit of the Dead Watching)* of 1892, Gauguin wrote:

> **To sum up: The musical part: undulating horizontal lines; harmonies of orange and blue, united by the yellows and purples (their derivatives) lit by greenish sparks. The literary part: the spirit of a living person linked to the spirit of the dead. Night and Day.[24]**

Influenced by Gauguin, Maurice Denis had summed up the inevitable implication of such an outlook three years earlier, prophesying the abstract compositions which would soon follow: 'It is well to remember that a picture – before being a battle horse, a nude woman, or some anecdote – is essentially a plane surface covered with colours assembled in a certain order.'[25]

See: CHIAROSCURO, EFFECT, *ESQUISSE*

[1] Delécluze, pp. 221-2

[2] *Lectures on Sculpture*, 1829, see Holt, 1986, p. 23

[3] *Observations on Viewing a Collection of Paintings Largely by Living or Recently Deceased Artists*, 1841, in Harrison and Wood, p. 51

[4] In Harrison and Wood, p. 374

[5] In Delaborde, p. 155

[6] *Lectures on Sculpture*, 1829, in Holt, 1986, pp. 22-3

[7] *Ibid*, p. 23

[8] *Ten Lectures on Art*, 1879, in Craig Harrison, p. 85

[9] *Ibid*, p. 86

[10] *Lectures on Sculpture*, 1829, in Holt, 1986, p. 23

[11] Armitage, p. 217

[12] In Delaborde, p. 152

[13] *Ten Lectures on Art*, 1879, in Craig Harrison, p. 125

[14] In Delaborde, p. 152

[15] *Ibid*

[16] 7 May 1824, in Delacroix, 1995, p. 39

[17] 23 April 1854, *ibid*, p. 240

[18] *Du vrai, du beau et du bien*, 1836, in Harrison and Wood, p. 196

[19] See Cartwright, p. 383

[20] 24 May 1883, in Cézanne, p. 209

[21] 'The Impressionists and Edouard Manet', *The Art Monthly Review and Photographic Portfolio*, 1876, in Harrison and Wood, p. 589

[22] *La nouvelle peinture*, 1876, in Harrison and Wood, p. 584

[23] 15 April 1904, in Cézanne, p. 301

[24] *Cahier pour Aline*, 1893, in Chipp, p. 69

[25] 'Définition du Néo-traditionisme', *Art et Critique*, 1890, in Chipp, p. 94

Croquis

MANY NINETEENTH-CENTURY TEXTS MADE NO CLEAR DISTINCTIONS between the terms *ÉBAUCHE, POCHADE, ESQUISSE* and *CROQUIS*. Significantly, in English the single word 'sketch' serves for them all. Nevertheless, the *croquis* was generally understood to denote summary notations either of ideas or from observation which could provide a vivid reference for future works. Intended purely for the artist's personal use, such thumb-nail sketches were usually made in sketchbooks, most frequently in pencil or other graphic media such as chalk or charcoal. Speed was of the essence, so that the practice would hone acuteness of response. Delacroix advised:

> **...if you are not skilful enough to sketch a man falling out of a window during the time it takes him to get from the fifth storey to the ground, you will never be able to produce monumental work.**[1]

Most nineteenth-century art academies and *ateliers* followed the French practice of encouraging students to carry sketchbooks, in which they were to note down daily events as an extra-curricula activity. The spontaneity and individuality with which such sketches were made provided a welcome antidote to the laborious, formulaic processes of formal DRAWING and painting tuition. Couture, for example, stressed the immediacy of the student's personal response: 'A few rapid strokes, your own observations and notes made under the heat of your impressions will guide you far better than those dreadful models which lead you astray.'[2]

While recognising the validity of a quick response, Ingres also advocated developing a sketch at greater length as a means of becoming familiar with the motif:

Always have a sketchbook in your pocket and note down the objects which strike you in a few strokes of the pencil, if you don't have the time to fully depict them. But if you do have the leisure time to make a more precise sketch, seize the model with love, study it and reproduce it in all its forms so as to embed it so firmly in your mind that you have come to own it.[3]

Although the practice of making *croquis* dated back to the Renaissance and beyond, it took on added meaning in the nineteenth century, when the depiction of contemporary life was seen as a way of escaping stereotypical themes. For Manet and the Impressionists, the speed of the act of notation, as well as of the subject matter, became an issue. Antonin Proust recalled:

Direct observation played such an important part in Manet's work that Paris had never known a *flâneur* who spent his time so profitably... [In the Parisian streets]...he used to sketch any trifle – a profile, a hat – in a word, any fleeting impression that took his fancy, and when, on the following day, a comrade, thumbing through his sketch-book, would say, 'You ought to finish that,' he would double up with laughter and reply, 'You take me for an historical painter.'[4]

See: DRAWING, *ÉBAUCHE*, *ÉTUDE*, FINISH, *POCHADE*

[1] Cited in Boime, p. 35

[2] T. Couture, *Méthode et entretiens d'atelier*, 1867, in Boime, p. 34

[3] Delaborde, p. 129

[4] Courthion, p. 5

Drawing

WHEN INGRES DECLARED DRAWING TO BE 'THE INTEGRITY OF ART' he was aligning himself with a long tradition which had claimed a moral dimension for the activity of drawing.[1] The debate concerning the respective virtues of drawing as opposed to COLOUR can be traced back to antiquity and had acquired great importance during the late Renaissance. In the seventeenth century the newly-formed Académie des Beaux-Arts stressed the aesthetic and moral values associated with drawing and installed it at the centre of its education system. Neo-classical artists returned to these ideals in the late eighteenth century. They equated drawing with the philosophical high ground, exemplified by the male qualities of the cerebral, the spiritual, the rational and the ascetic. In the following century, in his widely read *Grammaire historique des arts du dessin* (1867), Charles Blanc would still emphasize the pre-eminence of drawing over colour:

> **The union of drawing and colour is necessary for the engendering of painting, just as is the union between man and woman for engendering humanity, but it is necessary that drawing retains a dominance over colour. If it were otherwise, painting would court its own ruin; it would be lost by colour as humanity was lost by Eve.**[2]

Both the noun and the verb acted as generic terms for a wide gamut of media, practices and functions which ranged from the quick thumb-nail sketch (*CROQUIS*) to the highly polished life drawing. That the latter was known as an 'academy' signifies the centrality of such drawings within nineteenth-century education and aesthetics. Since the previous century drawings had been collected in their own right, yet their primary functions within fine art were still tied to the education of artists and the preparatory work for finished paintings and sculptures. Skilful drawing, particularly of landscapes and plants, was also considered a suitable accomplishment for middle-class women. Moreover the accurate description of the visible world in line engravings was widely used in the field of illustration.

As the century opened the influence of David and the Neo-classicists on French academic art ensured the dominance of line rather than colour. His grandson told of David's stress on drawing in his teaching: 'Everything began with drawing, either from casts, or from the model, before taking up the brush, the point chisel or the burin.' In his daily visits to the *ATELIER*, David would restrain the 'the young draughtsmen burning with desire to exchange their modest stools for the painter's easel.'[3]

For over half a century David's pupil Ingres kept the flame alight:

> **Over three quarters of what constitutes painting is comprised of drawing. If I had to put a sign above my door I would write: '*School of Drawing*', and I'm sure that I would produce painters.**[4]

As Ingres pointed out, drawing was central as a means of assessing the proficiency of a forthcoming member of the profession. It was seen as the guardian of professional rigour and competency and so it was placed at the heart of a rational outlook which could be taught and assessed. The ÉCOLE DES BEAUX-ARTS (which served as the model for most other western academies) taught only drawing until the reforms of 1863.

During the opening decades of the century artists as diverse as David, Flaxman, Canova and Ingres adhered to the Neo-classical stress on the supremacy of line, or contour as it was also termed. Even the visionary William Blake argued that:

> **If losing and obliterating the outline constitutes a Picture, Mr. B. will never be so foolish as to do one. Such art of losing the outlines is the art of Venice and Flanders; it loses all character, and leaves what some people call expression; but this is a false notion of expression; expression cannot exist without character as its stamina; and neither character nor expression can exist without firm and determinate outline...**
>
> **The great and golden rule of art, as well as of life, is this: That the more distinct,**

> **sharp, and wirey [sic] the bounding line, the more perfect the work of art, and the less keen and sharp, the greater is the evidence of weak imitation, plagiarism, and bungling.**[5]

However, what had begun as revolutionary purity in the late eighteenth century rigidified into academic dogma, and during the July Monarchy independents such as Delacroix challenged this orthodoxy. In later life Delacroix listed both 'contour' and 'drawing' among the initial terms for his projected dictionary and uncompromisingly defined the former as:

> **_Contour_. Should come last, contrary to the usual practice. Only a very experienced eye can place it accurately.**[6]

A few entries further down he cryptically summed up the debate: '_Drawing_: from the centre or from the contour.'[7] However, he was also respectful of the importance of contour and in a youthful diary entry had admonished himself:

> **The first and most important thing in painting is the contour. Even if all the rest were to be neglected, provided the contours were there, the painting would be strong and finished. I have more need than most to be on my guard about this matter; _think constantly about it, and always begin that way_.**[8]

Moreover, countless statements by teachers throughout the western academies would continue to echo the idea expressed by Ingres:

> **...never let a single day go by without drawing a line, said Apelles. What he meant by that, and I repeat it, line is drawing, that's all.**[9]

During the second half of the century the dominance of line over mass gradually loosened, partly through the freedoms won by the independents combined with the influence of lithographic and, later, of photographic reproduction processes. As line engraving gradually lost its place as the primary means of producing and reproducing multiple imagery, so there was less demand for the skill needed to produce clear line drawings from which to make prints. By the same token, the need to make paintings which relied on clear contours became less crucial. Balzac's dictum 'there are no lines in nature' was widely repeated.[10] Yet as late as 1886 Van Gogh could express the miseries endured by a multitude of art students throughout the western world, when he wrote to his brother whilst studying at the Antwerp ACADEMY:

> **I am glad after all that I went to the academy, for the very reason that I have abundant opportunity to observe the results of _prendre par le contour_ (proceeding from the contour). For that is what they do systematically, and that is why they nag at me. 'Faites d'abord un contour, votre contour n'est pas juste, je ne corrigerai pas ça, si vous modelez avant d'avoir sérieusement arrêté votre contour' ('First make a contour, your contour is not correct, I will not correct your work, if you insist on modelling before you have seriously determined your contour').**[11]

Nevertheless the second half of the century was less dominated by stress on purity of line and many an artist would have shared the French academician Jules Breton's view on the importance of modelling as a means of conveying EFFECT:

> **...it must, above all, express the intimate appearance of objects, their essential or accidental being...the links which join and harmonise them... It adapts itself to the feelings of every artist, or rather it is the chief carrier of his feelings... Modelling, combined with**

proportion, is the whole of drawing; and, combined with the relationship of values, it forms the whole splendid orchestration of the effect which is improperly called chiaroscuro.[12]

For many artists the stress on contour was seen as a necessary stage in their education, which was later outgrown. Hence with a touch of guilt at having dropped the disciplines of his youth Meissonier confessed: 'I have lost the habit of drawing outlines myself, for in painting I always block out the relief at once.'[13]

Whatever the favoured technique, drawing nevertheless dominated art teaching until the end of the century. Hence it continued to be seen as the crux of professional competence. It is thus not surprising that women artists became increasingly impatient with the academies for excluding them from drawing classes, particularly in life drawing, but they had to fight for official acceptance. In the late 1850s British women artists petitioned the Royal Academy Schools to accept women students, by emphasising the harm which exclusion from advanced teaching in drawing did to the increasing number of professionally active women artists:

It thus becomes of the greatest importance that…they should be enabled to gain a thorough knowledge of *Drawing* in all its branches, for it is in this quality that their works are invariably found deficient. It is generally acknowledged that study from the Antique and from Nature, under the direction of qualified masters, forms the best education for the artist.[14]

The tendency to seek scientific objectivity which characterised the 1850s and 1860s also contributed to moves away from classical line. Drawing was increasingly seen as a means to reach an understanding of the motif in terms of its empirical characteristics. Such was the message of Ruskin's book *The Elements of Drawing in Three Letters to Beginners*, first published in 1857, which would be widely used as a teaching manual well into the twentieth century in British and American art schools. In it Ruskin gave very practical advice and stressed the importance of drawing directly what one saw:

If you will not look at what you see, if you try…to cover the paper with 'characteristic' lines, or to produce anything, in fact, but the plain unaffected, and finished tranquility of the thing before you, you need not hope to get on. Nature will show you nothing if you set yourself up as her master. But forget yourself, and try to obey her, and you will find obedience easier and happier than you think.[15]

Nor did Ruskin insist on the primacy of line over mass. On the contrary he stressed the importance of mass. But what truly mattered was accuracy of perception and depiction. His aim was to teach students to draw so that they may love NATURE, rather than teaching them to love nature that they may learn to draw. He thus maintained that the activity of drawing had a moral and a social function. In an address to the students of the Working Men's College, where he had begun to teach drawing in 1854 he said:

I have not been trying to teach you to draw, only to *see*. Two men are walking through Clare Market, one of them comes out at the other end not a bit wiser than when he went in; the other notices a bit of parsley hanging over the edge of a butcher-woman's basket, and carries away with him images of beauty which in the course of his daily work he incorporates with it for many a day. I want you to see things like these.[16]

When giving evidence about his drawing classes to the Royal Commission on art education in 1857 he said that his efforts were 'directed not to making a carpenter an artist, but to making him happier as a carpenter.'[17]

Pissarro was equally convinced that drawing was a crucial means of forming visual perception for the student, despite his own commitment to working directly with colour without under-drawing. His incessant advice to his son Lucien was simply that 'one must draw, and draw often.'[18] These letters were written during his pointillist phase, and at times he suggested that contour was useful, but what he mostly stressed was the importance of the activity itself, particularly drawing from the motif:

> **While you have the time – time should not be wasted – make drawings; it will do you more good than you can imagine. If you just made copies of bas reliefs or Egyptian statues, but did them with scrupulous care, you would make progress...not photographs, the originals themselves...*and do not neglect nature.*[19]**

In Paris Lecoq de Boisbaudran's unique approach to teaching drawing was to make the École Royale de Dessin et de Mathématiques famous among fine artists.[20] From 1841 to 1869, first as a teacher and then as director, his method of teaching was based on asking students to draw from memory rather than from the plaster casts or academic models favoured by the *ateliers*. While developing accuracy and acuteness of observation the method also allowed students the freedom to express character. Lecoq de Boisbaudran's grateful pupils, many of whom had failed to win entry to the École des Beaux-Arts, included the sculptors Rodin, Dalou and Carpeaux, and the painters Fantin-Latour and Legros.

In the closing decades of the century, the innovations of Seurat's vibrant divisionism and of Cézanne's facets of colour dealt a further blow to traditional drawing methods. In both cases the contour was truly broken, but in a manner which also rejected academic notions of shading as a means of depicting mass. During the same period, the debate was reopened on the relative importance of colour and line. The emphasis that the Impressionists placed on working directly with colour from the motif without preliminary drawing, led to accusations that the AVANT-GARDE could not draw. For example, when Tolstoy saw paintings by Pissarro in 1894 (by which time the artist had rejected pointillism as an overly rigid method of working) he felt that the drawing 'was so indefinite that you were sometimes unable to make out which way an arm or a head was turned.'[21]

At the same time, the Symbolist and Expressionist currents within the avant-garde questioned Impressionist naturalism and explored the expressive potential of line, the most obvious manifestation of this being seen in Art Nouveau artifacts. Max Klinger argued that painting was more tied to describing the joys of the real world because of its colour, whereas the monochrome arts – such as various forms of printmaking and drawing – were best suited to communicating the artist's experiences of 'the mighty impressions with which the darker side of life inflict him.'[22] Precisely because of the greater possibility of expressive distortion, drawing could 'take on characteristics which may strike the synthesis of poetic perception more strongly than they do the eye itself.'[23]

Although they shared Klinger's belief in the importance of the artist's subjectivity, other avant-garde artists such as Degas and Gauguin argued that it was impossible to separate drawing from colour since they were interdependent. Hence among Degas' aphorisms were the following: 'I am a colourist with line' and 'To colour is to pursue drawing into greater depth.'[24] Gauguin noted in a sketch book:

'Sir you must draw properly before painting' – this is said in a pedantic manner; but then all the great stupidities are said that way.

Does one wear shoes instead of gloves? Can you really make me believe that drawing does not derive from colour, and vice versa?[25]

It could be argued that the contour versus mass debate of the early century had simply been transmuted into one of colour versus line and that this in turn was bequeathed to the early twentieth century in the guise of Expressionist emotion versus Cubist analysis. The impact of PHOTOGRAPHY together with an increased scepticism about positivist philosophical outlooks may have helped to undermine the need for clear, descriptive drawings. Yet it is equally significant that the very name of the new technique explained the process as a light drawing (photo = light, graphis = drawing), while Fox Talbot entitled his book about the process *The Pencil of Nature* (1844). Furthermore drawing continued to occupy a central place within art education until the end of the century and beyond. In his lectures at the Royal Academy Schools delivered from 1876 to 1882 Edward Armitage voiced a widely-held view:

Drawing is the backbone of all great work, and it is an art which, if neglected when you are young, does not appear ever to be acquired in after life.

Most artists improve in colour, and particularly in execution, as they get older, but in drawing they seldom acquire greater correctness. They acquire facility, but not accuracy.[26]

See: ANATOMY, *ATELIER*, COLOUR, *CROQUIS*, ÉCOLE DES BEAUX-ARTS, *ÉTUDE*, NUDE

[1] Delaborde, p. 123

[2] Frascina, 1993, p. 285

[3] David, I, pp. 495, 499

[4] Delaborde, p. 123

[5] *A Descriptive Catalogue*, 1809, in Eitner, I, p. 157

[6] Journal, 11 Jan 1857, in Delacroix, 1995, p. 352

[7] *Ibid*

[8] 7 April 1824, *ibid*, pp. 28-9

[9] Delaborde, p. 123

[10] *Le chef-d'œuvre inconnu*, 1832, in Harrison and Wood, p. 91

[11] Jan 1886, in Van Gogh, 1963, p. 256

[12] J. Breton, *Un peintre paysan*, 1896, in Boime, p. 29

[13] O. Gréard, *Meissonier*, 1897, in Boime, p. 32

[14] Published in the *Athenaeum*, 1859, see Cherry, p. 224

[15] Ruskin, XV, 1904, p. 51

[16] Cited by E.T. Cook, in Ruskin, XV, 1904, pp. 20-21

[17] *Ibid*, p. 20

[18] Letter 16 June 1883, in Pissarro, p. 36

[19] July 1883, *ibid*, pp. 37-8

[20] This school was founded during the reign of Louis XV to train craftsmen. It was known as the *petite école* to differentiate it from the *grande école*, the École des Beaux-Arts

21 L. Tolstoy, *What is art*, 1898, in Harrison and Wood, p. 817

22 *Malerei und Zeichnung*, 1891, in Harrison and Wood, p. 1053

23 *Ibid*

24 In Kendall, p. 319

25 'Notes synthétiques,' c1889-90, in Chipp, p. 64

26 *Lectures on Painting: Delivered to the Students of the Royal Academy*, 1883, in Craig Harrison, p. 107

Ébauche

DERIVED FROM THE ITALIAN TERM *ABOZZA* (ROUGHING-IN), the word *ébauche* in French nine-teenth-century studios came to denote the process of under-painting (or laying-in) on the pre-pared surface of the final work. However, artists and critics often used the terms *ESQUISSE, CROQUIS, ÉTUDE* and *ébauche* interchangeably and this has been perpetuated in later texts. In the *Dictionnaire de l' Académie des Beaux-Arts*, published from 1858, the *ébauche* was defined as follows:

> **...the initial stage of the realisation of a projected painting; the careful preparation, on broad lines of emphasis, of the characteristic masses, forms, action, effect and colour-scheme of the scene represented.**[1]

The favoured technique was to lay in broadly brushed areas resembling a mosaic of coloured patches, which would later be modified with half tones. The standard studio advice was to 'impasto the lights, brush the darks in lightly.'[2]

The academies considered that the *ébauche* should retain signs of the artist's original inspira-tion, as expressed in the *croquis* (thumb-nail sketch) and *esquisse* (oil sketch). For this reason it was worked up quickly and with as much spontaneity as possible. However, unlike the sketch its fate was obliteration. The *ébauche*, if satisfactory, would be rubbed down and worked over to arrive at the finished painting. That the *ébauche* formed part of the private, preparatory process was made quite clear: 'the *ébauche* is gradually concealed as the execu-tion of the picture progresses, and it disappears almost completely as the final touches are applied to the finished work.'[3]

The Romantics began to question such careful distinctions. They fretted over the inevitable loss of spontaneity involved in such a laborious and methodical academic procedure. When working on his *Entombment* (1848) Delacroix noted in his diary:

> **I'm satisfied with the sketch, but when I come to put in the details how am I going to pre-serve this impression of unity that results from very simple masses? Most painters, and I myself did so in the past, begin with the details and deal with the effect last. But howev-er distressing it is to see the impression of simplicity in a good sketch vanish as one adds the details, there still remains far more than could be obtained with the other method.**[4]

Delacroix's emphasis on retaining the characteristics of the *ébauche* in the finished work was adopted by Couture in his influential *ATELIER*:

> **You may produce a fine *ébauche* which captivates those who see it...yet you feel obliged to put more into it and finish it off....When this happens you should stop, take another**

canvas and copy the *ébauche* on to it. Keep the original which was such a success, use it as a guide and unhesitatingly put anything you like into the copy.[5]

He emphasised the importance of retaining purity of COLOUR and immediacy of TOUCH, and advocated retaining the freshness of the *ébauche* by allowing far more of it to show in the finished work than was acceptable in standard academic practice. His students, who included Manet, Puvis de Chavannes, and the American painters Mary Cassatt and William Morris Hunt, took heed. In turn, in his own busy Boston teaching studio Hunt advised his students:

If we would only work simply! If a bit of canvas uncovered has a better effect than it would have if paint were on it; if something half-done looks better than anything finished; in a word, if the Lord helps us in that way, let us say, 'Much obliged!' and take the help.[6]

The Impressionists essentially conflated the *ébauche* and the final work. Moreover they signified their questioning of academic procedure by sometimes referring to their exhibited works as *études, ébauches* or *esquisses*. Hence what had been seen as a private, preparatory activity had come out into the public arena. It is thus understandable that the more conservative academic painters found such activities to be a shocking betrayal of trade secrets.

See: *CROQUIS, ESQUISSE, ÉTUDE*, FINISH

[1] In Boime, p. 88

[2] J.N. Paillot de Montabert, *Traité complet de la peinture*, 1828-9, in Boime, p. 37

[3] *Dictionnaire de l'Académie des Beaux-Arts*, in Boime, p. 89

[4] 1 March 1847, in Delacroix, 1995, pp. 70-1

[5] T. Couture, *Méthode et entretiens d'atelier*, 1867, in Boime, p. 73

[6] See Hunt, p. 11

École des Beaux-Arts

OF ALL THE INSTITUTIONS WITHIN WHICH ART COULD BE STUDIED, none was as prestigious or influential as the École des Beaux-Arts in Paris. Students flocked to study there from all over France and beyond. The list of its alumni is a roll call of illustrious artists, including the painters David, Ingres, Delacroix, Millet, Manet, Degas, Renoir, Seurat, Bonnard, Denis, Bouguereau, Gérôme, Breton, and the sculptors Bourdelle, Carpeaux and Dalou. Foreign students included the Americans Thomas Eakins and Robert Henri and the Dutchman Joseph Israëls. The close links between the École and other sectors of the art establishment, such as the Académie des Beaux-Arts, the Académie de France in Rome and the Salon jury, conferred added status and promised professional success to its students. It served as an exemplar for art schools in provincial France, as well as in most other European countries and their colonies.

For most of the nineteenth-century students at the École had to be between 18 and 30 years of age, and they had to be male. Women were excluded until 1897. From their outsiders' perspective the École could appear a wondrous place, as the aspiring Russian artist Marie

Bashkirtseff confided to her diary:

> **We saw the École des Beaux-Arts. It is enough to make one cry.**
> **Why cannot I go and study there? Where can any one get such thorough teaching as there?...If ever I am rich I will found a School of Art for women.**[1]

Generally speaking, young bourgeois women like Bashkirtseff could study at independent fee-charging schools and *ateliers*, such as the Académie Julian where she was studying, or with private tutors. Young men followed the rigorous instruction provided free by the state-funded art schools, where they learned to be professional fine artists. Many boys started off in the provincial art schools. Cézanne, for example, attended the École Municipale de Dessin in Aix-en-Provence, while Bouguereau went to the École Municipale de Dessin et de Peinture in Bordeaux. For working-class and petit-bourgeois boys and girls there were schools devoted to the training of artisans, which taught utilitarian DRAWING. Under Louis-Philippe France had 55 art schools or schools of drawing.

With its roots in the seventeenth century, the École was newly established after the Revolution in the spirit of egalitarianism. David was instrumental in seeking to destroy the despotic, monopolistic teaching previously organized by the ACADEMY. Admittance was via a bi-annual entrance competition, the intention being that there was no bias on the grounds of class or wealth. All that mattered was talent. In practice the situation was far more chaotic and open to favouritism and corruption, while many of the artists of the nineteenth-century AVANT-GARDE, including Cézanne, Fantin-Latour and Rodin, failed to win acceptance as students. From 1883 there was both a practical and a written entrance examination. But the recommendation of a master was usually sufficient to gain admission to the school and attend lectures. Marie Bashkirtseff, under the pseudonym of Pauline Orell, protested in an article for *La Citoyenne*:

> **I will astonish no-one by saying that women are excluded from the École des Beaux-Arts, just as they are almost everywhere... not only do we hinder women's studies with antiquated procedures, not only are they excluded from the State school, but they don't even have access to courses in anatomy, perspective, aesthetics, etc.**[2]

Whereas, she continued, these courses were open to men even if they did not belong to the school. However, only students formally enrolled at the École who were successful in its semestrial competitions actually advanced through the system. These competitions were at the heart of the school's curriculum. Some of them, including studies of the male torso and expressive heads, dated back to the previous century. Prize-winning students progressed towards the most prestigious competition of all, the coveted PRIX DE ROME, though this was in theory open to any Frenchman less than 30 years of age. In his 1824 Salon commentary Stendhal complained of the aridity of such a system:

> **Whenever I visit these competitions, I see artists advanced in years gravely occupied in assessing the extent to which various young people have successfully imitated their own method of painting. Twenty of David's pupils gather together in order to examine a painting by one young man. If, like Prud'hon the young painter in question has any talent, and refuses to copy David, whose manner fails to meet the requirements of his soul, then David's pupils, standing on their dignity, declare unanimously, in a manner unquestioningly accepted by the public, that Prud'hon has no talent whatsoever.**[3]

The competitive system kept students in a permanent state of rivalry and often of anxiety and disappointment. The American Kenyon Cox, who spent seven years at the École, wrote home dejectedly of the easel position which he was allocated for a contest:

> **Instead of being no 11, as I had expected, I was no 30, the result was that I got a very bad place jammed in close to the stove, and with an uninteresting and difficult view of the models. My brains were so baked by the heat that, after starting three drawings and a painting of the head, all melancholy failures, I cut the whole thing and determined to rest for a day or two and go to work again on Monday with a determination to do something or 'bust'.[4]**

The prestige of the school stemmed from its being closely aligned with the Academy, which supervised all the competitions and selected the professors from its own members. Until 1863 there were twelve professors, each of whom taught for one month, for two hours a day. The institution was interdependent with the private *ateliers* in Paris, which were often led by the same academicians who taught as professors. The *ateliers* concentrated more on the practicalities of technique. Students would aim to develop their drawing skills in order to win a place at the École. Moreover, the private studios prepared those enrolled at the École for its various contests. It was not unknown for academicians who ran *ateliers* to favour their own pupils at the École, above all by voting for them in the Prix de Rome competitions. Competition and corruption were at the heart of the school's culture.

The school was divided into two: one section for painting and sculpture and one for architecture. Apart for a few changes, the curriculum remained similar to that of the eighteenth century. In 1816 a Prix de Rome for LANDSCAPE was created, together with a preliminary competition in compositional sketches for HISTORY PAINTING. In 1819 the inauguration of new classes in ancient history emphasized the importance of erudition in art. There were also some lectures on ANATOMY and perspective. But drawing, either from plaster casts or the male MODEL, was by far the most important element of an artist's training at the École.

So central was drawing to the intellectual tradition of French academic art that painting was not on the official curriculum until 1863. In that year other major reforms were instituted by the government of Napoleon III. It was decreed that henceforth the Minister of Arts would appoint the staff, and the rotating system of professors would be replaced by a fixed number of studios headed by a single master to create greater continuity of teaching. The rather vague theoretical courses were replaced by compulsory classes in art history, anatomy, perspective, archaeology and aesthetics. In practice staff continued to be chosen from among the Academy's members, as the heirs and guardians of traditional classical standards. Hence Gérôme headed one of the three painting studios for 39 years (1864-1903), while Bouguereau ruled with a firm hand from 1888. Cabanel, Lehmann and Cormon also ran popular studios. There was a continuing emphasis on drawing, line, clarity and high FINISH, which remained the hall marks of the academic aesthetic throughout the century. As a student in Gérôme's studio, Thomas Eakins complained to his father about the narrowness of this approach:

> **The big painter sees the marks that Nature's big boat made in the mud & he understands them & profits by them... Then the professors as they are called read Greek poetry for inspiration & talk classic & give out classic subjects & make a fellow draw antique not**

> **to see how beautiful those simple hearted big men sailed but to observe their mud marks which are easier to see & measure than to understand.**[5]

Yet he corresponded with Gérôme for several years after he returned to America, and his mature work, despite its powerful Naturalism, continued to be based on the Beaux-Arts tradition of working from preparatory drawings and sketches.

A distrust of the possibility of art being teachable was frequently voiced – often, it has to be said, by those who had themselves benefitted from the social and professional advantages of such an education. It originated partly in the Romantics' belief that GENIUS was innate. To Delacroix, an ex-student who had managed to win acceptance by the skin of his teeth, the school's dry approach was antipathetic to inventiveness and the conveying of emotion. Yet late in life, when he was finally accepted as a member of the Academy, he wrote to his painter friend Pignon:

> **When they made me an Academician they did not make me professor at the École, for that is just where the danger would lie in the eyes of our learned colleagues. Around a green table, where everyone speaks his opinion informally, words do not carry great weight, particularly when they are addressed to people whose minds are already made up, after a fashion; it is from a teacher's desk, by correcting the mistakes of the young, that one can teach something,... This is the situation which detracts vastly from the value of my new post.**[6]

The later avant-gardes shared the Romantics' search for freedom and individuality. The most radical public stance was taken by Courbet, both in his decision not to study at the École and in his response to a request from some of its frustrated students to direct an alternative Realist teaching studio: 'I cannot teach my art, or the art of any school whatsoever, because I deny that art can be taught, or, in other words, because I maintain that art is entirely individual.'[7] Courbet did, however, briefly run a radical, independent *atelier*. In 1871, as elected President of the Artists Commission during the Paris Commune, he called for the abolition of the Institut and the École des Beaux-Arts. The school's building was to be 'left at the disposal of students so as to cultivate the development of their studies by allowing them totally free choice among their professors.'[8] The Commune was crushed and the École des Beaux-Arts lived on.

By mid-century the École des Beaux-Arts and its professors' works had become so synonymous with academicism that it was avoided by radical young artists. Monet stubbornly refused his parents' entreaties that he enrol there even when they withdrew his allowance. He chose the greater freedom of Gleyre's *atelier* and the Académie Suisse. Edmond Duranty, the champion of Naturalist modernity, scoffed:

> **Do the[se] artists of the École really believe that they have created great art because they have rendered helmets, footstools, polychrome columns, boats, and bordered robes according to the latest archaeological decrees?...What is it, then, this world of the École des Beaux-Arts, even taken at its best? One sees reflected in it the melancholy of those who sit without appetite at a table laden with wonderful things...there they only copy old paintings, everyone having rid himself of nature.**[9]

But most artists looked for professional success rather than rebellion, and none of the alternatives to the École des Beaux-Arts provided as thorough an education or conferred such status at the start of a career. The feminist sculptor Mme Bertaux launched her campaign for women to be admitted to the school in 1889, and much of the ensuing debate revolved around the perceived impropriety of allowing bourgeois women to study alongside men. When the expense of building new *ateliers* for women was cited as an obstacle, she asked that a small number of women be allocated to a separate studio. In 1890 Bertaux expressed delight that the authorities had accepted in principle that women may enter its portals:

> **If I had had such help during my youth, I would certainly have made my way in a better fashion and have left better works behind because I would not have had to suffer and have lost so much time in isolated struggles.**[10]

In fact administrative, moral and financial obstacles delayed the admission of women until 1897, and it would be 1900 before they were given their own *ateliers* where they could work from the naked model. By then the school's influence and the values which it embodied were no longer crucial to the critically acclaimed high art of the day.

See: ACADEMY, ANTIQUE, *ATELIER*, DRAWING, NUDE

[1] 20 Oct 1878, *The Journal of Marie Bashkirtseff*, 1887, in Harrison and Wood, pp. 767-8

[2] 20 Feb 1880, in Sauer, p. 8

[3] 'Salon de 1824', *Œuvres complètes, mélanges III. Peinture*, 1972, in Harrison and Wood, p. 32

[4] 3 Oct 1878, H. Wayne Morgan, ed., *An American Art Student in Paris: the Letters of Kenyon Cox, 1877-82*, in Groseclose, pp. 18-20

[5] 6 March 1868, in Harrison and Wood, p. 420

[6] 21 Jan 1857, in Delacroix, 1971, p. 340

[7] 'Letter to the Young Artists of Paris', *Courrier du Dimanche*, 29 Dec 1861, in Courbet, p. 203

[8] 'To the Artists of Paris', *Le Rappel*, 7 April 1871, in Courbet, p. 410

[9] E. Duranty, *La nouvelle peinture*, 1876, in Harrison and Wood, pp. 577 and 581

[10] Letter 9 Oct 1890, in Sauer, p. 16

Effect

THE TERM CHANGED ITS MEANING AS THE CENTURY PROGRESSED, but it was in the last three decades that it took on an important critical resonance. In the early century the term tended to refer to the overall ensemble of a work of art and its impact on the viewer: as, for example, in a lecture planned in 1830 by Washington Allston, the pioneer of Romantic painting in America:

> **What is the minimum of truth in order to [cause] a pleasurable effect? We reply, So much only as will cause us to feel that the truth exists.**[1]

According to academic theory this meant achieving the pictorial unity in the relationships between planes of dark and light. The British landscape painter David Cox considered this question in his teaching manual, *A Treatise on Landscape Painting and Effect in Watercolours from the First Rudiments to the Finished Picture with Examples in Outline, Effect and Colouring* (1807), which offered the following advice to students:

The outline being completed in the manner prescribed by the forgoing instructions, LIGHT, SHADE and EFFECT, should be studied in sepia or Indian ink, by which a clearer conception of each will be acquired than if practised in colours; the variety of the latter tending to perplex the mind, and to divert it from the main object.[2]

Cox's treatise was republished in 1840, when it influenced another generation of painters.

In their attitude to the effect the Romantics focussed on the degree to which punctilious attention to detail could be sacrificed in the interests of communicating the essence of the subject to the viewer. Hence in Balzac's novel, *Le chef-d'œuvre inconnu* (*The Unknown Masterpiece*, 1845), the master Frenhofer exclaims:

Effects! effects! Why, they are the accidents of life, and not life itself... Neither the poet nor the painter nor the sculptor should separate cause and effect, which are inextricably bound up in each other! There is the real struggle![3]

He then launches into a speech about the need to go beyond the simulation of surface appearance in order to arrive at the heart of the subject. Delacroix repeatedly dwelled upon the problem of retaining the overall harmony and purity of the sketch despite its greater detail. Of his *Entombment* (1848) he commented in his journal: 'One of the great advantages of a lay-in by tone and general effect, without worrying about the details, is that you need to put in only those which are absolutely essential.'[4] Ten years later he used the word as a heading in his notes towards his dictionary:

Effect **on the imagination... It is the same with poetry as with pictures. They must not be too finished; the great art is the effect, no matter how it is produced.[5]**

In the 1860s Courbet was still using the term in a similar sense. Reminiscing about working alongside him on the Channel coast as a young man, Monet recalled:

Courbet always painted upon a sombre base, on canvases prepared with brown, a convenient procedure, which he endeavoured to have me adopt. 'Upon it,' he used to say, 'you can dispose your lights, your coloured masses; you immediately see your effect.'[6]

The term effect was also widely used in a more general sense to describe the overall characteristics of a motif. In the 1850s the painter Mary Howitt described her experience of a routine journey from her lodgings:

We see on our way numbers of beautiful groups and effects... we came upon a peasant woman with a reaping hook in her hand. Behind her was a background of foliage, a magnificent tangle of vines; she had a sun-burnt, handsome, strong face, brawny brown arms, loose white chemise sleeves, a black handkerchief on her head, whilst over her breast was crossed an orange kerchief, on which the sunlight fell dazzlingly in its brilliancy. Such colouring I never saw before; and beyond, above the vines, was deep blue sky, which heightened the effect wonderfully.[7]

It was in Italy that the term *effetto* really took on a central critical role. In 1862, one year before Delacroix's death, the philologist Giuseppe Rigutini reviewed the work of a group of Florentine painters, which he named the Macchiaioli:

...what are the Macchiaioli? I propose to explain. They are young painters, some of them undeniably gifted, who have put it into their heads to reform art, starting from the

principle that effect is everything.[8]

The group worked in 'spots' or broad brushstrokes with little concern for FINISH, albeit only in their sketches. This departure from the academic concern with a high degree of finish and illusionism was fully achieved in France by the Impressionists, where the concept of effect thus took on an unprecedented importance in the evaluation of AVANT-GARDE art. Reminiscing about his work of the late 1860s, Monet told the critic Thiébault-Sisson that he was 'experimenting with effects of light and colour.'[9] Indeed from the mid-1870s he took to titling his works *Effect of Snow*, *Effect of Fog* etc., a practice pioneered by Pissarro in the late 1860s.

The term effect came to mean the quality in a painting which conveyed the atmospheric look of a subject. This was derived partly through the way the work was painted and partly from the look of the motif itself. This position was clearly enunciated by Théophile Thoré:

> **...most landscapists stubbornly try to explain everything in their pictures rather than strive for an effect of the whole. They forget that the individuality of trees, fields, monuments, or figures is almost always drowned in the light or in the shadow, that is in the air. From nearby one sometimes perceives details, but at the slightest distance only the shapes of objects are revealed, leaving the rest to conjecture.**[10]

The meaning of the term effect came to encompass the distinctive sensations which the artist had in the presence of the motif. His or her originality was defined by these sensations, so the effect was linked to the artist's TEMPERAMENT and spontaneity of response. Pissarro explained to his son Lucien the difficulties involved in achieving such spontaneity when working *en PLEIN-AIR*:

> **...the weather is always changing, it is very discouraging... These two canvases are fairly well advanced, but I still need one session in fine weather without too much mist to give them a little firmness. Until now I have not been able to find the effect I want, I have even been forced to change the effect a bit, which is always dangerous.**[11]

See: *ÉBAUCHE*, FINISH, SENSATION, TEMPERAMENT, TONE

[1] W. Allston, *Lectures on Art and Poems*, 1850, in Harrison and Wood, p. 95

[2] In Orr, p. 163

[3] In Harrison and Wood, p. 89

[4] 2 March 1847, in Delacroix, 1995, p. 71

[5] 25 Jan 1857, *ibid*, p. 370

[6] M. Elder, *A Giverny chez Claude Monet*, 1924, in Rewald, p. 131. In fact Monet did not accept this old master technique, but adopted the white primer pioneered by Manet

[7] Howitt-Watts, I, p. 37

[8] *Gazzetta del Popolo*, 1862, in Harrison and Wood, p. 538

[9] *Les Temps*, 1900, cited by Rewald, p. 150

[10] P. Grate, *Deux critiques d'art de l'époque romantique – Gustave Planche et Théophile Thoré*, 1959, in Rewald, p. 210

[11] 19 Oct 1883, in Pissarro, p. 42

Esquisse

THE CONNOISSEURS OF SIXTEENTH-CENTURY VENICE VALUED THE CHARMS OF THE SKETCH, but it was Diderot who in the 1760s praised it in its own right. At the turn of that century the relative merits of sketchiness versus high finish became opposed when David's earnest Neo-classicism discredited Boucher's rose-petalled nymphs as frivolous bravado. The polarisation was exacerbated by the Romantics, and what became one of the major debates of the period culminated in the blurring and elimination of the distinction between sketch and FINISH by the Impressionists in the century's last three decades.

Derived from the Italian term *schizzo*, by the nineteenth century the term *esquisse* was often used interchangeably with *CROQUIS, ÉBAUCHE* and even *ÉTUDE*. However, the Academy's dictionary of fine arts defined it as 'the preliminary work, a work similar to an *ébauche* in small format; a future work of painting, engraving or sculpture.' The entry went on to define the purpose of the *esquisse*:

> **...to render the appearance of the future picture, the work in process of gestation in the painter's mind and to give a foretaste of its character as regards the composition, effect and colour-scheme.**[1]

Working broadly, usually on a small scale, the artist laid in the overall COMPOSITION and EFFECT, organising areas of darks and lights or masses and voids and dispensing with half tones or fine finish of surface texture. Sculptors would produce a small clay maquette. For major commissions and competitions the sketch was a means of showing the artist's intentions, while it also acted as a useful point of reference while working on a large and sometimes massive scale in the final work. In comparison with an *ébauche* an *esquisse* was thus more finished and not destined to be obliterated.

The making of a spontaneous work that captured the highly prized *première pensée* (first thought) was encouraged by academicians, including Ingres, as an essential part of the creative process. For students it was seen as a chance for them to work in a less rigid manner: it was also a good exercise for developing the imagination and skills in composition. More contentious was the privacy of sketches and their status as merely preparatory works. The Salon painter Jules Breton wrote:

> **An experienced painter...will start by making a lively sketch expressing the feeling he wishes to convey; then he will lay it in on canvas, taking his time and preparing all the materials he needs.**[2]

Yet for the Romantics, what made the sketch so attractive was its ability to retain the enthusiasm of inspiration and so convey the artist's personal emotions and inner world. Their preoccupation with the artist as genius set a premium on qualities of individuality, imagination and originality, all of which were felt to be expressed in their purest form in the spontaneity of the sketch. They thus initiated the idea that the sketch might in some respects be superior to the finished work. The British painter C.R. Leslie, Constable's friend and first biographer, agreed that qualities of imagination and facility of execution contributed to the pleasure that viewers derived from the sketch, then added:

...but these are lesser matters, there is often a one-ness of effect, and a beauty and truth of colour in a sketch, that are apt to be lost in the elaboration and timidity of finish; – and indeed I have noticed that the sketches of some painters have always more true finish than their pictures, because they have more of those essentials to finish, unity and breadth.[3]

When Constable's works were exhibited at the Paris Salon in 1824 French critics were excited by the freshness retained in his *Hay Wain* (1821), but they referred to it as a sketch. Delacroix, an admirer of Constable's 'sketchiness', commented in his journal: 'in painting, a fine indication, or a sketch infused with great feeling can be equal in expression to the most finished product.'[4]

From Delacroix to Cézanne independents fretted over the means of retaining the characteristics of the sketch in their final work. As a young man in the 1820s Delacroix had admonished himself against impetuous working procedures:

We should do everything calmly and only react emotionally to great works of art or noble deeds. Work quietly and without hurrying. As soon as you begin to sweat and to get excited, be careful. Slack painting is the painting of a slacker.[5]

But he increasingly came to value the scope for imagination and the largesse of overall effect embodied in the very incompleteness of the sketch. By the 1840s he concluded that he could dispense with the *esquisse* since a good *ébauche* (under-painting) would do the trick:

My ébauche is very good. It has lost some of its mystery; that is the drawback of the methodical ébauche. With a good drawing for the lines of the composition and the placing of the figures, one can do away with the esquisse, which represents a needless repetition of the work. One obtains the qualities of the esquisse in the picture itself, by means of the vagueness in which one leaves the details.[6]

Delacroix also grasped that the power of the fragment or incomplete lay in the scope it allowed for the imaginations of both artist and spectator: 'Perhaps the only reason why the sketch for a work gives so much pleasure is that each beholder can finish it as he chooses.'[7] Nevertheless, like other Romantics including Constable he was aware of the need to go beyond the first sketchy idea: 'The first idea, the sketch – the egg, or embryo of the idea, so to speak – is nearly always far from complete.'[8]

During the 1830s and 1840s the most innovative technical experiments occurred in the unsung category of LANDSCAPE painting. Working beneath the ever changing skies of northern Europe the Barbizon painters quickly realised that only by working quickly could they ever hope to capture the overall effects of light on their motifs. Their concern with sincerity to their sensations led them to value sketches made rapidly in the open air, as Corot pointed out:

I am never keen to arrive at detail; the overall masses and the character of a painting are what interest me above all....Only when that has been well established, do I begin to seek refinements of form and colour.[9]

And like the Romantics the Barbizon painters valued the immediacy of the first response. It was sometimes difficult to establish the precise cut-off point between the two states of FINISH and sketch. Théophile Thoré summed up the dilemma from a critic's viewpoint:

> **It is hard to tell the moment in a master's production when an ébauche or an esquisse turns into a picture. Is a picture in fact ever finished? For my part, I do not find Gerard Dou's painstaking efforts 'finished': they are over-finished. Perhaps they were more complete, that is to say more expressive of what the painter was trying to convey, at an earlier stage of preparation, thanks to delicate brush work.**[10]

Critics and patrons began to value the charms of incompletion. The progressive critic Castagnary wrote about Jongkind's evanescent landscapes:

> **In his case you do not think in terms of sketch or picture, you do not bother any longer about the execution: it is eclipsed by the power or charm of the effect.**[11]

Landscape sketches and studies were increasingly exhibited and sold, so provoking academicians. For them the *esquisse* was strictly a private preparatory process, not to be publicly paraded or merchandised. Yet the Barbizon painters still distinguished carefully between the two stages by also working on larger, more detailed finished works, and seeing their *esquisses* as lesser (and usually smaller), preparatory works.

Changing attitudes to the *esquisse* formed part of a wider appreciation of the informal, the incomplete and the lively surfaces shared by the various preparatory processes in art. From the mid-century onwards collectors began to snap up the studies and sketches to be found in the sales of studio contents after artists' deaths, for example Chenavard in 1845 and Delacroix in 1863. This trend became widespread during the 1860s and 1870s, when the Barbizon painters began to pass away and such works were thus available for view to the budding Impressionists. Couture's teaching from 1847 until his death in 1879, with its emphasis on freshness of response and execution, was also influential.

By the mid-1860s Manet and the Impressionists were using a sketchy, unrefined technique to convey the power of their first impressions as well as of the ephemerality of modern life. Jacques-Emile Blanche, who was tutored by Manet recalled:

> **Although he took a lot of trouble over the pictures he submitted to the Salon, you would think they were esquisses, so little has subsequent working (since the first stage of the ébauche) impaired their freshness of tone.**[12]

Moreover they adopted this approach not only in landscapes but also in large-scale figure paintings, which therefore challenged traditional values associated with HISTORY PAINTING. Antonin Proust recalled that in 1879 Manet was obsessed by two ideas, one of which was to paint a figure subject entirely outdoors and the other to paint Proust himself on an unprepared white canvas at one sitting:

> **After using seven or eight canvases, the portrait came off in 'one go'. Only the hands and certain parts of the back-ground remained to be done.**[13]

As Duranty explained in his pamphlet *La Nouvelle Peinture* (1876), the sketch-like, technically innovative quality of their works might be equated with MODERNITY:

> **Why are they forgiven for too often producing – and with a touch of laziness – nothing but sketches, abbreviated summaries of works?...**

What, then, do these painters contribute?

A new method of colour, of drawing, and a gamut of original points of view.

Some of them limit themselves to transforming tradition, striving to translate the modern world without deviating too far from the superannuated and magnificent formulas that served earlier eras. Others cast aside the techniques of the past without another thought.[14]

Towards the end of his article he returned to the theme of sketch versus finish:

The artist, enchanted by the delicacy or brilliance of colour, or by the character of a gesture or a grouping, is much less concerned with the finish and the correctness, the only qualities valued by those who are not artists.

***Laisser faire, laisser passer.* Do you not see the impatience in these attempts? Do you not see the irresistible need to escape the conventional, the banal, the traditional?**[15]

By the last two decades of the century the Naturalism spawned by such ideas was widespread throughout the west, partly thanks to the teachings of artists such as the American William Morris Hunt who had studied with both Couture and Millet:

To finish, stop fooling over your work! Don't blister it all over with facts! Facts are not poetry! And stop this eternal going back to correct![16]

See: *CROQUIS, ÉBAUCHE, ESQUISSE, ÉTUDE*, FINISH, *PLEIN-AIR, POCHADE*

[1] *Dictionnaire de l'Académie des Beaux-Arts*, 1858-[1900], in Boime, p. 88

[2] J. Breton, *La vie d'un artiste*, 1890, in Boime, p. 107

[3] C.R. Leslie, *A Handbook for Young Painters*, 1855, in Boime, p. 201, n. 37

[4] 4 April 1854, in Delacroix, 1995, p. 237

[5] 22 or 23 Dec 1823, *ibid*, p. 18

[6] 15 Feb 1847, in Boime, p. 90

[7] 20 April 1853, in Delacroix, 1995, p. 183

[8] 23 April 1854, *ibid*, p. 239

[9] C. Corot, Carnet 68, in Cailler, I, p. 86

[10] T. Thoré, *Salons de W. Bürger*, 1870, in Boime, p. 99

[11] J. Castagnary, *Salons, 1857-1879*, 1892, in Boime, p. 100

[12] J.-E. Blanche, *Manet*, 1924, in Boime, p. 76

[13] A. Proust, *Edouard Manet, Souvenirs*, 1913, in Courthion, p. 87

[14] In Harrison and Wood, p. 580

[15] *Ibid*, p. 585

[16] In Hunt, p. 22

Étude

IN THE SECOND HALF OF THE NINETEENTH CENTURY THE *Dictionnaire de l'Académie des Beaux-Arts* defined an *étude* as:

... a summary piece of work, a scribbled sketch indicating some general attitude, the rhythm of a group or the principal traits of a figure, or, in the case of landscape, the char-

acteristic lines of a site, with indications of the effects caused by the light falling on it at a given moment.[1]

What differentiated the *étude* from other preparatory processes was that it was worked from NATURE. It had several functions, one of which was to allow the artist to become familiar with the visual characteristics of the subject to be rendered. Relating a conversation with Couture, Delacroix wrote in his journal:

He said, and I can well believe it, that he feels himself to be especially suited to work from nature, and he told me that he makes preparatory studies, so as to learn by heart the subject he wants to paint, and then sets to work on his picture with enthusiasm.[2]

The *étude* could also be a self-sufficient work: 'an *étude*, instead of being a preparatory study for a picture, may be a work in its own right, independently of any intention to use it elsewhere.'[3]

In relation to HISTORY PAINTING or GENRE, typically the artist would make studies of specific details such as a head or drapery. In a lecture delivered in 1872, the British academic painter Edward Poynter, who taught according to the principles of French Classicism, advised his Slade students on how to 'carry further' their compositional sketches for *Jacob Wrestling with the Angel*. After correction by the master they should be composed from nature:

Studies of the action of the figures should be made from models, and persevered in till the required action is obtained. Where necessary two models should be used together. Then must follow separate studies of the hands, feet, heads, and draperies; of wings, if the angel is to be represented with wings, and of any other accessories that may be required in the picture.[4]

However, in relation to LANDSCAPE painting the primary function of the *étude* was to capture the overall effect of the motif, particularly in relation to light. It was a more resolved version of a *POCHADE*. As such it was in the forefront of the sketch/finish debate. In 1800 the classical landscapist Valenciennes had stressed that the importance of studies lay in the spontaneity and speed with which they were made: '…a good many painters,…fall into the grave error of wanting to finish studies that should be only sketches made in haste, seizing nature in its actuality.'[5] Of course he saw these as preliminary works which would act as *aides-mémoires* when working on the finished canvas in the studio. However as the Romantic landscapist Huet pointed out:

If the scene has made a profound impression on you, and you have grasped and recorded its main features at once, it is unlikely that you will not make good use of it. But the time to do so is later on: sometimes it is a good idea to let it mature. When you come to work it up, you see the difference between a study and a picture.[6]

In contrast, Corot in France and Constable in England valued their studies and sketches as primary works of art and sold them, although they also considered them to be preludes to more finished works. Huet expressed the exasperation of his academic contemporaries:

Under the Empire, landscapists seldom or never used *études*. Nowadays, do they not fall into the opposite extreme, and sometimes pass off their *études* as paintings?[7]

The Barbizon painters so valued the artist's sincerity that working fast when seizing the first impression took on added importance; it was then that spontaneous response was at its purest:

Whatever the site or the object; we should submit to our first impression. If we have been

genuinely touched, the sincerity of our emotion will be transmitted to others.[8]

Both academic and independent painters believed that the artist's choice of motif reflected his or her personal sensibility: hence the first, heart-felt response to it took on added value. This attitude was to become central to Impressionist art. Hence Pissarro advised the aspiring painter Louis Le Bail: 'Look for the kind of nature that suits your temperament.'[9] The Impressionists challenged, but did not dissolve, the academic distinction between a study and a finished work. It is notable that in a letter of 1906, the last year of his life, Cézanne was still referring to his works simply as studies:

> **...now it seems to me that I see better and that I think more correctly about the direction of my studies. Will I ever attain the end for which I have striven so much and so long?... I am always studying after nature and it seems to me that I make slow progress.**[10]

See: *CROQUIS*, *ÉBAUCHE*, *ESQUISSE*, FINISH, *POCHADE*, SENSATION, TONE

[1] *Dictionnaire de l'Académie des Beaux-Arts*, 1858-[1900], in Boime, p. 149

[2] 10 Feb 1847, in Delacroix, 1995, p. 69

[3] *Dictionnaire...*, *op. cit.*, in Boime, p. 150

[4] E. Poynter, *Ten Lectures on Art*, 1879, in Craig Harrison, p. 87

[5] P.-H. de Valenciennes, *Élémens de perspective pratique à l'usage des artistes, suivis de Réflexions et conseils à un élève sur la peinture, et particulièrement sur le genre du paysage*, 1800, in Taylor, p. 253

[6] R.P. Huet, *Paul Huet*, 1911, in Boime, p. 155

[7] *Ibid*

[8] C. Corot, 'Notes jetées sur la garde d'un album', in Cailler, I, p. 89

[9] L. Le Bail, Unpublished notes, in Rewald, p. 456

[10] 21 Sept 1906, Cézanne, pp. 329-30

Exhibition

THE INDUSTRIAL AND POLITICAL REVOLUTIONS OF THE LATE EIGHTEENTH CENTURY initiated change in traditional patronage systems. By the nineteenth century the dominance of commissions by church and state was displaced by the ascendancy of the open market patronised by the rising bourgeoisie. Reaching the general public via the display of works in exhibitions thus became crucial to the artist's achievement of critical and financial success. As a young Delacroix confided to his journal, 'Please God! the Salon will soon bring in enough to allow me to start on my travels.'[1] For most of the century the dominant exhibitions were those held by official organisations like the Paris Salon or the Royal Academy in London. The private dealers only began to seriously challenge their power in the century's closing decades, despite their existence throughout the century.

The Paris Salon, so-called because it was held in the Salon Carré in the Louvre during the eighteenth and early nineteenth centuries, was by far the largest and most prestigious of all these exhibitions. It served as an exemplar for others in the provinces and abroad. In France the state had long supported, and so controlled, the arts. The Salon was initiated by the state in the 1660s to display works by members of the ACADEMY, and it remained exclusive to academicians until the Revolution. In 1791 the Republican government, advised by David's artists' group, opened it to all artists, 'whether French or foreign and whether or not they are members of the Academy' – unless, that is, they transgressed public morals.[2]

In 1804 the tradition whereby major government commissions were given to artists who distinguished themselves at the Salon was replaced with the system of the state giving out 'inexpensive honoraria' and purchasing some works from those displayed. The Salon became even more of a market place, while the number of works shown increased dramatically, from 350 in 1789 to 794 in 1791. By 1824 it had risen to 2,180. While these liberalisations gave access to previously excluded artists such as women and foreigners they also opened up a contradiction in the Salon's function which was to plague it throughout the century. Was it displaying pictures to be seen and admired, or was it a market place?

The aesthetic conservatives argued that flooding the Salon with small paintings of the lower genres was a vulgarisation of the function of art that should be concerned with the elevated values embodied in the Grand Tradition (i.e. HISTORY PAINTING). From the 1820s onwards Etienne Delécluze, a student of David who became a conservative critic, battled against the commercialisation of the Salon:

> **It must be acknowledged that the exhibitions in the Louvre, created to serve the interests of those who make painting into a trade, have contributed much more powerfully to diminish the importance of this art. Since their institution, the Salons of the Louvre have, year by year, assumed the character of a bazaar at which each merchant is obliged to present the most diverse and bizarre objects to provoke and satisfy the whims of the customers.[3]**

There was little demand for history painting from the ever-growing domestic market and the majority of artists produced the traditional still lifes, portraits, landscapes and GENRE paintings which sold well. For them as much as for the AVANT-GARDE the Salon and its honours system was the main way of reaching the public and establishing a professional reputation. In general, the buyers trusted only works which had received its approval. Painters found its honours system to be a useful spring-board for a successful career: for example, the genre painter Rosa Bonheur, who won a third-class medal at the Salon of 1845: 'That prize made it easier for me to sell my paintings.'[4] Three years later she got a gold medal which led to such a plethora of sales and commissions that she soon had no need to show regularly in the Salon. She told her official biographer: 'Almost all my biographers claim that I owe my gold medal to *Ploughing in the Nivernais*. Just the opposite – my gold medal won me the commission for that painting.'[5] Even for artists with a private income such as Manet, Salon acceptance was important since it signified official approval.

At the heart of the century-long controversy about the Salon was the jury system. It had an extensive pedigree, having been introduced in the eighteenth century. After the Revolution the increase in the sheer number of works submitted led to a selection committee being appointed. The number of submissions continued to grow throughout the century so that selection became a practical necessity. The only jury-free Salon was that of the Second Republic in 1848, which still had to appoint a committee to hang the record 5,362 works (compared to the 2,321 works of the previous year's Salon). The following year a jury was reinstated. The selection of the jury itself was highly contentious. Despite many attempts to make it either fairer, more liberal or more aesthetically discriminating, overall the jury continued to be dominated by academicians who tended to be aesthetic conservatives. As late as 1875, when the Naturalist painter Daubigny wanted to give all artists the right to vote, that year's jury president, the academician Cabanel replied: 'My dear Daubigny, you are only interested in bad painters: the jury does not make mistakes today!'[6] Yet juries in the 1870s were still rejecting works by the avant-garde.

Until the last decades of the century the power of the Salon system was such that it was constantly under attack by conservatives as much as by innovators. Ingres voiced the doubts of the former. In the winter of 1848-9 he told the Second Republic's Standing Commission on the Fine Arts 'that there should be complete freedom of entry...because rejection of a mediocre work often reduces to despair a man who can provide for himself and his family only by his art.'[7] However, in private notes probably made at that time, he pointed out the often discussed impossibility of finding a foolproof jury and of the bad luck many artists had even if accepted, in terms of their pictures being badly hung. The best thing would be to abolish the Salon:

> **The Salon stifles and corrupts all feeling for greatness and beauty; artists are impelled to exhibit by the lure of profit, by the desire to be noticed at any price, by the presumed good fortune of an eccentric subject designed for effect and with a high price in mind. The Salon is, literally, the merest shopful of pictures.[8]**

In the 1863 reforms all exhibitors who had received a first or second-class medal were pronounced exempt from examination by the jury. Millet wrote:

> **I am very glad to think I shall not have to go through the ordeal of trial by jury for the Exhibition... I shall now be able to exhibit my *Man with a Hoe*, which would most certainly have been refused by the jury whom we know but too well![9]**

Sad stories of blighted careers abounded. A buyer returned a painting to Jongkind when he discovered that it was rejected by the jury a few days after the sale. Since these were marked on the back with a large 'R' the rebuff was deepened because the canvas would have to be relined if it had any hope of finding a buyer. The story of Jules Holtzappel was to haunt Parisian studios. Although accepted in 1864 and 1865 his work was rejected in 1866. He killed himself, leaving a note: 'The members of the jury have rejected me; therefore I have no talent.'[10]

There were contradictory situations, yet broadly speaking the number of works accepted reflected the state of play between the aesthetic and political conservatives and progressives. The former argued for an infrequent, stringently selective Salon of pictures for the public to see and admire, while the latter demanded an annual, accessible Salon of pictures for sale. In 1880 the last government-sponsored Salon showed a record 7,289 works. The Third Republic then handed the Salon to a newly-formed Society of French Artists. Its policies were not very different from that of its predecessors, although it had less influence.

Comparable – though not identical – situations existed elsewhere. The Royal Academy Exhibition in London, which relied on private funds, gave preferential treatment to members of the Academy. Their works were automatically accepted and hung in the choicest places.

Others could submit their works anonymously and some of these were selected and hung by a council of the Academy's all-male members. Yet outsiders outnumbered members. Louise Jopling recalled the anxiety felt by many an applicant when her picture was neither accepted nor rejected outright:

> **It was in the 'Doubtful' class. For the benefit of the uninitiated, I will explain that when the Council is sitting in judgement on the pictures sent in by outsiders, a few are accepted, and are bound to be hung, and they have the magic letter 'A' chalked by one of the assistants on the back of the canvas; others are summarily rejected, and have an ugly cross marked on them. The rest – more than could possibly be hung – are marked with a 'D', and are utilised to fill any vacant space. In these 'Doubtful' pictures, Luck is a dominant factor.[11]**

There were alternatives to these official exhibitions: in France, for example, there were the *cercles* (circles) such as the *Société des amis des arts*. But these existed largely as charitable organisations or artists' mutual aid societies. In France and elsewhere artists also grouped together to exhibit according to shared professional concerns. In England these included the Old Watercolour Society, established in 1804, and The Society of Female Artists, formed in 1857. But until the last two decades of the century none could compete with the status accorded to the major official exhibitions.

However, dissatisfaction with this situation led artists to seek alternatives by organising their own solo exhibitions. As early as 1799 David had responded to the lack of state funds for art caused by the Revolution by ignoring the Salon and organising his own, paying exhibition. This allowed him to control the way in which the paintings were seen. In contrast to the customary high hanging of large-scale pictures in the Salons, he displayed the gigantic *Intervention of the Sabine Women* (1799) at eye level and placed a mirror opposite so that the spectators could see themselves as participants in the scene, as well as being able to see an entire view of the narrative. This theatrical public display remained open for five years and was followed by other private exhibitions using mirrors which provided the artist with a substantial source of income.

David justified his exhibition of the *Sabine Women* by pointing out that Zeuxis and other ancient Greeks showed works in exchange for rewards; the ensuing riches enabled them to donate works to the nation. Secondly, artists incurred costs for models, costumes etc., and poverty led some to prostitute their talents to private patronage. Showing work to the general public for money would prevent this:

> **How happy I should consider myself... If the habit of exhibition could offer to the gifted a means of release from poverty, and if, as a result of this first opportunity, I might help to bring the arts nearer to their true destination which is to serve morality and to elevate the soul.[12]**

Furthermore there would be considerable social benefits in that access to art would be widened, works would not leave the nation to be sold abroad and the public would now be the artist's judge:

> **What holds us back, then, from introducing into the French Republic a custom which the Greeks and the modern nations have given to us? Our old prejudices no longer oppose us**

in the exercise of public liberty. The nature and the development of our ideas have changed since the Revolution, and we shall not return, I hope, to the false delicacy which had for so long constrained genius. As for myself, I recognise no honour higher than that of having the public as judge.[13]

David pointed to precedents in England. In a country which had weaker institutional links between art and the state than in France there was less division between commercial and critical approval. The practice of single-artist exhibitions had evolved there during the late eighteenth century, organised for example by Gainsborough and Copley. Benjamin West and Fuseli set up fee-charging, semi-permanent galleries in their studios. In 1804 Turner, who was already an academician, opened his free, private gallery primarily for aesthetic reasons – he wanted to control the way in which his works were hung and lit. In contrast, William Blake exhibited his own works partly from Republican idealism, to make art available to all, and partly in the hope of attracting customers for works which had been refused by the Royal Academy and the British Institution. In his advertisement for his 1809 exhibition he wrote:

I therefore invite those Noblemen and Gentlemen, who are its Subscribers, to inspect what they have excluded; and those who have been told that my Works are but an unscientific and irregular Eccentricity, a Madman's Scrawls, I demand of them to do me the justice to examine before they decide.[14]

In 1820 Géricault took advantage of the more developed commercial exhibition facilities in England to recuperate the expense of painting *The Raft of the Medusa* (1819), which had been denied state support by the Bourbon monarchy. He showed it in a successful paying exhibition in the recently-opened private museum, Bullock's Egyptian Hall, which offered exhibition rooms to artists. During the year-long exhibition Géricault's painting was seen by 30,000 people and the receipts enabled the artist to live in England for two and a half years.

During the first decades of the century artists organised studio exhibitions for connoisseurs: in France these included Isabey in 1800, Regnault in 1801 and Vernet in 1822. In Rome guidebooks published the addresses of artists whom rich patrons might visit as part of their Grand Tour. By the second half of the century some artists had turned their studios into elaborate *cabinets de curiosités* to entice buyers. Some, such as Harriet Hosmer, became adept self-publicists. The novelist Nathaniel Hawthorne visited her Rome studio in 1859:

…the bright little woman [was] hopping about her premises... She has a lofty room, with a skylight window; it was pretty well warmed with a stove; and there was a small orange-tree in a pot, with the oranges growing on it, and two or three flower shrubs in bloom.[15]

Travelling exhibitions provided artists with an income and wider public exposure, particularly in America where many regions had little access to original art. John Vanderlyn, who painted *The Death of Jane McCrea* (1804), showed the work in 'pay as you enter' exhibitions in major American cities. Catlin organised many of his paintings of Indian life together with costumes and objects into an Indian Gallery which toured the country in 1837-40 and then went to Paris and London in the 1840s. Edmonia Lewis, the African/Native American sculptor, took her work 'on the road', showing it in western fairs in booths which had the shape of wigwams to show her links with her parentage. The practice of touring exhibitions existed in Europe too. For example, Rosa Bonheur's works caused a mid-century sensation on their tour of England. Elizabeth Thompson's academic battle painting *Calling the Roll after an Engagement, Crimea* (1874) was highly successful at the Royal Academy, but it also toured the country where it attracted massive audiences. Such fame was an unusual achievement for a woman artist at that time.

During the first half of the century artists mostly saw such exhibitions as an additional way of showing their work and as a means of boosting sales of prints rather than as alternatives to the official venues. However, in the second half of the century the avant-garde used them to challenge the power of the official exhibitions. In France an early example was Courbet's Realist exhibition of 1855, a retrospective of 39 works that included the massive *Burial at Ornans* (1848-9) and *The Painter's Studio* (1855), both of which had been rejected by the jury of the Exposition Universelle that year. Taking a self-consciously avant-garde stance, he sited it provocatively outside the entrance to the fine art section of the exhibition. Eleven smaller works had been accepted but Courbet saw his exhibition as an assertion of his creative independence. To his patron Bruyas he wrote:

> **The paintings that I have in the Exhibition are horribly placed and I cannot even get them to put them together, as the rules dictate. In a word, they wanted to finish me off. For a month I have been desperate. They have systematically refused my large paintings announcing that it was not the painting they refused but the man. My enemies will make my fortune. That has given me the courage of my ideas...**
>
> **I am winning my liberty, I am saving the independence of art.**[16]

It was not well attended and got little critical attention. In a spirit of malice laced with generosity Delacroix noted of *The Painter's Studio*:

> **I went to the Courbet exhibition. He has reduced the price of admission to ten sous. I stayed there alone for nearly an hour and discovered a masterpiece in the picture which they rejected.**[17]

Art exhibitions were a highly popular part of the cornucopia of public display and entertainment provided by the growing urban culture. The 1855 Exposition Universelle was France's answer to Britain's Great Exhibition of 1851, which had been the first of a plethora of increasingly dazzling international exhibitions of arts, manufacturing and raw materials to be held in the major cities of Europe and America. Exhibitions of contemporary art were mass events, on a scale never known before or since. Over the six months of the 1855 exhibition in Paris, nearly 2,000 works by 700 painters were seen by almost one million people of all social classes. On Sundays when entry was free, more than 50,000 visitors would visit. Of the 1867 exhibition Taine wrote:

> **They come as they would to a pantomime or a circus. They want melodrama or military scenes, undressed women and trompe d'oeil [sic]; and they get it: battles and auto-da-fé, scenes of slaughter in Roman arenas, Andromeda on the rocks, stories about Napoleon and about the Republic, illusionistic jugs and dishes.**[18]

In his novel, *L'œuvre* (1886), Zola described the Sunday crowds under the Second Empire:

> **There were even groups of countryfolk, and soldiers and nursemaids, pushing their way through the exhibition on free days to account for the truly staggering figure of 50,000**

visitors on some fine Sundays. There was a whole army of them, the rearguard of the lower classes.[19]

In the continuing battle of exclusivity versus accessibility the State had persuaded the jury of the 1863 Salon to be extra selective. Of the approximately 5,000 works submitted by 3,000 artists more than 70% were rejected. Hence the calls to the Emperor Napoleon for the unprecedented state-sponsorship of a *Salon des Refusés* (1863) in which all the rejected works were to be shown unless artists withdrew them. Many did do so from the fear of being considered inept bunglers by the public, which saw jury approval as a sign of competence. The English painter-critic P.G. Hamerton rued their decision to do so:

The Emperor's intention of allowing the rejected painters to appeal to the public has been in great measure neutralised by the pride of the painters themselves. With a susceptibility much to be regretted, and even strongly condemned, the best of these have withdrawn their works, to the number of more than six hundred.[20]

He added that giving the same jury responsibility for the hanging of both Salons had also been a mistake; it had contributed to a distorted understanding of the works. Wanting to justify themselves to the public, the jury had given pride of place in the *Salon des Refusés* to what they considered to be the worst pictures. These included Whistler's *White Girl* (1862) and Manet's *Déjeuner sur l'herbe* (1863) and these duly became the focus of public ridicule both at the exhibition and in the press. Of Whistler's painting Hamerton wrote:

...the hangers must have thought her particularly ugly, for they have given her a sort of place of honour, before an opening through which all pass, so that nobody misses her.

I watched several parties, to see the impression the 'Woman in White' made on them. They all stopped instantly, struck with amazement. This for two or three seconds; then they always looked at each other and laughed.[21]

This intermingling of their works with those of mediocre or incompetent traditional artists placed the avant-garde in a difficult position, yet some joined the calls for the event to be repeated. For Cézanne this formed part of a conscious confrontation with the art establishment, and in 1866 he wrote to Nieuwerkerke, the Emperor's Superintendent of the Fine Arts, asking for a second *Salon des Refusés*:

I cannot accept the unauthorised judgement of colleagues to whom I myself have not given the task of appraising me... I wish to appeal to the public and to be exhibited at all costs. My wish appears to me not at all exorbitant and, if you were to interrogate all the painters who find themselves in my position, they would all reply that they disown the Jury and that they wish to participate in one way or another in an exhibition which would perforce be open to all serious workers.[22]

For others it was a matter of economic survival. In fact there had been previous Salons for refused works in 1827 and in 1841, but these had been small, privately arranged exhibitions which got little public or critical attention. The 1863 event was important partly because it was initiated by the state and partly because it became a *succès de scandal* – something which eluded the subsequent quasi-official or independent *Salon des Refusés* held in 1873, 1875, 1876 and 1886.

Manet's stance towards the art establishment was more ambivalent than Courbet's. Yet he too became frustrated by the inconsistent judgements of the Salon jury. In 1867, having been ignored in the preparations for a large exhibition of French art at the Paris World's Fair, he set up a private retrospective exhibition near the site of the official one. In the accompanying catalogue he echoed Courbet's plea that the public be allowed to assess his work:

Official recognition, encouragements and rewards are in fact regarded as a hallmark of talent; the public have been informed already what to admire and what to avoid, according to whether the works are accepted or rejected. On the other hand an artist is told that it is the public's spontaneous reaction to his pictures which makes them so unwelcome to the various selection committees. In these circumstances the artist has been advised to wait; but wait for what? Until there is no selection committee? He would be much better off if he could thrash the question out directly with the public.[23]

A similar desire motivated a group of independent artists, which included the future Impressionists, to organise their own independent group exhibition under the name of The Anonymous Society of Painters, Sculptors, Engravers, etc. By taking economic control they would achieve artistic independence. The group's constitution, written by Pissarro, was based on that of a baker's co-operative:

A Co-operative Joint Stock Company, with variable personnel and capital, is being formed between artists in painting, sculpture, engraving and lithography,...having as its object: (1) the organisation of free exhibitions, without a jury or honorary remuneration, where each member can exhibit his work; (2) the sale of the aforementioned works; (3) the publication, as soon as possible, of a journal, exclusively devoted to the arts.[24]

The journal never appeared. Held in Nadar's photographic studio in 1874, the exhibition included avant-garde painters such as Monet, Renoir, Sisley, Degas, Cézanne and Morisot, but also the experienced Salon exhibitors Boudin, Bracquemond and A.F Cals, as well as the amateur artists Henri Rouart and Latouche. This was to be the first of eight exhibitions, the last being in 1886, although membership varied: for example, Cassatt joined the group in 1879, while Monet broke with it to join the Salon in 1880.

The situation remained complex and sometimes contradictory. Manet, although seen as the leader of the avant-garde by the 1860s, continued to seek the approval of the official Salon and refused to exhibit with the Impressionists. Conversely, some more traditional artists such as A.F. Cals and A. de Molins exhibited with them. Enthusiastically drumming up support, Degas's letter to the more traditional painter Tissot justified the group's existence by pointing out its respectability:

Look here, my dear Tissot, no hesitations, no escape. You positively must exhibit at the Boulevard... Manet seems determined to keep aloof, he may well regret it. Yesterday I saw the arrangement of the premises, the hangings and the effect in daylight. It is as good as anywhere. And now Henner (elected to the second rank of the jury) wants to exhibit with us.[25]

Cassatt was more idealistic. She later advised a younger artist:

As for this years [sic] exhibition, I saw from a letter in the Herald that only one American was on the jury & only five American pictures were accepted. The American artists have the remedy in their own hands, let them refuse to send until the conditions of admission

are changed – Our group were the founders of the 'Independents'. After we gave up our exhibitions the name & principles were adopted by a younger set & have prospered – Our profession is enslaved, it is for us to set it free.

The jury system has proved a failure since hardly a single painter of talent in the last fifty years in France has not been a victim to the system.[26]

Renoir's approach was pragmatic. Having shown with the group in their first three exhibitions (1874, 1876, 1877) he submitted work to the Salons in 1878 and 1879. Having had considerable success at the latter he refused to exhibit with his erstwhile colleagues in their exhibitions of 1879 and 1880. From Algiers he wrote to his dealer Durand-Ruel:

I should explain to you why I am submitting to the Salon. In Paris there are scarcely fifteen art-lovers able to appreciate a painter outside the Salon. And there are 80,000 who wouldn't buy a picture of the nose on their face if it wasn't painted by a Salon painter. That is why I submit a couple of portraits every year, little though that is... My approach to the Salon is entirely commercial.[27]

By the time this letter was written the omnipotence of the Salon as the central arbiter of taste in France had in fact been broken. This was partly due to the increasing numbers of artist-controlled exhibiting groups. These did have precedents but took on greater importance in the last quarter of the century. The diversification of aesthetic outlooks mushroomed as the market for art continued to grow, both in France and elsewhere in Europe. Earlier calls for artistic independence blossomed to produce avant-garde exhibition groups such as La Société des Vingts, Brussels (from 1884), The New English Art Club (1886), the Munich Secession (1892), the Festa Modernista, Sitges, near Barcelona (1892) and the Vienna Secession (1898). In France the most influential was the Société des Artistes Indépendants. This was founded in 1884 by painters who had become impatient with the Salon, which remained narrow in its outlook even though it had been run by artists since 1880. It was with this group that Seurat made his debut in 1884. Although it is now associated with the avant-garde, the Société was set up as a jury-free Salon; in the name of aesthetic freedom it exhibited a wide range of styles, from the avant-garde to the traditional.

Other groups were socially or politically motivated. In England an early pioneer was the Society for Female Artists, founded in London in 1857 to combat the bureaucratic and institutionalised prejudice of the male-dominated Royal Academy, British Institution and other prestigious exhibition venues. In Russia the Society for Circulating Art Exhibitions (the Wanderers) held its first exhibition in 1871 in St. Petersburg, the aim being to raise consciousness by exhibiting social realist works in the provinces.

Some organisations grouped artists according to shared subject-matter or medium, for example the Société des Peintres Orientalistes Français founded in 1893, which held a yearly Salon, or the long-established Royal Watercolour Society in England. Yet these independent groups created their own exclusivities: The Society of Women Artists in England changed its name to The Society of Lady Artists in 1872 and restricted its membership to 23 professionals to confront the patronising categorisation of women's work with accomplishment art. Conversely, the conservative Symbolist group the Salon de la Rose + Croix claimed to be too respectful of the artist to have a jury, yet its manifesto excluded all works by women.

During these last decades of the century exhibitions held by private dealers became increasingly influential. Compared to the populist, crowded Salon or Royal Academy exhibitions these were held in lavishly decorated, exclusive environments to flatter the upper bourgeois buyer. Some were purpose-built. The Grosvenor Gallery, London (1877), for example, had an elaborate façade modelled on a Renaissance palace and richly decorated, glazed galleries. Its rival, the Fine Art Society (established 1876), had its façade remodelled by the Aesthetic movement architect Godwin in 1881 to make it look less like an ordinary shop front. Similarly in Paris, Georges Petit's new gallery (1882) impressed critics with its luxurious marble floors, velvet carpets, antique busts, flower displays and high ceilings.

From the artists' point of view these new venues became both a form of control and a source of increasing artistic freedom. A pioneer was Whistler who organised one of the first commercial solo shows at the Flemish Gallery, London in 1874 where he set a precedent for his future exhibitions by preparing his own catalogue and invitations and insisting on painting the gallery walls a plain grey and on hanging the pictures with plenty of space between them, something viewed askance by the Victorian public. When the editor of *The Hour* criticised Whistler for his unwillingness to hang his work alongside that of other artists the painter replied:

> **My wish has been, though, to prove that the place in which works of art are shown may be made as free from 'discordant elements which distract the spectators' attention' as the works themselves.**[28]

For the avant-garde such an approach was inspiring. Of Whistler's 1883 exhibition at the Fine Art Society, Pissarro wrote:

> **How I regret not to have seen Whistler's show; I would have liked to have been there as much for the fine drypoints as for the setting... I should say that for the room white and yellow is a charming combination... As for urging Durand-Ruel to hold an exhibition in a hall decorated by us, it would, I think, be wasted breath. You saw how I fought him for white frames, and finally had to abandon the idea.**[29]

However, only three months later he celebrated the degree of autonomy he enjoyed in arranging a solo show with Durand-Ruel:

> **We can only have a good exhibition if we ourselves arrange it. The Paris exhibition is pretty good though the hall is poor. I placed the pictures quite far apart. – I am fairly well satisfied with my arrangements, Durand gave me complete freedom.**[30]

The art market was becoming increasingly international. Practical to the last, Renoir remarked to his son that the exhibition organised by Durand-Ruel in New York in 1885 had brought the Impressionists a wider market: 'We perhaps owe it to the Americans that we did not die of hunger.'[31] The dealers' shows were claiming superiority over the Salon, which began to appear tawdry and lacked the exclusivity which the art buying public craved. In Zola's novel, *L'œuvre* (1886), the fashionable artist Fagerolles refused to bother submitting to the Salon. In agreement with his dealer, he said: 'I didn't want to exhibit there, it lowers the value.'[32]

See: ACADEMY, AVANT-GARDE

[1] 20 April 1824, Delacroix, 1995, p. 34

[2] Mainardi, 1993, p. 16

[3] *Ibid*, p. 18

[4] Klumpke, p. 123

[5] *Ibid*, p. 128

[6] Lethève, p. 111

[7] 'L'opinion d'Ingres sur le Salon', *La Chronique des arts*, 1908, in Harrison and Wood, p. 469

[8] H. Delaborde, *Ingres: sa vie, ses travaux, sa doctrine*, 1870, in Harrison and Wood, p. 470

[9] Letter to Sensier, 20 Jan 1863, in Cartwright, pp. 237-8

[10] Lethève, p. 108

[11] L. Jopling, *Twenty Years of my Life*, 1925, in Nunn, p. 91

[12] *The picture of the Sabines, exhibited to the public at the National Palace of the Sciences and the Arts, Hall of the Former Academy of Art, by the Citizen DAVID, member of the National Institute, Paris, Year VIII*, Holt, 1986, p. 6

[13] *Ibid*, p. 7

[14] Holt, 1979, p. 137

[15] Groseclose, p. 28

[16] 11 May 1855, in Courbet, pp. 140-1

[17] Delacroix, 1995, p. 308

[18] H. Taine, *Paris-guide*, 1867, in Lethève, p. 120

[19] Lethève, p. 119

[20] *Fine Arts Quarterly Review*, 1863, in Harrison and Wood, p. 513

[21] *Fine Arts Quarterly Review*, 1863, in Whistler, p. 80

[22] 19 April 1866, in Cézanne, p. 104

[23] Courthion, p. 60

[24] Harrison and Wood, p. 570

[25] Kendall, p. 102

[26] 13 Sept 1905, in Mathews, p. 297

[27] Harrison and Wood, pp. 601-2

[28] 10 June 1874, in Whistler, p. 48

[29] 28 Feb 1883, in Pissarro, pp. 22-3

[30] 13 May, 1883, *ibid*, p. 32

[31] Renoir, p. 226

[32] Cited in Mainardi, 1993, p. 138

Exotic

THROUGHOUT THE CENTURY ARTISTS COMMITTTED TO DIVERSE AND SOMETIMES contradictory aesthetics shared a fascination for the exotic. Early century 'PICTURESQUE' peasants, mid-century Orientalist slave girls and Gauguin's *fin de siècle* Tahitian Edens were all manifestations of the desire to escape into worlds and cultures far removed from the dreary familiarity of the urbanised west. In many cases, artists and critics did not distinguish clearly between the various source cultures. Thoré in 1857 listed the range of exotic sights which were then available to the modern travelling artist: from flocks glimpsed in a Swiss ravine to Arab horsemen and Moorish dancers. What mattered was difference from the urban, bourgeois norm experienced by both artists and public. The pursuit of the exotic can be attributed to several co-existing currents, including the search for originality and the imperative need to find new motifs which might attract a public in the competitive market place.

The rapid expansion of colonialism and trade in the second half of the eighteenth century had already led to a fascination with the landscapes, peoples and artefacts of distant lands, as the discoveries of voyagers such as the British Captain Cook and the Frenchman Louis de Bougainville were recounted in sometimes lavishly illustrated publications. Rococo designers had revived the taste for *Chinoiserie* and *Turkeries* (based on imprecise sources) and it became fashionable to have one's portrait painted in similarly exotic costumes. Jean-Jacques Rousseau's concept of the noble savage was fed by such accounts and it in turn fed the hunger for the exotic throughout the next century.

At the beginning of the nineteenth century the Napoleonic wars further expanded knowledge of distant lands, particularly about Egypt and Syria, since Napoleon's army was accompanied by a contingent of 175 *savants* (artists, scientists, botanists, geographers etc.) who provided topographical and scientific surveys which formed the basis for eagerly perused publications. The numerous objects brought back to France for the Musée Napoléon proved to be equally influential. Similarly, British colonialism led to an influx of artefacts and documentation from India, the Orient, Oceania and Africa with which to furnish British museums and to inform British publications.

In the early decades of the nineteenth century exoticism was often European, as the picturesque aesthetic led artists to search out local peasants in regional costumes with which to spice up their works. In France, the craze for such subjects had been initiated by Pauline Chatillon who had exhibited two portraits of Italian peasant women in 1798. She died young and the genre was developed by Madame Haudebourt-Lescot, whose paintings of the costumes and customs of the Italian *popolino* were very popular on the French art market, so that many artists followed in her footsteps. However, from the Romantic era until the mid-1860s exoticism was largely characterised by Orientalism. Until the term 'Middle East' was coined in 1902, the terms 'Orient' and 'Near East' referred to north Africa and the Ottoman Empire (Turkey, Asia Minor, Egypt, Syria and the Holy Land). For the western European traveller this was the closest, non-Christian region to which they could travel.

For the Romantics, the lure of unconsummated experience and escapism often formed part of the Orient's attraction. Hence Delacroix, fired by his passion for Byron's poetry, painted the *Massacre at Chios* (1824) and the *Death of Sardanapalus* (1827) before his visit to north Africa. Géricault and Bonington never travelled to the Near East, but the two artists depicted Oriental themes. These offered liberation from the restrictions of classical rules. Delacroix was one of the first painters to actually visit the region. There he felt himself to be surrounded by antiquity itself, so that it ceased to be an ideal canon mediated through the art of the ancients. From Meknes in Morocco he wrote to Armand Bertin (editor of *Le Journal des Débats*):

> **The picturesque is here in abundance. At every step one sees ready-made pictures, which would bring fame and fortune to twenty generations of painters. You'd think yourself in Rome or in Athens, minus the Attic atmosphere; the cloaks and togas and a thousand details are quite typical of antiquity. A rascal who'll mend the vamp of your shoe for a few coppers has the dress and bearing of Brutus or Cato of Utica.**[1]

From a twenty-first-century viewpoint such attitudes appear patronising and Eurocentric.

However, in the nineteenth century the appreciation of non-classical physiognomies, architecture and landscapes was equated with a progressive stance. As Gautier explained, in his utopian enthusiasm for the new age inspired by the 1848 revolution, hopes of revitalising an exhausted tradition could be found in the exotic cultures of the Orient, Tahiti, India and America, all of which he envisaged as contributing to a melting-pot of humanity:

> **A race greater than that of the fabled Titans or the biblical giants will soon cover the globe, and we shall build not Babels of confusion but towers of harmony...**
>
> **What an endless field of possibility is today open to the artist! Past is the age of three or four tired Greek and Roman ideals, degraded by servile reproduction, and artists today have at their disposal all the types of the huge family of man.[2]**

Yet both Gautier and Delacroix voiced the widely-held European assumption that the unfamiliar beauty which they discovered was that of the Rousseau's unspoiled, but child-like, noble savage. Gautier's article continued:

> **The mysterious Orient is finally becoming accessible, lifting a corner of its veil; those beautiful, pure faces, so calm and dreamy, pale and fresh from the cool shadow of the harem, or bronzed coppery gold by the fiery sun, faces which previously blossomed in a forgotten, secret solitude, leaving no silhouette in our memory, will soon present their perfect lines and noble profiles for artistic study, to the admiration of the people.[3]**

From Tangier, Delacroix wrote to the landscapist Théodore Gudin '...of the marvellous grace and beauty of these unspoilt, sublime children of nature.'[4]

In their dark, splenetic moods the Romantics sought solace in the idea of worlds far removed from their own. Hence, for many, the very attraction of the Muslim world stemmed partly from their perception of it as having remained untainted by the scepticism and rationalism of the Enlightenment. In idealising the exotic, the Romantics followed Rousseau's pastoral dream of the purity and nobility of the 'uncivilised'. The painter Catlin was happy to renounce the sophisticated stimulation and interaction with other artists provided by city life, in favour of his extended travels in the American wilderness:

> **...in this country, I...have little to steal my thoughts away from the contemplation of the beautiful models that are about me...I feel an unceasing excitement of a much higher order – the certainty that I am drawing knowledge from the true source. My enthusiastic admiration of man in the honest and elegant simplicity of nature, has always fed the warmest feelings of my bosom, and shut half the avenues to my heart against the specious refinements of the accomplished world.[5]**

Yet perhaps the greatest attraction was that the exotic was perceived as allowing for the suspension of rigid European moral and social norms; it made permissible deviations into the irrational, the erotic and the barbaric. When Delacroix first arrived in Tangier, he felt that he was indeed in a dream:

> **We landed in the midst of the strangest crowd of people... The Jewesses are quite lovely. I'm afraid that it will be difficult to do more than paint them: they are real pearls of Eden... I'm like a man in a dream, seeing things he's afraid will vanish from him.[6]**

Through these realms of otherness the Romantics could indulge their predilection for wild fantasies: violent scenes of carnage, fights to the death between wild stallions and lions, female bondage, rape and human sacrifice – the essence of male adolescent dreams.

In the first half of the century, the few artists who travelled to the Orient tended to go as part of military or diplomatic parties: such was the case with Delacroix and Horace Vernet. By the 1850s the region was becoming more accessible. A nascent tourist industry and greater trading and diplomatic contacts allowed a flood of self-financed visits by European artists. Some did so on an ambitious scale: Gérôme took 47 camels, 200 servants and six companions on his trip to the Sinai desert in 1868. For many the attraction remained that of the stimulus to the imagination provided by the unfamiliar. In 1856 the British artist Barbara Bodichon wrote to George Eliot from the Isle of Wight expressing a wish to visit some 'wilder country to paint.'[7] The following autumn she made her first visit to Algeria, from which she wrote:

> **I have seen Swiss mountains and Lombard plains, Scotch lochs and Welsh mountains, but never anything so unearthly, so delicate, so aerial, as the long stretches of blue mountains and shining sea; the dark cypresses, relieved against a background of a thousand dainty tints, and the massive white Moorish houses gleaming out from the grey mysterious green of olive trees.[8]**

In the sober, realist mood of the mid-century an exoticism which valued observed fact appeared to displace Romantic yearnings. The era was dominated by an obsession with accuracy of detail. Paul Lenoir, who accompanied Gérôme on his travels, explained the purpose of his 1868 Egyptian trip in these terms:

> **Without having pretensions to seeing everything, we wanted to look carefully in order to paint dal vero that which we saw.[9]**

The preoccupation with making precise records of their travels was encouraged by the recent invention of PHOTOGRAPHY. It is no coincidence that this tendency was pioneered by Horace Vernet, who arrived in Egypt armed with a daguerreotype camera in 1839, only three months after Daguerre had first demonstrated his revolutionary process. Vernet used the daguerreotype as a quick means of notation, as did the many Orientalists after him, including Gérôme, Holman Hunt, and William James Müller. Moreover, the painters often worked alongside the pioneer photographers who quickly fulfilled the public's thirst for anthropological and topographical photographs, in itself a vivid form of exoticism.

Many artists delighted in the sheer range of humanity to which their travels introduced them. Led by Gérôme they prided themselves on their ability to distinguish between the various ethnic types, as well as the finer points of architectural styles and decorative details, and a subgenre 'ethnographic painting' evolved. Charles Gleyre, for example, was commissioned to accompany the American traveller John Lowell Jnr. in order to produce such works, as well as topographical landscapes. The trend was reinforced by a growing cosmopolitanism in the European cities and contact with a wide range of peoples and their artefacts at the World Exhibitions. For progressives such developments were evidence of a new universality. The critic Théophile Thoré enthused:

> **One can no longer remain mewed up in philosophical, religious, literary or artistic systems, in little symbols and little mythologies, at a time when all religions and institutions, all thoughts, and all forms first confront then pervade each other in a chain of reciprocal influence,...when China is open to Europeans, and the Chinese up sticks and invade**

Western America; when Indians and all the inhabitants of old Asia come to visit European exhibitions, those meeting-places of the entire world. Ancient stigmata of race, old local superstitions, ancient forms embalmed by each people within the shadows of its frontier: these things have had their day. There is but one race and one people, one religion and one symbol: – Humanity![10]

Nevertheless, the Orient was largely seen as an unchanging world whose peoples had remained the same since Biblical days. This was a powerful attraction for painters of the Holy Land. Vernet was among the first artists to realise that when he observed the peoples of the Orient, he was seeing the actual physiognomies of Biblical characters, which had hitherto been based on European models. He thus pioneered a campaign for authenticity in Bible paintings, apparently insensitive to the potential conflict between this and his depictions of French military campaigns launched to subjugate the Algerian people:

Once the connection between Arab manners and customs and those of the ancient Hebrews takes hold of your thoughts...then the richest vein is yours to be mined!...Here is the way to do something new that's not merely freakish.[11]

His counterpart in Protestant England was David Wilkie, who articulated his own mission in travelling to the Holy Land in 1841: '...a Martin Luther, in painting, is as much called for as in theology, to sweep away the abuses by which our divine pursuit is encumbered.'[12] In a letter from Alexandria he specified his intention to fulfill this aim:

My object in this voyage was to see what has formed the scenes of so many pictures – the scenes of so many subjects painted from the Scripture, but which have never been seen by the painters who have delineated them.[13]

The most widespread and commercially successful exotic works were in the area of GENRE and LANDSCAPE, although these were often also evocative of Biblical themes by virtue of their topographical or physiognomic references. Far from embodying Thoré's humanist melting pot, most of these works would now be seen as reactionary, racist and/or sexist in content. Artists such as Gérôme, John Frederick Lewis and Leopold Müller used a highly illusionistic visual language, based on precise detail, which appeared to convey accurate representations of life in the Orient but was often factually inaccurate. For example, Gérôme's *The Dance of the Almah* (1864) offers a glimpse of the characteristic pink and yellow brothels of Cairo. Yet prostitutes had been banned from the city in 1834. Ignoring the squalor, poverty, exploitation and disease upon which most eye-witness accounts remarked, academic artists presented titillating, fantasy worlds for the European and American art market in which 'barbarian' warriors were uninhibitedly ferocious, all children were well fed, girls attended schools and near-naked slaves or prostitutes gladly displayed themselves to their occidental viewers.

For the AVANT-GARDE of the 1860s and 1870s, so concerned with grasping the MODERNITY of their own world, such Orientalism was anathema. Castagnary called for its demise in his 1872 Salon review, while in 1876 he disparaged the Egyptian scenes exhibited by Eugène Fromentin:

In this make-believe High-Egypt, a chocolate Nile flows between chocolate banks, while women with chocolate complexions plunge chocolate vases into chocolate waves.[14]

He hoped that Orientalism would soon die, so that he and others could '...erect a stone and engrave upon it these comforting words: "Orientalism has lived in French painting".'[15] But it did not. Such works continued to sell and many an artist made a good living from them until well into the early decades of the twentieth century. Indeed, during the Catholic revival that manifested itself during the conservative backlash to progressive thought in 1870s France, the sub-genre of Muslim piety was particularly favoured on the grounds that the Muslim world had bypassed the scepticism of the modern era. Lenoir wrote:

> **The thing that strikes you most when you visit mosques is their exclusively religious, almost poetic, atmosphere. These are not our pretty-pretty Parisian cathedrals, nor our phoney Greek temples, which are just theatres where the performance is the Mass. Seeing quiet, serious Arabs prostrate themselves without affectation before the wall of the *mihrāb*, I could not help thinking of my good old Madeleine, where the one o'clock service is just like the opening night of a show... In Cairo, it's fanaticism if you like, but at least it's real religious faith, and it expresses itself without any of that elegant, frivolous piety that characterises the Roman Catholic mosque back home.[16]**

The very avant-garde which dismissed the Orientalists, had since the early 1860s turned to the art of Japan for its own thrill of 'otherness'. A fashion for things Japanese developed soon after the opening of trade with the west in the 1850s. Kimonos, fans, blue and white porcelain etc. were sold at the *Porte Chinoise*, the inaccurately named shop opened in the Rue de Rivoli in 1862, and appeared as attributes or picturesque motifs in the paintings of Salon artists such as Tissot and Alfred Stevens. As they also did, initially, in works by the avant-garde: examples included Whistler's *Princess from the Land of Porcelain* (Salon 1865) and Monet's *Japonnerie* (1876), showing a woman in a brightly embroidered kimono. In their exploitation of decorative Japanese accessories, these works were also a form of exoticism.

Avant-garde calls for such an unfamiliar realm to be recognised echoed similarly idealised justifications for Orientalism. Hence, Renoir praised the Japanese in terms similar to those employed by Orientalist artists about the peoples of the Near East:

> **The Japanese still have a simplicity of life which gives them time to go about and to contemplate. They still look, fascinated, at a blade of grass, or the flight of birds, or the wonderful movements of fish, and they go home, their minds filled with beautiful ideas, which they have no trouble in putting on the objects which they decorate.[17]**

Duranty praised the positive influence which Japanese art had on the works of the Impressionists, but then linked it to that of other, non-European cultures:

> **Was there not, in the proud, melancholy eye of the Hindus, in the great, languorous, contemplative eye of the Persians, and in the lively, narrowed eye of the Chinese and Japanese, a masterful ability to blend exquisite harmonies of delicate, soft, neutral tones with bold, bright colours?[18]**

However, what had changed was that the avant-garde was responding primarily to the formal characteristics of Japanese art itself, particularly the woodcuts, which Félix Bracquemond had been one of the first to discover in 1856. Artists as diverse as Manet, Monet, Degas, Cassatt, Morisot, Whistler, and later Gauguin, Van Gogh and Seurat took an interest in Japanese prints. They absorbed the economy of means, the sharp observation of motifs, the asymmetry, the flatness, the bold outlines and freshness of colour, which characterised the work of Hokusai,

Utamaro and Hiroshige. Impressionists like Morisot acknowledged these artists as their counterparts: '... only Manet and the Japanese can indicate a mouth, eyes, a nose with a single stroke of the brush, so concisely that the rest of the face models itself.'[19]

While Monet later said of the Japanese artists:

> **Their refinement of taste has always pleased me and I approve of the suggestions of their aesthetic code, which evokes presence by means of a shadow, the whole by means of a fragment.**[20]

Manet and the Impressionists also empathised with the subject matter of Japanese prints: the secular pleasures of late eighteenth and nineteenth-century Japan seemed to echo that of the urban sophisticates of Second Empire Paris, with its brothels, theatres, crowded streets, convivial sharing of food and drink as well as its tributes to the pleasures of NATURE. Very few artists visited Japan; what they were inspired by was its art. Pissarro wrote to his son Lucien:

> **Admirable, the Japanese exhibition. Hiroshigé is a marvellous impressionist. Monet, Rodin and I are enthusiastic about the show. I am pleased with my effects of snow and floods, these Japanese artists confirm my beliefs and our vision.**[21]

Nevertheless statements were often couched in an adulatory tone: Mallarmé claimed that Japanese perspective was superior to that of 'civilised education', while the Goncourts went further, claiming that Japanese art was superior to that of the Greeks. While this can be interpreted as Eurocentric and patronising, it can also be understood as a combative device. When Whistler ended his 'Ten O'Clock Lecture' by equating Greek classicism with Japanese art, he was self-consciously aware of the controversy which this would cause:

> **...the story of the beautiful is already complete – hewn in the marbles of the Parthenon – and broidered, with the birds, upon the fan of Hokusai – at the foot of Fusiyama.**[22]

In the closing decades of the century the lure of PRIMITIVE artefacts and cultures added yet another twist to exoticism. The sophisticated and self-conscious avant-garde sought out and reassessed ever more unfamiliar sources for their works in Egyptian, Persian, Indian, Javanese, Peruvian, Japanese and Celtic cultures. The pursuit of the 'primitive', and so of the exotic was an important element within the avant-garde shift from naturalism. In the Symbolists' search for an authentic expression of their inner worlds, all that was contrived and illusionistic was condemned as insincere. The exaggerations and distortions of form, colour and line which they found in 'primitive' works, allowed them to take the risks which enabled them to create equivalents for ideas and inner states of mind which avoided naturalism.

The Symbolists admired not only the works of non-western cultures, but also what they perceived to be more authentic, less corrupt ways of life, untainted by the pretensions and hypocrisies of the bourgeoisie in the industrialised and urbanised west. Access to artefacts and peoples from remote parts of the world and in particular from the colonies was widened in the last quarter of the century. Such works and peoples were being exhibited at increasingly lavish international world exhibitions and in the ethnographic museums, most of which were founded during this period. Again, these displays constituted a form of objectification, which exoticised peoples, their cultures and their objects. Gauguin haunted the Paris Exposition Universelle of 1889, where he drooled over the Javanese dancers:

You were wrong not to come the other day. There are Hindu dancers in the Javanese village. All the art of India is there, and my photographs of Cambodia literally are found there, too. I will go there again on Tuesday, as I have a rendezvous with a mulatto girl. [23]

The desire to escape to a simpler, purer way of life often involved tourism within Europe. Gauguin, Emile Bernard and others escaped to Pont-Aven in Brittany, while Paula Modersohn-Becker joined Fritz Mackensen and others in the artists' colony in rural Worpswede. When Stanhope Forbes discovered the Cornwall fishing village of Newlyn in 1884, what delighted him was that it was 'a sort of English Concarneau.'[24]

Gauguin soon dreamed of a more distant refuge. From Pont-Aven he wrote:

I am going soon to Tahiti, a small island in Oceania, where the material necessities of life can be had without money... A terrible epoch is brewing in Europe for the coming generation: the kingdom of gold. Everything is putrefied, even men, even the arts. There, at least, under an eternally summer sky, on marvelously fertile soil, the Tahitian has only to lift his hands to gather his food; and in addition he never works...happy inhabitants of the unknown paradise of Oceania... To live, for them, is to sing and to love.[25]

Yet, as Pissarro pointed out, if unmediated the reliance on alien formal languages could be interpreted as plagiarism, and when divorced from their cultural context the resulting works could become reactionary in content. In his critique of Aurier's article about Gauguin, Pissarro offered an anarchist analysis, explaining that he did not object to the expression of ideas via colour or symbols, as such, but sensed a lack of authenticity in Gauguin's work:

The Japanese practised this art, as did the Chinese, and their symbols are wonderfully natural, but then they were not Catholics, and Gauguin is a Catholic. – I do not criticise Gauguin for having painted a rose background...what I dislike is that he copped [sic] these elements from the Japanese, the Byzantine painters and others. I criticise him for not applying his synthesis to our modern philosophy which is absolutely social, anti-authoritarian and anti-mystical. – There is where the problem becomes serious. This is a step backwards; Gauguin is not a seer, he is a schemer who has sensed that the bourgeoisie are moving to the right.[26]

Pissarro returned to this point a couple of years later:

I saw Gauguin... I told him that this art did not belong to him, that he was a civilised man and hence it was his function to show us harmonious things. We parted, each unconvinced... He is always poaching on someone's ground; now he is pillaging the savages of Oceania.[27]

Catholic revivalists esteemed in the supposed primitive piety of Breton people a 'savage', untutored, uncritical naivety bypassed by the scepticism of the Enlightenment and similar to that admired in Muslims of the Near East. Jules Breton wrote in his autobiography that the austere landscapes of the region, together with the PHYSIOGNOMY and costumes of its people, evoked religious sentiments:

I was profoundly struck by Finistère, under all its aspects, maritime, rural and religious. The dreary moors, the granite crosses of the Calvaries erected at the solitary cross-roads, expressing the rude fervour of the inhabitants...the wan light of the crepuscule and of cloudy days that cast a leaden hue, like a gray tan, over the thin faces of the peasants with

their fierce eyes and their long, thick hair, falling down their backs, over their stooped shoulders; the women that looked like pictures of the Virgin, with their mitre-shaped head-dresses,…and their cotton petticoats trimmed with gold or silver braid – this monastic rusticity, this mystic wildness.[28]

A similar impetus drew the French public to Gérôme's paintings of Arabs at prayer and those naturalist depictions of earnest, white-faced peasants at religious festivals in Brittany, as in *The Pardon* by Dagnan-Bouveret and versions of this subject by other artists. This theme also featured in self-consciously Symbolist paintings, for example Gauguin's *Jacob Wrestling with an Angel* (1888) and Bernard's *Breton Women at a Pardon* (1888). However, the exoticism of a Dagnan-Bouveret consisted in representing the subject as if untouched by technological or political change. Like the Orient, Brittany was portrayed in the traditional academic manner, as a timeless world, admired for its supposedly unchanging, eternal qualities and social relations, so affirming conservative values. The Symbolists' exotic subject matter may have had equally socially and politically conservative overtones and their assimilation of the formal simplifications and distortions of their exotic sources may indeed have been Eurocentric plagiarism. However, the very awkwardness and savagery of the visual language with which they portrayed their subjects conveyed a jagged disjunction from their own society which could also be interpreted as a critique of its social and moral outlooks. Ironically, it was that same corrupt, urban civilisation that sustained the experimentation and distortions of the avant-garde as well as the traditionalism of the academic artists.

See: AVANT-GARDE, GENRE, PEASANT LIFE, PICTURESQUE, PRIMITIVE

[1] 2 April 1832, Delacroix, 1971, p. 192

[2] 'L'art en 1848', *L'Artiste*, 1848, in Harrison and Wood, p. 316

[3] *Ibid*, pp. 316-7

[4] 23 Feb 1832, Delacroix, 1971, p. 184

[5] Letter to the editor of the *New York Commercial Advertiser*, first published 24 July 1832, see Harrison and Wood, pp. 134-5

[6] Letter to J.B. Pierret, 25 Jan (1832), Delacroix, 1971, p. 181

[7] 14 Jan 1856, in Orr, p. 179

[8] *Ibid*, p. 180

[9] P. Lenoir, *Le Fayoum, le Sinaï et Pétra*, 1872, in Stevens, p. 21

[10] 'New Tendencies in Art', 1857, in Harrison and Wood, pp. 380-1

[11] Letter of 1840, in Stevens, pp. 32-3

[12] A. Cunningham, *The life of Sir David Wilkie*, 1843, in Stevens, p. 33

[13] See Scharf, p. 79

[14] In Stevens, p. 135

[15] *Ibid*, p. 22

[16] Lenoir, *op. cit.*, in Stevens, p. 38

[17] Renoir, p. 217

[18] E. Duranty, *The New Painting*, 1876, in Harrison and Wood, p. 581

[19] B. Morisot, Carnet Vert, c.1885, in Shennan, p. 41

[20] See Rewald, p. 209

[21] 3 Feb 1893, Pissarro, p. 207

[22] 'Ten O'Clock Lecture', 1885, Whistler, p. 159

[23] Letter to E. Bernard, n.d. (March 1889), in Chipp, p. 78

[24] Letter cited in House and Stevens, p. 188

[25] Letter to J.F. Willumsen, Autumn 1890, in Chipp, p. 79

[26] Letter to L. Pissarro, 20 April 1891, Pissarro, p. 164

[27] 23 Nov 1893, Pissarro, p. 221

[28] J. Breton, *The Life of an Artist*, London, 1891, p. 308

Finish

IN THE EIGHTEENTH CENTURY DIDEROT HAD INITIATED THE DEBATE about the relative aesthetic merits of the sketch and the finished work and this raged on into the Romantic era, before culminating in the Impressionists' conflation of the two. Yet the Davidian belief in a high degree of impersonal, timeless finish was to be staunchly upheld by academicians from Moscow to Boston until the late nineteenth century and beyond. In terms of mainstream bourgeois taste it was probably the most favoured manner of the century.

It was partly a matter of professionalism. Before photography arrived, a major criterion of an artist's competence was the ability to render convincing, and therefore detailed, illusions of space, light and surface texture: the gleam in a sphinx's eye, the sheen on the fur of Oedipus's cloak. Delécluze, ex-student of David, criticised Delacroix's first Salon painting *Dante and Virgil* (1822) for being merely 'a sketch composed and painted with verve,' while he derided the *Massacre at Chios* (1824) for its technical imperfections, its 'impetuousness and spirited lack of correctness'.[1]

A highly finished surface, in which the spontaneous *ÉBAUCHE* (under-painting) had been rubbed down and reworked with careful half tones so that evidence of brush-marks were eliminated, denoted a seriously crafted work that appeared effortless: the concealment of manual labour broke with art's artisanal past. Yet in practical terms, such work would stand the test of time: the surface of the canvas would be less fragile than those of paint be-spattered, highly textured works. In keeping with such self-conscious professionalism, perfection of finish was the aim and, as Ingres noted, this would be achieved by high precision:

> **The completion of form comes from finish. In drawing, some are happy to leave it at sentiment; once that has been expressed, that is enough for them. Raphael and Leonardo de Vinci are here to prove that sentiment and precision can be allies.[2]**

Of equal importance was the nineteenth-century work ethic. The high moral value attached to conscientious and arduous work informed both the artists' and their publics' criteria for evaluating art. This was evident in the laborious methodology of academic teaching, which warned against the slapdash and the easily achieved, as opposed to high precision. In his teaching manual, first published in 1851, Etex warned:

> **A drawing, like a painting, cannot be done straight off. A notebook sketch is done in this way, and the skilful artist may put a great deal into a drawing tossed off in this manner. But the pupil must go to work more humbly, starting with simple elements and working up to more complex, keeping the main aim in view and achieving delicacy by degrees.[3]**

Moreover, one does not wash one's dirty linen in public. The spontaneous soups and slurries of the *ÉBAUCHE* and the *ESQUISSE* belonged to the private world of the studio. To parade the personal, inspirational process in the public market place was seen as cheap, self-aggrandizing behaviour and the concurrent display of brushstrokes as flashy posturing. The sober good manners of the professional entailed quiet self-effacement. In 1866 the British academician Henry O'Neil would still be stating this view:

> **Above all, beware of slovenliness of manner, which is too often regarded by the superficial observer as the mark of genius; whereas, in truth, it is the unerring sign of a want of real power, and is but an attempt of the artist to exhort by audacity that attention which he could not excite by more justifiable means.**[4]

Finally, and perhaps most crucially, the surface and the execution should not get in the way of communicating the idea. Ingres warned:

> **What gets called 'touch' is an abuse of execution. It is nothing but the mark of fake talents, fake artists, who depart from imitating nature just to show off their skill. Touch, however skilful, should not be visible, it prevents illusion and freezes everything. Instead of representing the object it shows the process, instead of showing the thought it betrays the hand.**[5]

The price paid for such impersonal, detailed exactitude was high. As Diderot had pointed out, originality and therefore genius were most evident in the spontaneous first thought as expressed in the preparatory *CROQUIS, esquisse* or *ébauche*. Not surprisingly, Delacroix was much preoccupied with the sketch/finish dilemma and his position changed as he matured, from an adherence to academic notions in the early 1820s towards seeking ways of retaining the qualities of the *croquis* and the *ébauche* in the finished work. By the 1840s he wrote of dispensing with the *esquisse*. However, his ideas on the subject were complex, subtle and sometimes contradictory. In his mature years he summed up the dilemma in a diary entry for 1854:

> **The precise quality that renders the sketch the highest expression of the idea is not the suppression of details, but their subordination to the great sweeping lines that come before everything else in making the impression. The greatest difficulty therefore, when it comes to tackling the picture, is this subordination of details which, nevertheless, make up the composition and are the very warp and weft of the picture itself.**[6]

Despite his high regard for the sketch, like other independents of the July Monarchy as well as Constable and Turner in England, Delacroix never regarded any of these preparatory processes as finished works: 'an artist does not spoil a picture by finishing it, but when he abandons the vagueness of the sketch he reveals his personality more fully, thereby displaying the full scope of his talent, not its limitations.'[7]

Delacroix's challenge to accepted notions of finish was felt as a particularly strong affront by academicians because he was a history painter. In contrast, since landscapes were considered lowly in the hierarchy of subject matter, greater leeway was accorded to them in terms of finish. Early in the century it became increasingly acceptable for landscapists to exhibit sketches. Constable, for example, showed *Studies from Nature* at the Royal Academy in 1803, yet he was careful to distinguish between these and his finished works, which were completed from oil sketches in the studio as academic procedure required: 'My dear Fisher...I am most anxious to get into my London painting-room, for I do not consider myself at work unless I am before a six-foot canvas.'[8] It was when he set out to retain the rough facture of the oil sketch in large-scale works that he encountered opposition.

The demands of remaining true to NATURE while it incessantly changed according to light and weather conditions were particularly difficult for landscapists, who had long worked on studies, *esquisses* and *POCHADES* directly from the motif as part of their preparatory work. For the Barbizon painters, as for Constable and the Italian Macchiaioli group, it was thus a matter of re-evaluating the importance of the spontaneous first impression against the demands of the well crafted, considered finished work. Corot for example ruminated on the need for spontaneity but also stressed the importance of not slacking when working on initial sketches:

> **I've noticed that everything that was done in one go was franker, more lovely in form and allows us to make the most of many chance occurrences; whereas, when we go back over things, we often lose that harmonious, primitive hue. I think that this method is very good for vegetation, which allows for a bit more leeway. Manufactured objects and bodies, generally well defined always need to be very precise. I see also how strict we must be in front of nature and not to be satisfied with a hastily drawn thumb-nail sketch. When looking at my drawings, how often have I regretted not having had the will to spend another half hour on them![9]**

Sensier, Rousseau's biographer, tells us that the Barbizon landscapist worked on his first Salon submission with care because he was afraid of 'showing himself to the public by way of the indecorous and blunt qualities of an étude which was only a preliminary to his actual work.'[10]

Despite the opening up of the debate, in the first four decades of the century most independents continued to adhere to studio ethics in terms of carefully differentiating between their sketches and their finished studio works, although they challenged the definition of finish as being a glassy Ingresque surface in which brush marks were invisible. Reviewing Corot's landscapes in his 1845 Salon, Baudelaire questioned the academic understanding of finish as meaning a highly detailed, glass-like, 'licked' surface, and defended the possibility of a spontaneous, roughly surfaced painting also being brought to a state of completion. Confronting the frequent accusation that 'M. Corot does not know how to paint,' he argued:

> **...a work of genius (or if you prefer, a work of the soul), in which every element is well seen, well observed, well understood and well imagined, will always be very well executed when it is *sufficiently* so. Next, that there is a great difference between a work that is *complete* and a work that is *finished*; that in general what is *complete* is not *finished*, and that a thing that is highly *finished* need not be *complete* at all.[11]**

With customary incisiveness, by distinguishing between finish and completion, Baudelaire had found a way out of the sketch/finish impasse.

The debate polarised during the mid-century decades. As the invention of PHOTOGRAPHY first made its impact many artists vied with the accuracy obtained by the new medium. Intertwined with this development was the taste of the new middle-class patrons for art of the seventeenth-century Dutch Republic. Both occurred in an increasingly commercialised art world. A multitude of artists throughout the west fulfilled this demand for highly detailed, illusionistic, prosaic descriptions of their subject-matter, as exemplified by French *juste-*

milieu artists such as Delaroche and his pupil Gérôme, the German portrait painter Winterhalter or the English genre painter William Powell Frith. Moreover the influential writings of Ruskin equated accuracy of detail, in describing specific motifs, with moral purpose and Christian virtue:

> **It is not...detail sought for its own sake, not the calculable bricks of the Dutch house-painters, nor the numbered hairs and mapped wrinkles of Denner, which constitute great art, they are the lowest and most contemptible art; but it is detail referred to a great end, sought for the sake of the inestimable beauty which exists in the slightest and the least of God's works.**[12]

It was during the same mid-century decades that the AVANT-GARDE combated such outlooks. As Courbet wrote of one of his works to his friend Francis Wey:

> **...the public admires only what is finished. If the tiniest detail is missing, the work no longer exists for them. That landscape was not finished, the leaves were not picked out, they existed only as a mass. It would have been successful only among artists.**[13]

Yet there were artists, critics and collectors who did appreciate the informal, the incomplete and the lively surfaces of the various preparatory processes. Couture's innovatory approach to teaching in his *ATELIER* from 1847-63, then privately until his death in 1879, stressed spontaneity, personal expression and freshness of COLOUR rather than the laborious methodical practices of over-intellectualising academicians: 'Make sure first of all that you have mastered material procedures; then think of nothing and produce with a fresh mind and hearty spirit whatever you feel like doing.'[14]

In the 1860s and 1870s Manet and the Impressionists challenged the very concept of making sharp distinctions between preparatory stages and finished works. This resulted partly from the Romantics' legacy of valuing the incomplete and the spontaneous as marks of the artist's individuality, but also from a distrust of pretentious fussiness. Antonin Proust recalled Manet often saying:

> **I loathe all that is unnecessary in painting, but the snag is how to see what is necessary. We have been led astray by painters' tricks-of-the-trade. How can we rid ourselves of them? Who will show us the way to make paintings simple and clear? Who will get rid of all these trimmings? Look, my friend, the truth of the matter, what we've got to do, is to go right ahead without bothering about what other people think.**[15]

The Impressionists made a point of exhibiting their works under the titles of *ébauche, étude* or *esquisse* and signed them, so showing their readiness to put the process of making art on display. For them, acceptance of the state of incompletion could be a mark of the fluidity and speed of contemporary life and of our perception of it. In the 1870s resistance to academic facility of technical finish had become a badge of avant-garde sincerity. Cézanne wrote to his mother of his struggle to avoid facile finish:

> **I have to work all the time, not to reach that final perfection which earns the admiration of imbeciles. – And this thing which is commonly appreciated so much is merely the effect of craftsmanship and renders all work resulting from it inartistic and common.**[16]

The debate reached its apogee in the Whistler-Ruskin trial. In 1877 Ruskin's review of a Grosvenor Gallery exhibition accused 'the modern schools' of 'indolence' and 'eccentricities'.

Above all, Whistler's *Nocturne in Black and Gold* (1875) should not have been shown, because:

> **...the ill-educated conceit of the artist so nearly approached the aspect of wilful imposture. I have seen and heard much of cockney impudence before now, but never expected to hear a coxcomb ask 200 guineas for flinging a pot of paint in the public's face.**[17]

Whistler sued. In the ensuing trial the court's criteria were those of the academicians. They relied on the Victorian work ethic: if something was done quickly it was worth less than if it took skill and patience to achieve. The Attorney General asked Whistler how long it took him to 'knock off' the picture, which led to the following famous exchange:

> **[Attorney General]: 'The labour of two days, then, is that for which you ask two hundred guineas!'**

> **[Whistler]: 'No: – I ask it for the knowledge of a lifetime.'** (*Applause*)[18]

Eminent practising painters such as Burne-Jones and Frith were called into the witness box in the court's attempt to define the term 'finish'. Burne-Jones testified as follows:

> **In my opinion complete finish ought to be the object of all artists. A picture ought not to fall short of what has been for ages considered complete finish.**[19]

When pressed, he admitted that Whistler's painting was:

> **...bewildering in form; and it has no composition and detail. A day or a day and a half seems a reasonable time within which to paint it. It shows no finish – it is simply a sketch...it would be impossible to call it a serious work of art. Mr. Whistler's picture is only one of the thousand failures to paint night. The picture is not worth two hundred guineas.**[20]

Frith agreed. Although Whistler won the case, he was further insulted by the court when it awarded him just one farthing in damages. The cost of the trial and the subsequent loss of buyers ruined him financially.

Whereas Whistler was claiming technical audacity as a means of achieving the formal and moral autonomy of art, Signac would argue, at the end of the century, that technical innovations were an act of political radicalism. He used the lack of finish pioneered by the Impressionists as his example:

> **It would therefore be an error...systematically to require a precise socialist tendency in works of art; this tendency will be found much stronger and more eloquent in pure aesthetes – revolutionaries by temperament, who, departing from the beaten track, paint what they see, as they feel it, and, often unconsciously, give a solid pick blow to the old social edifice, the which, worm eaten, cracks and crumbles like some abandoned cathedral.**[21]

Ironically, by the closing decades of the century the roughly textured surfaces favoured by Delacroix and Constable and the sincere responses to the motifs of the Impressionists were becoming the hackneyed formulaic techniques used by Salon artists. Yet the tradition of high finish dependent on careful studio practice lived on into the twentieth century in commissioned portraits and popular art.

See: *CROQUIS, ÉBAUCHE, ESQUISSE, ÉTUDE, PLEIN-AIR, POCHADE*

[1] R. Baschet, *E.-J. Delécluze, témoin de son temps (1781-1863)*, 1942, in Boime, p. 89

[2] In Delaborde, p. 126

[3] *Cours élémentaire de dessin*, 1877, in Boime, pp. 32-3

[4] H.N. O'Neil, *Lectures on Painting Delivered at the Royal Academy*, 1866, in Craig Harrison, p. 66

[5] In Delaborde, p. 150

[6] 23 April 1854, in Delacroix, 1995, p. 239

[7] 20 April 1853, *ibid*, p. 183

[8] Letter to John Fisher, 23 Oct 1821, in Holt, 1986, p. 114

[9] Italian journey notebook, in Cailler, I, p. 87

[10] A. Sensier, *Souvenirs sur Th. Rousseau*, 1872, in Boime, p. 93

[11] *Salon de 1845*, in Baudelaire, 1965, p. 24

[12] Preface to the second edition of *Modern Painters*, 1844, in Harrison and Wood, p. 207

[13] 20 April 1861, in Courbet, p. 194

[14] See Boime, p. 69

[15] A. Proust, *Edouard Manet: souvenirs*, 1913, in Courthion, p. 3

[16] 26 Sept 1874, in Cézanne, p. 142

[17] *Daily News*, 1878, in Harrison and Wood, p. 834

[18] In Whistler, p. 5

[19] *Ibid*, p. 14

[20] *Ibid*, p. 15

[21] *La Révolte*, 1891, in Harrison and Wood, p. 797

Genius

WHEN QUESTIONED BY A CUSTOMS OFFICER AS HE STEPPED OFF A SHIP AT NEW YORK harbour in 1882, Oscar Wilde famously declaimed: 'I have nothing to declare, except my genius.'[1] Such a statement could be interpreted as bravado, concealing the insecurities of a nineteenth-century artist operating without direct patronage in a mostly philistine society. The Romantics were the first to give the concept of genius a central place within the century's aesthetics. Yet it originated in the ideas of the Enlightenment, which had led artists to question received ideas and to place much greater stress on their own individuality and on the concept of innate qualities that could not be taught.

Taking a social view, David explained that only exceptional artists would be able to portray the glories of the Revolution: 'To paint the energy of the people which, in breaking its chains, has voted to liberate human kind, it takes proud colours, an energetic style, a bold brush, a volcanic genius.'[2] The Ancien Régime had crushed true genius:

> **...it is through this atrocious politics that the satraps have come to veil genius, to dry out the germ of true talent, to keep out the artist-philosopher whose brave pencils would have dared to show the people the dazzling image of liberty alongside the hideous one of slavery.**[3]

The early death (aged 26) of Jean-Germain Drouais, David's favourite pupil, was reputedly due to his obsessive pursuit of artistic virtue. The incident created a powerful legend that influenced artists such as Anne-Louis Girodet and Théodore Géricault, who also sought to arrive at early success via precocious genius rather than training and experience. In an undated notebook Géricault attributed David's reputation to his genius:

David…owes the success which has brought him to the attention of the whole world to nothing but his own genius. He owes nothing to any school; on the contrary, the influence of a school might have been extremely detrimental to his talent.[4]

He went on to argue that truly great artists did not simply echo the teachings of the ACADEMY and that therein lay some of their greatness. Moreover, whatever obstacles were placed in its path, genius always prevailed:

…although obstacles and difficulties frighten mediocre men, they are the necessary food of genius. They cause it to mature, and raise it up; if the way is easy it withers and dies. All that obstructs the path of genius irritates it and inspires a state of feverish agitation, upsetting and overturning those obstacles, and producing masterpieces.[5]

Whereas the upright Republicans, guided by David, had talked of genius as the articulation of shared, civic beliefs, the Romantics discussed the state of their individual souls. The first to value genius above all else, they defined it in terms of creative originality, IMAGINATION and personal independence, distinguishing it from mere talent. As the market place replaced traditional systems of patronage by church and state, artists were expected to fulfill the conflicting social roles of unworldly seer and sharp entrepreneur. Perhaps they could only survive by willing themselves into a high degree of self belief. William Blake, working in Britain where state patronage had never been on such a large scale as that of France, voiced his sense of alienation from potential patrons and the need to believe in his own genius:

Imagination is My World; this world of Dross is beneath my Notice & beneath the Notice of the Public. I demand therefore of the Amateurs of art the Encouragement which is my due; if they continue to refuse, theirs is the loss, not mine, & theirs is the Contempt of Posterity. I have Enough in the Approbation of my Fellow labourers; this is my glory & exceeding great reward. I go on & nothing can hinder my course:
> **and in Melodious Accents I**
> **Will sit me down & Cry I, I…** [6]

Delacroix, like most male artists of his generation, was very much preoccupied with the concept of genius. He took its existence for granted but sought to understand its essence:

Dimier thinks that great passions are the source of all genius! I think that it is imagination alone,…Dufresne made a very true remark. He said that fundamentally, what made a man outstanding was his absolutely personal way of seeing things… Hence, no rules whatsoever for the greatest minds; rules are only for people who merely have talent, which can be acquired. The proof is that genius cannot be transmitted.[7]

The following month he seized the moment of his thought and jotted down:

…Saturday 15 May, during the course of the day.

What moves men of genius, or rather, what inspires their work, is not new ideas, but their obsession with the idea that what has already been said is not enough.[8]

The Romantics equated genius with the breaking of rules; that is why they venerated Shakespeare as a playwright who did not conform to the classical rules of drama.

By mid-century the Realists and Naturalists looked askance at the grandiose claims and self-absorption of the Romantics, preferring to see themselves as workmanlike recorders of the TRUTH. Yet some of them assimilated the Romantics' definition of the social role of artists as rebellious, outrageous or eccentric, while most believed that their works must stem from freedom and individualism. Constable for example, who called for humility on the part of artists and rarely used the term 'genius', wrote: 'Whatever may be thought of my art, it is my own; and I would rather possess a freehold, though but a cottage, than live in a palace belonging to another.'[9] Courbet consciously cultivated the public persona of the bohemian outsider. In the essay he wrote in 1852 to help the writer Théophile Silvestre, who was preparing a book about living artists, he expressed a provocative arrogance:

> **I am a Courbetist, that is all; my painting is the only true one; I am the first and the only artist of this century; the others are students or drivelers. *Everyone* may think the way he wants *I do not care about it*. I am not only a *painter*, but also a *man*; I can make my judgement in morality, politics and poetry, as well as in painting... Before everything else, I do what I have to do. They accuse me of vanity! I am indeed the most arrogant man in the world.**[10]

In the following decade the critic Émile Zola would stress the importance of individualism in art: 'It is no longer a matter of pleasing or not pleasing: it is a matter of being oneself, of baring one's heart, of energetically creating an individuality.'[11] Despite his rationalism he clung to his search for 'the genius of the future' from his first Salon review in 1866 through to his last in 1896. As with most artists and critics Zola was loath to apply the term directly to a living artist, but he did refer to living 'masters', and having named Manet and referred to the Impressionists in his call for a free jury in 1876, he alluded to the question of genius in the following terms:

> **Alas! I'd love to hail a new genius. But I can only call up the shadows of Delacroix and Ingres, these obstinate giants who have left this world without betraying their gifts. These giants have left no heirs and we are still waiting for the genius of the future... Among the living barely one or two managed to raise themselves to the rank of creators.**[12]

The term genius was most commonly used simply to denote greatness, particularly when applied to past masters. Throughout the century the statements of a wide range of artists were dotted with praise for the supremacy of illustrious predecessors. Redon, for example, proposed an altruistic view of genius. In a section of his journal entitled 'Ingres', he disparaged the painter for having a barren mind and compared him with artists of genius, which he described as an ability to convey inspirational motivation to others:

> **His products do not constitute that real work of art whose value lies in its ability to enhance our moral being or in its greater power to influence others.**
>
> **Such is the modern work of art: the roughest sketch by Delacroix, Rembrandt or Albrecht Dürer inspires us to take up our brush and start working in spite of everything: it is as if they conveyed and infused life itself to us; that is their decisive achievement, their supreme import. Whoever has this effect on others is a genius.**[13]

It was left to the aesthetes and Symbolists of the latter decades of the century to push the concept of the genius to its extremes. The Romantic artist had occasionally been perceived as an individual of genius bordering on madness – the protagonist in Balzac's *Unknown Masterpiece* (*Le chef-d'œuvre inconnu*) (1845) was insane. When this vision was combined with a late nineteenth-century concern with states of mind, the result was an equation between AVANT-GARDE genius, social exclusion and insanity. By the 1870s Rimbaud could just as well have been defining the visual artist when he wrote:

The Poet becomes a seer by a long, enormous and reasoned derangement of all his senses. All the forms of love, of suffering, of madness; he seeks himself, he exhausts himself every poison, retaining only their quintessence. Ineffable torture, in which he requires supreme faith, superhuman strength, in which he becomes among all men the great invalid, the great criminal, the great accursed – and the supreme Sage. Because he arrives at the *unknown*.[14]

This was a stance embraced by the Symbolist writer Albert Aurier who, in the first published article about Van Gogh, linked the artist's character to his paintings, defining him in terms of pathological excess:

...his exalted temperament is the enemy of bourgeois sobrieties and of minutiae. He is a sort of drunken giant, more likely to move mountains than to handle bibelots on shelves, his feverish brain spewing lava into all the hollows of art. He is a terrible maddened genius, often sublime, sometimes grotesque, always verging on the pathological. Finally and above all, he is affected by an extraordinary sensitivity, perceiving as he does with abnormal, perhaps even painful, intensity, the subtle hidden character of lines and forms, and even more of colours, lights, nuances invisible to healthy eyes.[15]

Although he was committed to expressing subjectivity in his works, Van Gogh himself identified his social role as an artist with that of a humble worker and wrote that he would prefer to be an honest cobbler rather than a poet in colour. This unpretentious stance was one partly inherited from the Impressionists; Pissarro had similarly unassuming views while Cézanne prided himself on being a recluse:

But I curse the Geffroys and the few characters who, for the sake of writing an article for fifty francs, have drawn the attention of the public to me... Certainly, an artist wishes to raise himself intellectually as much as possible, but the man must remain obscure.[16]

The *fin de siècle* view of the living artist as a precious, almost sacred being perhaps reached its apogee in Joséphin 'Sâr' Péladan's 'Symbolist Manifesto and Rules of the Salon de la Rose + Croix'. Written in a seer-like, posturing and obtuse style, it either reviled artists for being mundane and realist or venerated them as demigods: 'The Salon de la Rose + Croix will be a temple dedicated to Art-God, with masterpieces for dogma and for saints, geniuses.'[17] Since women were excluded from this Salon such a definition was not open to them. Throughout the century the characteristics of the genius were those associated with masculinity – inspiration, inexplicable ability, virility, seminality and precociousness. Art critics and artists would often point out that women could not attain these, that they could be accomplished but that they could not excel. The originality which was linked to genius was thought to be outside their capacities. Even at the end of the century George Moore could express the still widely held view that:

...in the higher arts, in painting, in music and literature, their achievements are slight

indeed – best when confined to arrangements invented by men – amiable transpositions suitable to boudoirs and fans... Women have created nothing, they have carried the art of men across their fans charmingly, with exquisite taste, delicacy, and subtlety of feeling, and they have hideously and most mournfully parodied the art of men.[18]

Women's art was rooted in their compliant natures: 'it is just because man can raise himself above the sentimental cravings of natural affection that his art is so infinitely higher than woman's art.'[19] Moreover the degree of self-absorption and arrogance demanded of the genius was inimical to social expectations for women. In his 1865 lecture on the ideal of womanhood Ruskin voiced the prevalent view that the woman's place was to provide a haven of peace in the home:

> **[She]... must be enduringly, incorruptibly good; instinctively, infallibly wise – wise, not for self-development, but for self-renunciation; wise, not that she may set herself above her husband, but that she may never fail from his side: wise, not for the narrowness of insolent and loveless pride, but with the passionate gentleness of an infinitely variable, because infinitely applicable, modesty of service.**[20]

This self-effacing nurturer would have little time or energy for an ego-centred search for her inner self.

Among those who questioned such assumptions was the painter and feminist Barbara Leigh Smith: 'There is no reason at all why a woman should not build a cathedral if she has the instruction and the genius.'[21] When the American Neo-classical sculptor Harriet Hosmer was accused of not having created her own works, she defended herself in an article, explaining defiantly that all Neo-classical sculptors depended on skilled artisans to carve the stone from maquettes provided by the artist: 'The artist is a man (or woman) of genius: the artisan merely a man of talent.'[22]

Moreover a few exceptions were made, the most famous of whom was Rosa Bonheur. She was hailed as a genius, and in 1865 became the first woman to be awarded a cross of the Legion of Honour, one of France's highest civic awards. As the Empress Eugénie gave Bonheur the cross she pronounced: 'genius has no sex.' Heads of state visited her studio, American girls were given Rosa Bonheur dolls, she was awarded a plethora of public honours on an international scale and in 1894 she became the first woman to be promoted to the rank of officer of the Legion of Honour. Significantly she adopted the attitudes of her male counterparts, telling her companion and official biographer:

> **My whole life has been devoted to improving my work and keeping alive the Creator's spark in my soul. Each of us has a spark, and we've all got to account for what we do with it.**
>
> **I try to follow in Schiller's footsteps. He said that what we have to give art comes from inside, and that what we take from outside must be reborn within. If you neglect the divine inspiration that has to make your canvas breathe, you feel nothing and your work remains lifeless.**[23]

While the concept of genius was undoubtedly defined as a masculine preserve, male artists were nevertheless also having a difficult time finding a social and economic basis from which to function. The male Romantics' arrogance was perhaps necessary as means of survival.

See: AVANT-GARDE, IMAGINATION, SENSATION, SUBLIME, TEMPERAMENT

[1] M. Fido, *Oscar Wilde*, London, 1973, p. 50

[2] Projet du Comité de salut public pour les Beaux-Arts, in David, I, p. 193

[3] *Ibid*, p. 194. Satraps were tyrannical rulers

[4] In Harrison and Wood, p. 24

[5] *Ibid*, p. 26

[6] Manuscript of a Public Address, 1810, in Eitner, I, p. 108

[7] Journal, 27 April 1824, in Delacroix, 1995, pp. 35-6

[8] 15 May 1824, *Ibid*, p. 41

[9] Unpublished paper, in Leslie, p. 240

[10] In Rubin, p. 109

[11] 'Le Moment Artistique, Mon Salon', *L'Événement*, 1866, in Zola, 1959, p. 61

[12] 'Deux Expositions d'Art au Mois de Mai', *Le Messager de L'Europe*, 1876, *ibid*, p. 178

[13] 23 April 1878, in Harrison and Wood, p. 848

[14] Letter to Paul Demeny, 15 May 1871, in P. Pia, ed., *Rimbaud: poésies complètes*, Paris, 1960, p. 220

[15] 'Les Isolés – Vincent Van Gogh', *Mercure de France*, 1890, in Dorra, p. 222

[16] Letter to Gasquet, 30 April 1896, in Cézanne, p. 245

[17] *Le Figaro*, 1891, in Harrison and Wood, p. 1055

[18] *Modern Painting*, 1893, in Cherry, pp. 74-5

[19] *Ibid*, p. 74

[20] *Sesame and Lilies The Two Paths and the King of the Golden River*, London, 1907 (first edition, 1865), p. 60

[21] *Women and work*, 1857, in Nunn, p. 4

[22] *Atlantic Monthly*, 1864, in Chadwick, p. 218

[23] In Klumpke, pp. 220-1

Genre

THE ORIGINAL MEANING OF THE FRENCH WORD *GENRE* (KIND OR TYPE) IN RELATION TO ART, was to denote the different categories of subject matter. In 1791 Quatremère de Quincy defined a new use: 'genre properly speaking, [is] scenes of everyday life.'[1] By the mid-nineteenth century this meaning was widespread. Tracing its ancestry back to Caravaggio's paintings of contemporary life, genre had first truly flourished in the Dutch seventeenth-century Republic. It was no coincidence that this tradition, along with the eighteenth-century genre paintings of Chardin, Greuze and Hogarth, was reappraised during the nineteenth century, when a new bourgeois public preferred depictions of daily life on a domestic scale to the elevated posturings and erudite references of HISTORY PAINTING. Yet according to the academic hierarchy of subject-matter, genre continued to be considered a minor category, situated below history painting and PORTRAITURE, but above LANDSCAPE and STILL LIFE. Widely reproduced in print form it was the popular art form of the century.

A plethora of sub-genres evolved encompassing works as diverse as Wilkie's rustic cottagers, Landseer's anthropomorphic animals, Meissonier's *ancien régime* cavaliers, Gérôme's dancing Arab boys, Frith's urban crowds, Tanner's Afro-Americans or Tissot's *hautes bourgeoises*. Genre was entangled with a range of artistic preoccupations, including MODERNITY,

URBAN LIFE, PEASANT LIFE, literature, Orientalism, exoticism and historicism, and it was also marked by national and regional differences. It is not, therefore, always clear whether a work can be described solely as a genre painting, and the question of definition was equally problematic in the nineteenth century. However, specific characteristics of genre can be identified. It did not aspire to the elevated scale, generalised effects or high moral truths of the grand manner; rather it sought to be entertaining (and often humorous), anecdotal and sentimental. Moreover, it depicted in telling detail non-heroic, anonymous, 'ordinary' people going about their daily lives, whether they be contemporary and 'real', historical or literary. Significantly such works in Britain were often referred to as 'incident pictures'.

The fissure between the demand of public taste and the relatively low prestige accorded to genre by the profession was a source of tension and tragedy. It is thought that Benjamin Haydon's suicide was caused by his reluctant production of anecdotal genre such as *Punch on May Day* (1829), which he believed to be a betrayal of the artist's elevated destiny to create grand history paintings for which, to his dismay, there was little demand in his native Britain. In contrast, William Mulready very quickly abandoned early attempts at high art, settling in 1809 for a successful career as a painter of mostly rustic genre. He justified his own attitude by noting: 'in the present state of the art almost any subject matter may be raised to importance by TRUTH and beauty of light and shade and colour and with an unostentatious mastery of execution.'[2]

Genre was often equated with Dutch art which, despite its reappraisal, was still considered inferior to the Italian school by the academies because of its lack of finesse and discrimination. Hence the English visionary Samuel Palmer was anxious to avoid its banalities, writing to fellow painter John Linnell:

> **...in the fine old works the Heads are always most elaborated; – on the Flemish canvas, the least finished of any part; and yielding to the perfected polish of stew-pans and chamber pots: a preference most religiously observ'd by the cleverest disciples of that style at present. An instance of this appear'd in the last exhibition.[3]**

Having then described his enthusiasm for depicting a new subject he hoped that 'if I can atal [sic] succeed, it will be nothing Dutch or boorish.'[4]

Yet its practitioners and supporters justified genre on moral grounds, arguing that it encompassed universal truths about the human condition, shared by all social classes, by depicting situations and narratives with character, sentiment and truth. In Britain during the first half of the century, many felt that rustic genre, in which pious, sober and industrious peasant families populated clean and tidy cottages, would entertain the upper classes while improving the sensibilities of the lower classes. An anonymous writer expressed this attitude in 1851:

> **There is a fine moral tone in the works of Wilkie, and their circulation among all classes of the community cannot fail of producing, together with a taste for art, refining and humanising influences. They deal with the common things of life, and, with subtle penetration, but not unkindly feeling, satirise our common infirmities and foibles, detect and exhibit the humorous and ridiculous, and throw an interest over the simple and joyous amusements of domestic life.[5]**

The effect of gazing at Wilkie's work is thus to draw out the spectator's emotions, 'and he becomes, in a measure, more gentle, refined, and charitable in his tastes and feelings.'[6] While Wilkie himself wrote: '...private patronage...[calls] alike on art to decorate the dwelling of the noble, and embellish the abode of the peasant – to pour a ray or two of its light on the thick darkness of sullen ignorance, and mingle its fuller and brighter beam with the sunshine of learning and taste.'[7]

Despite such claims, overall the popularity of genre rested primarily on the undemanding qualities of its content; it was intended to be entertaining and avoided references to the unpleasant or to specific contemporary social conditions. Hence, in France the Realists and Naturalists were keen to differentiate their depictions of unvarnished everyday life from mere genre. For example, having pointed out that Courbet's works were not caricatures, burlesques or satires, Pierre-Joseph Proudhon wrote:

> **It would be no truer to call him a genre painter, like the Dutch and Flemish, whose paintings, though pleasant or comic, are insubstantial; they rarely go to the heart of things, reflect no philosophical concerns, and reveal more imagination than observation ... Courbet's pictures are mirrors of truth; qualities and defects of execution apart, their merit, till now unequalled, lies in the profundity of the idea.**[8]

By mid-century this was beginning to be as much a matter of formal means as of choice of subject matter.

While national and regional differences abounded, there was throughout the west a certain naivety to the subject matter of genre during the first half of the century which gave way to more diversity later on. This included the adoption of urban subjects from the late 1850s. In the 1860s and 1870s British artists such as Thomas Faed, Frank Holl, Luke Fildes and Hubert von Herkomer depicted the hardships endured by the urban and rural poor in a manner which sought to raise the social conscience of the middle class. In America the national character of genre in works by George Caleb Bingham or William Sidney Mount began to seem parochial and unsophisticated, and gave way to more universal subjects in an increasingly international market for originals and prints. For example, having built his success with genre scenes of American farm life during the 1830s, in the mid-1840s Mount considered widening his range to include urban subjects, such as 'A poor widow about to part with relics of better days in order to supply bread for her starving children,' 'Please give to me a penny,' and 'Cold victuals.'[9]

In Britain some began to see the idealisation of the pious poor as patronising, while others saw it as signifying a lost golden age. In 1887, reminiscing about the British genre of Wilkie, Webster and others, the genre painter John Evan Hodgson wrote:

> **On the evidence of Webster's pictures, we feel inclined to accept the fact that there was a period in English history – a not very remote one either – when the agricultural labourer was satisfied with his lot, and did not quarrel with his employer about his wages – when he did not spend these in the public-house, to the detriment of his family, when he was content to live at home and enjoy the frugal blessings which were graced by the lustre of the paternal salt-cellar. Webster's peasants...belong to an ideal world, but it is a beautiful one, and his art has a neatness and precision, limpid translucent quality of colour which is in strict keeping with the nature of the conception, and seems in an equal degree to minister to the soul's needs.**[10]

Moreover, the timelessness suggested by a reliance on long-established stylistic conventions, which characterised much genre in the first half of the century, began to be superseded by an increasing emphasis on high FINISH and attention to details of dress and context, as painters vied with PHOTOGRAPHY to produce meticulous illusionism. Hence genre came to be defined in terms of formal means that conformed to academic principles, including the continuation of 'pleasing' groupings within an illusionary space.

The predilection for portraying sentiment and pathos manifested itself throughout the century. Marguerite Gérard pioneered sentimental, moralising genre paintings showing improving scenes of contemporary bourgeois life during the first Republic. Sentimental pathos was widely admired by a surprisingly diverse range of commentators. Ruskin, for example, praised the Pre-Raphaelite James Campbell's genre painting *The Wife's Remonstrance* (1858) as 'by far the best picture in the Suffolk Street Rooms this year, full of pathos, and true painting,' although he also chided the artist for 'the fate of loving ugly things better than beautiful ones.'[11] Writing about himself in the third person, the African-American painter, Henry Osawa Tanner, explained his choice of subjects such as *The Banjo Lesson* (1893), partly on the grounds of sentiment:

> **Since his return from Europe he has painted many Negro subjects, he feels drawn to such subjects on account of the newness of the field and because of a desire to represent the serious and pathetic side of life among them, and it is his thought that other things being equal, he who has the most sympathy with his subject will obtain the best results. To his mind, many of the artists who have represented Negro life have only seen the comic, the ludicrous side of it and have lacked sympathy with and affection for the warm big heart within such a rough exterior.[12]**

In a similar vein Van Gogh, referring to his lifelong admiration for the English social genre painters Herkomer, Fildes and Holl whose works were illustrated in the *Graphic*, wrote:

> **...the reason why they still mean more to me than Gavarni and Daumier, and will continue to, is that while the latter seem to look on society with malice, the former – as well as men like Millet, Breton, de Groux, Israëls – chose subjects which are as true as Gavarni's or Daumier's, but have something noble and a more serious sentiment. That sentiment especially must remain, I think. An artist needn't be a clergyman or a churchwarden, but he certainly must have a warm heart for his fellow men.[13]**

Nevertheless most of the AVANT-GARDE were suspicious of overt sentiment, seeing it as all too often tipping over into the mawkish, and so as untruthful or insincere. Again, it was not only the choice of subjects from everyday life but the approach to them that marked out a work as genre. Right at the end of the century Signac still found it important to address the *way* in which subjects were treated, contrasting genre unfavourably with the sincere and 'overwhelmingly real' studies of everyday life and working-class suburbs depicted by the Impressionists and Seurat:

> **Now it can hardly be denied that the reproduction of such subjects elicits a more sincere sentiment of justice and more fertile thoughts than a melodramatic composition showing a 'Family Fallen on Hard Times' where the father has an Italian-style beard, the mother wears the head of the Virgin, and the children have cherubic hairstyles, all this painted**

on a background of rags and utensils straight from an *Opéra Comique* stage-set.[14]

Genre's frequent lack of profundity made it appealing to the public, while acting as a source of embarrassment to a profession keen to claim intellectual status untainted by crass commercialism. It grew in popularity throughout the century and so exposed the essential contradiction of a market-led society, which claimed to demand high-minded history painting yet actually preferred sentimental anecdotes in its homes. Accusations of frivolity were frequent even by mainstream commentators such as the conservative painter/critic P.G. Hamerton who wrote:

> **Let anyone examine the catalogues of our exhibitions, and he will be surprised by the predominance of trifling subjects, chosen purposely to hit what the artists evidently suppose to be popular taste. I do not insist upon any necessity for nobility of subject, for much of the greatest art has displayed itself in perfect grandeur with scarcely any subject at all... But I say that when the subject is at the same time trivial and obtrusive, as it is in this popular art I am just now writing about, the whole picture is likely to be vulgar from beginning to end, and unredeemed by any elevated thought whatever.**[15]

Calling on cultivated people to discourage 'those lower kinds of incident-painting which abound in the modern schools,' he took the moral stance that 'Art which is only pretty and amusing is always a degraded kind of art, which does no good to the mind in the way of refinement or elevation, though it may do some good as a harmless diversion for the thoughts from the anxieties of daily life.'[16]

Some artists justified their works precisely in terms of providing necessary escapism. During the last quarter of the century George Dunlop Leslie, who specialised in works spectacularly devoid of high moral purpose, in which beautiful women (often in frilly eighteenth-century dresses), engaged in domestic tasks such as testing their maid's mixture of pot-pourri, unashamedly stated that he had always aimed:

> **...to paint pictures from the sunny side of English domestic life... The times are so imbued with turmoil and misery, hard work and utilitarianism, that innocence, joy, and beauty seem to be the most fitting subjects to render such powers as I possess useful to my fellow-creatures.**[17]

In France the art establishment frequently cast genre as unprincipled, commodified art in contrast with high-minded history painting. In 1871, for example, in a post-war report to the Minister of Public Instruction, Charles Blanc (*directeur des beaux-arts*) wrote: 'the state exhibits works and not products; it sponsors a Salon and not a bazaar.'[18] He went on to attack 'familiar, anecdotal, imitative art addressing itself to individuals.'[19] Yet this report provoked a petition from over one hundred artists from a wide range of the aesthetic spectrum (apart from history painters), including Daubigny, Daumier, Corot and Manet as well as now unknown artists such as Coffetier and Petitgrand etc. In a direct reference to history painting the petition stated:

> **French art today is composed not only of a few competent and learned pensioners that the state can employ for the decoration of monuments and gardens. It consists also, and most particularly, of a brilliant and enormous legion of landscape and genre painters, more numerous each day, whose original works are sought after by the entire world and whom our neighbouring countries envy.**[20]

Despite some genre painters undoubtedly having a seriousness of intent, overall genre was intended to be entertaining or humorous. Its moral messages of homely, unchallenging, generally acknowledged 'truths' were based on upholding conservative, God-fearing principles and on taking an idealised view of its protagonists. Not surprisingly, it became the *bête noire* of avant-garde artists since it stood for everything they hated, and this legacy lived on into the following century.

See: EXOTIC, HISTORY PAINTING, MODERNITY, PEASANT LIFE, URBAN LIFE

[1] In M. Clarke, *The Concise Oxford Dictionary of Art Terms*, Oxford, 2001, p. 105

[2] In Gaunt, pl. 18

[3] 21 Dec 1828, in Harrison and Wood, p. 126

[4] *Ibid*, p. 126

[5] *The Wilkie Gallery*, in Payne, 1998, p. 8

[6] *Ibid*

[7] A. Cunningham, *Life of Wilkie*, 1843, in Payne, 1998-9, p. 28

[8] *Du principe de l'art et sa desintation sociale*, 1865, in Harrison and Wood, p. 408

[9] Sketchbooks, cited in Johns, p. 58

[10] *Fifty Years of British Art, as Illustrated by the Pictures and Drawings in the Manchester Royal Jubilee Exhibition*, 1887, in Payne, 1998, p. 83

[11] *Academy Notes*, 1858, in Ruskin, XIV, 1904-12, pp. 187-8

[12] See Eisenman, p. 186

[13] Letter, 1 Nov 1882, in Pickvance, p. 39

[14] *La Révolte*, 1891, in Harrison and Wood, p. 797

[15] P.G. Hamerton, *Thoughts about Art*, 1873, in Craig Harrison, 1999, pp. 45-6

[16] *Ibid*, p. 46

[17] In Cowling, p. 54

[18] In Mainardi, 1993, p. 42

[19] *Ibid*

[20] *Ibid*

History Painting

STRICTLY SPEAKING HISTORY PAINTING CONSISTED OF THE REPRESENTATION of narratives from classical history or mythology, but biblical subjects were also included since they encompassed equally elevated concepts. Situated at the pinnacle of the hierarchy of subject matter by academic theory, history painting was the ultimate hurdle which an artist had to jump in order to make a serious reputation. Significantly the PRIX DE ROME, the highest prize given by the ÉCOLE DES BEAUX-ARTS, was awarded for an historical COMPOSITION, the most difficult form of art. Often referred to as the grand style or grand manner, it embodied the highest aesthetic values. A report of the Institut de France in 1808 on progress in science, letters and arts since the Revolution underlined the importance of history painting:

> **We believe that it is important to encourage in particular the most elevated categories of art... It is the degree of perfection of history painting that establishes the level for all the secondary variations of this art.**[1]

However, its elevated status and power contained the seeds of its destruction. In a century in which progressive thought was increasingly linked to the democratisation of ideas and to grasping the massive changes caused by industrialisation, history painting was soon accused of elitism and of remoteness from or irrelevance to contemporary life. Since it epitomised academic theory and institutional power it provided the focus for anti-establishment opinion, becoming the hated oppressor against which AVANT-GARDE art rebelled and so, defined itself. Its supremacy was equally challenged by the conservative GENRE and LANDSCAPE easel paintings which fed the art market's growing dominance.

Academic theory saw history painting as the noblest form of art because its subject-matter offered the opportunity to explore the passions and the intellect, and so to address the essence of spiritual, moral or political dilemmas. History painting had been a vehicle for conveying philosophical and ideological stances since the seventeenth century, so that powerful institutions, not least the state, recognised its importance. At the dawn of the nineteenth century it was still associated with the high-minded, revolutionary idealism with which it had been reinvigorated by David. In 1793, as an elected deputy, he addressed the young Republic's National Convention on the composition of a new jury to select works for the Salon:

> **Citizens... It is not only in charming the eyes that works of art have achieved their end; it is in penetrating the soul, in making a profound impression, like that of reality, on the spirit. Then the traits of heroism, and of civic virtues, offered to the eyes of the people electrify their souls and bring forth in them the passions of glory, of devotion to the well-being of their country. The artist, therefore, must have studied all the qualities of humankind; he must have a great knowledge of nature; he must, in a word, be a philosopher.[2]**

The choice of subject as well as the manner in which it was portrayed gave both artists and their public the opportunity to display their erudition: when the curriculum of the École des Beaux-Arts was reformed in 1819 the study of ancient history was added. Because of the large scale of the works, history painting also enabled artists to display their competence in the imaginative composition of complex narratives as well as in depicting the idealised male NUDE engaged in heroic action, so satisfying the Academy's classical criteria of excellence. Quatremère de Quincy, a contemporary of David's at the French School in Rome who went on to become Permanent Secretary of the Académie des Beaux-Arts (1816-39), and whose writings were influential in France and in England, defended these principles well into the nineteenth century:

> **The subject of a painting may form a good moral lesson, and yet the mode of treating it occasions us no other kind of pleasure than that limited to the senses. Such, for instance, would be the case, in the representation of the fable of the labourer and his children trying to break the bundle of sticks. Suppose the scene be presented to us as the interior of a poor and rustic cottage, with the costume and portraits of its peasant inhabitants, and if you will, let Teniers be the painter, the imitation of an incident in itself so moral, will in that case produce only the physical pleasure of imitation. Suppose now the same scene expressed by the historical painter, with all the nobility of character, beauty of form, variety of expressions and attitudes that the subject will admit of, the mind will then enjoy the moral pleasure of imitation. Nay more, the same effect may even be produced in the representation of events stamped with a character of the greatest immorality. I shall be**

content to cite the massacre of the innocents of Raffaello.[3]

Although the academies of other western nations tended to emulate the lead of the ACADEMY in France, the response by the state and the public was not uniformly enthusiastic. For example in England, where there was less state patronage than in France, the conceptual basis of such art was not widely accepted despite the Royal Academy's teachings. Benjamin Haydon's devotion to working in the grand manner was a lifelong struggle, though he began his career with high hopes. In his autobiography he described the early stages of work on his first monumental history paintings, when he was aged 20:

> **Ordered the canvas for my first picture (six feet by four) of 'Joseph and Mary resting on the road to Egypt'; and on October 1st, 1806, setting my palette and taking brush in hand, I knelt down and prayed to God to bless my career, to grant me energy to create a new era in art, and to rouse the people and patrons to a just estimate of the moral value of historical painting.**[4]

Similarly, in North America history painters such as John Trumbull and John Vanderlyn aspired to raise art in their young nation to the heights of history painting but despaired at the scant commissions which this attracted.

Even in France history painting was never widely popular and it depended on the strong traditions of state patronage for its survival. Works on such a scale required lengthy working processes and were almost always commissioned or bought from the Salon by church or state. The Academy defended the genre as the standard bearer of a disinterested, non-commercial ideal to which art and artists should aspire. State and church supported it for its didactic function. But few artists could make their entire living from it and even successful history painters painted smaller easel pictures; both Ingres and Delacroix, for example, took private portraiture commissions. In the early 1820s a young Ary Scheffer showed his recent painting *The Soldier's Widow* to his master Guérin. The latter exclaimed:

> **Ah! Scheffer, is it possible that you would abandon great painting in this fashion? Have you renounced in advance all the success I predicted for you? ...[Scheffer replied] 'Sir, I love my mother and I need money, both for her and for myself. Do not be concerned if I take a different direction. When I have made a name and my position is secure I shall return and then perhaps I shall do my teacher greater honour than he seems to expect from me now.'**[5]

The widening of permissible subject matter to include heroic contemporary events can be traced back to Benjamin West's late eighteenth-century paintings, and was pursued vigorously in France by Antoine-Jean Gros in his glorification of Napoleon's victories in the opening years of the nineteenth century, for example *Napoleon in the Plague House at Jaffa* (1804). What made Géricault's *Raft of the Medusa* (1819) so controversial was that its contemporary subject was a human action that had been far from heroic, that its participants were unknowns and that it exposed government corruption. Unusually for such a large-scale work it was not commissioned and not surprisingly the Bourbon Monarchy refused to buy it from the Salon. Yet its large scale and its complex pyramidal composition of a mass of idealised, nude male figures conformed to academic criteria. Despite its credentials as a Romantic work concerned with emotive states of mind and contemporary life it was also indebted to the classicism of David.

The aesthetic conservatives called for a return to a more rigorous definition of history painting. One of these was Ingres, who attacked the Romantics – even though he himself produced several historical genre pictures over the course of his career:

> **Modern painters call themselves history painters: it is essential to destroy this claim. A history painter is one who represents heroic deeds, and such deeds are only to be found in the history of the Greeks and the Romans; and it is through them that the artist can display his skill in painting nudes and draperies; all other periods only yield *genre paintings* because the costume conceals the body. It is because of costume that so-called Romantic painters are able to construct their pictures so easily without having learned the first thing about the structure of the human body.[6]**

The young Delacroix, who had posed for one of the figures in Géricault's *Raft*, was torn between the attractions of contemporary subjects and those of traditional history painting. He voiced the torment which the new-found freedom of choice could pose for the artist. Having resolved on Wednesday 7 April 1824 that he must make some drawings of contemporary figures, the following Sunday he noted:

> **The trouble is, that with a roving and impressionable mind like mine, one idea drives another out of my head quicker than the changing wind alters the direction of a windmill's sails. And when I have a number of different ideas for subjects in mind at once, what am I to do?...I believe that when one needs a subject, it is best to hark back to the Classics.[7]**

What further muddied the waters was that from the 1820s artists such as Vernet, Scheffer and Delaroche created sentimental, anecdotal celebrations of the lives of historical figures or the daily experience of past times in their desire to satisfy the demands of the Salon public. Delaroche showed an awareness of the prosaic character of his era:

> **The great masters have exploited the field of poetic invention with such success, that only a few scraps remain to be gleaned from their traces. From now on the harvest has been gathered. Religious ideas have long found their definitive form... What is there that still remains to be attempted? The analysis of purely human events, the representation of the facts from a purely dramatic point of view and from their most probable, if not their most imposing aspect. Instruction which is direct and to a certain extent familiar – that is what will be most appropriate to the conditions of modern art and to the intellectual needs of our time.[8]**

Contemporary critics distinguished between this *genre historique* (historical genre) as opposed to the philosophically rigorous elevated aims of *la peinture historique* (history painting), yet the municipal councils and other official bodies which offered lucrative commissions were often less discriminatory. Such works suited the sentimental escapist mood of the *juste-milieu* art of Louis-Philippe's reign (1830-48) and continued to be popular right through the century. They were also widespread in other countries. In 1873 the British painter/writer P.G. Hamerton commented:

> **...the majority no longer think it necessary to attempt high art, which is always too high to be within their reach. A young man, in the present day, who adopts the profession of art, soon perceives what is most likely to be a remunerative investment of his time. He learns to paint faces and costumes as prettily and cleverly as possible, and then seeks**

some incident such as Queen Elizabeth's toothache, or King Charles knighting the sirloin, which will at the same time amuse the public and afford a proper opportunity for costume painting. All this is very excusable, but really, when you reflect upon it, does it seem a quite adequate employment for men of grave and serious genius?[9]

For the mid-century avant-garde both historical genre and grand history painting were simply outdated. In his assessment of art in 1848 the Romantic Théophile Gautier boldly stated:

What used to be called history painting...no longer exists. Or rather, it no longer exists in the form practised by David, Guérin, Girodet, Gros, Meynier and other luminaries of the Empire and the Restoration, where a noble, solemn subject was treated in epic fashion, in a highly stylised manner, on a canvas of huge dimensions. The painters who were practised in this art were profoundly disdainful of genre painting and landscape, and we were lucky to get a portrait out of them, or a painting of a sovereign or dignitary treated in some pseudo-historical fashion. Other artists and the general public regarded these masters with a humble sort of terror...

Now we seem to have recovered somewhat from our infatuation with history painting, and we believe that Andromache has mourned Hector long enough... No one today has room to give up twenty feet of wall to mythology.[10]

He went on to recommend that the only place for such works was a public building, a view surprisingly shared by Ingres, who drew a clear distinction between public and domestic art:

The government has no obligation to encourage any genre other than history painting. Genre strictly speaking – scenes of family life, modern scenes, fruit and flowers, still life etc. – should be left to private individuals, to collectors. This is how things were done last century... Thus the state's task is simply to encourage history painting in the present and the reproduction of the most beautiful monuments of the past; the rest is none of its business.[11]

Courbet self-consciously attacked history painting head on with his *Burial at Ornans* (1848-9), which he advertised on posters in Besançon and Dijon as 'the history painting' of a funeral at Ornans, but which showed small-town life on an epic scale. A decade later, when he was seen as the leader of the avant-garde, he published an open letter to disaffected students in which he made clear his opposition to history painting:

Every age should be represented only by its own artists, that is to say, by the artists who have lived in it. I hold that the artists of one century are totally incapable of representing the things of a preceding or a subsequent century, in other words, of painting the past or the future. It is in this sense that I deny the possibility of historical art applied to the past. Historical art is by nature contemporary. Every age must have its artists, who give expression to it and reproduce it for the future. An age that has not managed to find expression in the work of its own artists has no right to be expressed by later artists. That would be falsifying history.[12]

The elevated status of history painting excluded the majority of artists from its sanctum and women in particular. Women were considered incapable of abstract thought and so incapable of producing the required universal truths. The influential critic John Ruskin expressed a widely shared outlook when he explained that women could imitate rather than originate. Secondly, they were far less likely to have had the necessary formal education in history and the classics that would enable them to explore its subject matter. Thirdly the large scale of the genre was physically daunting to most women artists of the era. Finally and crucially the exclusion of women from life DRAWING and ANATOMY classes for the first three quarters of the century put them at a serious disadvantage.

There were exceptions. During the revolutionary period David fiercely defended his right to have women students, as did Regnault and Guérin. Several women, including Sophie Guillemard, Contess Benoist and Angélique Monguez exhibited history paintings in the early years of the century. In mid-century Britain feminist artists contested the male bastion. But the battle could prove disheartening. In 1856 two artist friends, Mary Howitt and Joanna Boyce, sent their large-scale history paintings to the Royal Academy. Mary Howitt felt that her *Boadicea Brooding over her Wrongs* would 'embody her ideals and be her masterpiece.'[13] But both painters were rejected. Undaunted, Howitt sent her work to the Crystal Palace exhibition where it was hung and where it got a mixed critical response. Ruskin chose to respond privately. In a letter to Howitt he advised that she give up her aspirations and turn to the more suitable subject of STILL LIFE:

> **What do *you* know about Boadicea? Leave such subjects alone and paint me a pheasant's wing.**[14]

Mary Howitt's mother testified that the effect of this experience was so devastating that she withdrew from any more attempts at carving out a career for herself. Yet others continued to try. By the last quarter of the century women were exhibiting history paintings, and in 1872 Jessie Macgregor won a gold medal for one. Yet she recalled the resentment of her male peers:

> **I was under great disabilities compared with my fellow competitors. Perhaps it was this that made the men students so enraged (as they were) at the success of a 'chit of a girl' as I was called; feeling was so high that in their wrath the students smashed a cast that night.**[15]

By this stage history painting had lost much of its prestige. While historical genre continued to thrive until the early twentieth century, the status of history painting was declining quickly in Europe. Even so, innovative artists such as Manet, Renoir, Cézanne and Seurat continued to search for a way to reinterpret the principled ideals of history painting but in a modern idiom. Much of Manet's work of the 1860s consisted of attempts to re-energise it in terms of contemporary life and Georges Rivière saw that that was also true of Renoir:

> **M. Renoir has every right to be proud of his '*bal*'... This is a historical document, a priceless monument to Parisian life, scrupulously faithful... This painting has important implications for the future...M. Renoir and his friends have realised that history painting isn't just the more or less comical illustration of stories from the past. They have shown the way forward, and others will have to follow. Let those who want to do history paintings show the history of their own times rather than scrabbling in the dust of past centuries. What do we care for comic opera kings got up in blue or yellow robes with sceptre in hand and crown on head!**[16]

Yet the desire to convey generalised and philosophical ideas persisted. In the late 1880s and 1890s Symbolists sought to return to art the cultural significance that it had lost since the demise of classical history painting. Many trawled through mythological subjects in their attempts to return art to the elevated realms beyond realist and naturalist descriptions of everyday life. However, they did so mostly on the scale of domestic easel painting and without the didactic or moral earnestness of the early century. Moreover many were concerned with conveying states of mind, primarily through formal means rather than through communicating declamatory narratives which elucidated moral truths. This is why they admired the often non-specific allusions to a past golden age in the works of Puvis de Chavannes. As Maurice Denis explained:

Let us analyse the hemicycle of Chavannes at the Sorbonne that necessitates a written explanation for the vulgar. Is it literary? Certainly not, for that explanation is false: the examiners of the baccalaureat should know that the beautiful form of Ephebus that droops down toward a semblance of water symbolises studious youth. It is a beautiful form, is it not, aesthetes? And the depth of our emotion comes from the ability of these lines and of these colours to explain themselves as uniquely beautiful and divine with beauty.[17]

Although Seurat rejected many aspects of Denis's art theory, his large scale, carefully composed *Grande Jatte* (1884-86) vied with David's history paintings in its revolutionary intent. Of this painting Seurat told Signac: 'In another vein I would just as willingly have painted the struggle between the Horatii and the Curatii.'[18] Indeed, it could be argued that some of the most memorable nineteenth-century paintings by Géricault, Courbet, Manet, Seurat and Gauguin are attempts to challenge, vilify or modernise the dying tradition, so that in this sense its power continued to haunt the century's art.

See: ACADEMY, ANTIQUE, BEAUTY, GENRE, NUDE, PRIX DE ROME, TRUTH

[1] Mainardi, 1993, p. 15

[2] See Taylor, p. 44

[3] *Essai sur la nature, le but et les moyens de l'imitation dans les beaux-arts*, 1823, in Taylor, pp. 87-8

[4] In Eitner, II, p. 84

[5] C. Lenormant, 'A Scheffer', *Le Correspondant*, 1859, in Lethève, pp. 62-3

[6] Lethève, p. 63

[7] Delacroix, 1995, pp. 30-1

[8] In Duffy, p. 12

[9] *Thoughts about Art*, 1873, in Craig Harrison, p. 45

[10] 'L'art en 1848', *L'Artiste*, 1848, in Harrison and Wood, p. 318

[11] Notes recorded by Delaborde, probably 1848-9, in Harrison and Wood, pp. 470-1. Ingres was serving on a fine arts commission set up by the government of the Second Republic.

[12] 25 Dec 1861, in Courbet, p. 203

[13] Orr, p. 40

[14] In Cherry, p. 187

[15] *Ibid*, p. 61

[16] *L'Impressioniste. Journal d'art*, 1877, in Harrison and Wood, p. 594

[17] 'Définition du Néo-traditionnisme', *Art et Critique*, 1890, in Chipp, p. 99

[18] Cited in Eisenman p. 276

Imagination

CLOSELY ALIGNED WITH THE CONCEPTS OF INVENTIVENESS AND ORIGINALITY, imagination was at the centre of the major nineteenth-century debates about naturalism versus idealisation as well as individualism versus the continuing authority of the ancients. Voicing the dominant view of the academies, Ingres warned against untrammelled innovation:

> **What do these alleged artists mean, who preach the discovery of the 'new'? Is there anything new? Everything has been done, everything discovered. Our task is not to invent but to continue, and we have enough to do if, via the examples of the masters, we use those innumerable types which nature constantly offers to us, interpreting them with wholehearted sincerity, and ennobling them through that pure and firm style without which no work has beauty.**[1]

It was the Romantics who first questioned such outlooks. For them imagination was an essential requisite of GENIUS and was intertwined with the progressive calls for artistic freedom. Discussion centred around the degree to which the artist should work from the motif as opposed to the imagination, begging the question of individual inventiveness, as the English visionary William Blake pointed out:

> **Men think that they can copy nature as correctly as I copy imagination. This they will find impossible: and all the copies, or pretended copies, of nature, from Rembrandt to Reynolds, prove that nature becomes to its victims nothing but blots and blurs. Why are copies of nature incorrect, while copies of imagination are correct? This is manifest to all... I know my execution is not like anybody else's. I do not intend it should be so. None but blockheads copy one another... To what is it that gentlemen of the first rank both in genius and fortune have subscribed their name? To my inventions. The executive part they never disputed.**[2]

Delacroix often mulled over this theme in his journal. Conceding the great importance of working from NATURE, he concluded that nevertheless it should ultimately be overruled by imagination. Of Rubens he wrote:

> **When an artist is very learned and very intelligent the use of a model, if properly understood, allows details to be suppressed which a painter who works from his imagination always includes too lavishly for fear of leaving out something important... Rubens is a remarkable illustration of the abuse of details. His painting, which is dominated by the imagination, is everywhere superabundant, the accessories are too much worked out... And yet, if you compare his exuberant manner, not with the dryness and poverty of modern painting, but with really fine pictures where nature has been imitated with restraint and great accuracy, you feel as [sic] once that the true painter is one whose imagination speaks before everything else.**[3]

A few days later he returned to this dilemma:

> **When Courbet painted the background of the woman bathing, he copied it faithfully from a study which I saw hanging near his easel. Nothing could be colder; it is like a piece of mosaic. I began to make something tolerable of my African journey only when I had forgotten the trivial details and remembered nothing but the striking and poetic side of**

the subject. Up to that time, I had been haunted by this passion for accuracy that most people mistake for the truth.[4]

In questioning 'this passion for accuracy' he was considering the outlooks of the emerging Realist AVANT-GARDE with its faith in scientific observation and disdain for flights of fancy. Already in the 1830s, Constable in England and the Barbizon painters in France had considered an alternative to the Classicists and the Romantics. In his introduction to the first of four lectures on landscape painting, at London's Royal Institution, Constable had said: 'I hope to show that ours is a regularly taught profession; that it is *scientific* as well as *poetic*; that imagination alone never did, and never can, produce works that are to stand by a comparison with *realities*.'[5] While among his personal papers the following note was found:

'Is it not folly,' said Mr Northcote to me in the Exhibition, as we were standing before — —'s picture, 'for a man to paint what he can never see? is it not sufficiently difficult to paint what he does see?' – This delightful lesson leads me to ask, what is painting but an imitative art? an art that is to *realise*, not to *feign*. I constantly observe that every man who will not submit to long toil in the imitation of nature, flies off, becomes a phantom, and produces dreams of nonsense, and abortions. He thinks to screen himself under 'a fine imagination' which is generally, and almost always in young men, the scapegoat of folly and idleness.[6]

In mid-century France the issue was politicised. Max Buchon's *Annonce*, published in 1850 to advertise Courbet's provincial exhibitions of that year, praised *The Stonebreakers* (1849-50) for its objective realism. The work's lack of fancifulness and sentimentality conveyed its left-wing message:

Yet this man, who in no way is the product of the artist's imagination, this man of flesh and bones who is really living in Ornans, just as you see him there, this man, with his years, with his hard labour, with his misery, with his softened features of old age, this man is not yet the last word in human distress. Just think what would happen if he would take it into his head to side with the Reds: He could be resented, accused, exiled, and dismissed. Ask the prefect.[7]

A decade later, Courbet published (probably with Castagnary's help) a carefully considered artistic credo in the form of an open letter, in which he accorded imagination a role subservient to the depiction of tangible subject matter:

I also maintain that painting is an essentially concrete art form and can consist only of the representation of real and existing things. It is an entirely physical language that is composed, by way of words, of all visible objects. An abstract object, not visible, nonexistent, is not within the domain of painting. Imagination in art consists of knowing how to find the most complete expression of an existing thing, but never of inventing or creating the thing itself.[8]

This outlook reached its apogee in the works of the Impressionists, which were conceived in terms of rendering the motif in an objective, quasi-scientific fashion. Monet was often praised primarily for his acuteness of sight, as in Cézanne's reported remark in the late 1880s: 'What an eye Monet has, the most prodigious eye since painting began! I raise my hat to him.'[9]

By the 1860s and 1870s imagination had been relegated to musings about possible choices and interpretations of subject-matter by attention-seeking Salon artists. So much so, that when

Baudelaire boldly ennobled imagination in his Salon of 1859, he was for once out of step with the avant-garde. Echoing the views of his hero, the now ageing Delacroix, he wrote:

> **How mysterious is Imagination, that Queen of the Faculties! It touches all the others; it rouses them and sends them into combat... It is both analysis and synthesis... It is sensitivity....It is Imagination that first taught man the moral meaning of colour, of contour, of sound and of scent. In the beginning of the world it created analogy and metaphor. It decomposes all creation, and with the raw materials accumulated and disposed in accordance with rules whose origins one cannot find save in the furthest depths of the soul, it creates a new world, it produces the sensation of newness.[10]**

Yet the poet still differentiated between the Classicist's claims to the faculty of imagination and the modern commitment to observation:

> **In spite of all the magnificent privileges that I attribute to the imagination, I will not pay your readers the insult of explaining to them that the more it is helped in its work, the more powerful it is, and that there is nothing more formidable in our battles with the ideal than a fine imagination disposing of an immense armoury of observed fact.[11]**

Three years later, he could praise Manet's work despite its uncompromising realism, because he saw it as being informed by the imagination:

> **MM Manet and Legros combine a vigorous taste for reality, modern reality – already a good symptom – with that lively and abundant imagination, both sensitive and bold, without which, it must be emphasised, even the finest gifts are no more than servants without a master.[12]**

In fact, Baudelaire's eulogy to the imagination anticipated the outlook of the Symbolists and Post-Impressionists, who claimed the liberty to explore themes and ideas in a way that went beyond the recording of external appearances. As early as his Salon of 1868 Redon questioned current avant-garde outlooks:

> **One wonders why Mr Corot, who knows so well how to be realist, still dares, a great audacity, to paint cupids or nymphs. This is not the place to open the eyes of those who are set on restricting the painter's art to reproducing only that which he can see. Those who remain within these narrow-minded boundaries condemn themselves to an inferior ideal.[13]**

He went on to argue that an artist who has taken from nature the necessary means of expression is liberated:

> **...free, legitimately free to borrow his subjects from history, from the poets, from his imagination, the million sources of his imagination. Here lies the superior artist: a painter in front of nature, a poet or thinker in his studio. Mr Corot is one of these.[14]**

It is not surprising that Baudelaire and Redon would become heroes to the younger Symbolists. They went further than their predecessors in that they explored the imaginative exaggeration of colour, line and form to convey meaning, as suggested in Gauguin's legendary advice: '...do not paint too much after nature. Art is an abstraction; derive this abstraction from nature while dreaming before it, and think more of the creation which will result than of nature.'[15] In his journals Gauguin warned against the pitfalls to be found when working from life:

> **It is better to paint from memory, for thus your work will be your own; your sensation,**

your intelligence, and your soul will triumph over the eye of the amateur. When you want to count the hairs on a donkey, discover how many he has on each ear and determine the place of each, you go to the stable.[16]

However, as Van Gogh's agonised attempts to heed Gauguin's advice showed, this was by no means the only possible way of arriving at an expressive manner of working. Having attempted to work from the imagination, in a way which he referred to as 'abstractions', he concluded that working from nature was a more powerful way of conveying meaning:

As you know, once or twice, while Gauguin was in Arles, I gave myself free rein with abstractions,...and at the time abstraction seemed to me a charming path. But it is enchanted ground old man, and one soon finds oneself up against a stone wall... So I am working at present among the olive trees,...really, above all, the great thing is to gather new vigour in reality, without any preconceived plan or Parisian prejudice.[17]

Yet he shared the avant-garde suspicion of the academic painters' literal approach to subject matter, warning Bernard 'that one can try to give an impression of anguish without aiming straight at the historic Garden of Gethsemane;...it is not necessary to portray the characters of the Sermon on the Mount in order to produce a consoling and gentle motif.'[18]

See: GENIUS, MODEL, NATURE, TEMPERAMENT

[1] Delaborde, p. 112

[2] 'An Address to the Public', 1810, in Protter, p. 103

[3] 12 Oct 1853, Delacroix, 1995, p. 207

[4] 17 Oct 1853, *ibid*, p. 210

[5] Lecture I, 26 May 1836, in Leslie, p. 259

[6] Leslie, p. 235

[7] Harrison and Wood, p. 365

[8] 'Letter to the Young Artists of Paris', *Courrier du dimanche*, 29 Dec 1861, in Courbet, p. 204

[9] Gasquet, p. 164

[10] Baudelaire, 1965, p. 156

[11] *Ibid*, p. 157

[12] 'Painters and Etchers', 1862, *Ibid*, p. 218

[13] 'Salon de 1868', in Lemaire, p. 229

[14] *Ibid*

[15] Letter to Schuffenecker, 14 Aug 1888, in Chipp, p. 60

[16] Gauguin, p. 27

[17] Letter to Emile Bernard, beginning Dec 1889, in Chipp, p. 44

[18] *Ibid*

Landscape

IT COULD BE ARGUED THAT OF ALL SUBJECTS LANDSCAPE PAINTING EPITOMISED nineteenth-century outlooks. Like the hero of a Victorian novel it rose from humble beginnings, battled with obstacles and triumphed in a blaze of official acceptance and popularity. The impact of industrialisation was to change attitudes to the countryside as well as the physical landscape.

Despite changes in the forms, meanings and status of landscape painting, the viewpoint was always that of the urban dweller. What united artists as diverse as Friedrich, Constable, Cole, Morisot and Gauguin was their idealisation of landscape as a refreshing, pure antidote to the stresses and excitements of the city.

At the beginning of the century landscape was still seen as a minor category of painting, situated below portraiture and genre in the hierarchy of subjects adhered to by the academies. It was thought that landscape could not convey the profound truths of HISTORY PAINTING. Moreover, it was considered to be a suitable subject for the 'accomplishment art' practised by genteel amateurs. This contributed to the low regard in which landscape painting was held by artists self-consciously seeking to elevate their own professional status.

Landscape presented a dilemma particularly for women artists, since ridicule of landscape as amateurish was often linked to its being produced by women. As late as 1891 the usually progressive Signac expressed the prejudices of the age:

> **I went to Pont-Aven yesterday. It is a ridiculous place full of little corners with waterfalls for the English lady watercolourists.**[1]

Landscape was more accessible for women since it required neither the classical erudition nor the study of the human figure from which women were mostly excluded until the last quarter of the century. Moreover, such non-contentious subject matter was socially acceptable for middle-class women. Its lowly status facilitated their entry into the profession yet condemned them to its lowlier levels.

This lack of importance gave the landscapists relative leeway in the degree of expertise with which they were expected to finish their works, but by the same token they were expected to work on a suitably modest scale. Yet artists such as Turner and Valenciennes, following the classical tradition of Poussin and Claude, successfully evaded this limitation by painting large landscapes with mythological or biblical themes. In his treatise on perspective and landscape painting, first published in 1800, Valenciennes explained the superiority of the classical landscape:

> **There are two ways of looking at nature... The first is that in which we see Nature as it is and represent it as faithfully as possible... The second is that in which we see Nature as it ought to be and in the way enriched imagination presents the view to the eyes of men of genius who have seen much, compared carefully, and analysed and reflected upon the choice that one must make; men who recognise all the beauties and faults; who warm, inspire, and identify themselves through readings with the celebrated poets.**[2]

Having pointed to the importance of familiarity with such poets as Homer, Plutarch, Virgil and Ossian, Valenciennes argued that the first method merely produces the PICTURESQUE, whereas the second was much more difficult because it required genius and erudition to produce works 'that interest the philosopher and the educated man.' He went on:

> **It is then that a man produces successfully in his works all the sensations he himself has felt... The artist does not thus make a cold portrait of insignificant and inanimate nature. He paints it speaking to the soul.**[3]

The eighteenth-century division of landscape painting into the SUBLIME and the picturesque was still common during the early decades of the next century. The concept of a past golden age of landscape painting continued to haunt artists well into the century, whether by default or by compliance. Yet it was the challenges to such dogma that shaped the works of both Romantics and Realists. Far from denigrating 'insignificant' NATURE the Romantics accorded it an almost divine status. For example, the German landscape painter Caspar David Friedrich wrote:

> **Art occupies the role of mediator between nature and man. The original is too great and too sublime for the majority to be able to grasp it. But the copy is the product of human hands and so lies closer to human frailty.**[4]

In his influential *Nine Letters on Landscape Painting*, published in 1831, the painter Carl Gustav Carus shared the views of his friends Friedrich and Goethe, arguing that landscape painting was a modern subject, that it revealed the infinite within the finite and that as such it was a manifestation of the divinity of human creativity:

> **And thus the creative power of Art engenders ever more extensively, and the world, as it lies formed before our senses, emerges anew in her hands... Sun and moon, sky and clouds, mountain and valley, trees and flowers, the most varied animals and the even more varied and higher individuality of man show themselves to be reborn, with the power particular to each of them affecting us – now gloomily, now cheerfully, but always lifting us high above what is commonplace through the perception of divinity, of the creative power of man.**[5]

Asking himself why this type of art developed so late, he concluded that in earlier times mankind had been too self-obsessed and that landscape painting presupposed a high level of culture.

Far more down-to-earth were the attitudes of Friedrich's contemporary Constable, though he shared with the Romantics an impatience with historicism, a fascination with science and an insistence on the artist's individual response as a basis for the creation of original works. In his introduction to *English Landscape* (1833), a collection of mezzotints of his own paintings, he opposed the classical attitude:

> **In art, there are two modes by which men aim at distinction. In the one, by a careful application to what others have accomplished, the artist imitates their works, or selects and combines their various beauties; in the other, he seeks excellence at its primitive source, nature. In the first, he forms a style upon the study of pictures, and produces either imitative, or eclectic art; in the second, by a close observation of nature, he discovers qualities existing in her which have never been portrayed before, and thus forms a style which is original.**[6]

Constable's break with convention lay first of all in his choice of unglamorous subjects. Secondly, his modest scenes from his native surroundings were devoid of overt narrative. Thirdly, he made technical innovations such as the use of bright tonal contrasts and surfaces seething with the texture of exuberant brush marks, and finally, from the 1820s onwards, he began to submit 'six-footers' to the Royal Academy. To present informal landscapes on the same scale as history painting was to question current academic theory.

However, Constable's insistence on the superiority of his native landscape can be seen as the expression of a widely shared patriotism, the celebration of the English countryside being a source of pride for many artists as well as their public. For example, he explained that his aim in publishing landscape prints was 'to increase the interest for and promote the study of the rural scenery of England, with all its endearing associations, and even in its most simple localities.'[7]

The American painter Thomas Cole saw the embodiment of American values in the characteristics of the young nation's landscape, which he compared with the ancient landscapes of the classical European tradition:

American associations are not so much of the past as of the present and future. Seated on a pleasant knoll, look down into the bosom of that secluded valley, begirt with wooded hills – through those enamelled meadows and wide waving fields of grain, a silver stream winds lingeringly along... – from yonder dark mass of foliage the village spire beams like a star. You see no ruined tower to tell of outrage – no gorgeous temple to speak of ostentation; but freedom's offspring – peace, security, and happiness, dwell there, the spirits of the scene.[8]

The French landscapist Corot's example of choosing to work in the French countryside, despite his having been trained in the classical tradition in Rome, was to be influential. He set off on his *Tour de France* in 1829 and discovered charms to equal those of the ancients in the hitherto rarely depicted landscapes and people of Brittany and Normandy. From Fontainebleau he wrote:

I frolic, I go to weddings and village fairs. I leap about with the dryads, the hamadryads of the valley. They are charming: they all adore me. I don't know which way to turn. To hide my tears, I plunge into the deepest part of the forest. If I don't meet any of these beauties there, I find at least, the purity, the *frigus opacum* of the ancients, which suits my state of mind.[9]

It can be argued that the increasing vogue for exotic and oriental landscapes by artists such as Decamps, Gleyre and Guillaumet from the 1830s onwards was the other side of the same patriotic coin, in that it paraded evidence of imperial conquests in far-off lands. The discovery of the humble, undramatic landscapes of Northern Europe were also the product of the wider shift by Naturalists towards the unassuming values of the Dutch realist tradition as opposed to those of the Italianate classical schools so venerated by the academies. Hence Millet marked the following passage in his copy of Michelet's *Histoire de la peinture Flamande* (History of Flemish Painting) published in 1865, which made the following claim of Flemish painting:

[It] seeks another kind of beauty than that of Italian art. It amplifies the true characteristics of nature. It exaggerates living forces.[10]

During the 1830s and 1840s landscape painting increased in popularity with the public and the number of landscapes submitted to the Salon grew considerably. By the end of the decade Corot's battles with the jury were over and his career was firmly established. It was no coincidence that the 1840s also witnessed the growth of topographical PHOTOGRAPHY and some soon believed that this new technology would release painting from its more tedious mimetic function. Lady Eastlake, amateur artist and patroness of The Society of Female Artists, was one of the first to articulate this publicly in 1857. Turning her attention to landscape photography she praised the medium's ability to record precise detail but concluded that only art could convey an idea of completeness. But landscapists were all too sensitive to accusations that they were no better than 'mere' photographers and stressed the originality of their interpretations of the motif. In 1854 Dutilleux wrote:

> **...the reproduction we make of nature is never an exact, mathematically precise copy such as one can expect from a machine like the daguerreotype. It can only, and should only, be an interpretation in which the artist brings to bear his knowledge, his skill, but above all his temperament, his own ideas and inner responses; his feelings!**[11]

By the 1850s the Romantics' celebration of nature and of the IMAGINATION had entered mainstream artists' attitudes to landscape. When recalling her student years working in Germany in the early 1850s, Mary Howitt was voicing a now commonly held view of the countryside:

> **I have no words to describe the delight which these walks are to me: the air is pure, keen, and bracing; the ground hard and crisp, and morning and evening I find some lovely, fresh picture painted for me by that most wonderful of all artists – Nature.**[12]

By mid-century, 'Romantic landscape' had become a recognised sub-category. Coupled with the increasing facility of travel brought by steam ships and trains it led to a search for ever more exotic, extreme and dramatic subjects. For example, when the feminist painter Barbara Bodichon painted *Eruption of Vesuvius from Naples* (1855) she enthused:

> **It is really a grand and awful sight to see it even as I have seen it, from the shores of the bay, looking across the water to the dark mountain at night, and watching its crown of fiery vapour, and the long lines of the rivers of lava running down its sides... To think there is a hole right down into the red-hot centre of the earth, to the very place where the devil is! That is strange! Strange, very strange, it is to find hot water and hot steam and hot air everywhere about here. One feels terribly close to hell.**[13]

Since landscape was still viewed as a relatively unimportant genre by the academies, it had become a 'safe' area within which to make technical innovations during the 1830s and 1840s, for example the sketchiness, or lack of finish in Turner, Constable and Corot's works. In his exhibition works Corot continued to conform to the classical convention of manipulating his sources, but his stress on the importance of a sincerely felt response when sketching directly from the motif was to be influential on the Barbizon and Impressionist painters. An undated comment in one of his notebooks states:

> **While I conscientiously seek imitation, I don't for a single moment lose touch with the emotion which grips me. The real is part of art; sentiment completes it.**
>
> **If we have been genuinely touched, the sincerity of our emotion will be conveyed to others.**[14]

From the mid-century onwards, as industrialisation led to the rapid growth of cities, landscape painting continued to grow in popularity among a public nostalgic for its rural roots. It was supported by progressive critics: for example, Baudelaire devoted an entire section of his 1846 Salon to it, while in 1848 Gautier identified it as one of the subjects for the new modern age, which would oust history painting.

The Romantic and Barbizon painters' calls for sincere responses and TRUTH to nature formed the background for the mid-century Realist emphasis on a scientific objective accuracy in both England and France. For the English Pre-Raphaelite Brotherhood the major impetus came from reading the first volume of Ruskin's *Modern Painters* (1843), which was written in defence of Turner. Ruskin claimed that this artist had overcome convention to create works unsurpassed in their sincerity, so making contact with the truth of nature in all its aspects. Attacking the generalisations called for by the academic Grand Manner, he believed that 'every class of rock, earth, and cloud, must be known by the painter, with geologic and meteorologic accuracy.'[15] Each landscape had its own character because of its specific geology and climate:

> **...it is as utterly futile to talk of generalising...impressions into an ideal landscape, as to talk of amalgamating all nourishment into one ideal food, gathering all music into one ideal movement, or confounding all thought into one ideal idea.**[16]

Ruskin ended by finding a moral dimension for sincere accuracy, attacking Claude's 'ideal' alterations to the landscape:

> **It cannot...be expected, that landscapes like this should have any effect on the human heart, except to harden or to degrade it, to lead it from the love of what is simple, earnest, and pure, to what is sophisticated and corrupt in arrangement, as erring and imperfect in detail. So long as such works are held up for imitation, landscape painting must be a manufacture.**[17]

In France, Zola praised the future Impressionists for their adherence to simple scientific objectivity. For example, when reviewing the landscapes in the 1868 Salon he accused the majority of being lifeless, concocted 'poems' by insincere, crowd-pleasing artists who used their brushes as if they were a pen. In contrast, he praised Pissarro for working with honesty, directly from the motif: '...creators of skies and fields. Day dream if you want to, this is what he has seen.'[18] Not based on lies about nature, his works were the product of a temperament '...made of precision and gravitas'.[19] In his landscapes one could hear the voices of the earth:

> **...the austerity of the horizons, the disdain for showiness, the utter lack of titillating detail gives the whole an epic grandeur. Such a reality is on a higher plane than reverie.**[20]

It was partly this concern to convey the world as they found it which prompted accusations that the Impressionists produced ugly landscapes. Pissarro in particular refused to ignore the encroachments of industry into the countryside. As late as 1891 the English painter/critic P.G. Hamerton attacked his works on these grounds:

> **...he has so little objection to ugly objects that in one of his pictures the tower of a distant cathedral is nearly obliterated by a long chimney and the smoke that issues from it, whilst there are other long chimneys close to the cathedral, just as they might present themselves in a photograph. By this needless degree of fidelity, M. Pissarro loses one of the great advantages of painting.**[21]

Of equal importance to the Impressionists was the spontaneity of their response to the motif. Pissarro wrote to his son: 'One should not seek in the studio what cannot be found there, even as outdoors one should strive only for direct and spontaneous sensations.'[22]

This priority meant that they had to work at speed as they sought to capture the movement of nature and that of figures in the landscape. In 1875, when she was in Cowes on the Isle of Wight in England, Berthe Morisot conveyed her frustration to her sister Edma:

> **...it is the prettiest place for painting – if one had any talent. I have already made a start,**

but it is difficult. People come and go on the jetty and it is impossible to catch them. It is the same with the boats. There is extraordinary life and movement, but how is one to render it?[23]

The vagaries of changing light and weather conditions became in a sense the main subjects of landscape painting, even as they provided its chief thrills and despairs. As Monet wrote:

I am feeling bleak and am deeply disgusted with painting... the weather has not ceased to be appalling for these past two months. It is enough to drive you mad, when you seek to render the weather, the atmosphere, the ambience...[24]

In turn, such a concern led to a greater emphasis on the technical means with which the landscape was represented, on the *how* instead of the *what* of the works.

By 1875, Zola could report that the battle for truth had been fought and won and that landscape painting now 'constitutes the glory of the modern French school.'[25] Yet the Salon juries continued to discriminate in favour of history painting, rarely giving landscapists the most prestigious national awards. As late as 1877 Duranty complained that although still life and landscape made up more than a third of the Salon the state had only bought four landscapes.

By the mid-1880s a tame form of Naturalism had seeped into academic art. For the vanguard what now mattered were departures from scientific accuracy in the interests of self-expression or symbolism. Having himself moved on from his Impressionist beginnings, Gauguin wrote that they remained shackled to verisimilitude:

For them the dream landscape, created from many different entities, does not exist... They heed only the eye and neglect the mysterious centres of thought, so falling into merely scientific reasoning.[26]

In 1898 Signac confided to his journal:

This mania for painting from nature is quite recent. We should collect material, not copy... What a difference there is between one who goes out for a walk, stops at random in a shady corner and 'imitates' what he finds in front of him, and the one who tries to recall on a sheet of paper or a canvas, by means of beautiful lines and colours, the feelings he experienced at a given moment before a beautiful landscape.[27]

For some the whole idea of landscape had become so synonymous with mindless naturalism that they attacked the genre itself as inane. Joséphin 'Sâr' Péladan excluded landscape from his Symbolist Salons. Toulouse-Lautrec wrote:

Landscape is nothing and should be nothing else but an accessory. The pure landscape painter is a fool. The function of landscape should be nothing more than to make the character of the figure more understandable. Corot is great only because of his figures. The same is true of Millet, Renoir, Manet, Whistler, and all the others... If Monet had not given up figure painting, what might he not have accomplished![28]

Those who did gain the respect of the younger generation were Cézanne, Van Gogh and Gauguin who were willing to distort the motif in order to convey their inner feelings. Of the role played by landscape in the gestation of *The Scream* (1893) Munch wrote the now famous explanation:

I was walking along a road with two friends. The sun set. I felt a tingle of melancholy.

> **Suddenly the sky became blood red. I stopped and leaned against the railing, dead tired, and I looked at the flaming clouds that hung like blood and a sword over the blue-black fjord and the city. My friends walked on. I stood there trembling with fright. And I felt a loud unending scream piercing nature.**[29]

It is tempting to give the last word to Cézanne who, while not given to lengthy theorising, saw the drawbacks and advantages of both the Impressionist and Symbolist approaches and admonished the young Emile Bernard:

> **Your need to find a moral, an intellectual point of support in your works, which assuredly will never be surpassed, keeps you constantly on the qui vive, incessantly on the search for the means, only dimly perceived, which will surely lead you, in front of nature, to sense your own means of expression.**[30]

See: NATURE, PICTURESQUE, *PLEIN-AIR*, SENSATION, SUBLIME

[1] See Lethève, p. 103

[2] P.-H. de Valenciennes, *Élémens de perspective pratique à l'usage des artistes, suivis de Réflexions et conseils à un élève sur la peinture, et particulièrement sur le genre du paysage*, 1820, in Taylor, p. 250

[3] *Ibid*, p. 251

[4] 'Observations on Viewing a Collection of Paintings Largely by Living or Recently Deceased Artists', c1830, in Harrison and Wood, p. 50

[5] Taylor, p. 272

[6] Leslie, pp. 153-4

[7] *Ibid*, p. 153

[8] 'Essay on American Scenery', *American Monthly Magazine*, 1 Jan 1836, in Harrison and Wood, p. 137

[9] Letter to A. Osmond, July 1831, in Cailler, I, p. 192. Hamadryads are wood nymphs.

[10] In Herbert, 1976, p. 196

[11] In Scharf, pp. 94-5

[12] In Howitt-Watts, I, p. 150

[13] In Orr, p. 175

[14] In Cailler, I, p. 86

[15] In Taylor, p. 294

[16] *Ibid*, pp. 294-5

[17] *Ibid*, p. 296

[18] 'Mon Salon: Les Naturalistes', *L'Evénement Illustré*, in Zola, p. 127

[19] *Ibid*

[20] *Ibid*

[21] 'The Present State of the Fine Arts in France', *The Portfolio*, 1891, in Pissarro, p. 151, n. 1

[22] 13 May 1891, *ibid*, p. 169

[23] Morisot, p. 101

[24] 21 July 1890, in Geffroy, p. 188

[25] 'Une Exposition de tableaux à Paris', *Le Messager de l'Europe*, 1875, in Zola, p. 166

[26] 'Divers choses', 1896-7, in Chipp, p. 65

[27] Lethève, p. 107

[28] Letter cited in Protter, p. 171

[29] Mackintosh, p. 41

[30] 23 Dec 1904, Cézanne, pp. 309-10

Mise en trait

IN A PROCESS WHICH HAD BEEN ESTABLISHED SINCE THE SEVENTEENTH CENTURY, novice art students were taught to draw by copying from a *MODÈLE DE DESSIN* (drawing model). They first had to orientate their subject along its principal axes which had to be indicated by lines. Then the student was shown how to make a *mise en trait*, a layout of the main lines of direction which set the motif within a horizontal or vertical grid. This summary would act as a kind of diagram, a guide to the main directional shapes, within which the student would make a finished copy. There were variants. In Germany this preliminary drawing stage favoured a geometric base, whereas in France clear directional lines were the main objective. This process was frequently carried over into drawing from NATURE. For example Thomas Couture taught that:

> **To establish, either in imagination or in reality, a horizontal and a vertical line in front of the objects one is reproducing – this is an excellent maxim to which one should always adhere. When with the aid of light indications, you have decided upon the layout, then you screw up your eyes and look at the natural object. By so doing, you simplify it and eliminate detail, so that you can see only the basic contrasts of light and shadow. Having thus established and made sure of the basic outline, you open...your eyes and fill in the details within the design you have set yourself.**[1]

Such an approach was widespread. The American painter William Morris Hunt, who had studied with Couture and Millet in the late 1840s and early 1850s, subsequently opened a French-style *ATELIER* (teaching studio) in Boston in the 1860s where he told his students:

> **...let me give you a few simple rules for learning to draw: –**
> **First, see of what shape the whole thing is!**
> **Next, put in the line that marks the movement of the whole. Don't have more than one movement in a figure! You cannot patch parts together.**
> **Simple lines! Then simple values!**
> **Establish the fact of the whole. Is it square, oblong, cube, or what is it?...**
> **Find the middle of the figure, and then hold up vertical and horizontal lines across it. See what parts come under the same line.**[2]

See: DRAWING, *MODÈLE DE DESSIN*

[1] Couture, *Méthode et entretiens d'atelier*, 1867, in Boime, p. 26

[2] In Hunt, pp. 10, 27

Model

SINCE THE HUMAN FIGURE WAS CENTRAL TO ART SO WAS THE MODEL, and the search for suitable ones was a frequent preoccupation. Indeed, the Pygmalion myth in which the artist's model comes to life was a popular subject in the century's art and literature. To save money artists sometimes modelled for each other: for example the young Delacroix served as a model in Géricault's *Raft of the Medusa* (1819), the Impressionists frequently posed for each other, and many artists used their lovers or spouses as models.

In his influential *ATELIER* David broke with the traditional academic practice of posing models in 'academic poses' (*attitudes académiques*) with the help of cords to hold their arms and blocks of wood to secure their feet. Delécluze recalled David demonstrating the importance of creating more natural movements. The artist posed the model as if he were in the act of throwing a stone. When the man complained that he could only hold that pose for five or six minutes, David retorted:

> **Well! Who told you any different?...if you don't like it go and pose in your Academy; they will tie cords to your feet and hands as if you were a puppet.**[1]

With the same intent to widen the student's experience of natural poses and physiognomies David initiated the practice of asking the students to pose for each other. Ingres continued this practice and took it further. Not satisfied with one of his student's attempts to pose as Seleucus for his *Stratonice* he undressed and took up the pose himself, asking his students to draw him.

The search for interesting 'types' was often a justification for travel. In 1868, when Mary Cassatt and Eliza Haldeman travelled into the countryside outside Paris to find picturesque peasants who would pose cheaply, they were following in the footsteps of the 1840s Barbizon artists. A few years later Cassatt went to Seville from where she wrote to Emily Sartain:

> **All the three heads are foreshortened and difficult to pose, so much so that my model asked me if the people who pose for me live long... The great thing here is the odd types and peculiar rich dark colouring of the models, if it were not for that I should not stay.**[2]

Two years later she wrote to the same friend from Antwerp in Holland: 'Models are not pretty and difficult to find, so after all I might have chosen a better place.'[3]

This search for unfamiliar physiognomies was frequently interlinked with the Romantics' taste for the EXOTIC and its legacy. After Delacroix made his Moroccan journey in 1832 numerous artists travelled to the Near East, while at the end of the century Gauguin sought non-European models in Martinique and Tahiti.

Models were usually working-class men, women and children. Often enough, they might be persuaded to become the artists' sexual partners. When working on *The Massacre at Chios* (1824), Delacroix wrote of one of the models for the painting:

> **I saw Sidonie, last Tuesday. What ravishing moments! How lovely she looked lying naked on the bed! It was mostly love-making and kisses.**
>
> **She is coming back on Monday.**[4]

The loose morality which was associated with modelling also stemmed from the social and moral stigma attached to nakedness. Alice Michel, the shadowy author of a memoir about modelling for Degas at the end of the century, may have been a model or possibly a journalist, but she certainly had first-hand experience of the model's way of life. She related a conversation with the artist:

> **'Monsieur Degas, do you remember the first time I visited you? Louise had brought me here so that you could tell me if I looked good enough to pose as a model.'**
>
> **'Yes indeed, I remember that I was the first to see you naked. But it didn't all happen easily. You didn't want to take off your shift; Louise had to tear it off you. You looked so**

chaste; it was charming.'

'Just think! Taking all your clothes off in front of a man!'

'Is an artist a man?' replied Degas, shrugging his shoulders.[5]

Moral outrage at nudity and lax sexual mores were even more strictly upheld outside Paris. In a mawkish tale which conveys the moral tone of the Victorian era, the painter William Powell Frith recalled seeing a young model crying during a life class at the Royal ACADEMY. A few months later, he engaged her privately, presumably to act as a clothed model. Realising that she was a 'respectable' person, he asked:

'Now tell me why you did such a thing?'

'I did it,' said she, 'to prevent my father going to prison. He owed three pounds ten, and if he couldn't have paid it by that Saturday night, he was to be arrested. The Academy paid me three guineas for the week, and saved him. I never sat in that way before, and I never will again!' and I believe she never did.[6]

In his role as an enlightened, cosmopolitan aesthete, Whistler mockingly published the text of a lecture given by the Royal Academician J.C. Horsley R.A. to the Church Congress on 7 October 1885:

If those who talk and write so glibly as to the desirability of artists devoting themselves to the representation of the naked form, only knew a tithe of the degradation enacted before the model is sufficiently hardened to her shameful calling, they would for ever hold their tongues and pens in supporting the practice. Is not clothedness a distinct type and feature of our Christian faith? All art representations of nakedness are out of harmony with it.[7]

The following year, Van Gogh wrote from Antwerp:

It struck me in a chapter from 'L'Oeuvre', by Zola, printed in the Gils Blas, that the painter, Manet of course, had a scene with a woman who had posed for him, and afterwards he had become indifferent to her, oh – curiously well described. What one can learn in this respect from the academy here is never in that light to paint women.

They hardly ever use nude women models. At least not at all in the class, and only most exceptionally in private.[8]

His later letters often refer to the difficulty of finding models. Similarly, Pissarro who lived in the French countryside, had cause to complain to his son:

I have also prepared several compositions of *Peasant Girls Bathing* in a clear stream under a shade of willows....What hampers me is the impossibility of getting a model, otherwise I could do things which would be new and rare.[9]

For women artists there was the added problem of the models' prejudice against them. From Rome Mary Cassatt complained to Emily Sartain:

My great difficulty here is the models, can't find a model, oh! how I regret Spain! All the good models are taken for the winter and of course would rather pose for men.[10]

Until the closing decades of the century much of the struggle of women to gain professional status revolved around their attempts to gain admission to the life class, from which they were excluded on the grounds of modesty. Jessie Macgregor, prize-winning student for HISTORY

PAINTING at the Royal Academy in 1872, looked back on her experiences in later life:

> **...in those days none of the advantages in figure study, now freely open to students of both sexes, were open to us – so that I was under great disabilities compared to my fellow competitors.**[11]

Although women-only life classes became quite widespread by the latter decades of the century even in these sessions the dilemma continued to be solved by partially draping the model. This was particularly true when male models were used. In Gleyre's *atelier*, one of the few which did permit women into the mixed-gender life room, this was a matter of economic survival. Renoir recalled that 'Old Gleyre had made the model wear a pair of short drawers so as not to offend the female students.' One of the women students had repeatedly asked that these be removed, saying: 'But Mr Gleyre, I know what it looks like, because I have a lover.' Her teacher reputedly answered, in his Swiss accent: 'Put I don't wand do lose my sdudenz from the Vaubourg Saint-Germain.'[12]

Alice Michel's narrative also points to the tensions and frustrations of the artist/model relationship from the model's point of view. Artists were often rude or intolerant of the tedium and discomforts which models endured:

> **'Good God, you really are posing badly today!' shouted Degas to his model, accompanying his words with a furious blow on the turntable. 'If you're tired, say so.'**
>
> **'Yes, I am,' admitted Pauline, who had been making a last effort over the past few moments to stay balanced on her left leg, while struggling to hold her raised right foot behind her with her right hand.**
>
> **'Well, have a rest then. You can try to get the right position later.' ...**
>
> **Why had he been grumbling at her all afternoon? 'Stand better than that!' 'Lift your foot!' 'Shoulders back!' 'Don't go all limp.' Wasn't she doing her best to pose properly?**[13]

Studio legends abounded, for example of a young girl fainting while posing for David and of his restraining his assistants from reviving her because he found her new pose so apt for his work. Yet models could be frustrating for the artists too. Marie Bashkirtseff complained in her journal about the street children she employed:

> **After a thousand perplexities, I have spoilt my canvas. The boys did not sit, so attributing these failures to my incapacity. I commenced again and again, and at last...it is very fortunate [sic]: those dreadful monsters moved, laughed, cried and fought.**[14]

The competitiveness which characterised the French education system spread to the models' terms of employment. At the ÉCOLE DES BEAUX-ARTS they had to win the work by stripping off and striking up various poses in the hope of being selected by the students for a class. Some male professional models had lengthy careers, for example the legendary Dubosc modelled from the age of seven to sixty two. He recalled posing as a child with the quiver of Cupid in David's day, wearing a toga in the 1830s and military uniform in the 1850s. Women were paid more than men because their working lives were shorter. In 1852 the rate was 4-5 francs for 4 hours for women and 3 francs for men. Some took pride in their profession: for example Baure, who had modelled for the young boy in Rude's *La Marseillaise* (1833-36), was proud to say 'My portrait is on the Arc de Triomphe.'[15] But it is likely that most were driven to the work by necessity.

From the early 1850s artists could purchase photographs of naked male and female models. These were a cheap alternative to a living model and were widely used. When advertised, photographs of naked models were discreetly called *Académies, Études Photographiques, Études Académiques* or *Services des Élèves de l'École des Beaux-Arts*, yet they were often passed around soldiers' barracks and smoking rooms as erotica.

The issue of whether or not to work directly from the model was related to the Romantic call for greater realism and emotional involvement with NATURE. In his diaries Delacroix returned several times to the dilemma posed by the conflicting attractions of, on the one hand, selecting and generalising from the model, and, on the other, needing to respond directly to him or her:

> **If one is in the habit of working without a model – however happy the original conception – one misses those striking effects which the great masters obtained so simply, because they rendered an effect in nature.**[16]

Yet he also battled with the distractions of working from the model. Sympathising with tales that the painter Decamps found it impossible to paint from a model, he reflected:

> **You must have complete freedom of imagination when you are painting a picture. The living model, compared with the figure which you have created and harmonised with the rest of the composition, is apt to confuse you and to introduce a foreign element into the ensemble of the picture.**[17]

Yet for the Realists and Impressionists it was imperative that they work from life. In the late 1860s, Eliza Haldeman and Mary Cassatt were planning to move from Courance to another Barbizon village in their search for a French master. Haldeman explained their reasons in a letter to her father:

> **We were at Barbizon last week but she (Miss Cassatt) was not pleased with the Master she intended taking. You can imagine the horror we were seized with on hearing he painted without models, a sort of french [sic] Rothermel. Of course he don't [sic] draw well and though a very celebrated painter would not be good as a master on that account.**[18]

Yet the issue of how open an artist should be about disclosing his or her sources was one of the major reasons for the scandal of Manet's *Déjeuner sur l'herbe* (1863), in which the artist had made no attempt to conceal the fact that the naked woman was a model. Nor had he idealised from nature. However by the end of the century the Symbolists were warning against slavish naturalism and even daringly suggesting that the model be dispensed with: 'It is well for young people to have a model so long as they draw a curtain over it while they paint.'[19]

See: ACADEMY, *ATELIER*, HISTORY PAINTING, NATURE, NUDE

[1] See Delécluze, p. 48

[2] 1 Jan 1873, in Mathews, p. 114

[3] 25 June [1875], *ibid*, p. 121

[4] 15 April 1823, in Delacroix, 1995, p. 12

[5] In Kendall, p. 312

[6] Frith, p. 38

[7] Whistler, p.193

[8] Jan 1886, in Van Gogh, 1963, p. 257

[9] 3 July 1893, in Pissarro, p. 209

[10] 26 Nov 1873, in Mathews, p. 123

[11] Letter, 21 Nov 1912, in Cherry, p. 57

[12] In Renoir, p. 95

[13] Kendall, p. 312

[14] 27 Feb 1882, in Bashkirtseff, 1890, II, pp. 248-9

[15] In Lethève, p. 77

[16] 29 Jan 1847, Delacroix, 1995, p. 64

[17] 26 April 1853, *ibid*, p. 185

[18] April 1868, in Mathews, p. 51

[19] Gauguin, 'Divers Choses', 1896-97, in Chipp, p. 65

Modèle de dessin

IN A SYSTEM WHICH ORIGINATED IN RENAISSANCE PRACTICE and was not peculiar to France, the novice student in an *ATELIER* or school of DRAWING would be set the task of copying from a *modèle de dessin* (drawing model). These were engravings (and occasionally lithographs) in which the subject was clearly delineated with accentuated contours, while the tonal parts were shown by hatching or cross-hatching in clear marks. The objective was to make a painstaking copy of these lines and marks.

The subject matter was systematically graded. Initially the student copied individual parts of the face and body; usually the first series consisted of eyes, noses and lips. This would be followed by a combination of all three, after which the student would progress to copying a profile and front view of this combination. He or she would then be promoted to working from a second sequence which usually consisted of chins, followed by ears and culminating in a combination of all five features. The third series consisted of entire heads, after which the students would move on to parts of the body (hands, feet, legs etc.), and then finally the entire figure. Students would only be allowed to proceed to the next stage, drawing from plaster casts, when their teacher decided that they had fully mastered this process.

There were two kinds of *modèle de dessin*: the *dessin au trait* (line drawing), in which only the contours were shown, and the *dessin ombré* (tonal drawing), in which shading was added to the contours to suggest mass. In the latter, simple *hachure* (hatching) would be further cross-hatched to convey deep relief. In the first decades of the century academicians defended this system of teaching shading, but cross-hatching became controversial as independent artists argued that the representation of solidity was better achieved by the less rigid *estompe* – smudging the charcoal or pencil line with a stump of paper or parchment. In his nine-volume guide to painting, Paillot de Montabert agreed that cross-hatching could lead to 'wretched mechanical studies' but explained its practical aspects as a teaching tool:

> **The hachure is not a device invented to enhance the beauty or expressiveness of a pictorial work, but a necessity imposed by the nature of the imitating process: a method to which one resorts in suitable cases to make up for the faint lines produced by a pencil or brush.[1]**

Delacroix was among the independents who opposed this method, preferring his 'system of eggs', that is avoiding the contour as a starting point in favour of working from within, in scribbled oval shapes. An *atelier* satire of the period dramatises his attempts to be admitted by the ACADEMY after repeated rejections. He is described repenting for his sketchy works and being given the penance of copying a classical figure *gravé en hachure* (engraved with hatching) in black pencil, two hundred times. When Delacroix's pleas for mercy are rejected he timidly asks 'With the cross-hatching?' The unrelenting academician's reply is 'With the cross-hatching'.[2]

Partly as a result of the Romantics' questioning of the lack of spontaneity inherent in such a process, and partly due to the influence of the more fluid imagery provided by lithographic prints, the *estompe* became more prominent by the mid-nineteenth century. The process exemplified the importance given to diligent application and hard work from the very start of the artist's education. Moreover, if a student showed natural facility for drawing, he or she would be set to copy a complicated shaded engraving, to force them to develop a tighter, more studiously worked technique (hence the Delacroix parody). Copying from endless *modèles de dessin* taught patience and accuracy of observation, and provided artists with the confidence to render the most complex forms.

See: *ATELIER*, DRAWING, ÉCOLE DES BEAUX-ARTS, *MISE EN TRAIT*

[1] *Traité complet de la peinture*, 1829, in Boime, p. 25

[2] Laurent-Jan, *Légendes d'atelier*, 1859, in Boime, p. 192, n. 11

Modernity

ONE OF THE FEW AUTHENTICATED COMMENTS MADE BY DAUMIER was that 'One must be of one's times.'[1] The saying became a rallying cry for artists such as Courbet, Manet and Cassatt because it embodied the spirit of the third quarter of the nineteenth century. Statements referring to the superiority of contemporary art can be traced back as far as Charles Perrault in the seventeenth century. However, the self-conscious sense of modernity in relation to art emerged only in the mid-nineteenth century, as artists engaged with the experiences of fast changing social conditions generated by political change and the Industrial Revolution. It was Baudelaire who would define the concept and coin the term *modernité*.

The Romantics were the first to consider it an advantage for art to be of its times. As early as 1817 Stendhal had embarked on a long tract entitled *Le beau idéal antique*, as opposed to *Le beau idéal moderne*, and the latter was to form a major element in his definition of Romanticism. Seven years later he would uncompromisingly state: 'The Romantic, in all the arts, is the man who represents people as they are today, and not as they were in those heroic times so distant from us, and which probably never existed.'[2] Comparing a classical battle painting by Salvator Rosa with a Romantic one by Horace Vernet he praised the latter and mocked the former by asking: 'What sympathy can be felt by a Frenchman of today, who has himself carried a sword, for men who fight *stark naked*.'[3]

By the 1830s the German Romantic landscapist, Caspar David Friedrich showed an historical awareness of art's development over time:

> **...if today a painter such as Raphael or some other excellent artist of an earlier age were to appear...he would...not paint as they did. His works would...bear the imprint of his times and the paintings of the second Raphael would be very different from those of the first, even if they depicted the same subject. For this reason, you gentlemen from A to B who continually imitate Raphael, Michelangelo and others, your works will no more be taken to resemble the products of these masters than the works of an ape who imitates a man... Be sensible and reflect, then, and recognise yourselves and the time in which you live.[4]**

Yet the Romantics were chiefly preoccupied with questioning the Classicists' subservience to past canons of taste, while their commitment to originality and imagination led them to avoid repeating what had already been done before. Even those few works which took contemporary events for their subject matter, such as Géricault's *Raft of the Medusa* (1819) or Delacroix's *Massacre of Chios* (1824), selected them and portrayed them in such a dramatised and emotive fashion that the works were far removed from everyday experience.

It was the Realists in the mid-nineteenth century who pushed these ideas towards the depiction of modern times in a modern manner, by portraying everyday people going about their lives in an undramatised fashion. In the statement which prefaced the catalogue of his works in his controversial Pavilion du Realisme outside the Exposition Universelle of 1855, Courbet wrote:

> **To record the manners, ideas and aspect of the age as I myself saw them – to be a man as well as a painter, in short to create a living art – that is my aim.[5]**

After the 1848 Revolution even conservative artists working in a conventional academic manner had begun to accept that working people could become suitable subject matter, so that Couture for example would recommend it, and artists such as Jules Breton would build their careers from the practice. The taste of the growing bourgeoisie for GENRE and LANDSCAPE provided a market for anecdotal and sentimentalised portrayals of contemporary life. However, the academic painters felt constrained by the concepts of BEAUTY which held that modern clothes were ugly. The British genre painter William Powell Frith recalled his early work:

> **One of the greatest difficulties besetting me has always been the choice of subject. My inclination being strongly toward the illustration of modern life, I had read the works of Dickens in the hope of finding material for the exercise of any talent I might possess; but at that time the ugliness of modern dress frightened me, and it was not till the publication of *Barnaby Rudge*, and the delightful Dolly Varden was presented to us, that I felt my opportunity had come, with the cherry-coloured mantle and the hat and pink ribbons.[6]**

To achieve modernity was not simply a matter of depicting contemporary subjects; appropriate formal means had to be found. What made Courbet's *Burial at Ornans* (1849-50) a modern work was partly the choice of anonymous, life-size, provincial protagonists, but also the lack of idealisation with which these figures were portrayed. Moreover the work's simplified COMPOSITION was reminiscent of those in the popular woodcuts that were the art of the people. Hence Courbet's champion, the critic Champfleury, praised the work for its contemporaneity of PHYSIOGNOMY and dress and for its lack of idealisation:

> **It has pleased the painter to show us the small-town domestic life. He has said to himself**

that printed cotton dresses and black suits are as good as Spanish costumes, the laces and feathers of the time of Louis XIII...

As for the alleged ugliness of the bourgeois of Ornans, he has not exaggerated anything...

Mr. Courbet can boldly state that the three women's heads, the children, the grave digger, and several other figures, are characteristic of modern beauty.[7]

But Champfleury also commended the work's formal innovations:

from a distance, when one enters the room, the Funeral looks as if it is framed by a doorway; everybody is surprised by that simple painting, as one is surprised at seeing those naive woodcuts, carved by a clumsy hand, that head the broadsides describing murder cases, printed in the Rue Gît-le Coeur.[8]

Yet the Realism of Courbet and the Barbizon artists was centred on subjects from rural France which, despite technological and political changes, was still linked with traditional ways of life. Modernity was associated above all with urban subjects, as the AVANT-GARDE of the 1860s and 1870s engaged with the major social changes engendered by the rapid growth of Paris, London and other major cities from the mid-century. Baudelaire, who coined the term *modernité*, used it as an important criterion for evaluating beauty in art and defining it in terms of the experience of the urban and the quintessential newness which that implied. Already in his Salon of 1846, he had defined the new beauty to be found in the heroism of modern URBAN LIFE:

The life of our city is rich in poetic and marvellous subjects. We are enveloped and steeped as though in an atmosphere of the marvellous; but we do not notice it.

The *nude* – that darling of the artists, that necessary element of success – is just as frequent and necessary today as it was in the life of the ancients; in bed, for example, or in the bath, or in the anatomy theatre. The themes and resources of painting are equally abundant and varied; but there is a new element – modern beauty.[9]

In 1859 Baudelaire expanded this theme in his seminal essay 'The Painter of Modern Life', which was first published in *Le Figaro* in 1863 and which continued to influence artists well into the next century. Taking the illustrator Constantin Guys as his example of the archetypal painter of modern life, he defined this modern artist as a spectator, half invalid, half child, an anonymous *flâneur*, responding to the spectacle provided by the swirling crowds in the new public spaces of the city. Entitling the fourth section of his essay 'Modernity' he explained that Guys's works embodied this quality: 'He makes it his business to extract from fashion whatever element it may contain of poetry within history, to distil the eternal from the transitory.'[10] He went on to denigrate the academicians' lazy retreat into historicism:

...it is much easier to decide outright that everything about the garb of an age is absolutely ugly than to devote oneself to the task of distilling from it the mysterious element of beauty that it may contain, however slight or minimal that element may be. By 'modernity' I mean the ephemeral, the fugitive, the contingent, the half of art whose other half is the eternal and the immutable.[11]

It was to be Manet, Degas and the Impressionists whose works most embodied these characteristics, since they understood that the new experiences offered by the city would require not only new subjects but also new ways of depicting them. For example Degas in his notebooks planned all manner of new viewpoints, fugitive effects, odd compositions as well as new subjects:

> **...a severely truncated dancer – do some arms or legs, or some backs – draw the shoes, the hands of a hairdresser, the built-up hairstyle, bare feet in the act of dancing etc...**
>
> **On smoke – smokers' smoke, pipes, cigarettes, cigars – smoke from locomotives, from tall factory chimneys, from steam boats etc. Smoke compressed under bridges – steam.**
>
> **On evening – infinite variety of subjects in cafés – different tones of the glass globes reflected in the mirrors...**
>
> **Neither monuments nor houses have ever been done from below, close up as they appear when you walk down the street.**[12]

Unlike the idealised types to be seen in academic genre, the Impressionists kept faith with the Realist commitment to untempered TRUTH. This refusal to avert their eyes from the perceived vulgarities of their own age contributed to the modernity of their works. In her old age, Mary Cassatt wrote:

> **So you think my models unworthy of their clothes? You find their types coarse. I know that is an American newspaper criticism, everyone has their criterion of beauty. I confess I love, health & strength... Paul Veronese had a jacket which he took about with him & constantly painted on all his models, I doubt if they were 'cultured' how I hate the word, these are elemental things which no culture changes. Then who do you think makes the fashions? The uncultured girls & they are launched by the 'free lances' also uncultured but copied by the sheltered women.**[13]

In *La Nouvelle Peinture*, first published as a pamphlet in 1876, the writer Edmond Duranty brilliantly summed up the Impressionists' preoccupations:

> **And, as we are solidly embracing nature, we will no longer separate the figure from the background of an apartment or the street. In actuality, a person never appears against neutral or vague backgrounds. Instead, surrounding him and behind him are the furniture, fireplaces, curtains, and walls that indicate his financial position, class, and profession. The individual will be at a piano, examining a sample of cotton in an office, or waiting in the wings for the moment to go on stage, or ironing on a makeshift table. He will be having lunch with his family or sitting in his armchair near his worktable, absorbed in thought. He might be avoiding carriages as he crosses the street or glancing at his watch as he hurries across the square.**[14]

Middle-class women artists could not take on the role of the urban *flâneur* – for them it was socially unacceptable. Marie Bashkirtseff voiced her frustration with this situation:

> **Ah! how women are to be pitied; men are at least free. Absolute independence in everyday life, liberty to come and go, to go out, to dine at an inn or at home, to walk to the Bois or the café: this liberty is half the battle in acquiring talent, and three parts of every-day happiness.**
>
> **But you will say, 'Why don't you, superior woman as you are, seize this liberty?' It is impossible, for the woman who emancipates herself thus, if young and pretty, is almost tabooed; she becomes singular, conspicuous, and cranky; she is censured, and is, consequently, less free than when respecting those absurd customs.**[15]

One solution for avant-garde women was to turn their attention to sheltered domestic life, which *was* their domain. Within it, they too discovered new subjects devoid of the sentimentalised, narrative aspect so beloved by academic painters. Moreover, like their male colleagues, women artists captured the fugitive aspects of these subjects. In some of the very few references to her own work which appear in her correspondence, Berthe Morisot wrote:

> **I am to decide how to pose the lady with the parrots. If I am satisfied, I'll try to paint it very quickly; if not, I shall not do anything at all under the pretext that I must leave in a hurry.**[16]

She then developed this idea more fully:

> **...the desire for posthumous glory seems to me an inordinate aspiration. My ambition is limited to trying to record something fleeting, anything, the least of things. Yet even this ambition is excessive. A pose struck by Julie, a smile, a flower, a fruit, the branch of a tree, one of these would be enough.**[17]

Certain public places such as the theatre and the park could be frequented by women as long as they were chaperoned. Cassatt and Morisot did turn to these subjects.

By the end of the century, official national EXHIBITIONS from New York to Moscow were teeming with works that depicted scenes of every day life, yet their anecdotal, or narrative content would disqualify many of these from epitomising the concept of modernity. Nevertheless, so ubiquitous and clichéd had such subject matter become that many avant-garde artists at the end of century repudiated it.

See: BEAUTY, URBAN LIFE, GENRE, PEASANT LIFE

[1] In Nochlin, 1971, p. 103

[2] 'Salon de 1824', *Journal de Paris*, 1824, in Harrison and Wood, p. 37

[3] *Ibid*

[4] 'Observations on Viewing a Collection of Paintings Largely by Living or Deceased Artists', c.1830, see Harrison and Wood, pp. 51-2

[5] In Harrison and Wood, p. 372

[6] In Frith, p. 56

[7] 'L'Enterrement d'Ornans', *Messager de l'Assemblée*, 1851, in Harrison and Wood, pp. 368-9

[8] *Ibid*, p. 368

[9] *Salon de 1846*, in Baudelaire, 1965, p. 119

[10] 'Le peintre de la vie moderne', *Figaro*, 1863, in Baudelaire, 1995, p. 12

[11] *Ibid*

[12] Notebooks, c1876, in Kendall, p. 112

[13] Letter to Theodate Pope, 19 Feb 1911, in Mathews, p. 306

[14] In Harrison and Wood, p. 583

[15] Journal, 20 June 1882, in Harrison and Wood, pp. 768-9

[16] Letter to Eugène Manet, 1882, in Morisot, p. 126

[17] 'Carnet noir', in Shennan, p. 260

Museum

THE COLLECTION AND CLASSIFICATION OF OBJECTS FOR THE PURPOSE OF STUDYING them originated in the ancient Greek *Mouseion*. Originally meaning anything from a shrine to a textbook which was consecrated to the muses, the word came to be associated more specifically with temples to the arts and sciences. In the fourth century BC Aristotle collected and classified zoological specimens for the purpose of study in the *Mouseion* which he started for his school, so giving it an educational function. Museums became an established part of the ancient world and the Romans transmuted the Greek word into the Latin 'museum'. Aristocrats, rich merchants and the church continued to accumulate collections of natural history, curiosities, books, manuscripts, precious objects and works of art throughout the centuries. During the Renaissance artists would be admitted to study from collections of antiquities such as the Belvedere and Capitol in Rome and this practice was adopted elsewhere in later centuries. But it was only in the nineteenth century that museums became part of the creation of a mass public culture. Like the great exhibitions they educated, elevated and entertained all the social classes.

Before the nineteenth century most museums and art collections were privately owned. When Catherine the Great of Russia had the Hermitage built in the eighteenth century she did so 'for myself and the mice'.[1] Although it was increasingly possible from this period to gain admittance by appointment to private museums, in practice this was only granted to the respectable middle and upper classes. In 1753 the British Museum became the first to be established by a government with the specific function of being a public museum. It opened its doors in 1759. Yet the nucleus of its collection was a bequest to the nation (subject to the payment of £20,000) of Sir Hans Sloane's collection of drawings, coins, books and natural history. This set a precedent in Britain of public museums relying mostly on private bequests.

During the French Revolution the transformation of part of the Louvre royal palace into a museum for the now publicly-owned royal art collection was a potent symbol of Republican ideals of equality, liberty and fraternity. In the opening decades of the nineteenth century the idea that the general public might be given access to major art collections was still viewed as dangerously democratic. The didactic and political function of the project was made clear by David in his Plan of the Committee of Public Safety of the Arts. Art was to be publicly displayed so that it might educate and elevate the people:

> **It is time to substitute for the lecherous pictures which adorned the luxurious apartments of the satraps and the powerful, of the courtesans' voluptuous boudoirs...for these dishonourable productions, paintings worthy of the gaze of a republican populace which cherishes moral standards and rewards virtue.**[2]

The Napoleonic conquests added to the richness of the French collections. In 1794 booty from the Belgian campaign had been added to the Louvre and this began a government policy of systematic looting. The French army was accompanied by commissioners who selected treasures from churches and princely collections in conquered territories. In 1798 the Louvre was renamed the Musée Napoléon and works looted from the Vatican Museum were escorted to it in a triumphal procession complete with bands and military parades recalling those of the

Roman conquerors. David's pupil Delécluze marvelled as carts filled with rare manuscripts, precious minerals and live, exotic animals trundled past the crowds:

These were followed by a long line of carts filled with crated paintings, inscribed with the titles of the most famous works, such as Raphael's *Transfiguration* and Titian's *Christ...* Finally, on specially constructed, heavy carts followed the sculptures and marble groups: the *Apollo Belvedere*, the *Nine Muses*, the *Antinous*, three or four statues of *Bacchus*, the *Laocoon*, the *Gladiator* and other specimens of the best antique sculpture. These carts and their precious cargoes bore numbers and were bedecked with laurel branches, bouquets and wreaths of flowers, and with flags taken from the enemy.[3]

During the peace of Amiens in 1802 artists and connoisseurs including Turner, Flaxman, Fuseli and Benjamin West travelled from all over Europe to marvel at the riches contained in the Musée Napoléon. The British painter Martin Shee was overwhelmed by the experience:

The extraordinary assemblage of works of Art deposited in the Louvre at Paris appears in this respect on the first view quite embarrassing. All is confusion and astonishment, the eye is dazzled and bewildered, wandering from side to side, from picture to picture; like a glutton at a feast, anxious to devour everything, till the intellectual stomach, palled and oppressed by variety, loses the pleasure of taste, and the power of digestion.[4]

The French example was soon emulated, albeit without the same overt political intentions. In 1809 the King of Spain established the Prado museum in Madrid to publicly exhibit the royal art collection. By mid-century European royal art collections were being incorporated into public museums, with the exception of the British one which is still privately owned today. Art museums became a matter of national pride and prestige and prestigious buildings to house the collections were commissioned. Most commonly these were built in the classical style to express the dignity and seriousness with which their contents were viewed. Museums truly became temples of art. For example England's first purpose-built public art museum, the Dulwich Picture Gallery, opened to the public in 1817, while Smirke's Neo-classical building for the British Museum was commissioned in 1823. Not to be outdone, Friedrich Wilhelm III King of Prussia paid the architect Karl Friedrich Schinkel to visit the British Museum and the Louvre in order to be well-informed before undertaking the commission to build the Altes Museum in Berlin, which opened in 1830. Reporting to the king, Schinkel wrote:

The impression the Paris Museum gives is as great in the excellence of the art works as in the method of exhibition and decoration of the rooms.

The Museum of the Vatican in Rome gives the same effect. The Museum in Berlin, so richly provided for by Your Royal Majesty's favour will have an important place among the other museums because of its contents. In the manner of its arrangement as well as the furnishing of the rooms, it will be distinguished in its simplicity and organic plan. The greatest effort will be made to achieve this simple dignity so that the building's appearance before the world may correspond to the intention of its great founder.[5]

The National Gallery in London (opened in 1824) moved to its purpose-built home in Trafalgar Square in 1834-7. In the second half of the century provincial public museums began to spread in Europe and in the colonies while the great American public museums were established during the last quarter of the century, for example the Museum of Fine Arts, Boston (1870), The Metropolitan Museum of Art, New York (1870), and the Art Institute of

Chicago (1879).

During the French Revolution the artist-citizen Alexander Lenoir organised the display, classification and preservation of sculptures, confiscated by the new government from the church and aristocracy, within a Museum of French Monuments. In doing so he set the precedent for later nineteenth-century museums by classifying the works in a scholarly manner and arranging them chronologically. Unlike the 'picturesque' hanging most commonly practised in the previous century, which relied on aesthetically pleasing groupings of paintings, this was intended to set a more serious and educational tone. The system was soon followed in the Louvre and was later widely adopted elsewhere in Europe. In his catalogue Lenoir explained that museums could become major places of study both for the public and for artists:

> **Versed from my infancy in the art of drawing, I became convinced that collections were of more service to the progress of the arts than schools, where the pupils never see any works of art... A museum... ought to have two objectives in view, the one political, the other that of public instruction.**[6]

Art museums became repositories of treasures and knowledge carefully classified and catalogued in a manner that expressed the century's positivist confidence in furthering human understanding. But they were still understood to play an important social role in providing a civilising and edifying influence on the population. In the mid-nineteenth century Baudelaire wrote:

> **You the bourgeois – be you king, lawgiver, or businessman – have founded collections, museums and galleries. Some of those, which sixteen years ago were only open to the monopolists, have thrown wide their doors to the multitude...**
>
> **And what you have done for France, you have done for other countries too. The Spanish Museum is there to increase the volume of general ideas that you ought to possess about art; for you know perfectly well that just as a national museum is a kind of communion by whose gentle influence men's hearts are softened and their wills unbent, so a foreign museum is an international communion where two peoples, observing and studying one another more at their ease, can penetrate one another's mind and fraternise without discussion.**[7]

The museum's role was central to academic teaching. The Neo-classical belief in learning from the perfections of the ANTIQUE and approved old masters survived in the academies throughout the century, and almost all art students copied in museums. It was hoped that exposure to these works would form and refine the students' discernment and taste. This had long been a tradition within the accomplishments expected of gentlemen and some gentlewomen, hence the required museum visits of the Grand Tour. At the beginning of the century Lenoir had already understood that the academies themselves could be substituted by 'a clear and easy method of teaching' in museums:

> **Such means of study naturally present themselves in a museum chronologically arranged, where youth will find, by the comparisons which they themselves make, certain and proper models to direct their studies.**[8]

The Louvre's Salon Carré, where the most important paintings were hung, was alive with students and professional copyists and the National Gallery in London was opened exclusively to artists on Fridays and Saturdays until 1880. This facility was of particular use to women artists who were excluded from most of the official art colleges until the latter decades of the century. For Caroline Luise Seidler, for example, winning permission to work in the private Dresden Picture Gallery in the early nineteenth century (where few were allowed at that time) was an important triumph. Rosa Bonheur was another woman for whom study in the museums was an essential stage in her battle to become a painter. Taught privately by her father, she told a biographer about her education during the 1830s:

> **Soon he agreed to set me up in the Louvre. Now I could work in this sanctuary to my heart's content! I was so happy that the whole first day my hand shook like a leaf and I couldn't draw a single stroke.**[9]

By allowing her to study in the Louvre unchaperoned her father was aware that he was breaking social taboos. That he did so was probably because he was a progressively minded Saint-Simonian, yet he had to warn her against the likelihood of improper advances by fellow male students. More than two decades later, when the upper-bourgeois Morisot sisters gained permission to copy in the Louvre in 1858 they were chaperoned by their mother. As late as 1879 the independent-minded Marie Bashkirtseff, who also came from the upper class, raged against social restrictions in her diary:

> **Do you imagine I can get much good from what I see, chaperoned as I am, and when, in order to go to the Louvre, I must wait for my carriage, my lady companion, or my family?**
>
> **Curse it all, it is this that makes me gnash my teeth, to think that I am a woman!... It is the sort of liberty that I need, and without it I can never hope to do anything of note.**[10]

However, in England pioneering feminist artists stepped out unchaperoned in defiance of such social restrictions on their professional development and in the 1850s their studies in the British Museum and National Gallery provided them with the added attraction of congenial meeting places. Laura Herford, Ellen Clayton and other signatories to the 1859 petition to be admitted to the Royal Academy would meet in these two museums.

The massive international collections built up by the imperial powers permitted students and artists to study a wide range of works. The American painter and influential teacher William Morris Hunt, who studied with Millet during the late 1840s and early 1850s, wrote of the latter:

> **Sometimes we would go up to Paris, to the Louvre, and he would lead me up to a Mantegna or an Albrecht Dürer, and show me what were the great things... Always said he did not care to go to Rome. He could see great pictures enough in the Louvre.**[11]

Yet for those artists who could afford it, travelling to visit the major European collections was understood to be an important part of their formation as well as providing a lifelong source of stimulation. Many are the letters and journals in which artists enthuse about their discoveries. Manet, who as a young man had already visited the museums in Belgium, Holland, Germany, Austria and Italy, wrote to Fantin-Latour from Madrid in 1865 about the Prado's collection:

> **Oh what a pity you are not here; what pleasure it would have given you to see Velazquez, who alone is worth the whole journey... He is the painter to beat all painters. He didn't astonish me, he enchanted me.**[12]

As a mature artist Berthe Morisot wrote to her mother from Madrid:

> **So far we have seen only the museum, which is magnificent, as you know. The city has no character... I have no intention of exerting myself to see anything but paintings.**[13]

Furthermore copying from 'the masters' was a source of income for impoverished students, so that even those progressive teachers who did not approve of the practice turned a blind eye to it. For women artists in particular copying religious old masters for provincial churches provided a modest income. Such subjects were considered respectable for middle-class women, and since copying did not require invention or passion there was no perceived threat to the social norms expected of their gender. The art museums became increasingly crowded with copyists: when Seidler wrote her memoirs she gloated that in her youth she had had the Dresden Picture Galleries to herself, whereas '[nowadays] the masterpieces are so thickly barricaded with easels and scaffolds that one cannot enjoy a view of them.'[14]

Such was the veneration with which the old masters were viewed that major museums such as the Louvre and London's National Gallery excluded the work of living painters. However as the century wore on and the status of contemporary art grew it was increasingly shown in museums. A pioneer was the Luxembourg Museum in Paris, founded in 1815 with the purpose of exhibiting contemporary art bought by the state. The works would graduate to the Louvre upon the artists' deaths, so ensuring their place in future art history. The conservatism of the Académie des Beaux-Arts ensured that the AVANT-GARDE was excluded from such official accolades; works by Salon artists dominated museums in Paris and in the provinces.

From the mid-century onwards a similarly conservative taste informed the contemporary art shown in museums elsewhere. Many were based on collections amassed by private entrepreneurs: for example the Mappin Art Gallery Sheffield (1887) bore the name of the Sheffield brewer who had donated his collection of contemporary British genre to the museum, while the Tate Gallery London (1897) was founded by the sugar magnate Henry Tate to be a 'British Luxembourg'. In America the Walters Art Gallery was founded by a Baltimore railway baron from his collection of mostly French academic and Barbizon art, while in Russia Pavel Tretyakov bequeathed his collection of paintings by the 'Wanderers' to the city of Moscow in 1892.

Even at the end of the century Van Gogh's intention to move to Paris was partly motivated by the attractions of the Louvre and the Luxembourg. So excited was he by the prospect that he journeyed earlier than arranged and headed straight for the Louvre's Salon Carré when he got there. Such was the respect for tradition that even the most ardent innovators continued to be well versed in the works of 'the masters' seen in museums and churches, and the writings of artists as diverse as Delacroix and Ingres, Constable, Cassatt, Millet and Whistler are liberally peppered with references to them. In late-middle age, finding himself in a period of creative doubt, Pissarro turned to the Louvre for succour:

> **How can one combine the purity and simplicity of the dot with the fullness, suppleness, liberty, spontaneity and freshness of sensation postulated by our Impressionist art?... I'm constantly pondering this question, I shall go to the Louvre to look at certain painters who are interesting from this point of view. Isn't it senseless that there are no Turners [here].**[15]

However, the calls for greater naturalism led to debates over the conflicting pulls of direct perception versus the thrills to be found in the art of the museums. Pissarro himself had as a young man called for the closing down of the Louvre. As early as 1822, when the possibility of building a National Gallery was being discussed, Constable had foreseen its potential dangers:

> **Should there be a National Gallery (which is talked of) there will be an end of the art in poor old England, and she will become, in all that relates to painting, as much a nonentity as every other country that has one. The reason is plain; the manufacturers of pictures are then made the criterion of perfection, instead of NATURE.**[16]

Yet as Constable's biographer Leslie pointed out, in later letters and especially in his lectures (1833) Constable frequently referred in glowing terms to previous masters such as Claude and to the pleasures of seeing their works in the National Gallery.

The debate came to a head with the Impressionists in the 1860s. Renoir told his son that a major preoccupation throughout his life was the tension between working from museum art and working from nature. Cézanne voiced the preoccupations formed in his youth when as an old man he told Emile Bernard that he aimed: 'to make of Impressionism something solid, like the art in the museums.'[17] But he also wrote:

> **The Louvre is a good book to consult but it must only be an intermediary. The real and immense study to be undertaken is the manifold picture of nature.**[18]

By the closing decades of the century the avant-garde began to beat on the doors of the museums. After Manet's death (1883) Monet organised a subscription among artists and patrons to buy the *Olympia* (1865) from the painter's widow in order that it be presented to the Louvre. Explaining that he and other subscribers saw Manet as a great master, whose paintings belonged alongside those in a national museum, Monet argued that they had chosen *Olympia* because it was 'one of the most beautiful and the most characteristic of the master's overall body of work.'[19] The ensuing correspondence shows both the admiration with which Manet was held by the avant-garde and continuing official resistance to their works. As Berthe Morisot replied to Monet:

> **Everything I have heard confirms the administration's hostility which you have mentioned before... I was told that someone (whose name I do not know) had gone to see Kaempfen to sound him out, that Kaempfen had angrily assured him that so long as he was there no Manet would be admitted to the Louvre, and that thereupon his visitor rose angrily saying: Very well then, we shall try to get rid of you, and then we shall bring in Manet.**[20]

At the close of the century the Impressionist painter-collector Caillebotte caused a scandal when he bequeathed his important collection of Impressionist art to the nation, on condition that the works be hung in the Louvre on their creators' deaths. The administration was embarrassed and the academicians were furious. Among the latter Jean-Léon Gérôme was bluntly dismissive:

> **I do not know these gentlemen and of this donation the only thing I know is its title. It includes paintings by Monet, Pissarro and others doesn't it? For the State to accept such filth would be the sign of great moral decline.**[21]

Only at the very end of the century did the American collectors buy avant-garde works for their museums. Public art museums epitomised nineteenth-century attitudes to art and to society. They were to be temples of art untainted by the crass ephemera of the modern world. They were to act as guardians of good taste to educate and elevate the sensibilities of the population and so to fulfill the century's preoccupation with earnest self-improvement.

See: ACADEMY, ANTIQUE, EXHIBITION, NATURE

[1] In Brettell, 1999, p. 68

[2] Projet du Comité de Salut Public pour les Beaux-Arts, *Le Moniteur*, 1794, in David, I, p. 193

[3] In Delécluze, *Louis David, son école et son temps*, 1855, in Eitner, II, p. 8

[4] *The Elements of Art*, 1809, in Eitner, II, p. 9

[5] 24 Oct 1826, in Holt, 1986, p. 292

[6] *Description historique et chronologique des monuments…réunis au Musée des Monuments Français*, 1803, in Eitner, II, p. 7

[7] *Salon de 1846*, in Baudelaire, 1965, p. 42

[8] In Eitner, II, p. 7

[9] In Klumpke, p. 110

[10] 2 Jan 1879, in Bashkirtseff, II, 1890, p. 21

[11] In Hunt, p. 170

[12] In Courthion, p. 14

[13] 1872, in Morisot, p. 89

[14] *Memoirs*, 1874, in Greer, p. 305

[15] Letter to Lucien Pissarro, 6 Sept 1888, in Pissarro, p. 132

[16] Letter to Mr Fisher, 6 Dec 1822, in Leslie, p. 82

[17] In Eisenman, p. 345

[18] Letter to Bernard, 12 May 1904, in Cézanne, pp. 302-3

[19] Letter to Antonin Proust , 22 Jan 1890, in Geffroy, p. 126

[20] Nov 1889 (?), in Morisot, p. 171

[21] In Harding, p. 19

Nature

THE RELATIONSHIP OF NATURE TO ART WAS WIDELY DEBATED IN THE NINETEENTH CENTURY, and it was closely linked to ideas of truth and beauty. All three were considered essential to great art. The term nature could refer to many things, and its meaning varied depending on time, place and cultural context. In general the idea of nature was gendered as feminine, with the attendant implications of its being a compliant or a treacherous seductress ready to be tamed or modified by the (male) artist.

Probably the most common usage was in the straightforward sense of representation, the phrase *d'après la nature* denoting a work from life, whether this be from the MODEL, the LANDSCAPE, a still-life motif, or any other visible phenomena. Hence nature meant the world out there, the raw material from which artists took their information. According to the classical theories perpetuated by academicians such as Quatremère de Quincy, nature was but a starting point. He had studied sculpture at the Académie de France in Rome at the same time as David. Later on he exerted considerable influence in his support for Ingres and the classical ideal owing to his writings and his post as Permanent Secretary of the Académie des Beaux-Arts. In his *Essai sur la nature, le but et les moyens de l'imitation dans les beaux-arts* (An Essay on Nature, the End and Means of Imitation in the Fine Arts) (1823) he argued that a blind imitation of nature entailed reproducing the vulgar; art existed on another plane of experience:

> **By one mode then nature is partially imitated, from a model which is everywhere. Of such the sole result is the pleasure the senses experience from resemblances which are not elevated above the reality of objects. This kind of imitation is that, which to judge, gives the mind the least possible labour, which leaves the imagination idle, in which sentiment has little share, reason little employ, and which has for its admirers, the vulgar...**

> **By another mode nature is imitated generally, that is, from a model which is neither local nor individual, which cannot be arrested in any determinate place, nor, wholly, in any distinct object, because it resides in the higher and invisible region of principles, of causes, and of the intelligent reason, the true source of all the effects which possess any active influence on the faculties of our minds.[1]**

The academic assumption that the study of nature led to work that accorded with classical ideals survived within western academies until late in the century. For example, the British Royal Academician Sir Edward Poynter told the students at St Martin's School of Art in 1875:

> **...the imitation of nature is the principal object, only it is an imitation which leaves out of sight all that is weak, ungainly, or ignoble, and delights only in beauty, strength, and life, as is the case in the noble works of the Greek and Italian schools. For the student of to-day there is accordingly but one thing to aim at, and that is so to study nature as to receive and retain the most complete and distinct impressions.[2]**

During the first half of the century the Classicists' belief in the need to improve upon nature according to the ideals established by the old masters was challenged by the Romantics' and Realists' encroaching calls for TRUTH to the sensory experience of nature. Although they too used the term to denote working from the observable world, for the Romantics nature was deified as the rural, unspoiled environment, the organic world of fauna and flora untouched by the harmful effects of manufacture and industrialisation. Delacroix dwelt on this aspect of nature over and over again in his diaries. He recorded his own love of being in the countryside, closely observing the most humble of natural phenomena as well as the most dramatic; he stood and stared at sunsets, at the sea in all its humours, but also looked closely at insects, rocks, and the quiet landscapes around his country retreat.

The Romantics' response was many faceted and contradictory, yet there was a shared sense that to be in the presence of nature was to be at one's most human. Artists would express their individual, emotional responses to it. The German landscapist Caspar David Friedrich bemoaned the prevalence of imitations of the old masters in contemporary painting and the rule-bound inhibition which distracted painters from presenting 'nature in its simple nobility and grandeur – as it actually is when one has the sensibility, character and feeling to grasp it and recognise it as such.'[3]

Delacroix wrote frequently of the need to distinguish between mimicking or copying nature, which he argued was not great art, and the need to express its essence, by being selective, which was great art. While Goethe pointed out that only by understanding how nature functions could artists hope to transgress the limitations of imitating outward appearances:

Nature is separated from Art by an enormous chasm, which genius itself is unable to bridge without external assistance.

All that we perceive around us is merely raw material... in the practice of art we can finally vie with Nature only when we have learned from her, at least to some extent, her method of procedure in the creation of her works.[4]

Although they rejected the classical rules the Romantics still saw nature as raw material to be transformed into art. Since a personal response via the senses was imperative, the results were predictably varied. For example Turner, whose works sought the SUBLIME, praised the transformation of the mundane in art in a lecture delivered at the Royal Academy:

Of the Flemish School approaches to individual nature... only two, Rembrandt and Rubens, dared to raise her above commonality. Rembrandt depended upon his chiaroscuro, his bursts of light and darkness, to be felt. He threw a mysterious doubt over the meanest piece of Common.[5]

In contrast his fellow countryman, Constable felt that the artist should humbly accept 'the Primitive Source' of nature as he found it; indeed he argued that nature was greater than art: 'It appears to me that pictures have been over-valued; held up by a blind admiration as ideal things, and almost standards by which nature is to be judged rather than the reverse.' He went on to argue that 'selection and combination are learned from nature herself, who constantly presents us with compositions of her own, far more beautiful than the happiest arranged by human skill.'[6]

For Constable, an unpretentious depiction of the untamed meant recording faithfully the chaotic and mundane configurations of the landscape, regardless of the classical rules of composition. Yet this involved a nostalgic idealisation of nature as untarnished by the interfering hands of humanity at a time of increasing industrialization, when the English countryside was being heavily farmed. In contrast, within a very different geographical context, nature truly was a wilderness for North American painters of the Hudson River School such as Thomas Cole, striding out with his paint box and sketch book into unmapped territories. American Romanticism would praise the wildness of the American landscape in terms of a nascent national pride. Cole berated those who belittled it for its lack of associations and vestiges of antiquity, which supposedly made European landscape superior. On the contrary he argued, its very unspoiled state was what rendered it sublime:

The most distinctive, and perhaps the most impressive, characteristic of American scenery is its wildness...there are those who regret that with the improvements of cultivation the sublimity of the wilderness should pass away; for those scenes of solitude from which the hand of nature has never been lifted, affect the mind with a more deep toned emotion than aught which the hand of man has touched. Amid them the consequent associations are of God the creator – they are undefiled works, and the mind is cast into the contemplation of eternal things.[7]

By the mid-nineteenth century the Realists and the Naturalists challenged such Romantic outlooks, which by then had been watered down by *juste-milieu* Salon art. The danger was that directness of vision and openness to one's response to nature would be hampered by false striving after EFFECT. Courbet combatively wrote to Emile le Girardin, the editor of *La Presse*, complaining that the catalogue of the 1851 Salon mistakenly listed him as the student of Hesse, whereas he argued that he was in fact a student of nature: 'constant effort has been devoted to the preservation of my independence.'[8] Millet echoed this vision in a letter of 1851: 'if I could only do what I liked, or at least try to, I would do nothing that did not result from impressions from nature, either in landscape or figures.'[9] A decade and a half later, when he had become an established artist, he rued the current state of mainstream art:

> **It seems to me that you might show, by going back a little, that Art began to decline from the moment when the artist no longer leant directly and simply upon impressions taken from nature. Then clever execution rapidly took the place of nature, and the decadence began.**[10]

In fact by mid-century a host of artists, often working in artists' colonies, were following in the steps of the Barbizon pioneers. For example, the British painter Barbara Bodichon who would work in the Fontainbleau forest for up to twelve hours outdoors, wrote impatiently when on a visit to Rome in 1854:

> **Oh! the waste of time in studios here! I wish I could turn all the artists out into the country. I am quite disgusted, and feel that for an artist Rome is a very dangerous place.**[11]

Yet like other Barbizon and Realist artists she would then work her sketches into finished paintings in the studio. It was the Impressionists who pushed these ideas further. For them truth to nature meant working from the motif (*d'après le motif*), there and then, often in the open air. Clearly voicing the newer generation's impatience with Romanticism's dramatisations and posed compositions, Renoir noted:

> **The artist who uses the least of what is called imagination will be the greatest.**
>
> **To be an artist you must learn the laws of Nature.**[12]

Yet he also extolled the virtues of learning from the old masters and echoed Zola's stress on the individuality of the artist's response to the motif:

> **Go and see what others have produced, but never copy anything except Nature. You would be trying to enter a temperament that is not yours and nothing that you would do would have any character.**[13]

Mirbeau recalled a young man asking to become Monet's pupil. Monet refused, reputedly by replying:

> **...since the beginning of the world,...there has been and always will be only one professor, – and he ignores all our aesthetics, – it is this...(He showed him the sky and the surrounding scenery)... Go and question him and listen to what he tells you. If he tells you nothing, well start studying law.**[14]

It is easy to forget that these battles had to be fought before the naturalism of the later century could rest on these premises. Castagnary titled his review of the 1863 Salon 'The three contemporary schools' and summed up the current situation with clarity:

> **Classic school, Romantic school, Naturalist school, all three are in agreement about the point of departure: nature is the foundation of art.**

But:

The classic school states that nature must be corrected under the guidance of antiquity or the masterpieces of the Renaissance. Reality alarms and frightens it. Claiming to purify and idealise, it weakens or deforms; when it is not merely conventional, it invariably diminishes.

The Romantic school states that art is free; that nature must be interpreted freely by the liberated artist. It is not afraid of reality, but escapes reality by travestying it as the whims of imagination dictate; when it is not merely sleepwalking, it is invariably rather hit and miss.

The Naturalist school states that art is the expression of life in all its forms and all its degrees, and that its only goal is to reproduce nature by bringing nature to its maximum power and intensity; it is truth counterpoised by science.[15]

However as with Constable's approach, this new 'scientific' and 'objective' view of nature (in the sense of 'nature' meaning pastoral subject matter) also continued to harbour the urban dweller's nostalgia for a vanishing rural idyll. Yet within the Impressionist group, artists such as Manet, Degas, Cassatt and Fantin-Latour avoided working entirely from the motif, preferring the seclusion and weather-proof conditions of the studio. That was where a painter could manipulate subjects and effects, which to the purist Impressionist was tantamount to lying. With customary acid acuity Degas was heard to say, at one of Berthe Morisot's Thursday soirées:

Art is deception... An artist is only an artist at certain times, by an effort of will...the study of nature is a cliché: isn't Manet the living proof? For although he prided himself on slavishly copying nature, he was the most inadequate painter in the world, not making a single brushstroke without reference to the old masters.[16]

Baudelaire may have shocked the mid-century bourgeoisie's sentimental attachment to an idealised concept of nature, by declaring that nature was nothing but a dictionary, but he attached great importance to this claim partly because it had been one of Delacroix's. It might appear like an anachronistic Romantic cry from the perspective of Zola's and Castagnary's scientific world of accuracy, but it took on a vital role in the aesthetics of the Symbolists. By the 1880s the limitations of working directly and precisely from nature began to appear restrictive and the ideals of both Romanticism and Classicism were reassessed. For the aesthetes and Symbolists who flocked around Oscar Wilde and Mallarmé, nature once more became merely a source of information from which the noble IMAGINATION of the GENIUS would fashion a more concentrated, emotive and evocative art. In his Ten O'clock Lecture, delivered in Oxford, Cambridge and London in 1885, Whistler said:

Nature contains the elements, in colour and form, of all pictures, as the keyboard contains the notes of all music.

But the artist is born to pick, and choose, and group with science, these elements, that the result may be beautiful...

To say to the painter, that Nature is to be taken as she is, is to say to the player, that he may sit on the piano.

That Nature is always right, is an assertion, artistically, as untrue, as it is one whose truth is universally taken for granted. Nature is very rarely right,... the condition of things that shall bring about the perfection of harmony worthy a picture is rare, and not common at

all... Still, seldom does Nature succeed in producing a picture.[17]

Three years later, Gauguin expressed the ideas which he had been propagating among his young disciples in Pont-Aven in a letter to Emile Schuffenecker:

Some advice: do not paint too much after nature. Art is an abstraction; derive this abstraction from nature while dreaming before it, and think more of the creation which will result than of nature. Creating like our Divine Master is the only way of rising toward God.[18]

For the expressionist current that emerged in the work of artists such as Van Gogh, Toulouse-Lautrec and Munch, departure from strict anatomical or illusionistic mimicry was essential as a means of expressing feeling through formal means. Yet for many the situation was not so straightforward. Much of the creative dialogue between Van Gogh and Gauguin revolved around the artist's relationship with nature, and Van Gogh tried to follow Gauguin's approach of working from the IMAGINATION or memory. But he concluded that he needed to remain close to the motif. He could not work without a model. Yet the transformation of the motif by line and colour was still crucial, and in this sense he departed from the objective recordings of the Barbizon artists and the Impressionists just as Gauguin did.

Influenced by his son Lucien Pissarro and by Seurat, Camille Pissarro moved away from his earlier naturalist manner in 1886, working away from the motif in the studio, in a pointillist manner. Yet he was increasingly beset by doubts about the artificiality of this method and finally renounced these experiments in 1894; right at the end of the century he advised his son:

...you would have to disregard your friend Ricketts...who from the point of view of *art* seems to stray from the true direction, which is the return to *nature*. For we have to approach nature sincerely, with our own modern sensibilities; imitation or invention is something else again.[19]

The relationship with nature for Rodin was a playful one:

I often begin with one intention and finish with another. While fashioning my clay, I see in fancy something that had been lying dormant in my memory and which rises up before me in what seems to be a vision created by myself. I know it is not this, but a suggested combination of form which I must have already perceived in nature, and which has never before aroused in me the image that corresponds to it. And then, as I go on, and the execution becomes more complete, there is a sort of reverse process in my mind, and that which I have made reacts on my perception of nature, and I find resemblances and fresh analogies which fill me with joy.[20]

Concurrently, from the mid-1880s onwards, a polite naturalism was spreading throughout the academies and becoming the new academicism of the *fin de siècle*. For the extremist hot heads who were inspired by the Post-Impressionists, nature became ever more of a starting point. Following Gauguin's dictum they dreamed in front of nature and in the angry canvases of Munch nature itself screams. Maurice Denis argued that the naturalism of recent art was merely literary and that the power of art lay in its transforming power:

It is through the canvas itself, a flat surface bathed in colour, that our emotions, whether bitter or soothing, are provoked. These emotions are 'literary', as painters say, and have no need to impose the memory of other past feelings (such as a familiar motif drawn

from nature).[21]

He ended his article by pointing out that 'those with aesthetic imagination triumph over those who attempt crude imitation, the emotions of Beauty triumph over the lies of Naturalism.'[22] During the 1890s, AVANT-GARDE studios adopted as a mantra the following dictum of Puvis de Chavannes:

> **Art completes what nature crudely sketches. How then can one succeed when one wishes to help nature to express herself? By abbreviation and simplification.**[23]

This is somewhat ironic, since Puvis de Chavannes's claim was itself derived from his Classical aesthetics. Sérusier, Klimt and Bonnard arrived at a form of flat, decorative, Symbolist painting, so far removed from the illusion of the visible world that it would have horrified David. Yet they all shared the view that the artist should transform nature in the process of creating art.

Throughout the century the debate revolved around the issue of whether to select from nature or to humbly record it. Yet almost all artists and critics invoked nature and no one dared to say that it was anything but fair and lovely until the very end of the century, when aesthetes and Symbolists found it distastefully earthy and blemished. It would be for the next century to divorce BEAUTY from nature all together. Cézanne wisely perceived that:

> **Art is a harmony which runs parallel with nature – what is one to think of those imbeciles who say that the artist is always inferior to nature?**[24]

See: BEAUTY, IMAGINATION, LANDSCAPE, MODEL, *PLEIN-AIR*, TRUTH

[1] In Taylor, p. 99. This influential book was translated into English in 1837

[2] *Lectures on Art*, 1885, in Harrison and Wood, pp. 646

[3] *Observations on Viewing a Collection of Paintings Largely by Living or Recently Deceased Artists*, 1841, in Harrison and Wood, p. 53

[4] Introduction to the *Propyläen*, 1798, in Eitner, II, pp. 41-2

[5] See Protter, p. 104

[6] Lecture at the Royal Academy, 16 June 1836, in Leslie, p. 274

[7] 'Essay on American Scenery', *American Monthly Magazine*, 1836, in Harrison and Wood, p. 137

[8] May 1851, in Courbet, pp. 101-2

[9] Letter to Sensier, 1 Feb 1851, in Herbert, p. 96

[10] Letter to Sensier, 29 March 1865, in Cartwright, p. 283

[11] In Orr, p. 175

[12] In Renoir, pp. 215-6

[13] *Ibid*, p. 218

[14] In Geffroy, p. 120

[15] 'Salon de 1863', in Harrison and Wood, p. 412

[16] In Shennan, p. 235

[17] In Whistler, pp. 142-3

[18] 14 Aug 1888, in Chipp, p. 60

[19] 19 Aug 1898, in Pissarro, p. 329

[20] In Elsen, pp. 141-4

[21] 'Définition du Néo-traditionnisme', *Art et Critique*, 1890, in Harrison and Wood, p. 867

22 *Ibid*, p. 869
23 In Jullian, p. 41
24 Letter, 26 Sept 1897, in Cézanne, p. 261

Nude

DESPITE FUNDAMENTAL CHANGES OF OUTLOOK, THE IDEALISED NAKED FORMS of men, women and children continued to personify ideas and ideals, myths and beliefs from David's austere Neo-classicism right through to the Symbolists' mannered, androgynous youths of the *belle époque*. During a century in which the baring of flesh was considered immodest, so that many people rarely saw naked bodies apart from those of babies, the nude was central to its art. Its mastery lay at the heart of art education; indeed many students studied little else. Even the Impressionists, who were primarily landscapists, did not find it incongruous that they should be drawing from the naked model at the Académie Suisse and in Gleyre's ATELIER. In the 1880s Pissarro would still advise his son:

> **...recognise fully that you do not draw well, my dear Lucien. I told you any number of times that it is essential to have known forms in the eye and in the hand... Don't despair. If you could work evenings in the free art schools where there are nude models you would make progress.**[1]

Such ideas can be traced back to the Académie des Beaux-Arts, for which the idealised nude had a central role in the teaching and practice of painting and sculpture. Since the Neo-classical period in particular, artists had depicted the nude to achieve a timeless and universal art that would be accessible to all peoples. When Canova made a statue of Napoleon in 1806, it was without irony or any sense of impropriety that he portrayed him naked.

Aware of the puzzlement some felt at seeing the nudity in *The Intervention of the Sabine Women* (1799) David added 'A Note on the Nudity of My Heroes' to his text explaining the public exhibition of the painting in 1800. Having pointed out 'how much easier it would have been for me to paint my figures clothed,' he concluded, 'my desire was to represent the customs of antiquity with such an exactitude that the Greeks and the Romans, had they seen my work, would not have found me a stranger to their customs.'[2]

As the ancients had already achieved the highest and purest depictions of the ideal nude, their selections from the imperfections of NATURE were to be emulated, hence the endless art school drawings from casts of Greek statues. Moreover, if a student could master this most difficult and subtle of forms from the living model, in movement, in repose, in every conceivable pose from every viewpoint, then he or she would be equipped to create the narratives of HISTORY PAINTING. In 1801 Ingres, a pupil in David's atelier, won the PRIX DE ROME with *The Ambassadors of Agamemnon Visiting Achilles* (1801) because of his proficiency in depicting the anatomically correct, but idealised male nude, under the strict exam conditions which forbade the use of models or preparatory drawings.

The legacy of David led the early Romantics to continue to stress the idealised male nude, for example Gros's *Napoleon in the Plague House in Jaffa* (1804) and Géricault's *Raft of the*

Medusa (1819), despite their break with classicism in depicting contemporary events and extreme states of mind. Although it told of extreme physical deprivation, which had led to cannibalism, no signs of starvation or exposure to the elements marred the ideally proportioned youths who populated Géricault's raft. Nevertheless, it was during the Bourbon Monarchy that impatience with the entire concept of the nude began. In his Salon review of 1824 Stendhal summed up the differences which were then emerging within French painting:

All those huge pictures, filled with some thirty naked figures, copied from antique statues, and those long and tedious five-act tragedies in verse are no doubt extremely respectable pieces of work, but whatever their merits they are beginning to pall, and if David's *Sabine Women* were to be exhibited today there is no doubt that people would note that the figures are painted without passion; moreover, in any country, it is absurd to set out for battle when not wearing any clothes... The time has come for good painters to try to be modern instead. The nude was pleasing to the Greeks: we on the other hand hardly ever see it, and what is more, I think we even feel some repugnance for it.[3]

Yet the classical nude prevailed in the less politically or socially motivated work of Ingres and other academic artists, though the domination of the male nude waned. Ingres adopted an aspect of Winckelmann's eighteenth-century theories of beauty which asserted that the male nude could have character but only the female nude could be beautiful, since beauty rests on continuity and smoothness. He produced highly influential classical female nudes: from the monumental *Valpinçon Bather* (1808) to the eroticism of the *Turkish Bath* (1862), which he proudly inscribed with his age 'Aetatis LXXXII' (82). While working on *The Age of Gold* (1840-8), a mural painting for the Château de Dampierre in which numerous female nudes recline and cavort, he noted:

One must not dwell too much on the details of the human body; the members must be, so to speak, like shafts of columns: such they are in the greatest masters.[4]

For seven decades Ingres pursued the path of antiquity, his influential views gradually rigidified into often reactionary dogma.

In 1847 Couture's *Romans of the Decadence* (1847) caused a sensation at the Salon, partly for its implied critique of the July Monarchy, and partly for infusing new life into the genre of monumental history painting, with the nude at centre stage. It was to be one of the most discussed and reproduced paintings of the second half of the century, though it has since been eclipsed by Courbet's and Manet's AVANT-GARDE battle with the problem of creating a modern nude. Courbet's *Bathers* (1853), which some have interpreted as a satire on the academic nude, exposed the central model's body as an undressed, sexualised woman rather than an idealised personification or allegory. Delacroix was appalled by such directness and lack of allegory or narrative:

...if only the idea (such as it is) had been made clear! But what are the two figures supposed to mean? A fat woman, back view, and completely naked except for a carelessly painted rag over the lower part of her buttocks, is stepping out of a little puddle scarcely deep enough for a foot bath. She is making some meaningless gesture, and another woman, presumably her maid, is sitting on the ground taking off her shoes and stockings... There seems to be some exchange of thought between the two figures, but it is quite unintelligible.[5]

Such was the work's importance to Courbet that he included it in the background of his anti-Academic manifesto painting *The Painter's Studio* (1855), at the centre of which he placed himself watched over by a young boy, a cat and a naked female model, all three being emblems of spontaneity, sensuality and freedom in progressive circles. The woman's figure above all would have signified ideas of nature.

While Courbet engaged directly with the ideologically loaded subject of the academic nude, Millet (who as a student had laboured for years in academic studios) self-consciously avoided it in his mature work:

> **As you will see by the titles of the pictures, there are neither nude women nor mythological subjects among them. I mean to devote myself to other subjects; not that I hold that sort of thing to be forbidden, but that I do not feel myself compelled to paint them.**[6]

In fact in both of Courbet's paintings the depiction of the model was dependent on his use of photographs. Since the early 1850s artists could work from photographs of naked male and female models. Delacroix had immediately realised the deceptive nature of the 'truth' offered by such images:

> **A daguerreotype is…in some ways false just because so exact. The monstrosities it shows are indeed deservedly shocking although they may literally be the deformations present in nature herself; but these imperfections which the machine reproduces faithfully, will not offend our eyes when we look at the model without this intermediary. The eye corrects without our being conscious of it.**[7]

Increasingly, whether artists used photographs or not, the nude could not so easily be portrayed without an awareness of the naked body's angularities and imperfections. Yet academic artists and their public were still steeped in the expectation of its idealisation according to classical canons. The scandal caused by the nudes in Manet's *Déjeuner sur l'herbe* (1863) and *Olympia* (1865) can be partly attributed to this. For example, the now forgotten critic, Amédée Canteloube wrote:

> **Nothing so cynical has ever been seen as this 'Olympia', a sort of female gorilla, an india-rubber deformity, surrounded by black, lying on a bed, completely nude... Her hand is clenched in a sort of indecent contraction... Truly, women about to become mothers, and young maidens, would do well, if they are prudent, to run away from this spectacle.**[8]

The accusations of indecency also stemmed from Manet's rejection of the academic pretence to high-minded allegorical or mythological subject matter. His direct portrayal of a naked woman on display for the delectation of the viewer reminded his male public all too frankly of their own moral double standards. Realists challenged the hypocritical concealment of lasciviousness behind a show of virtue. In 1864 Courbet submitted a speciously mythological subject to the Salon: *Psyche and Venus* (1864), which showed two naked women embracing. The work was probably rejected by the Salon jury for its impropriety. Referring to this incident, Millet wrote:

> **I find it very hard to imagine that any picture of Courbet's could be more improper than the indecent works of Cabanel and Baudry at the last Salon, for I have never seen anything that seemed to me a more frank and direct appeal to the passions of bankers and stockbrokers.**[9]

Rodin's *Age of Bronze* (1876), which depicted an unidealised male nude in so lifelike a manner that the sculptor was accused of having worked from casts of the body, was also denigrated on the grounds of its vulgarity.

Mallarmé acutely understood the subtleties of Manet's innovations in terms of form and subject:

> **'Olympia'; that wan, withered courtesan, who showed to the public for the first time, nakedness rather than the conventional nude of tradition. The bouquet, still wrapped in its paper, the gloomy cat,...and all the accessories were truthful, but not immoral – that is, in the ordinary and foolish sense of the word – but incontestably tending towards intellectual perversity. Rarely has any modern work been more applauded by the few, or more deeply damned by public opinion...We were surprised by it, as if by something long hidden, but brusquely revealed. Both captivating and shocking, eccentric and uncensored, the types he offers us answer a need among the circles in which we live.[10]**

Gauguin's early naturalistic *Nude Study* (1880), depicting a naked woman rather incongruously sewing, was praised by Huysmans in his review of the Impressionists' sixth exhibition in 1881 for its 'vigorously realistic note', its lack of idealisation and hence its utter modernity:

> **...she is a modern girl and not a girl posing for an exhibition, she is neither lascivious nor simpering, she is quite simply darning her clothes.**
>
> **In addition she is blatantly fleshly; we no longer have the flat, smooth skin that painters prefer, that skin with no marks, spots or pores, that uniform skin dipped in rose water and pressed with a smoothing iron;...in fact there is truth in every part of her body, in that stomach sagging slightly over her thighs, in the folds of flesh beneath pendulous breasts.[11]**

He went on to disparage the academic nudes which thronged the Salons as 'puppets with neat little pink breasts and slim hard stomachs, drawn up according to what passes for good taste and designed according to formulae learned from plaster casts.'[12]

By the 1870s the depiction of the female nude had become a hackneyed Salon device for attracting purchasers. In 1873 Mary Cassatt's friend the art teacher Emily Sartain, wrote:

> **Went to the Salon Monday afternoon. Although they refused 4000 pictures, there are so many left, that I brought away a very confused impression of them after my three hour examination of them....There are as usual, a great many crudities in colour, extravagant subjects, and nudities to attract the eye, – and perhaps in consequence, the landscapes seemed to me unusually fine, – they reposed the eye by their simplicity.[13]**

Adherence to moral propriety was the most common pretext for excluding women from the life class. This was a serious obstacle to their achieving parity with men in a profession in which the depiction of the nude was pivotal. There were exceptions. David insisted on teaching women in his *atelier*; those who could afford it were privately tutored and some women organised their own classes. By the 1860s the prejudice was seriously challenged especially in Britain, where 38 women petitioned the Royal Academy to admit women students in 1859. The humorist Ratier published a series of prints, *Pièces sur les Arts* (Items on Art), one of which showed an embarrassed young woman at her easel facing her model, an entirely naked man: 'Just imagine that you are painting history,' admonishes her male tutor.[14]

By the 1870s access to women-only life classes was quite possible, yet rarely were women permitted to draw from an entirely naked model. Edward Poynter's first address to the Slade School of Art, which showed an enlightened approach, nevertheless expressed current doubts:

> **There is unfortunately a difficulty which has always stood in the way of female students acquiring that thorough knowledge of the figure which is essential to the production of work of a high class; and that is, of course, that they are debarred from the same complete study of the model that is open to the male students...**
>
> **But I have always been anxious to institute a class where the half-draped model might be studied, to give those ladies who are desirous of obtaining sound instruction in drawing the figure, an opportunity of gaining the necessary knowledge...it is my desire that in all the classes, except of course those for the study of the nude model, the male and female students should work together.**[15]

Yet the idea of women depicting the nude remained of itself offensive to many and was easily pilloried. Despite the cool Neo-classicism of the American sculptor Harriet Hosmer's works, Thomas Crawford, also a sculptor, accused her of cheating:

> **Miss Hosmer's want of modesty is enough to disgust a dog. She has had casts for the entire female model made and exhibited them in a shockingly indecent manner to all the young artists who called upon her. This is going it rather strong.**[16]

The battle raged on until the end of the century. In 1886 Thomas Eakins, a rebel Naturalist who stressed the importance of direct, unidealised studies from the model, was forced to resign from the Pennsylvania Academy of Fine Arts, where he had been teaching for ten years, partly because he prioritised working from male and female models for students of both sexes.

In Paris Marie Bashkirtseff enrolled at the private Académie Julian, one of the few where women were permitted to draw from the naked male model. She argued in her diary that if the model were perfect we would see only the beauty and not be aware of the nudity and so we would not be shocked by it, and the model would not feel shame. Under the pseudonym Pauline Orell she made her public plea to allow women to work from the naked model:

> **We are asked with indulgent irony how many great women artists there have been. Well! Gentlemen, there have been some and that is astonishing, given the enormous difficulties they encounter. Try telling respectable people that they must send their daughters to study from the nude, without which no serious study is possible. Most of them will scream in horror, yet they do not hesitate to bring these same young ladies to the beach where they contemplate dancers in triton's costumes.**[17]

In 1884 with ebullient defiance she announced in her journal:

> **I have found a subject for a painting....As it happens I'd wanted a modern subject with a lot of people in it and in the nude and on a canvas that is not too big, well that's it, I'm going to do one. What? Well! fairground wrestlers with a crowd watching. There will be naked torsos to show that I can paint the nude...it will be very difficult, but it has grabbed me, that's all it needs, what delirium!**[18]

In the closing decades of the century the move towards subjectivity did not deter innovative artists as diverse as Munch, Klimt and Toulouse-Lautrec from continuing to see the nude as a legitimate subject through which to express emotions or suggest states of mind. As an old man Rodin explained to a Canadian journalist:

Nature gives me my model, life and thought; the nostrils breathe, the heart beats, the lungs inhale, the being thinks, and feels, has pains and joys, ambitions, passions and emotions. These I must express. What makes my *Thinker* think is that he thinks not only with his brain, with his knitted brow, his distended nostrils and compressed lips, but with every muscle of his arms, back and legs, with his clenched fist and gripping toes.[19]

Gauguin went further. His expression of intangible states of mind led to distortions of colour and form. Of his painting *Manao Tupapau* (*The Spirit of the Dead Watching*, 1892), he wrote:

A young Tahitian girl is lying on her stomach, showing part of her frightened face... Captured by a form, a movement, I paint them with no other preoccupation than to execute a nude figure. As it is, it is a slightly indecent study of a nude, and yet I wish to make of it a chaste picture and imbue it with the spirit of the native, its character and tradition.[20]

Such was the enduring popularity of the female nude that Degas, Renoir and Cézanne all returned to in the closing decades of the century. Meanwhile the more academic Symbolists and aesthetes such as Delville, Burne-Jones and Moreau produced androgynous male and female nudes that vied in the 1890s Salons with the Venuses and Danaës by academic painters such as Bouguereau and Carolus-Duran.

See: ACADEMY, ANTIQUE, *ATELIER*, DRAWING, ÉCOLE DES BEAUX-ARTS, HISTORY PAINTING, MODEL, NATURE

[1] 21 May 1883, in Pissarro, p. 32

[2] See Holt, 1986, p. 12

[3] 'Salon de 1824', *Journal de Paris*, 1824, in Harrison and Wood, p. 31

[4] 'Notes for the Age of Gold', in K. Clark, 1956, p. 147

[5] Journal, 15 April 1853, in Delacroix, 1995, pp. 181-2

[6] Letter to Sensier, probably winter 1849-50, in Cartwright, pp. 105-6

[7] *Revue des Deux Mondes*, 1850, in Scharf, pp. 119-20

[8] *Le Grand Journal*, 1865, in Courthion, p. 225

[9] See Thomson, pp. 168-9

[10] S. Mallarmé, *Les Impressionistes et Edouard Manet*, 1876, in Mallarmé, p. 310

[11] J.-K. Huysmans, *L'Art moderne*, in Harrison and Wood, p. 892

[12] *Ibid*

[13] Letter to John Sartain, 8 May 1873, in Mathews, p. 118

[14] Frascina, 1993, p. 241

[15] *Ten Lectures on Art*, 1879, in Nunn, p. 52

[16] See Chadwick, p. 217

[17] *La Citoyenne*, 1880, in Sauer, p. 8

[18] 2 June 1884, in Bashkirtseff, 1901, pp. 236-7

[19] Interview with a Journalist, 1917, in Elsen, p. 52

[20] 'Cahier pour Aline', 1893, in Chipp, pp. 67-8

Peasant Life

DURING THE LATER DECADES OF THE CENTURY UMPTEEN DEPICTIONS OF THE JOYS and sorrows offered by peasant life adorned the homes of the bourgeoisie. Yet at the 1850-1 Salon Millet's *Sower* (1850) was accused of spreading the seeds of radical revolution and during the preceding decades Constable and the Barbizon artists had to struggle to get the subject accepted by academic juries. The political and industrial revolution led to vast social and political changes in the relationship between the city and the countryside. By 1860, hordes of country-dwellers were moving to industrial centres every year. Many a peasant family had its life overturned by mechanisation or migration to the city; many a bourgeois art collector recalled a rural childhood. Paintings of peasant life were laced with references to the ambiguities and contradictions posed by the shifting relationship between town and country. Attitudes to the subject were highly charged both emotionally and politically.

Although there were precedents in the pastoral works of eighteenth-century painters such as Fragonard and Gainsborough, peasant life as subject matter answered the Romantic call for artists to portray the contemporary scene. Equally influential were the re-evaluated GENRE paintings of the seventeenth-century Dutch Republic. Inspired by these, traditional British painters such as Wilkie and Mulready specialised in rustic genre during the first half of the century. They shared the Romantic poets' belief that the rural poor, in its simplicity and naïvety, best displayed the fundamental human passions and specifics of character that the sophisticated city dweller concealed. Their sentimental homilies about the piety, industriousness and frugality of humble peasant life were intended to convey the supposed universality of the human condition.

In the century's opening decade the French painters Pauline Chatillon and Madame Haudebourt-Lescot pioneered the depiction of the 'exotic' clothes and customs of the Italian *popolino* for the French Salon. So well did such pictures sell that the genre became widely practised, for example by the academic painters Winterhalter and Lehmann, who both went to Italy in the 1830s.

However, during the 1830s and 1840s the AVANT-GARDE in France reappraised seventeenth-century Dutch peasant paintings, as well as those of the Le Nain brothers, from a more radical aesthetic and/or political point of view. This shift in values formed part of a wider re-evaluation of humble, everyday subjects and calls for un-idealised TRUTH in art, a trend which united artists as diverse as Constable, the Barbizon artists, the Realists and the Pre-Raphaelite Brotherhood. During a trip to the Auvergne in 1866, Millet would write to his patron Gavet:

> **The women spindle wool as they watch their cows, something I've never seen before, and which I intend to use. This has nothing in common with the little shepherdess threading her distaff in the pastorals of the last century.**[1]

Realist artists and writers shared the Romantics' veneration of peasant life. The progressive critic Théophile Thoré began his 1844 Salon with an open letter to the Barbizon painter Théodore Rousseau that expressed his utopian vision:

For my part, I would rather live in a beautiful countryside, half thinker, half peasant, in a peasant smock and wooden shoes, with baked bread, potatoes from my own garden, and a modest natural wine, than throw myself into an artificial and turbulent life amid luxury and material pleasures.[2]

By the late 1830s the Romantics' mantle of anti-academic outsider was being worn by Naturalist and Realist painters such as Corot, Daubigny and Troyon, partly grouped in an artists' colony around the Barbizon forest, a day trip away from the Salon in Paris. Primarily landscapists, they would feature a cowherd, or a shepherdess in their un-idealised paintings. Unlike the milk maids flirting with their suitors of the eighteenth-century pastoral, the Barbizon painters showed working people wearing drab, homespun clothes. They stood awkwardly in the distance, giving scale and a complementary note of red in the waistcoat or petticoat, to show off the fresh green of the growing corn or cow pasture. But some, such as Paul Soyer (Cassatt's teacher) and Millet were primarily figure painters and by the 1840s peasant subjects were no longer uncommon.

When such figure painters set out to portray the true life of the common people this was understood to have democratic implications. In his 1857 Salon, in which he defended Millet's *The Gleaners* (1857), the left-wing critic Castagnary explained:

Religious painting and history or heroic painting have gradually become weaker, alongside the weakening of the social organisms, theocracy and monarchy, to which they refer; their elimination, virtually achieved nowadays, brings with it the absolute domination of genre, of landscape, of portraiture, which heighten individualism, in art as in society, man becomes more and more man.[3]

The battle was not quite as easily won as Castagnary implied. The Barbizon artists and the Realists struggled to obtain equal status for peasant subjects until the 1860s. To depict peasants, often in the action of working, in some cases on the same scale as HISTORY PAINTING, was seen by conservatives as a threat to established cultural and political values. Claims that such unheroic subjects had parity with history painting were interpreted as yet another bohemian attack on the bastion of academic hierarchies. Also challenging was the lack of idealisation. Realist works were considered ugly, drab, lacking in nobility of character and devoid of significant narrative content. The American artist William Morris Hunt, one of the first buyers of Millet's works, first came across them in the late 1840s:

No one else cared for them. They were called '*des tristes affaires*' (sad jobs)...

He would not paint anything pretty or fascinating until the public should recognise his pictures of labourers. People said that his pictures were 'not elegant'.[4]

When Millet showed his *Man with a Hoe* (1860-2) at the Salon of 1863, the conservative critic Saint-Victor wrote:

For M. Millet art is limited to the servile copying of vile models. He lights his lamp and searches for a cretin; he must have searched for a long time before finding his 'Peasant with a hoe'. Similar types are not common, even in the Bicêtre lunatic asylum. Imagine a monster without a cranium, with deadened gaze and an idiotic grimace, rooted askew, like a scarecrow in the middle of a field. No glimmer of intelligence humanises this brute at rest. Has he come to work or to assassinate?[5]

In the decade before the 1848 revolution there were renewed calls for greater political and social justice: the new Republican hero was the common man, and the peasant came to symbolise radical politics. Regardless of the artist's outlook, simply to be a peasant painter was often understood, by the conservative press and its followers, as a sign of revolutionary Republicanism or Socialism. Delacroix dryly expressed this discomfort in his journal entry for 16 April 1853:

> **They brought Millet to my studio this morning. He spoke of Michelangelo and the Bible which, he says, is almost the only book he reads. This explains the rather pretentious look of his peasants. Moreover, he is a peasant himself and boasts of it. He belongs to that constellation or crew of bearded artists who made the revolution of 1848 or encouraged it, thinking, apparently, that it would bring equality of talent as well as equality of wealth.[6]**

With customary fair-mindedness he added: 'But Millet himself seems to me to be above this level.'[7] Delacroix conveyed the condescension with which the city-based bourgeoisie viewed the peasantry, although his response also hints at resentment of a younger radical by the former anti-establishment lion. The deliberate goading of the bourgeois public was a tactic of the recently emergent and highly self-conscious avant-garde.

It was at the Second Republic's free Salon of the winter of 1850/1 that scandal really erupted with the public display of Courbet's *The Stonebreakers* (1849-50) and *Burial at Ornans* (1849-50) and Millet's *Sower* (1850). Not long thereafter, Louis Napoléon's *coup d'état* of 1851 would re-establish the political and cultural conservatives. Taking a partisan political stance, Courbet deliberately set out to confound bourgeois conservatism. During the revolution itself, he explained that he saw his work as a form of political action. In 1849, while living in Ornans, he gave his reasons for painting the peasants in *The Stonebreakers*:

> **I had taken our carriage to go to the castle of St Denis to paint a landscape. Near Maizières I stopped to contemplate two men who were breaking stones on the road. It is not often that one encounters the most complete image of poverty, and so, right then and there, I got the idea for a painting.[8]**

Having described the picture he commented:

> **Yes M. Piesse, we must drag art down from its pedestal. For too long you have been making art that is pomaded and in 'good taste'. For too long painters, even my contemporaries, have based their art on ideas and stereotypes.[9]**

The very discomfort of the Salon-going public would be partly based on its reminder of the social misery engendered by the dislocation occurring in countryside and city. The new, urban factory workers would be landless peasants similar to the pair mending that country road.

In contrast, Millet claimed not to have political intentions. In a letter to his patron Alfred Sensier in 1863 about the scandal surrounding his *Man with a Hoe* (1860-2), which had caused him to be called a Saint-Simonist, he protested that he did not know what this meant and that he had known nothing but the life of the fields throughout his life: 'I try and say, as best I can, what I saw and felt when I worked there.'[10] Four years later he returned to this theme:

> **...glad that you laid stress on the *rustic* side of my art, for to say the truth, if this side is not brought out in my work, I have failed. I reject with my whole might the democratic**

idea, as it is understood in the language of the clubs, which some persons have tried to impute to me. I have only tried to make people think of the man whose life is spent in toil, and who eats bread by the sweat of his brow.[11]

Yet he frequently expressed humanitarian empathy for the hardships endured by his subjects. Of *Going to Work* (1851-3) he wrote to Sensier:

I must confess, at the risk of your taking me to be a Socialist, that the human side is what touches me most in art,.. The joyful side never shows itself to me, I know not if it exists, but I have never seen it.[12]

Furthermore, his social behaviour was that of a bohemian rebel rather than a pious peasant. The ambivalence of his political stance was echoed in the works: he painted *The Angelus* (1855-7) as well as the *Man with a Hoe*. Similarly, critics and public interpreted his works as Biblical, romanticised odes to the eternal values embodied by the nobility of labour but also as powerful indictments of social oppression.

More conservative artists, such as the award-winning Jules Breton took up peasant subject matter from the 1850s onwards, removing subversive 'ugliness' from their works by idealising the figures and giving the subjects a narrative or anecdotal dimension which reaffirmed the urban public's preferred romantic views of country life. Yet Breton also claimed to be the champion of the common man:

The causes that led to this revolution and the consequences that resulted from it exerted a powerful influence, as I have said, on my mind, and on that of every other artist, as well as on the general movement of art and literature. In every department new experiments were tried.

'The new social stratum', as Gambetta called it later on, together with its natural environment, became a subject of study. There was a deeper interest in life of the street and the fields. The tastes and the feelings of the poor were taken into account, and art conferred honours upon them, formerly reserved for the gods and the great.[13]

From the 1860s through to the end of the century and beyond the subject of peasant life became increasingly popular throughout Europe and America, existing between the two polarities of conservative nostalgia and socialist heroism. By the 1870s Millet's work sold well. The most popular with the art buying public were glorifications of traditional country life by artists such as Breton, Dagnan-Bouveret and Bastien-Lepage. These works showed pious, humble peasants for whom, it was felt, enduring poverty was a purifying experience. Often inspired by Millet's works, the paintings were frequently full of pathos but less uncompromisingly 'PRIMITIVE' and harsh in their execution, for example Bastien-Lepage's much reproduced *Poor Fauvette* (1881).

In the closing decades of the century Bastien-Lepage's influential peasant paintings provided a palatable halfway house between the idealisations of academic painting and avant-garde primitivism. He prided himself on the authenticity of his work, choosing to depict only the peasants and landscapes of his native northern French province. This intimate knowledge of his subject would contribute to what he perceived as the unvarnished truth:

...the peasant has his own fashion of being sad or joyous, of feeling and thinking... it mat-

ters little if your personages have irregular features, clumsy manners and coarse hands. They cannot fail to be beautiful because they will be living and thinking beings.[14]

However, the avant-garde was then beginning to question such *PLEIN-AIR* Naturalism. The English painter Sickert savaged Bastien-Lepage and others of his type:

[He is]...a painter of exhibition pictures... an inveterate *salonnier... Faire vrai* is the sum and aim of his intention. Realists he and his like have been jauntily labelled by the hasty journalist. But the truth in their work is truth of unessentials, and their elaborate and unlovely realities serve only to cover themes that are profoundly unreal... Your subject is a real peasant in his own natural surroundings, and not a model from Hatton garden. But what is he doing? He is posing for a picture as best he can, and he looks it. That woman stooping to put potatoes into a sack will never rise again.[15]

Artists from all over the world congregated around the mushrooming artists' colonies in France and elsewhere. Americans and their public were particularly attracted to the exoticism of European peasant life. Like W. M. Hunt some emulated Millet in affecting the dress and mannerisms of French peasants. Mary Cassatt and her fellow American Eliza Haldeman visited Barbizon but settled in Ecouen, a colony established by Pierre Edouard Frère and Paul Soyer. Their letters home conveyed the patronising attitude of their social class towards this source of cheaply available models:

It is surprising to see how polite the children are if we pass a group of boys playing, when we are walking, they all get up and take off their hats and say good morning though they are only pesants [sic], and some but five years old. The men and women are the same and invite us into their houses with as much grace as if they were ladys [sic].[16]

As the economics of art tourism encroached, there evolved a sophisticated, symbiotic relationship between artists and their host communities. The bourgeois, urban artists tended to adopt a romanticised but condescending attitude towards the lives and people among whom they chose to live. Laura Knight recalled:

One night [the American painter Joseph] Raphael, Harold [Knight] and I gave a party to our farmer and his wife. We all sat in our best clothes, so properly, round the table till twelve o'clock. They had never been up so late before. They understood as little of our conversation as we did of theirs, but we roared at their jokes as if we knew what they were about...just as they did at ours... Our party was a great success.[17]

As visiting artists became an additional source of income, they too were open to exploitation. Phil May worked in the Dutch colony at Volendam:

I saw a little girl in a doorway, the first after my arrival, and she was standing knitting; the whole thing was very pretty – the composition perfect. I made her understand that I wanted her to stay as she was while I made a rapid sketch. I was very pleased with the result, until I got back to the hotel and I found that every artist who had ever visited Volendam...had painted that same child, had been caught by the knowing kiddie in the same way as I had.[18]

Van Gogh, enthralled by Millet but also by Breton, had originally set out to become a peasant painter. Living among the peasants of Nuenen in Holland he produced his first major work *The Potato Eaters* (1885). He explained that he could express the harshness of his subjects' lives by formal means:

> **It might just turn out to be <u>a genuine peasant painting</u>. <u>I know that it is</u>. But anyone who prefers to have his peasants looking namby-pamby had best suit himself. Personally, I am convinced that in the long run one gets better results from painting them in all their coarseness than from introducing a conventional sweetness.[19]**

Yet his own attitudes echo some of the prejudices and contradictions of the era:

> **I wanted to convey a picture of a way of life quite different from ours, from that of civilised people...**
>
> **No, one must paint peasants as if one were one of them, as if one felt and thought as they do. Being unable to help what one actually is. I very often feel that peasants are a world apart, in many respects one so much better than the civilised world. Not in all respects for what do they know of art and many other things?[20]**

As the century drew to a close, the 'primitivism' of peasant life, which allegedly survived in relatively inaccessible regions like Brittany, attracted the Symbolists who gathered around Gauguin at Pont-Aven. They repudiated the corrupting influence of industrialisation, as Gauguin explained in a letter to the painter Emile Schuffenecker:

> **I love Brittany; I find there the savage, the primitive. When my clogs ring out on this granite soil, I hear the dull, muted, powerful tone which I seek in my painting.[21]**

In fact, by this time Pont-Aven was a well-established artists' colony. In 1891 Signac would report:

> **...it's a funny nest for Symbolism... Drunken hooligans of painters swagger round in velvet jackets. The tobacconist has a palette for a sign outside his shop and he sells artists' materials. The servants at the inn have 'painterly' ribbons in their caps.[22]**

During the same period partisan Socialists such as the sculptors Dalou and Meunier or the painters Giuseppe Pelliza and Segantini reassessed the revolutionary potential of the heroism of peasant labour. Again, they were often inspired by Millet: for example, Segantini drew a copy of Millet's *Sower* in 1897 for the Almanac of the Italian Socialist Party. Throughout the 1890s Pelliza worked on several versions of his epic scene of striking agricultural workers, *The Fourth Estate* (1901). Painted in an avant-garde pointillist style, the work was provocative in both its form and in its portrayal of active, politically organised peasants:

> **I am attempting Social painting...a crowd of people, workers of the soil, who are intelligent, strong, robust, united, advance like a torrent, overthrowing every obstacle in its path, thirsty for justice.[23]**

Pelliza's belief was that art 'must give the people a portrait of themselves, but embellished'.[24] However, a portrayal of individual peasant labour in the heroic manner of Millet was now officially acceptable. Meunier's monumental sculpture *The Reaper* represented Belgium at the Paris Exposition Universelle in 1900. Meanwhile a host of artists continued to provide idealised visions of rural idylls such Bouguereau's pearly toothed, idealised women and children riding well-fed donkeys in the Italian countryside.

See: AVANT-GARDE, EXOTIC, GENRE, LANDSCAPE, MODERNITY, PRIMITIVE, TRUTH

[1] Letter 1886, in Herbert, p. 192

[2] Taylor, p. 322

[3] In Herbert, p. 85

[4] Hunt, p. 168, 171

[5] In Herbert, pp. 137-8

[6] Delacroix, 1995, p. 182

[7] *Ibid*

[8] Letter to M. and Mme Wey, 26 Nov 1849, in Courbet, p. 88

[9] *Ibid*. M. Piesse was a critic and curator for the collection of the École des Beaux-Arts.

[10] 30 May 1863, in Cartwright, p. 240

[11] Letter to Sensier, 23 April 1867, *ibid*, p. 300

[12] Probably winter 1850-1, see *ibid*, p. 106

[13] Breton, pp. 184-5

[14] See House and Stevens, p. 30

[15] W.R. Sickert, *Modern Realism in Painting*, 1891, in Theuriet, pp. 138-40

[16] E. Haldeman, letter to her mother, 19-20 Feb 1867, in Mathews, p. 42

[17] See Lübbren, p. 58

[18] P. May, 'The Children of Volendam', *Magazine of Art*, 1900, in Lübbren, p. 74

[19] Van Gogh, 1996, p. 291

[20] *Ibid*, pp. 291, 292

[21] March 1888, in House and Stevens, p. 73

[22] Letter to Luce, in Lethère, p. 103

[23] See House and Stevens, p. 246

[24] *Ibid*

Photography

THE ROYAL ACADEMICIAN SIR WILLIAM BLAKE RICHMOND RECALLED that when the aged Turner was shown a daguerreotype he exclaimed: 'This is the end of Art. I am glad I have had my day.'[1] Of the century's technological inventions, the 'sun's drawings', as Ruskin called them, had the greatest direct impact upon art. Ever since Daguerre made his invention known to an astonished public in 1839, art and photography began a continuous dialogue. Many nineteenth-century artists used photographs either overtly or covertly: they included Delacroix, Ingres, Courbet, Millet, Corot, Millais, Frith, Rossetti, Gérôme, Tissot, Manet, Degas, Eakins, Gauguin, Cézanne and Toulouse-Lautrec. Most of the early photographers had themselves been trained as artists and this heightened the temperature of the debate, which veered between the polarities of hostile distrust and respectful admiration.

In the beginning many artists marvelled as enthusiastically as the general public. Initially they were astonished by the accuracy, detail, speed, and technical ease of the new 'light drawings.' Ingres remarked: 'This is the exactitude that I would like to achieve.'[2] He referred students including Hippolyte Flandrin and Amaury-Duval to the effects achieved in a photograph: 'Look at this, gentlemen! Which of you would be capable of such fidelity, such firmness of line, such delicacy of modelling?'[3]

In 1839 the French government entrusted the academician Paul Delaroche with the leadership of a committee to report on Daguerre's invention. Although he is reputed to have commented 'from today, painting is dead' when he first heard of the process, his report was enthusiastic, rejecting the often-voiced fear that it could undermine art and fine engraving. The report, delivered at the Académie des Sciences in August 1839, suggested that daguerreotypes might be eminently useful to artists, not least as preparatory tools:

> **The painter will discover in this process an easy means of collecting studies which he could otherwise only have obtained over a long period of time, laboriously and in a much less perfect way, no matter how talented he might be... To sum up, the admirable discovery of M. Daguerre has rendered an immense service to the arts.**[4]

Artists immediately seized on the process's potential as an *aide-mémoire* and optional substitute for sketch book notation. In 1839, only a couple of months after Daguerre's public announcement of his invention, Horace Vernet took a camera with him on his trip to the Near East, confiding to his journal that he and a colleague were making daguerreotypes 'like lions'.[5] Along with scientists and archivists, artists valued the medium's capacity to document information faithfully (not least in recording their own works). Théophile Gautier interpreted this aspect of the invention as part of the MODERNITY brought by technological advances:

> **[Art]...has set off in all directions on the wing of steam: new countries, unexplored climates, unknown types, unrecorded races present themselves to it in all its parts. After 6000 years, it takes possession of a real world which up until now it had only viewed indistinctly. The photograph, this humble servant, takes notes for [art], and the sun draws upon its travel notebooks the men, the animals, the plants, the rocks, the monuments, the statues, the remarkable sites with an infallible certainty and a mathematical precision; vast quantities of material, sketches, almost devoid of labour, are at the disposition [of art].**[6]

Delacroix, an early enthusiast, and one of the most perceptive of the early commentators on the medium, soon realised that it also actually offered new ways of seeing NATURE, and understood the enormous and ambivalent implications of this. When away from his studio, he confided in his journal how he filled his evenings in a hotel room: 'passionately, never growing weary, I study photographs of nude men – this human body, this admirable poem, from which I am learning to read – and I learn far more by looking than the inventions of any scribbler could teach me.'[7]

Five years earlier, in 1850, he had reviewed his friend Elizabeth Cavé's book *Drawing Without a Master*:

> **Many artists have had recourse to the daguerreotype to correct errors of vision...certain details almost always neglected in drawings from nature, there – in the daguerreotype – characteristically take on a great importance, and thus bring the artist into a full understanding of the construction. There, passages of light and shade show their true qualities, that is to say they appear with the precise degree of solidity or softness – a very delicate distinction without which there can be no suggestion of relief.**[8]

However, Delacroix argued that the photograph's very inability to be selective proved to be a double-edged sword, since it brought to light such shocking 'deformations' and imperfections, which our eyes unconsciously correct when we look at nature: 'The unfortunate discrepancies of literally true perspective are immediately corrected by the eye of the intelligent artist: *in painting it is soul which speaks to soul, and not science to science.*'[9] He concluded that the artist must depart from such truths so that the inner meanings of the subject could be conveyed: to imitate the subject's outward characteristics from a photograph produced mere mechanical copies.

> **Their work then is only the copy – necessarily cold – of a copy, itself imperfect in other respects. In a word, the artist becomes a machine harnessed to another machine.**[10]

This question would emerge as one of the central debates over art and photography for the rest of the century.

For other contemporaries, the issue was not so much whether artists should use photographs, but in what way they should be used. Even those who acknowledged their usefulness felt that their use by students would be pernicious. Sir William Newton, a portrait miniaturist, welcomed photographs as aids to the painter but recommended: '... the student in art *not* to take up the Camera as a means of advancement in his profession until he has made himself well acquainted with the true principles of his art, as well as acquired considerable power of hand, with a view to draw with ease and correctness the *outline* of any object he may wish to represent.'[11] Ironically Newton's own speciality – miniature painting – was to become the first casualty of the invention.

The mid-century Realists' preoccupation with portraying objective TRUTH was often equated with photography because of their perceived preoccupation with the ugly and 'artless' aspects of daily life. Delécluze based his attack on Courbet's *Burial at Ornans* (1848-9) partly on this stance: 'In that scene, which one might mistake for a faulty daguerreotype, there is the natural coarseness which one always gets in taking nature as it is, and in reproducing it just as it is seen.'[12] The Realists' active opposition to the classical ideal of BEAUTY was thought to have been fed by photography. Delécluze felt that:

> **The taste for naturalism is harmful to serious art...the constantly increasing pressure exerted during approximately the last ten years, on imitation in the arts, is due to two scientific forces which are fatal in action, that is to say the daguerreotype and the photograph (i.e. on paper) with which artists are already obliged to reckon.**[13]

In the 1850s Champfleury and Duranty defended Courbet against accusations of degrading art to this debased level by stressing that his work did indeed eschew the ideal of outdated classicism, but that it differed from photography because it portrayed nature through an individual TEMPERAMENT. Nevertheless, reservations about the influence of photography upon art became more frequent. In 1855 the American painter Edward Wheelwright recorded his conversations with Millet, who made the following comments on the new medium:

> **'[it was]...a good thing, and [he] would himself like to have a machine and take views. He would, however, never paint from them, but would use them as we use notes. Photographs, he says, are like casts from nature, which can never be equal to a good statue. No mechanism can be a substitute for genius. But photography, used as we use casts, may be of the greatest service!**[14]

Millet voiced a widely held objection, which stemmed partly from the fear of being accused of cheating, thus revealing artists' fear of the mechanisation of their professional expertise.

Hence few artists openly admitted to using photographs. This was particularly true in Britain (during the early decades of its invention, artists in France had been surprisingly open about their reliance on photography). For example, the British GENRE painter William Powell Frith was keen to stress that his laboriously detailed works were not dependent on photography. Of his famous urban genre painting *The Railway Station* (1860-62) he said: '...for the information of young painters…every object, living or dead, was painted from nature.'[15] Yet it is now known that Frith copied photographs, including one of the train engine in that painting. The French painter Hippolyte Flandrin rued the poverty of good DRAWING which he found at the Salon of 1863 and blamed the influence of photography:

> **Isn't it through drawing that everything noble in art is expressed? Perhaps I am mistaken but I am very much afraid that photography has dealt art a mortal blow.**[16]

From the late 1850s onwards, the honeymoon was over: the medium itself was no longer a novel and magical revelation, artists felt threatened by growing claims that photography was itself art and increasingly saw it as a vulgar and negative influence on the noble calling of high art. Yet it had perhaps become a victim of its own success. In practice, few artists were now working without some reliance on the medium, often secretively. For example Emily Sartain, who accompanied Mary Cassatt on a painting trip to Parma, expressed horror at the practice of an Italian contemporary in a letter to her father:

> **Signor Barbieri, the inspector, received a commission from Rome to make copies of the cherubs of the Hall of Diana – And imagine how he is doing it! He works in his room from photographs!**[17]

For LANDSCAPE painters photographs became major sources of documentation, so avoiding hours spent outdoors in all weathers making sketches and studies. For genre and history painters a market had soon formed for photographs of the human figure, either naked or in picturesque costume, denoting trades or regional origins, so providing cheap access to often obscure source material. Numerous portrait painters saw photogaphs as a useful economy, and they were, of course, now able to make posthumous portraits. Later in the century the British Pre-Raphaelite, John Brett, explained: 'The most frequent instances in which photographs have been copied by painters, occur in the practice of portraiture, where the sitter's time is precious.'[18]

Madame Cavé's and Delacroix's objection to unimaginative, unselective, machine-like copying had proved true, as numerous academic painters and sculptors vied with the medium in order to meet public taste, which now saw 'photographic' exactitude as a major criterion for assessing excellence in art. It was to this aspect of photography that the Goncourt brothers, the mature Ruskin and Baudelaire objected. Baudelaire above all acutely pinpointed the situation in his review of the 1859 Salon.Because of the stupidity of public demands that art imitate nature blindly, photography had become the barometer of verisimilitude against which art was measured:

> **I am convinced that the ill-applied developments of photography, like all other purely material developments of progress, have contributed much to the impoverishment of the French artistic genius, which is already so scarce... this industry, by invading the territories of art, has become art's most mortal enemy, and…the confusion of their several functions**

prevents any of them from being properly fulfilled.[19]

Baudelaire's solution was to put the medium firmly in a subservient role as 'the very humble servant' of both the arts and the sciences – a means of documenting and classifying information: 'But if it be allowed to encroach upon the domain of the impalpable and the imaginary, upon anything whose value depends solely upon the addition of something of a man's soul, then it will be so much the worse for us!'[20]

After an initial enthusiasm for the process, Ruskin arrived at a similar conclusion in his Slade Lectures (1870). For him, photography's inability to be selective was its downfall:

> **...photographs supersede no single quality nor use of fine art... They supersede no good art, for the definition of art is 'human labour regulated by human design' and this design, or evidence of active intellect in choice and arrangement, is the essential part of the work...they are not true, though they seem so. They are merely spoiled nature.**[21]

However, from the mid-1860s the AVANT-GARDE saw photography as neither rival nor oppressive taskmaster; for Manet and the Impressionists it proved to be both an inspiration from which they learned and a liberator. They rarely mentioned photography in their writings, yet their commitment to portraying the objective TRUTH led them to absorb visual effects derived from early photography into their works. The odd angles of vision, in some of the cityscapes, recall the photographs taken from top floor apartments; the blurring of figures and moving foliage, so typical of the relatively long exposures of early photographs, was appropriated by them as a modern means of conveying transience. The artlessness and awkwardness of human postures, revealed by the camera, which for Delacroix had been 'shocking monstrosities' of nature, were now equated with the unidealised truth of observed reality. The photograph's oddities of scale and perspective, and its often arbitrary, artless COMPOSITION of motifs (in which objects or figures were brutally cut off), provided them with a powerful visual equivalent for the fragmented evanescence of perception, which characterised the modern experience. Photography taught artists to see the world in a fresh manner.

At the same time, it liberated them from verisimilitude. Renoir's son recalled that his father expressed respect for Nièpce and Daguerre:

> **[They had]...freed painting from a lot of tiresome chores, starting with family portraits. Now the good shopkeeper has only to go to the photographer around the corner. So much the worse for us, but so much the better for the art of painting.**[22]

The Impressionists' lack of precision in describing objects, the impastoed broken brush work and use of juxtaposed, vivid pigment, all stressed the picture surface and *facture*, in a manner which carved out a path for painting independent of its traditional role as mirror of nature. Furthermore, photography's continuing technical inability to reproduce COLOUR permanently, despite numerous semi-successful experiments, gave them the licence to fully explore pure colour.

By the late 1870s even academic painters were learning from, rather than vying with the camera. In the winter of 1878/9 Edward Muybridge first published his consecutive photographs of horses in motion, which proved that, when galloping, at a certain point the animal's hooves all left the ground at the same time. The camera could see what the human eye could not. These, and Muybridge's subsequent explorations of animals in motion caused a major stir among artists, many of whom subscribed to his publication *Animal Locomotion, and Electro-Photographic Investigation of Consecutive Phases of Animal Movements* (1887). These included Leighton, Watts, Herkomer, Alma-Tadema, Fildes, Poynter, Sargent, Millais, Holman Hunt and Whistler in England, and Gérôme, Meissonier, Bouguereau, Puvis de Chavannes and Rodin in France. Many others, for example Degas, studied and worked from Muybridge's photographs. As John Brett acknowledged: 'The chief use of the camera to the artist, lies in its power of securing images of rapidly moving animals.'[23]

Even so, the ensuing controversy about the visual representation of movement continued to revolve around old issues such as the opposition between the soulless machine and the human being's imaginative powers of interpretation. While some, for example Meissonier, gamely changed their manner of depicting horses as a direct result of learning from Muybridge, others argued that the artist needed to lie in order to convey the essence of the truth. In a conversation with Paul Gsell, Rodin was asked to compare his figure of *St John the Baptist* (1878), which has both feet on the ground, with photographs of walking men, in which one foot leaves the ground. Rodin maintained that 'it is the artist who is truthful and it is photography which lies, for in reality time does not stop, and if the artist succeeds in producing the impression of a movement which takes several moments for accomplishment, his work is certainly much less conventional than the scientific image, where time is abruptly suspended.'[24] Turning to the debate about Géricault's pre-photography *ventre à terre* (flying gallop) depiction of galloping horses, Rodin went on: 'Now I believe that it is Géricault who is right, and not the camera, for his horses *appear* to run.'[25]

By the closing decades of the century it had become the norm for mainstream artists to comply with photographic verisimilitude as the main criterion for assessing and so producing their work. Working within such a visual culture, which was itself being flooded by mass-produced photographs and illustrations derived from photographs, the avant-garde was almost unanimously antagonistic to such accuracy. Yet it is as well to recall that artists such as Cézanne, Ensor, Gauguin and Toulouse-Lautrec did consider it legitimate to use photographs, albeit as sources from which to interpret their subjects. According to Emile Bernard, Cézanne 'did not object to a painter's use of photography, but he must interpret this exact reproduction as one interprets nature.'[26] Albert Aurier defended Gauguin's departures from verisimilitude on the grounds that he was one of the first to 'understand the futility of the petty little pursuits of realism and of photographic impersonality which is misleading contemporary painters and to attempt to re-establish in our society, so badly prepared for that revolution, true art, the art of the rebirth of ideas, of living symbols.'[27]

Baudelaire's 1859 article now appeared prophetic: the avant-garde IMAGINATION soared, free of the need to merely describe nature objectively. The move towards a concern with the expressive potential of formal means and the anti-naturalist desire to convey inner worlds can itself be attributed partly to the omnipotence of photographic objectivity. Yet the avant-garde artists mercilessly castigated their liberator. Gauguin wrote to Emile Bernard in 1888: 'I am far from thinking that photography can be favourable to us.'[28] Along with other Symbolist poets and painters, Gauguin felt that the new art (which he still called Impressionism) would act as an antidote to photographic illusionism and so rejuvenate art: 'I consider impressionism an altogether new departure which inevitably diverges from anything that is mechanical, such as photography etc.'[29] As Van Gogh explained to his brother Theo, such departures from verisimilitude would allow the artist to use colour and line expressively:

...you must boldly exaggerate the effects of either harmony or discord which colours produce. It is the same as in drawing – accurate drawing, accurate colour, is perhaps not the essential thing to aim at, because the reflection of reality in a mirror, if it could be caught, colour and all, would not be a picture at all, no more than a photograph.[30]

Even more radically, as early as 1878 Whistler had argued (like Walter Pater) that subject matter was now subservient to formal means: 'As music is the poetry of sound, so is painting the poetry of sight, and the subject matter has nothing to do with harmony of sound or of colour.'[31] Explaining that he had titled his portrait of his mother *Arrangement in Grey and Black* (c.1870), he argued that the identity of the sitter would be of no relevance to the wider public. He justified this stance by pointing out that:

The imitator is a poor kind of creature. If the man who paints only the tree, or flower, or other surface he sees before him were an artist, the king of artists would be the photographer. It is for the artist to do something beyond this.[32]

It would not be long before Maurice Denis would presage the next century's move towards abstraction, itself partly attributable to art's liberation by photography from its traditional mimetic function.

See: BEAUTY, FINISH, GENRE, MODERNITY, PORTRAITURE, TRUTH

[1] A.M.W. Stirling, *The Richmond Papers*, 1926, in Scharf, p. 102

[2] Cited by Coke, p. 12

[3] *Ibid*

[4] In Scharf, p. 37

[5] *Ibid*, p. 80

[6] 'Le Salon de 1857', *L'Artiste*, 1857, in Stevens, p. 22

[7] 5 Oct 1855, in Delacroix, 1995, pp. 323-4

[8] *Revue des Deux Mondes*, 1850, in Scharf, p. 119

[9] *Ibid*, p. 120

[10] *Ibid*

[11] 'Upon Photography in an Artistic View, and its Relation to the Arts', *Journal of the Photoraphic Society of London*, 1853, in Harrison and Wood, p. 654

[12] *Journal des Débats*, 1851, in Scharf, p. 128

[13] *Ibid*

[14] In Cartwright, p. 161

[15] In Scharf, p. 54

[16] H. Delaborde, *Lettres et pensées d'Hippolyte Flandrin...*, 1865, in Scharf, p. 153

[17] 12 Jan 1872, in Mathews, p. 88

[18] In Scharf, p. 55

[19] 'Lettre à M. le Directeur de la *Revue française* sur le Salon de 1859', *Revue française*, 1859, in Baudelaire, 1965, pp. 153-4

[20] *Ibid*, p. 154

[21] In Scharf, p. 99

[22] In Renoir, p. 161

[23] *British Journal of Photography*, 1889, in Scharf, p. 222

[24] In Scharf, p. 226

[25] *Ibid*

[26] Coke, p. 49

[27] 'Le Symbolisme en peinture: Paul Gauguin', *Mercure de France*, 1891, in Scharf, p. 251

[28] In Scharf, p. 250

[29] *Ibid*

[30] Probably summer 1888, in Scharf, p. 251

[31] 'The Red Rag', *The World*, 1878, in Whistler, p. 127

[32] *Ibid*, p.128

Physiognomy

THE PRACTICE OF PHYSIOGNOMY, THAT IS THE STUDY OF THE SHAPE, colouring, proportion and expression of the human head, dated back to the ancients when it had been used in medical diagnosis. Artists and caricaturists had long exploited the connection between the face and the personality, but it was the publication of Lavater's profusely illustrated *Essays on Physiognomy* (1775-7) which revived interest in the practice. Translated into English and French the work proved to be highly influential in the next century when other scientists, artists and medics developed ever more elaborate systems for reading the human countenance. Numerous nineteenth-century artists, schooled as many were in the French academic discipline of conveying emotions via facial expression, found Lavater's text crucial as a guide to conveying meaning. Hablot K. Browne, Dickens' primary illustrator, adopted the pseudonym 'Phiz' because it was an abbreviation of the word physiognomy.

Lavater's study of physiognomy had been driven by the *Sturm und Drang* (Storm and Stress) movement's concern with the individual and his/her states of mind. In mood the Romantic portrait dwelled upon the sitter's inner turmoil without resort to the more commonly used devices of dramatic posture, costume, setting and attributes. Much influenced by Lavater's theories, David d'Angers toured Europe to make his bronze portraits of contemporary geniuses. For example, in his *Portrait of Paganini* (1830) he elongated Paganini's forehead, giving it a protruding bump, and gave the virtuoso violinist suitably sunken cheeks and a determined, jutting chin. Perhaps the most profound explorations of physiognomy during the Romantic period were Géricault's portraits of the insane. Commissioned by his psychiatrist friend Dr Etienne-Jean Georget, who classified madness through physiognomic observation, it is thought that they may have been used as teaching material.

By the 1840s physiognomy had become interlinked with the new social science of anthropology (or ethnography as it was also known) as well as the more medical science of phrenology. These disciplines were increasingly important in the growing cities, as a means of assessing and classifying the multitude of strangers encountered in terms of region, race, nationality and social class. In his 1846 Salon, writing of the 'most appalling capacity for variety' in the human race, Baudelaire commented:

> **Without counting the major types which nature has distributed over the globe, every day I see passing beneath my window a certain number of Kalmouks, Osages, Indians,**

Chinamen and Ancient Greeks, all more or less Parisianized. Each individual is a unique harmony; for you must often have had the surprising experience of turning back at the sound of a known voice and finding yourself face to face with a complete stranger – the living reminder of someone else endowed with a similar voice and similar gestures... It is possible that Lavater was mistaken in detail; but he had the basic idea. Such and such a hand demands such and such a foot; each epidermis produces its own hair. Thus each individual has his ideal.[1]

From the 1840s onwards physiognomic or 'anthropological' observation became a popular pastime and it was common to classify people in terms of 'types'. When Hippolyte Taine visited London, he told of his system for deciphering and classifying the English crowd. He would 'note the most salient features or expressions, study them in all their variations and shades, graduations and mixtures; check that they are to be found in sufficiently numerous individuals; by this means, isolate the principal characteristic traits, then compare, interpret and classify them.'[2] He compared his method to that of zoologists and botanists, but also to painters and novelists who worked more instinctively in order to provide 'a resumé of their times and environment.'[3]

Numerous books and articles provided guides to physiognomic types, some even dwelling on specific features such as the expression of the eyes. In 1853 the British artist George Elgar Hicks published his *Guide to Figure Drawing*, in which he stated the commonly held belief that the shape of the forehead might be a guide to intelligence:

The erect forehead being peculiar to man, more than any other feature distinguishes him from the brutes. Its elevation is indicative of intellectual power, a projecting one of idiotcy [sic], and a low and receding one of deficiency of intellect.[4]

The portrayal of character via physiognomy was linked to social, spiritual and moral values in history painting and portraiture, but it truly flourished within the highly coded scenes of GENRE painting. William Powell Frith, for example, was a keen physiognomist and made specific use of well known types in his exceedingly successful crowd scenes *Derby Day* (1858) and *The Railway Station* (1862). Appealing to a public well versed in classifying physiognomic types, numerous mainstream genre paintings thus conveyed the specifics of nationality, character and class.

For the French AVANT-GARDE in the second half of the century, what mattered was not to establish one single canon of ideal BEAUTY, but rather to delight in the varieties of ethnic and physiognomic types. Hence Théophile Thoré could write the following in an 1857 article on recent tendencies in art:

What is the most beautiful type in the human race? The Greek type or the Roman type? The Arab type or the English type? Or possibly the Parisian type?
Phrenologists are often asked, What really is the most perfect type of cerebral organisation? Show me the head in which everything is 'just right'!...
To search for a standard type in art is absurd. How can one believe that the future lies behind us![5]

When Baudelaire defined the modern artist, he did so partly in terms of the convalescent enjoying the urban scene from behind the glass panes of a café, who finally cannot resist plunging into the urban crowd: '…in pursuit of an unknown, half-glimpsed countenance that has, on an instant, bewitched him.'[6] While aware of the more academic connotations of physiognomy, Degas could also view it as a continuing challenge, noting his intention to 'update' Lavater:

> **Make of the têtes d'expression a study of modern feeling – it's like Lavater, but a more relative Lavater in a way. – Study Delsartre's observations on those movements of the eye inspired by feeling. – Its beauty must be nothing more than a specific physiognomy.**[7]

Physiognomy also shaded off at one extreme towards the classification of entire social classes and ethnic groups as inferior or superior, and it led to widespread stereotyping: for example, the elongated 'aristocratic' physiognomies and indolent, patrician stances with which Singer Sargent and Boldini flattered the upper bourgeoisie in their PORTRAITURE. Nor were the avant-garde immune from falling into such traps. When visiting Vichy and the Auvergne in the late 1860s Millet could un-selfconsciously write:

> **The inhabitants of the countryside are quite different from the peasants of Barbizon. They have that good natured animal clumsiness which owes nothing to taking the waters, I assure you. The women have, in general, snouts which announce the exact opposite of wickedness, and which would be exactly the type of many of the physiognomies in gothic art.**[8]

Van Gogh admired and collected the types depicted in the *Heads of the People* commissioned by the *Graphic* from Herkomer, Small and other British social realists from 1875. He gave his *The Potato Eaters* (1885) the low brows, snoutish noses, sensuous lips and jutting jaws commonly identified by nineteenth-century physiognomists and anthropologists as typifying the coarse, undeveloped peasant. Yet in his later portraits of working-class sitters, such as those of the Roulin family, he found a means of conveying their individual inner lives without resorting to such stereotyping. Instead he expressed their essential selves in terms of COLOUR, as he told Theo:

> **And in my pictures I want to say something consoling, as music does. I want to paint men and women with a touch of the eternal, whose symbol was once the halo, which we try to convey by the very radiance and vibrancy of our colouring.**[9]

See: EXOTIC, GENRE, PORTRAITURE, *TÊTE D'EXPRESSION*

[1] *Salon de 1846*, in Baudelaire, 1965, pp. 80-1

[2] *Notes on England*, 1850-60, in Cowling, p. 96

[3] *Ibid*, p. 98

[4] In Cowling, p. 94

[5] *Salons de T. Thoré…*, 1868, in Taylor, p. 368

[6] 'Le peintre de la vie moderne', *Figaro*, 1863, in Baudelaire, 1995, p. 7

[7] Notebook no. 23, 1868-72, in Kendall, p. 37

[8] In Herbert, p. 183

[9] 3 Sept 1888, in Van Gogh, 1996, p. 394

Picturesque

IN AN ARTICLE PUBLISHED IN 1821-2 THE BRITISH CRITIC WILLIAM HAZLITT indulged in the still popular sport of identifying what was picturesque and what was not: 'A rough terrier-dog, with the hair bristled and matted together, is picturesque... A shock-dog is [not]... A goat with projecting horns and pendant beard is a picturesque animal: a sheep is not.'[1] Prior to Romanticism's attack on the idea of universal taste, there grew up a plethora of viewpoints and categories within the single, classical system for defining BEAUTY, the concept of the picturesque being the most influential. First mooted by the British artist-clergyman William Gilpin in the last decades of the eighteenth century, the term was widely used until the early decades of the nineteenth. In *Three Essays on Picturesque Beauty* (1792) Gilpin took issue with Edmund Burke's ideas on beauty and the SUBLIME, as set out in *A Philosophical Inquiry into the Origin of Our Ideas of the Sublime and the Beautiful* (1757). To allow for only two extreme forms of aesthetic experience seemed too narrow, and excluded consideration of the less powerful, yet still pleasurable, aesthetic experiences that lay between.

Gilpin's definition of the picturesque as 'worthy of a picture' was somewhat vague, and the use of the term remained inconsistent despite the efforts of his friend Sir Uvedale Price to articulate a systematic theory in *An Essay on the Picturesque* (1794). The precise meaning of the term was to be a source of endless polemical debate. However, it was generally agreed that at its core lay the irregular, the varied and the contrasting. Accepting Burke's definition of beauty as 'the *neat* and *smooth*', Gilpin continued: '*roughness* forms the most essential point of difference between the *beautiful,* and the *picturesque*.'[2] Unlike the SUBLIME, the picturesque was never overwhelmingly disconcerting; unlike beauty it was not utterly balanced and harmonious. Referring to an elegantly proportioned, symmetrical Palladian building Gilpin wrote:

> **Should we wish to give it picturesque beauty, we must use the mallet, instead of the chisel: we must beat down one half of it, deface the other, and throw the mutilated members around in heaps. In short, from a *smooth* building we must turn it into a *rough* ruin.**[3]

Nor were irregularities to go beyond a polite boundary. Such excess Gilpin termed 'romantic'. The city of Edinburgh, because of 'the odd misshapen and uncouth' Arthur's Seat, was romantic rather than picturesque: 'a view with such a staring feature in it, can no more be picturesque than a face with a bulbous nose can be beautiful.'[4] He busied himself travelling the British Isles seeking out picturesque experiences, which he duly recorded in his many topographical publications, beginning with *Observations on the River Wye* (1783), in which he did not differentiate between the aesthetic experience of viewing NATURE and that of viewing art. Dependent on the academic tradition, he had no objection to altering the natural scene when he found a vista wanting in charm or contrast. Nor was he concerned as Burke had been, with the associative properties of such experiences or scenes. The social or moral implications of the subjects viewed or depicted equally remained outside of both his and Price's concerns. The latter would write that no evidence of 'the works of man', including agricultural cultivation, should mar the picturesque scene, although quaint castles, hovels and cottages did qualify by virtue of their battered charms. While Gilpin wrote:

In a moral view, the industrious mechanic is a more pleasing object, than the loitering peasant. But in a picturesque light it is otherwise... even idleness... adds dignity to a character. Thus the lazy cowherd resting on his pole; or the peasant lolling on a rock, may be allowed in...[as may]... figures in long, folding draperies, gypsies, banditti, and soldiers.'[5]

So long, Gilpin added, as the soldiers were in tattered uniforms: his sole concern was with the formal qualities of a scene; his aim to refine and aestheticise the process of seeing. Thanks to Gilpin, it became fashionable for the landed gentry and the rising middle classes to engage in picturesque tourism. Armed with his guides they could aestheticize the act of perception, congratulating themselves on their educated discernment of the picturesque features in the vistas surveyed. Aesthetic tourism became so fashionable that it was satirised, for example in Rowlandson's prints and in the novels of Jane Austen. During the high patriotism of the Napoleonic wars, when travel abroad was severely curtailed, it also became a means of exoticising the native LANDSCAPE. The influence of the picturesque was felt in the compositional devices of numerous landscapists including Turner, and in informal landscape garden designs in Britain and abroad.

By the 1820s early naturalists such as Constable reacted against what they saw as the formulaic artifice of the picturesque, dependent as it was on emotionally facile academic recipes. They saw it as antithetical to their own concern for quasi-scientific TRUTH to specific visual experience. However it continued to influence the manner in which Turner composed many of his landscapes until his death in 1851 and the term in its original meaning was still being used in landscape gardening well into the century.

The search for new subjects within GENRE painting led to a craze for depictions of 'picturesque' European peasants in their regional costumes. This was initiated by paintings of Italians at the beginning of the century by Pauline Chatillon and Madame Haudebourt-Lescot. The French academic painter Jean-Jacques Henner reported of Italian women:

The most picturesque among them – and they know well they are picturesque – will come up to you when they see you with your box of colours and say: 'Signor, volete intratarmi,' that is: 'Do you want to paint my portrait?' They themselves ask nothing better and when you draw houses or monuments they deliberately stand beside them, so beautiful and in such graceful poses that you almost forget that the government has sent you here to do history painting.[6]

The objectification of people which was inherent in such attitudes was rarely questioned by artists and their publics. Rosa Bonheur expressed commonly held assumptions when she recalled her 1846 visit to the rural Puy-de Dôme region: 'I did a huge amount of work during that end-of-summer trip...my albums and portfolios were stuffed with sketches and studies of the region's picturesque sites, people and animals.'[7] As late as 1872 the American painter Mary Cassatt would write of the treeless landscape around Cordova in Spain: 'no houses, here and there a flock of sheep, a herd of cattle or swine, with the herdsman, wrapped in his cloak, immensely sad, vast and dreary, but infinitely picturesque.'[8]

Nevertheless, the term was increasingly used simply to indicate the quaintly pretty. In his journal Delacroix noted that the landscape between Ribérac and Montmoreau, with its vines 'clinging to trees, or to posts, in the Italian way [was]...very pretty and picturesque and would look well in a painting.'[9]

The place of the picturesque in cultural history is still contentious. Some argue that it was a form of early Romanticism, others that it was an offshoot of academic practice.

See: BEAUTY, EFFECT, EXOTIC, LANDSCAPE, NATURE, SUBLIME

[1] 'On the Picturesque and the Ideal, a Fragment', *Table Talk*, 1821-2, in Harrison and Wood, p. 115

[2] *Three Essays on Picturesque Beauty…*, 2nd ed., 1794, in Taylor, p. 50

[3] *Ibid*, p. 51

[4] *Observations on the Highlands*, 1808, in Vaughan, p. 38

[5] *Observations, Relative Chiefly to Picturesque Beauty…Particularly the Mountains, and Lakes of Cumberland, and Westmorland*, II, 1786, in Klingender, pp. 73-4

[6] In Lethève, p. 41

[7] In Kumpke, p. 125

[8] 27 Oct 1872, in Mathews, p. 109

[9] 17 Sept 1855, in Delacroix, 1995, p. 316

Plein-air

JEAN-JACQUES ROUSSEAU'S IDEALISATION OF THE GREAT OUTDOORS was carried into the nineteenth century by the Romantics, where it lingered. Describing the painter Barbara Bodichon to his sister, Dante Gabriel Rossetti said she would think 'nothing of climbing up a mountain in breeches, or wading through a stream in none, in the sacred name of pigment.'[1]

By the nineteenth century, working in the open air was hardly new: Dürer had made a study of a piece of turf, the seventeenth-century landscapists had drawn in the Roman campagna, the British eighteenth-century watercolourists' topographical surveys had captured a sense of place and the luminosity of natural light. The problem, in terms of producing studio-finished, exhibition landscapes was that light, atmosphere and the seasons change the aspect of the motif. As early as 1800 the classicist Valenciennes explained:

> **…it is absurd for an artist to spend an entire day copying a single view from Nature. He should realise that he would be painting the sky at dawn, the background a little later, and the third plane at noon, the second at four o'clock, and the foreground in the light of the setting sun.**[2]

Although Valenciennes advocated studio-produced historical landscapes, he realised the importance of the quick, *plein-air* STUDY for its ability to record EFFECTS of light in specific settings. This approach was advocated by the academies throughout the nineteenth century. The innovations came with the sketch-FINISH debate initiated by Constable, who sought to retain the qualities of the sketch in his finished paintings. Of his own work he wrote:

> **In some of these subjects of Landscape an attempt has been made to arrest the more abrupt and transient appearances of the CHIAR'-OSCURO IN NATURE; to shew its effect in the most striking manner, to give 'to one brief moment caught from fleeting time', a lasting and sober existence, and to render permanent many of those splendid but**

evanescent Exhibitions, which are ever occurring in the changes of external Nature.[3]

By the 1820s there was much enthusiasm for LANDSCAPE studies from the motif. From about this time numerous artists' colonies sprang up, many along the French Channel coast and in the Barbizon forest. Late in life Corot confided his thoughts to the critic Théophile Silvestre:

> **You have to go to the fields and not to the paintings. The Muse is in the woods: she wants silence; she no longer lives in the Poissonnière neighbourhood.**[4]

By the mid-1850s the practice of making outdoor studies was commonplace, and some artists even held that the first impression was the purest, most heightened of moments. As Boudin recorded in his notebook: 'Everything that is painted directly on the spot has always a strength, a power, a vividness of touch that one doesn't find again in the studio.'[5]

It was the English Pre-Raphaelites who first set out to paint an entire finished work outdoors, influenced by John Ruskin's emphasis on the need for accuracy, authenticity and detailed specificity. Ford Madox Brown had his wife modelling in all weathers so that he could paint *The Pretty Baa-Lambs* (1851-9) entirely out of doors. He said that it was 'painted in the sunlight, the only intention being to record that effect as well as my powers in a first attempt of this kind would allow.'[6] Yet the central figure was in historical costume, the lambs were brought to the outdoor location every morning, while the meticulously detailed execution, with its enamel-like finish and careful COMPOSITION, revealed a lengthy laborious working process, so making it impossible to note the vagaries of natural light or the movement of living figures. Brown's work was as contrived as any traditional studio picture.

It was the Impressionists, influenced by Manet, who retained more of the spontaneity of the first impression in the final painting. They did so by working quickly, experimenting with *plein-air* work on the whole painting, and accepting the ensuing lack of detailed finish. For his second major attempt at an outdoor figure painting, *Women in the Garden* (1866-7), Monet dug a trench so that he could retain the same viewpoint when working on both the lower and upper parts of the canvas. The aim was TRUTH to the first impression, born of the artist's individual SENSATIONS and TEMPERAMENT:

> **The search after truth, peculiar to modern artists, which enables them to see nature and reproduce her, such as she appears to just and pure eyes, must lead them to adopt air almost exclusively as their medium, or at all events to habituate themselves to work in it freely, and without restraint.**[7]

By the mid-1860s, others shared Monet's preoccupation with depicting figures and landscapes in the open air. In 1866, when still a young painter, Cézanne wrote to Zola of his intention to paint such a picture:

> **But you know all pictures painted inside, in the studio, will never be as good as those done outside. When out-of-door scenes are represented, the contrasts between the figures and the ground is astounding and the landscape is magnificent. I see some superb things and I shall have to make up my mind only to do things out-of-doors.**[8]

Plein-air painting had the distinct advantage of being able to best convey the evanescence, luminosity and transparency of natural light. Antonin Proust tells us that in 1879 Manet had two *idées fixes*: one was to paint a portrait in one sitting and the second was to paint a picture entirely outside, 'in which the features of persons would melt, as he put it, in the vibrations of the atmosphere.'[9] When he discovered the light of the south in Antibes Monet communicated his excitement to his friend Geffroy:

It is so beautiful here, so light, so luminous! One swims in blue light, it is frightening.[10]

Working quickly led the Impressionists to major formal and technical innovations. As Mallarmé realised, *plein-air* painting provided them with 'if nothing more, an incentive to a new manner of painting.'[11] Using a white ground without under-painting meant dispensing with CHIAROSCURO, which, in turn led to the discovery of the vibrancy of pure COLOUR and the expressive potential of visible, lively brushwork. Accepting the mobility of unposed figures led to informal compositions, while breaking with high finish outmanoeuvred the challenge of PHOTOGRAPHY, with its accuracy of detail. Unlike the Pre-Raphaelites the Impressionists found a contemporary visual language with which to speak of their contemporary subject-matter.

However, the practical difficulties encountered in such a working process were often tedious. People and objects moved, curious passers-by were distracting or intimidating, and the vagaries of the climate, especially in northern Europe, were a constant trial. With her customary melancholy, Berthe Morisot complained to her sister Edma during a visit to the Isle of Wight in 1875:

I have worked a little, but what rain we have had for a week! Today we have been to Ryde. I set out with my sack and portfolio, determined to make a water-colour on the spot, but when we got there I found the wind was frightful, my hat blew off, my hair got in my eyes. Eugène was in a bad humour as he always is when my hair is in disorder – and three hours after leaving we were back at Globe Cottage.[12]

In a subsequent letter she returned to the problems involved in working outdoors:

I made an attempt in a field, but the moment I had set up my easel more than fifty boys and girls were swarming about me, shouting and gesticulating. All this ended in a pitched battle, and the owner of the field came to tell me rudely that I should have asked for permission to work there... On a boat one has another kind of difficulty. Everything sways, there is an infernal lapping of water; one has the sun and wind to cope with, the boats change position every minute etc.[13]

Undeterred, from the late 1870s until the first decades of the twentieth century numerous artists throughout Europe, America and the colonies of the western Empires began to practise *plein-air* naturalism, often in a watered-down manner, which was nevertheless rooted in *plein-air* painting. By the 1880s advanced academies began to teach it. Not long before making his Salon début in 1878 with *The Harvest*, Bastien-Lepage wrote to his friend on Ascension Day, 1877:

15th August, your verses are just the picture I should like to paint. They smell of the hay and the heat of the meadow... If my hay smells as well as yours I shall be content... I have had hard work to set up my first ideas, being determined to keep simply to the true aspects of a bit of nature.[14]

Yet, as his admirer and fellow *plein-airist*, George Clausen conceded:

No doubt Bastien-Lepage worked for truth of impression and of detail too, but it is apparently impossible to get both; and this seems to show that the building-up or combining a number of facts, each of which may be true of itself and to the others, does not

in its sum total give the general impression of truth.[15]

It must be remembered that several major artists associated with Impressionism were never *plein-air* painters, notably Degas and Cassatt. By the mid-1880s AVANT-GARDE artists were questioning the limitations of naturalism. Oscar Wilde expressed their reservations:

> **There is far more to be said in favour of that newer school at Paris, the *Archaicistes*, as they call themselves, who, refusing to leave the artist entirely at the mercy of the weather, do not find the ideal in art in mere atmospheric effect, but seek rather for the imaginative beauty of design and the loveliness of fair colour, and rejecting the tedious realism of those who merely paint what they see, try to see something worth seeing.**[16]

Pissarro, one of the pioneers of *plein-air* painting, went through a period of doubt, when he recognised the advantages of working away from the motif, before returning to *plein-airism* in his late work: 'I am more than ever for the impression through memory, it renders less of the object – vulgarity disappears, leaving only the undulations of the truth that was glimpsed, felt…'[17]

Van Gogh also flirted with Gauguin's ideas of working away from the motif, on what he termed abstractions, before deciding that he felt a need for the humble facts of NATURE in front of him:

> **So I am working at present among the olive trees, seeking after the various effects of a grey sky against a yellow soil, with a green-black note in the foliage; another time the soil and the foliage all of a violet hue against a yellow sky;…Yes, certainly, this interests me far more than the above-mentioned abstractions.**[18]

See: EFFECT, FINISH, LANDSCAPE, NATURE, SENSATION, STUDY, TRUTH

[1] In Orr, p. 75

[2] *Élémens de perspective pratique à l'usage des artistes, suivis de Réflexions et conseils à un élève sur la peinture, et particulièrement sur le genre de paysage*, 1820, in Taylor, p. 254

[3] Introduction to *English Landscape*, 1833, in R.B. Beckett, ed., *John Constable's Discourses*, Ipswich: Suffolk Records Society, XIV, 1970, in Harrison and Wood, p. 128

[4] Cailler, I, p. 115. Corot's studio was in the Poissonière quarter.

[5] In Rewald, p. 38

[6] In Nochlin, 1971, p. 142

[7] S. Mallarmé, 'The Impressionists and Edouard Manet', *The Art Monthly Review and Photographic Portfolio*, 1876, in Harrison and Wood, p. 589

[8] c.19 Oct 1866, in Cézanne, pp. 112-3

[9] *Souvenirs*, in Courthion, p. 87

[10] 12 Feb 1888, in Geffroy, p. 117

[11] S. Mallarmé, *op. cit.*, p. 589

[12] Morisot, p. 102

[13] *Ibid*, p. 104

[14] Theuriet, p. 46

[15] *Ibid*, pp. 125-6

[16] *The Critic as Artist*, 1890, in Wilde, p. 1051

[17] 26 April 1892, in Pissarro, p. 195

[18] To Bernard, beginning of Dec 1889, in Chipp, p. 44

Pochade

ONE OF THE LEAST COMMONLY USED TERMS (which were sometimes interchangeable) for the various preparatory processes leading towards the creation of a finished painting, the *pochade* was a speedily executed summary of a motif. While a CROQUIS was most usually worked in one of the graphic media, the *pochade* would be executed in paint. Its primary purpose was to capture the overall EFFECT of the light values of a specific motif:

> **A *pochade* is a study of a complete theme, done from the point of view of correct values and conveying the impression of a motif that has caught the painter's attention...it is from the *pochade* that you establish the range of values...it helps you to remain true to the desired effect as your work proceeds.**[1]

The *pochade* was particularly valuable to landscape artists since they were encouraged to make observations directly from NATURE, and often had to work quickly because of the changing light. While it is not possible to make a clear distinction between an *ÉTUDE* and a *pochade*, the latter tended to be a less detailed and more hesitant first trial.

According to academic theory, the *pochade* was a preparatory stage that did not seek to create an illusionistic representation of the motif. However, by the 1840s they came to be valued in their own right, albeit as minor works, particularly in relation to the Barbizon painters. From the mid-1860s the Impressionists created controversy by going one step further and signing, exhibiting and selling works as finished paintings which academic artists would have called *pochades*, or *esquisses*. In 1869 Monet wrote to Bazille:

> **I have indeed a dream, a picture of bathing at *La Grenouillère*, for which I've made some bad sketches [*pochades* in the original letter], but it's a dream. Renoir, who has been spending two months here, also wants to do this picture.**[2]

Monet evidently reassessed these *pochades* since he later signed and exhibited them.

See: *CROQUIS*, *ÉBAUCHE*, EFFECT, *ESQUISSE*, *ÉTUDE*, FINISH, *PLEIN-AIR*, SENSATION

[1] K. Robert, *Traité pratique de peinture à l'huile*, 1884, in Boime, p. 153

[2] 25 Sept 1869, in Rewald, pp. 227-8

Portraiture

PORTRAITURE HAD AN IMPECCABLE HERITAGE, from the portrait busts of the ancients via old masters such as Titian and Raphael through to Rembrandt and Velazquez. That it ranked second in the hierarchy of subject matter of the Académie des Beaux-Arts reflected the high social status of its predominantly aristocratic sitters in the seventeenth century, when the pecking order was first formulated. In the nineteenth century the expansion of the middle class provided a new clientele, keen to affirm its social status by adopting upper-class trappings of 'tradition'. Portraiture became the most widely practised single category of subject-matter. For example about half of the works exhibited at the ACADEMY in London from 1823 to 1833 were portraits.

Ranging from the lowly paper silhouette to full-length, life-size statues, most portraits were commissioned. They provided a major source of income for artists at all levels, from the provincial limner to the society academician. In France the enlightened *ateliers* of the revolutionary period (for example those of David and Regnault) created a strong contingent of *citoyenne* portrait painters, including Marie Charpentier, Madame Romany and the Contess Benoist, who continued to exhibit in the opening decade of the nineteenth century. As the century progressed the increasing ubiquity of portraiture lowered its status within the profession, so that it became easier for women to practise it. Many miniaturists were women. It was a socially respectable subject which did not require the classical erudition or knowledge of the naked human figure provided by formal art education, from which most women were excluded until the last quarter of the century.

While some artists were content to devote themselves entirely to portraiture, many resented it as a necessary but tedious chore which drained their creative energies. An anecdote from Ingres's Rome years told of his proud reply to those who asked whether his studio was that of the portrait painter: 'No, Monsieur, he who lives here is an artist.'[1] Having laboured over numerous portrait commissions during the first quarter of the century, he only occasionally accepted them once he had established his reputation as a history painter, and only from high-ranking sitters such as the Duc d'Orléans, the heir to the French throne, whom he painted in 1841-2. Of the duke he wrote to his friend M. Gatteaux:

> **Between you and I, despite being honoured that the prince wants to be painted only by me, I still have to paint another portrait! You know how removed I am at the moment from this kind of painting; but still I'll do my best for this amiable person.[2]**

For ambitious artists, portraiture was seen as a necessary career move. Théodore Chassériau admitted with brutal transparency: 'I want to execute plenty of portraits first of all to become better known, then to make money, and finally to get the necessary independence that will allow me to fulfil the duties of a history painter.'[3] For many, it might be the only means of getting an income. Before the spread of the railways, the future genre painter William Powell Frith began his career in the 1830s as a travelling portrait painter. Word of mouth provided future commissions:

> **I went from house to house, chiefly among the higher class of gentlemen farmers, staying as long as my work lasted: sometimes flirting with the young ladies, who thought painting 'oh, such a beautiful art,' flattering their mothers – in their portraits, I mean.[4]**

Most portraitists faced the perennial conflict posed by the client's simultaneous desire to be flattered and be provided with a likeness. At the dawn of the century the legacy of Neo-classicism, with its concern for timelessness and cool perfection, permitted a degree of idealisation and generalisation. This opened the way for artists like Canova, Madame Vigée-Lebrun and Marie Charpentier to emphasise the nobility of the sitter's moral or temporal worth, rather than their physical attributes. Indeed the marble sculptures and busts of the late Neo-classical period portrayed their subjects in the ANTIQUE manner, as in Canova's over-life size marble statue of an idealised, naked *Napoleon* (1806).

The question of whether to depart from this classical convention preoccupied later artists such as the American sculptor Hiram Powers. His bust of *President Jackson* (c.1835) shows the unidealised head of the man atop a classical toga, but Powers later decided that he should 'take the actual costume of the age and [do] his best with it.'[5] Unimpressed, when Nathaniel Hawthorne visited the sculptor's studio in Rome in 1858 he voiced the reservations of the age: 'though [present] costume might not appear ridiculous to us now...two or three centuries hence, it would create...an impossibility of seeing the real man through the absurdity of his envelopment, after it shall have gone entirely out of fashion and remembrance.'[6]

Yet even the Neo-classical artist was expected to provide a resemblance, an expectation which increased as the century wore on. This requirement partly explains Ingres's frustration with the genre, so committed was he to the classical ideal. He noted: 'The history painter renders the specific in generalisation, while the portrait painter only represents the particular individual, consequently from a model who is often ordinary or full of defects.'[7] Even so, he accepted the need to provide a close likeness and provided some practical advice: 'A portrait often lacks likeness because the model was badly posed, because he was placed in a poor play of shadow and light, which would make the sitter unrecognisable to himself were he to see himself in the place where he was painted.'[8]

At the less elevated end of the market, such was the call for the mimetic that the humble New England journeyman, Rufus Porter, printed a handbill offering his service as a portrait painter simply in terms of providing 'Correct Likenesses: Taken with elegance and despatch [sic].' Moreover, he guaranteed his workmanship with the slogan 'No likeness, No Pay.'[9]

For the Romantics, the individual response of the artist in the encounter with the sitter was deemed to play a vital part in portraiture. The American Washington Allston, in his *Lectures on Art and Poems* (1850, begun in 1830) argued that TRUTH resided therein:

...suppose two portraits; simple heads, without accessories,...and both by artists of equal talent, employing the same materials, and conducting their work according to the same technical process...though in all respects equal, in execution, likeness &c ., we shall still perceive a certain exclusive something that will instantly distinguish the one from the other, and both from the original. And yet they shall both seem to us true. But they will be true to us also in a double sense; namely, as the living original and as to the individuality of the different painters...both artists must originate.[10]

For many, this truth was a matter of responding to the inner characteristics of the sitter rather than to their outward physical appearance. In the 1830s and 1840s Margaret Gillies painted portraits of the progressive British intellectuals of her age. She explained her approach to a client:

Artists in general seize every opportunity of painting the nobility of wealth and rank it would be far more grateful to me to be able to paint what I conceive to be true nobility that of genius long faithfully earnestly and not without suffering labouring to call out what is most beautiful and refined in our nature and to establish this as a guide and standard of human action.[11]

It is significant that the term *self-portrait* dates from the nineteenth century, although artists had painted pictures of themselves prior to this. The Romantics' preoccupation with self expression and self discovery led artists to delve into their own psyches or biographies, while the century's concept of the artist as GENIUS encouraged such aesthetically diverse artists as

David, Delacroix, Cassatt and Hodler to provide posterity with pictures of themselves –
Courbet made his Salon debut with one. In 1854 he wrote to his patron Alfred Bruyas of his
Self-Portrait with Pipe (exhibited 1852):

> **It is the portrait of a fanatic, an ascetic. It is the portrait of a man who, disillusioned by
> the nonsense that made up his education, seeks to live by his own principles. I have done
> a good many self-portraits in my life, as my attitude gradually changed. One could say
> that I have written my autobiography.**[12]

To paint oneself or one's family and friends was also a way of avoiding the restrictions of a
client's needs. On a more prosaic level, it was a source of free models and so of particular
appeal to the AVANT-GARDE, which suffered from lack of public support. Yet the preoccupation with the self (like the critics' and historians' preoccupation with the artist's personal
life) was also a manifestation of the age of individualism.

The single, most momentous challenge to portraiture came with the invention of PHOTOG-
RAPHY by Daguerre in France and Fox Talbot in England in 1839. The first daguerreotypes
were portraits and an industry of photographic portraiture developed almost immediately.
Since these images were cheaper even than miniatures, portraiture was now within the means
of the many. But from an artist's point of view the new technology posed a threat. The first
casualties were miniatures: 300 were exhibited at the Royal Academy in 1830, but by 1860 only
64 were shown (although the genre did enjoy a brief revival at the end of the century). Yet the
boundaries between painting and photography were not clear cut. Many of the early photographers had been portrait painters, and the practice of painting from photographs or even *over*
photographic prints was soon initiated. In the 1850s 'Beard's Photographic and Daguerreotype
Miniatures' were advertised as remarkable 'for breadth of effect and beauty of colour, and the
Photographs on Paper (finished as paintings in water colours or crayons) are equal to the best
Miniatures, with this advantage, that the likenesses are marvellously accurate.'[13]

It was their precision of detail and of likeness which most impressed the early public, and this
was to enhance an already existing demand for accuracy of resemblance in a pragmatic and
empirical age. Henceforth, a multitude of portrait artists would use photographs, either as reference material to save time and effort for sitter and painter, or to ensure an accurate likeness.
By the 1870s it was accepted practice, albeit one rarely admitted publicly. In his lectures at
the Royal Academy, delivered between 1876 and 1882, the painter Edward Armitage was
refreshingly frank:

> **I see no objection whatever to the practice...All portrait-painters know that it is not easy
> to get ladies and gentlemen to sit for their clothes, and it is far better to get help from a
> good photograph than from a model or lay figure whom the clothes do not fit. I have no
> doubt that if photography had been known in the time of Raffaelle [sic] he would have
> largely availed himself of it.**[14]

It could be argued that the invention of photography was not surprising, such was the thrust
towards mimesis during the nineteenth century. From the 1860s, and perhaps even earlier,
some painters even worked directly on their canvases from projected photographic images,
although this was frowned upon. Henceforth, to paint a portrait became a less straightforward
proposition, since artists had to ask themselves what they were doing that the camera could

not. Broadly speaking the effect was twofold: while academic artists vied with the camera to create verisimilitude, the avant-garde felt that it liberated them from such tedium. Baudelaire was quick to understand the implications. In his 1859 Salon he castigated the widespread infatuation with exactitude, which he saw as being exacerbated by photography:

> **...the disaster is verifiable. Each day art further diminishes its self-respect by bowing down before external reality; each day the painter becomes more and more given to painting not what he dreams but what he sees. Nevertheless it is a happiness to dream, and it used to be a glory to express what one dreamt. But I ask you! does the painter still know this happiness?**[15]

For the avant-garde the answer was clear. Manet and the Impressionists dispensed with half tones, glazes and other painstaking, illusionistic academic techniques. With deft bravura they emphasised TOUCH and the materiality of pigment on canvas, so putting the surface of the painting at a premium. To his friend Antonin Proust, Manet wrote:

> **Your portrait is painted with the utmost sincerity possible. I remember, as if it were only yesterday, the quick and simple way I treated the glove you're holding in your bare hand and how, when you said to me at that moment, 'Please, not another stroke,' I felt in complete sympathy with you and could have hugged you.**[16]

What mattered most was sincerity and this could best be achieved by speed of execution. Manet dreamed of executing a portrait in a single sitting. To fidget over a canvas would be to kill its freshness. With characteristic self-depreciation Berthe Morisot wrote to her sister in 1871: 'I am doing Yves with Bichette. I am having great difficulty with them. The work is losing all its freshness.'[17] The Impressionists were also inspired by the new ways of seeing which the camera introduced and by its ability to capture the fleeting moment. Degas wrote of his intention to exploit the new medium in a notebook (1877-83):

> **After having done portraits seen from above, I will do some seen from below – sitting very close to a woman and looking up at her. I will see her head in the chandelier, surrounded by crystals.**[18]

Turning his back on a centuries-old tradition, according to which artists had sought to convey the character, occupation, inner world and social status of their sitters, Whistler shockingly declared the identity of the sitter to be virtually redundant. Taking the most radical stance on the implications of photography, he argued that what truly mattered was not the sitter, but the formal arrangement of the painting:

> **Take the picture of my mother, exhibited at the Royal Academy as an 'Arrangement in Grey and Black'. Now that is what it is. To me it is interesting as a picture of my mother; but what can or ought the public to care about the identity of the portrait?**
>
> **The imitator is a poor kind of creature. If the man who paints only the tree, or flower, or other surface he sees before him were an artist, the king of artists would be the photographer.**
>
> **It is for the artist to do something beyond this.**[19]

For other members of the avant-garde, the exploration of formal elements provided the expressive means to convey the inner lives of their sitters. Van Gogh wrote to his sister:

> **What fascinates me much, much more than it does all the others in my trade – is the**

portrait, the modern portrait. I am attempting it with colour, and I am certainly not alone in attempting it this way... <u>I should like</u> to do portraits which will appear as revelations to people in a hundred years' time. In other words, I am not trying to achieve this by photographic likeness but by rendering our impassioned expressions, by using our modern knowledge and the appreciation of colour as a means of rendering and exalting character.[20]

The desire to document their own times had motivated artists as diverse as Catlin, Morisot, Eakins, Watts and Van Gogh to work on uncommissioned portraits. Empiricism and the accompanying mania for the meticulous collection and classification of information, together with colonisation, gave birth to the new discipline of anthropology. This led to documentary portraits uncommissioned by their sitters. While the bulk of such enterprises took the form of photographs, Catlin had begun his self-imposed, lifetime's task of recording the vanishing tribes of North America before photography was invented:

I have designed to visit every tribe of Indians on the Continent, if my life should be spared; for the purpose of procuring portraits of distinguished Indians, of both sexes in each tribe, painted in their native costumes; accompanied with pictures of their villages, domestic habits, games, mysteries, religious ceremonies, and so forth with anecdotes, traditions, and history of their respective nations.[21]

The impetus to classify and preserve the characteristics of his age informed the enterprise of the English painter George Frederic Watts, who in 1850 set out to create a hall of fame by painting uncommissioned portraits of his most eminent contemporaries. He continued until his death in 1904 and bequeathed the project to the National Portrait Gallery in London. This MUSEUM, founded in 1856, was in itself an expression of the century's celebration of individual achievement. Not unduly concerned with physical resemblance, Watts sought to express the excellent character of his subjects. Similarly the sculptor David d'Angers toured Europe making portraits of 'Men of Genius'. Influenced by the philosopher and physiognomist Johann Caspar Lavater, he exaggerated their features as a means of conveying their greatness, for example by giving Paganini a forehead higher than he actually possessed.

Countless GENRE paintings, particularly those of single figures, were thinly disguised portraits of anonymous, often humble people. At the end of the century Van Gogh was among the first to paint named portraits of working-class subjects, such as the postman Roulin's family, in an unpatronising manner which acknowledged the sitters' inner lives.

During the later decades of the century, as the bourgeoisie grew, the demand for commissioned portraits continued to increase. More expensive than photographs, portraits were status symbols and the artist could flatter and aggrandise the sitter's persona more easily than the photographer. At the end of the century, the detailed, glasslike finish typical of earlier painters such as Ingres, Franz Winterhalter or Edward Ward had given way to a looser Naturalism practised by Emile Carolus-Duran, John Singer Sargent and Giovanni Boldini. Yet the society painters continued to present flattering likenesses of their sitters in elegant clothes and well-appointed environments.

From the prosaic to the startling, portraits spun their tale of the times. Throughout the century, the majority were dull depictions of middle-class men by uninspired middle-class men. The odd exception dazzled. As Manet recognised of Ingres, the outstanding examples could encapsulate the ethos of an era, whatever their style:

What a masterpiece that Portrait of Bertin is!...Dry! Dry! Oh come, Monsieur Ingres chose le Père Bertin as representative of an epoch. He represented him as a Buddha of the well-to-do, self-satisfied and successful bourgeoisie.[22]

See: PHOTOGRAPHY, PHYSIOGNOMY, *TÊTE D'EXPRESSION*

[1] In Lethève, p. 141

[2] 6 Aug 1840, in Delaborde, pp. 258-9

[3] See Scharf, p. 49

[4] Frith, pp. 48-9

[5] In Groseclose, p. 41

[6] *Ibid*, p. 41

[7] In Delaborde, p. 153

[8] *Ibid*

[9] In Groseclose, p. 37

[10] In Harrison and Wood, p. 94

[11] Letter to Leigh Hunt, 1838-9, in Cherry, p. 208

[12] 3 May 1854, in Courbet, p. 122

[13] In Scharf, p. 43

[14] 'On Finish: Drapery and Detail', *Lectures on Painting Delivered to the Students of the Royal Academy*, 1883, in Craig Harrison, 1999, p. 120

[15] 'Lettre à M. le Directeur de la *Revue française* sur le Salon de 1859', *Revue française*, 1859, in Baudelaire, 1965, pp. 154-5

[16] In Courthion, p. 30

[17] In Morisot, p. 82

[18] In Kendall, p. 113

[19] 'The Red Rag', *The World*, 1878, in Whistler, p. 128

[20] 3 June 1890, in Van Gogh, 1996, p. 492

[21] 'Letter from the Mouth of the Yellowstone River', *New York Commercial Advertiser*, 1832, in Harrison and Wood, pp. 135 6

[22] In Courthion, p. 9

Primitive

THE TERM PRIMITIVE WAS USED TO MEAN DIFFERENT THINGS throughout the nineteenth century. In its first decade, the *barbus* (bearded-ones) of David's studio had been called *les primitifs*, or *les penseurs* (the thinkers). Led by Maurice Quaï, they sought a return to the purity of Greek art at the time of Phidias and advocated burning all other art, to revive the 'taste for the simple, the true, the *primitive*.'[1] They upheld the seriousness of art's purpose, which was to enclose grand and eternal truths in the envelope of BEAUTY. Moreover, they carried commitment to their beliefs over into their everyday lives by growing beards and long hair and dressing in the flowing white robes, long cloaks and buskin boots seen in Greek vase paintings. To nourish their spirit and their hearts they read only Homer, the Bible and Ossian, all written during 'primitive' times.

The term 'primitive' was used in a more general sense up to the mid-nineteenth century to describe early French, Italian and Flemish Renaissance artists such as Giotto and Jean Fouquet. To a lesser extent it denoted late-Medieval European artists, all of whom were re-evaluated and increasingly admired for their unassuming, formal simplicity and directness of narrative. Hence the views expressed by Mary Cassatt in reply to the author Carl Snyder's request for information about Degas: 'I will quote you a saying of Degas – "il faut s'incliner devant les Primitives, car ils ont tous fait (we must bow down before the primitives, because they have achieved everything)."'[2] With customary acuity she followed this quotation with her own reflection: 'One thing though which is required of us they did not have, each artist a distinct technique and personality.'[3]

Such demands did indeed drive the self-conscious AVANT-GARDE of the late nineteenth century to seek out ever more unfamiliar sources of inspiration. Thus, the final meaning of the term primitive evolved at the end of the century when it was extended to denote ancient Egyptian, Persian, Indian, Javanese, Peruvian, Japanese and Celtic societies and their artefacts. These were considered to be 'closer to nature' than those of industrialised, urban societies. The pursuit of the primitive was instrumental in the avant-garde shift from naturalism towards the expressive use of formal means. The lack of illusionism found in the art of unfamiliar cultures guided the avant garde's search for a more 'authentic' and direct communication of inner states of mind. Many artists also venerated and idealised non-industrialised cultures and societies as much as their artefacts and some, like Gauguin, sought escape from the corruptions of their age by moving to more 'primitive' parts of Europe or elsewhere.

Gauguin's desire to live and paint 'like a savage' was echoed in the aesthetic of the *fin de siècle* Symbolists who valued his works as well as those of Cézanne and Van Gogh for the awkwardness, raw savagery and innocence which they found there. Hence Emile Bernard sought out what few Cézannes he could find, their very rarity contributing to their attraction:

> **At Tanguy's, number 14 rue Clauzel, in a narrow and dark shop, childish landscapes can be found; red houses in a tangle of slender branches and primitive hedges, still-lifes: apples rounded as if by compasses, triangular pears, lopsided fruit dishes, napkins folded in a rage; portraits. And all of this: bottle-green, brick-red, ochre and a launderer's blue. Harsh, unpolished, acid, these canvases are staggering... Some of them, however, have a child-like quality that awakens the precise idea of a brilliant shepherd-child like Giotto who dabbles in colours.[4]**

Cézanne himself, now a wily old man, was not above playing up to such an image of himself. When asked about oddities of perspective in his works, he told Rivière and Schneb in 1905:

> **I am a primitive, I've got a lazy eye. I presented myself twice to the École [des Beaux-Arts], but I could never get the proportions right; a head interests me, and I make it too big.[5]**

It was often a matter of conflating the 'savagery' of the work with that of the chosen way of life. Maurice Denis's tribute to the influence of Gauguin fluidly moved from one to the other:

> **He was not the sort of 'gentleman artist' that had become so distasteful to us for the past fifteen years – indeed, his sensuality was uncommon – but his works were rugged and sound... Something of the essential, of the profoundly true, emanated from his savage art, from his rough common sense, and from his vigorous naïveté... he invigorated painting again. He was for our corrupt time a kind of Poussin without classical culture, who,**

instead of serenely going to Rome to study antiquities, became inflamed by a passion to discover a tradition beneath the coarse archaism of Breton calvaries and of Maori idols, or in the crude colouring of the *Images d'Epinal*.[6]

See: EXOTIC

[1] In Delécluze, p. 90

[2] 21 April 1904, in Mathews, p. 292

[3] *Ibid*

[4] 'Paul Cézanne', *Les Hommes d'aujourd'hui*, 1891, in Harrison and Wood, p. 986

[5] P.H. Dorran, *Conversations with Cézanne*, in House and Stevens, p. 55

[6] 'The Influence of Paul Gauguin', *L'Occident*, 1903, in Chipp, p. 104

Prix de Rome

SUMMING UP HIS ROLE AS MASTER OF A PARIS *ATELIER*, Baron Gros remarked: 'My job is to mould artists and send them to Italy at the government's expense.'[1] Competing for the Grand Prix de Rome lay at the heart of French nineteenth-century art education – the numerous other competitions were seen as successive stages towards it. Winners of this coveted prize, such as David, Ingres or Gros, saw it as a step towards a successful career. The sculptor David d'Angers set off for Paris with a 40-franc loan from his drawing master saying: 'In three years' time I shall have won the Prix de Rome.'[2] And so he did.

Dating back to the seventeenth century, the Prix de Rome provided artists with a state scholarship to spend several years at the Académie de France in Rome where they were free to work by themselves and to study the very best examples of art and architecture from Antiquity and the Renaissance. The only requirement was that the artists send works back to France each year for the approval of the academicians.

Held annually, the competition consisted of two preliminary trials followed by a third for the finalists. This last entailed making a HISTORY PAINTING from a set subject while working in isolation, without access to preparatory drawings or models. It thus acted as a severe test of the aspirants' erudition as well as their competence in ANATOMY, DRAWING, painting and COMPOSITION.

In theory contenders merely had to be unmarried Frenchmen under thirty years old. But in practice no contender would catch the attention of the jury unless he had previously succeeded in the semestrial competitions held at the ÉCOLE DES BEAUX-ARTS. Hence artists had first to be accepted as students of the École, which required their joining one of the *ateliers* run by Academicians, who formed the competition jury. Favouritism, nepotism and considerations of seniority rather than merit were rampant among the jury, and the prize tended to be awarded to the most diligent emulator of an influential master.

The process was gruelling, as indicated by the experience of Paul Baudry, a student in the *atelier* of Drölling (himself a winner of the Prix de Rome). Baudry first entered for the prize in 1847. From the original 95 contestants for the first painted sketch trial, he was placed sixteenth. This entitled him to enter for the second trial and in this he came eighth out of the ten, so qualifying for the final contest in which he won the Second *Grand Prix*. This was in itself an achievement, but his final work fell short of the requirements of the ACADEMY, as Baudry wrote to his parents:

> **I was so ill advised...as not to paint with the type of brush work that has served the École des Beaux-Arts so well for all these years – that is to say I got only the second prize because I painted in my own style, instead of riding gently in, according to the accepted formula.[3]**

Such was the prize's prestige that it was normal for students to endure the humiliation of repetitive failure several years running. Funding from an artist's home municipality often rested on achieving success. For example, Chapu's scholarship from Seine-et-Oise was increased from 200 francs to 1,000 francs when he won the prize. Baudry put himself through the same process again in 1848 and in 1849, when he informed his family:

> **'If I had enough to live on I would not try so hard, for you can be a great painter without going through the mill of the Ecole de France [sic]; but what with my pension, my obligations and your wishes, I must try to get the prize sooner or later.'[4]**

The following year he finally won the prize and his municipality increased his allowance. He duly spent the next five years at the Villa Medici in Rome and went on to receive major official commissions such as the decoration of the Paris Opera, and election to the Academy in 1870. Other alumni who obtained official accolades included the painters Hippolyte Flandrin, Alexandre Cabanel and William Bouguereau, and the sculptors David d'Angers, Henri Chapu, Jean-Baptiste Carpeaux and Alexandre Falguière.

Inevitably, those who failed were more numerous than those who succeeded. The prize fostered a high degree of competence but it also encouraged academic mediocrity (as Baudry had realised) and some rebelled against its tyranny. Some such as Géricault, having failed to win it, made their own way to Rome. This route was also favoured by women artists with private means, since they were not eligible for the Prix de Rome. Others like Delacroix eschewed the competition altogether, preferring to make their mark with a strikingly original Salon début. Much later in life Delacroix confided to his diary:

> **To draw upon the imagination in order to find a way of rendering nature and its effects, and then to render them according to one's own temperament are 'vain imaginings, profitless studies' that never lead students to the Prix de Rome or to the Institute: all they have to do is to imitate the execution of Guido or Raphael, according to which one happens to be in fashion.[5]**

Not surprisingly the Realists and Impressionists rejected the academic strictures demanded by the prize. When Manet berated the professional MODEL Dubosc for taking up exaggerated, academic poses, the affronted man replied:

> **...thanks to me there is more than one student who has gone to Rome,** to which Manet retorted: **We're not in Rome now and we don't want to go there. We're in Paris – let's stay here.[6]**

Even so, late in life Renoir could still recall the ditty sung by Gleyre's students about the prominent academic artist Gérôme (even though this artist had not in fact won the Prix de Rome):

Pick up your brush, Gérôme,
Don't miss the train to Rome,
Don't forget your yellow chrome.
These men have set off
On the hunt for the big prize.[7]

For those who needed to support themselves from their work the prize had an enduring status. It continued to symbolise the path to professional success. Even towards the end of the century, when its importance had been seriously challenged by the AVANT-GARDE, the sculptor Mme Léon Bertaux could point to the disadvantages caused by the exclusion of women:

To be a Rome prize winner! Apart from providing proof of your skill in the grand manner, this means being sheltered from the most awful misfortunes, it means having in the École des Beaux-Arts a family which protects you and gives you the best teaching, free, with the most illustrious professors, which supports you initially, then encourages you, and protects you at all times.[8]

It was not until 1903 that women became eligible for the prize.

See: ACADEMY, *ATELIER*, ÉCOLE DES BEAUX-ARTS

[1] J.-B. Delestre, *Gros, sa vie et ses œuvres*, 1867, in Boime, p. 23

[2] See Lethève, p. 15

[3] C. Ephrussi, *Paul Baudry, sa vie et son œuvre*, 1887, in Boime, p. 54

[4] *Ibid*, p. 55

[5] 25 Nov 1855, in Delacroix, 1995, p. 328

[6] See Courthion, p. 4

[7] Renoir, p. 103

[8] Extract from a report to the Congrès des Œuvres et Institutions féminines du 16.7.1889, in Sauer, p. 36

Rapin

The origins of the term *rapin* are obscure, but it came into general use during the first three decades of the century. Etienne Delécluze, who entered David's *ATELIER* in the late 1790s aged fifteen, left the following definition in his memoirs:

By this name are known, in the painting studios, pupils who are still only copying drawings, and those who are drawing from the relief, that is from plaster casts of statues. By extension, and in an epigrammatic sense, it is used to designate students who are more advanced but who have neither the disposition nor the talent for their art.[1]

Writing in the early 1860s, he then says that the *rapin* is happy now, but that 50 years ago he was 'a kind of vassal, a slave even', attending to the studio's housework, having to answer to the apprentice painters' every whim and even occasionally being beaten by them.[2] In fact, they still acted as studio servants during the second half of the century: humiliations and embarrassing or cruel initiation ceremonies continued to make many a *rapin* miserable. For example, they might be made to sing songs and perform balancing exercises in the nude while being daubed with paint. Other victims would be hung upside down from ladders for hours on end. Some such pranks ended in broken limbs, and in 1843 one young man died of a heart attack. Most of them would never fulfill their desire to make their names as artists – *rapin* was ultimately used as a term for all aspiring and unsuccessful artists. Defending Manet, Zola wrote: 'I hope that people will cease to treat the man whose physiognomy I have just sketched out, as a slovenly *rapin*...[this] committed and sincere artist.'[3]

See: *ATELIER*

[1] Delécluze, p. 86

[2] *Ibid*, p. 86

[3] 'Une nouvelle manière en peinture: Edouard Manet', *L'Artiste: Revue du XIXe siècle*, 1 Jan 1867, in Zola, p. 86

Sensation

'I paint as I see, as I feel,' Cézanne claimed, 'and I have very strong sensations.'[1] The move away from a preoccupation with interpretations of subject matter towards stressing the individual artist's response to it, which was to become a major characteristic of modernism, was pioneered in the 1860s by the Impressionists. Intertwined with the concepts of sincerity, spontaneity and the individuality of the artist's TEMPERAMENT, sensation became an important critical term during the second half of the century.

Already in the 1850s, Corot had dwelled upon the importance of a sincere, personal response to the motif:

> **Reality is a part of art, but it is feeling which makes it whole. When faced with nature, begin by looking for form; then values and tonal relations, colour and execution: and subordinate the whole to your original feelings. Our feelings are as real as anything else... Any landscape, any object; we should yield to our first impression. If we have really been moved, the sincerity of our feeling will be communicated to others.**[2]

By the 1860s, spurred on by the support of progressive critics such as Zola and Castagnary, the artist's sincere, naive openness to his or her sensory response to NATURE would emerge as an important criterion of aesthetic value. In contrast to the academic painters' concern with poetic EFFECT, the Naturalists' unpremeditated response to their sensation of the motif was seen as a measure of objective TRUTH:

> **What need is there to retrace history, take refuge in legend, or scan the archives of the imagination? Beauty lies before our eyes, not in the brain; in the present, not the past; in truth and not in dream; in life and not in death. The universe before our eyes is that which the painter must represent and translate. The poetry accessible to our souls is made of all the sensations that it transmits to us.**[3]

In order to achieve this the artist would need to achieve a state of receptivity untainted by previous experience. Hence spontaneity and individuality of response became highly prized faculties. Berthe Morisot felt that art should stem from 'new, personal sensations', and that in order to allow for these it was vital for the artist to cultivate a peaceful and contemplative life: 'to daydream, is to live.'[4]

In defence of Manet, Mallarmé wrote:

One of his habitual aphorisms then is that no one should paint a landscape and a figure by the same process, with the same knowledge, or in the same fashion; nor what is more, even two landscapes or two figures. Each work should be a new creation of the mind. The hand, it is true, will conserve some of its acquired secrets of manipulation, but the eye should forget all else it has seen, and learn anew from the lesson before it. It should abstract itself from memory, seeing only that which it looks upon, and that as for the first time.[5]

In the last decades of the century, Pissarro continued to stress the importance of remaining open to one's sensations in his exhortations to his son:

It is my hope that now that you find yourself back in London, you will concentrate energetically on your studies and be able to give free play to your sensations... your problem is to discover an execution appropriate to your spirit. Do not permit yourself to be discouraged. Do not overdevelop a critical sense, and trust to your sensations blindly.[6]

In other letters he used sensation as a criterion for evaluating BEAUTY, inspiration and artistic integrity. Conversely, he denigrated Signac's work as 'very correct, very well executed, but cold and monotonous,' and found that his use of 'interlaced ribbons of colour' in the background of *Portrait of Fénéon* (1890) had 'no value from the point of view of sensation.'[7]

Yet it is, of course, Cézanne's frequent references to his *petites sensations* (little sensations) which became the most often quoted and influential. Having honed his ideas with his childhood friend Zola, he remained convinced that such naïveté and openness to the motif was the path to follow, and he passed on this advice to the young, as in the following discussion with Emile Bernard: '[Cézanne] "One must make an optic, one must see nature as no one has seen it before you."' In line with current shifts in thought, Bernard asks Cézanne to differentiate between possible interpretations of the meaning of sensations:

'But of what sensations do you speak? Of those of your feelings, or of those of your retina?'

[Cézanne] 'I think that there cannot be a separation between them; besides, being a painter I attach myself first of all to visual sensation.'[8]

Most of Cézanne's statements on art date from his dialogues with young admirers such as Bernard, who sought him out in his old age, by which time the term had become associated with the degree of intensity of the artist's individual feelings and sensations, regardless of the truth to the motif. In a tribute to Gauguin, who had died that year, Maurice Denis recalled the revelation of Sérusier's *Talisman* painted according to the advice of the older man:

Thus was introduced to us for the first time, in a paradoxical and unforgettable form, the fertile concept of the 'plane surface covered with colours assembled in a certain order.' Thus we learned that every work of art was a transposition, a caricature, the passionate equivalent of a sensation received. [9]

See: EFFECT, TEMPERAMENT

[1] See Eisenman, p. 342

[2] Notebook entry, c.1855, in Harrison and Wood, p. 535

[3] J.A. Castagnary, 'Le Monde artistique. Salon de 1867', *Liberté*, 1867, in Harrison and Wood, p. 414

[4] In Yeldham, p. 355

[5] S. Mallarmé, 'The Impressionists and Edouard Manet', *The Art Monthly Review and Photographic Portfolio*, 30 Sept 1876, in Harrison and Wood, p. 587

[6] 7 June 1893, in Pissarro, p. 209

[7] 30 March 1891, *ibid*, p. 156

[8] E. Bernard, 'Une conversation avec Cézanne', *Mercure de France*, CXLVIII, 1921, in Chipp, pp. 12-13

[9] M. Denis, 'The Influence of Paul Gauguin', *L'Occident*, 1903, *ibid*, p. 101

Still Life

With supreme disdain Ingres made one of his rare references to the subject-matter which academicians had long regarded as being the lowest of them all: '...draw, paint, above all imitate, even if this be still life. Everything imitated from nature is a work, and this imitation leads to art.'[1] Academic theory placed still life at the very bottom of its hierarchy of subject-matter. Theorists and critics thus rarely discussed it and it had low professional status. Yet it was popular in the market-place. This ambivalent status can be traced back to the ancient Greeks. According to Pliny, the painter Pyreicus was supremely skilful but marred his own success by depicting only humble subjects, so earning the insulting name *rhyparagraphos* (a painter of filth or rubbish). Even so, his works sold for higher prices than bigger works by other artists.

Definitions differ but at its simplest, still life meant the depiction of inanimate, manufactured or organic objects. No paintings from Greek antiquity survived, and as a living tradition it evolved from depictions of attributes within religious and portrait paintings in the sixteenth century. It blossomed into a major category of subject-matter in the secular art of seventeenth-century Republican Holland, where the term *stilleven* (still life) first appeared in the later part of the century. Hitherto pictures had been identified according to the category of their subjects (e.g. kitchen pieces, flowers, products of the hunt). In France, the term *nature morte* (dead nature) did not emerge until the eighteenth century and only came into common use in the nineteenth century.

Still life was disparaged as an inferior GENRE by painters like Reynolds. According to academic theory it could not convey complex philosophical and moral themes – these were best shown by narratives of human endeavour. Moreover, still life had long been associated with meticulous renderings of the textures and surfaces of the material world; such technical virtuosity was considered a distraction from the generalisations demanded of serious subjects. In fact still lifes had long conveyed ideas and beliefs. For example, perishable fruit and flowers might symbolise the ephemeral seductions of earthly life in Dutch seventeenth-century *vanitas* paintings.

Such possibilities did not occur to those who considered it an eminently suitable subject for women artists. Still life needed no education in the classics, no knowledge of ANATOMY or of the NUDE, and its pursuit did not challenge the norms of social decorum. Above all, it demanded manual dexterity rather than abstract thought. Its appeal was to the 'female' realm of sensory pleasure rather than to the higher, 'male' realm of mental pleasure. By the second half of the eighteenth century, the art of still life (and flower painting in particular) was seen as a genteel accomplishment for bourgeois women, and this was still the case in the following century. The writer Léon Legrange explained:

Let women occupy themselves with those kinds of art they have always preferred... the paintings of flowers, those prodigies of grace and freshness which alone can compete with the grace and freshness of women themselves.[2]

Still life remained a popular subject for amateur and professional women painters throughout the nineteenth century. This association did nothing to enhance its official status. Reviewing Berthe Morisot's still life, in her second year of submitting work to the Salon, the critic Paul Mantz voiced widely held assumptions:

Since it is not necessary to have had a long training in draughtsmanship at the Academy to paint a copper pot, a candlestick and a bunch of radishes, women succeed quite well in this domestic type of painting. *Mlle Berthe Morisot* **brings to the task really a great deal of frankness with a delicate feeling for light and colour.**[3]

In the opening decade of the nineteenth century its prestige was at its lowest. David's civic idealism had little room for such a domestic, non-didactic genre, and few still lifes were exhibited at the official Salons, one of the exceptions being the late works of Anne Vallayer-Coster. However, the Romantics did turn to it. As young men Géricault and Delacroix had been inspired by Snyders's hunting still lifes at the Musée Napoléon (1802-15) and had painted some works in the same manner. Goya painted at least ten still lifes, mostly of birds, game and fish. It was an opportunity to celebrate the wonders of the natural world and to challenge academic canons. In 1849, when Delacroix exhibited some flower paintings at the Salon, he explained to the painter Constant Dutilleux the difference between his own approach and that of traditional flower paintings in the Louvre. These showed masterly execution, but the details were too highly elaborated:

I have been working in exactly the opposite way to the... works in question, and I have subordinated details to the whole as far as possible. I tried to get away from the convention which seems to condemn anyone who paints flowers to reproduce the same vase with the same columns of fantastic draperies to serve as background or provide contrast. I have tried to paint bits of nature as we see them in gardens, only assembling within the same frame and in a fairly probable manner the greatest possible variety of flowers.[4]

Nevertheless still life remained a minor preoccupation for him, as for other Romantics. It was the Realists who truly revived the genre in the 1850s and 1860s, to the extent that Manet could declare still life to be 'the touchstone of the painter'.[5] The Realist interest in depictions of everyday life led to the reappraisal of Chardin and Dutch seventeenth-century still lifes. The large collection of Chardin still lifes, which entered the Louvre with the La Caze bequest in 1869, provided further stimulation, notably for Manet and Cézanne. Motivated by progressive egalitarianism, the socialist Thoré published a pioneering, two-volume study of Dutch art, in which he devoted a section to 'painters of ordinary things.' He questioned the negative connotations of the term 'still life' and made a plea for raising its status:

It is in vain that we struggle against this nasty appellation *nature morte...* **everything is in a constant state of metamorphosis....The wine in this crystal glass evaporates in the sun**

and joins the invisible – this gold box erodes in contact with the Oriental rug on which it is placed. This sword of Damascus attracts moist atoms and becomes sheathed in an envelope of rust and this coat of rust will devour the blade of steel... Everything acts and reacts in the ongoing whirlwind of the universe. Everything is an object and a being at the same time, a work as well as a worker. There is no such thing as 'nature morte'.[6]

The Goncourt brothers also called for art to be of its time and championed Chardin and the Dutch school, but they were motivated by apolitical aestheticism and nostalgia for the Rococo era. In their reassessment, *Art in the Eighteenth Century* (published in instalments, 1859-75), they excluded David and praised Chardin for his sharp and true observation from the real world. His still lifes, they believed, had raised this 'second rate' genre to the highest consideration. Manet's justification for his love of still life showed similar impatience with the pretensions of history painting, as in this observation made during a trip to Venice in 1874:

These Italians bore one after a time with their allegories and their *Gerusalemme Liberata* and *Orlando Furioso*, and all that rubbish. A painter can say all he wants to with fruit or flowers or even clouds... You know, I should like to be the Saint Francis of still life.[7]

As with LANDSCAPE painting, the low status of still life provided a quiet backwater in which AVANT-GARDE artists could try out experimental techniques without courting controversy. Manet's advice to Philippe Burty links the genre with a concern for visual perception:

Concentrate on tonal values. While you are looking at it (the arrangement), and particularly as you are giving thought to the manner in which best to capture what has struck you about it, that is, in such a way as to have the same effect on the viewer that it had on you... when you focus on the whole, you wouldn't think of counting the individual scales on the salmon, right? You will see them as little pearls, their silver set against grey and rose. Isn't that so? Look at the rose tones of this salmon with its bone, white at the centre amid degrees of mother-of-pearl grey.[8]

A still-life motif was immobile; its moods and expression did not change; the objects could be relatively cheap and the painting could be executed in the relatively steady light of the studio. These were important advantages for the Realist committed to working from life. Fantin-Latour, whose reputation was built on his still lifes, wrote of his 'horror of movement, of animated scenes, and the difficulty of painting in the open air with the sun and the shade.'[9] Of all genres, still life gave the greatest aesthetic control over the motif. Artists could organize the formal aspects of their work before making a mark on the canvas. It was perfect for artists concerned with formal experimentation, and Cézanne for one made it central to his output. Louis Le Bail witnessed him carefully arranging some peaches, a napkin and a glass of red wine:

The cloth was very slightly draped upon the table, with innate taste. Then Cézanne arranged the fruits, contrasting the tones against the other, making the complementaries vibrate, the greens against the reds, the yellows against the blues, tipping, turning, balancing the fruits as he wanted them to be, using coins of one or two *sous* for the purpose. He brought to this task the greatest care and many precautions.[10]

The fast-growing bourgeoisie provided an avid market for still lifes, perhaps partly because it seemed to be more neutral in ideological meaning. What could be more suitable than innocuous bowls of fruit for the dining room, flower-pieces for the hall or hunt trophies for the billiard room? Even the avant-garde could find buyers relatively easily. As Courbet pointed out in a letter: 'I have done four...flower paintings. Flowers are making me a mint...'[11] Similarly, Monet turned to still lifes between 1878 and 1882 because they sold more easily than other types of painting.

Yet most of the public continued to favour a high degree of illusionism and the majority of artists catered for this demand. Moreover, the official art world continued to view still life as a minor art. As such it was sometimes used as a means of breaking into the Salon. The American painter May Alcott, for example, had her first Salon acceptance in 1877 for *Apples, blue jug and flask of Maraschino*. In a letter home she expressed surprise that it had not been rejected:

...these French students paint most elaborately arranged eastern stuffs, Venetian glass, brass, armour, on an immense scale, and give much time to it, finishing every detail most perfectly.[12]

In 1883 Edward Armitage made a plea for a mild degree of departure from high FINISH:

...a picture which is not an exact counterpart of the object portrayed, but leaves something to be imagined, is generally more interesting than a more perfect copy would be.

This fact is particularly noticeable in pictures of flowers, fruit and still life generally.[13]

By this time the avant-garde was moving from such naturalism towards the suggestive and expressive potential of the subject. Van Gogh began work on a series of sunflowers to welcome Gauguin:

Now that I hope to live with Gauguin in a studio of our own, I want to make a decoration for the studio. Nothing but big sunflowers... if I carry out this idea there will be a dozen panels. So the whole thing will be a symphony in blue and yellow.[14]

In the first article to be published on Van Gogh the Symbolist critic Albert Aurier discovered expressive and symbolic meaning in his work:

...he is...pressed by the need to give his ideas precise, palpable, tangible forms, dense, fleshy, physical envelopes. In almost all his canvases, under this form... there lies,... a thought, an Idea... As for the brilliant and dazzling symphonies of colour and line, whatever their importance in the eyes of the painter, they are but simple expressive *means* simple *processes* of symbolisation... Likewise this obsessive passion both for the sun, which he makes shimmer in the fiery glow of his skies and for that other sun, that vegetable heavenly body, the sumptuous sunflower, which he repeats tirelessly, like a monomaniac – how can one explain it without admitting his preoccupation with a vague and glorious heliomythical allegory?[15]

In a modest thank-you letter, explaining that Gauguin and Monticelli's works were more powerful than his own, Van Gogh nevertheless confirmed his intention to symbolise an idea. After Gauguin left, he wrote:

I tried to paint 'his empty place'.

It is a study of his wooden armchair, brown and dark red, the seat of greenish straw, and in place of the absent person, a lighted candle in a candlestick and some modern novels.[16]

The Symbolists held Cézanne's still lifes in such high regard that Maurice Denis placed one (owned by Gauguin), at the centre of his group portrait *Homage to Cézanne* (1900). They saw in them a wild abandon, a mystery, which delighted them. Huysmans wrote of Cézanne:

> **In full illumination, in porcelain compotes or on white cloths, brutal, rough pears and apples, shaped with a trowel, intensified with twists of the thumb. Seen close to, a rough assemblage of vermilion and yellow, of green and blue; from a distance, the correct one, fruits meant for Chevet's show windows, full-flavoured and savoury, enviable.**
>
> **And truths unnoticed, until then become apparent, strange and true tones, *taches* with a singular authenticity, shadings on the table linen, vassals of the shadows spreading from the curves of the fruits and scattered in vague and charming traceries of blue which make these canvases, works which initiate one into mysteries, when compared to the usual still lifes embossed in bitumen on unintelligible backgrounds.[17]**

Having entered the nineteenth century as the lowliest of subjects, still life left it under the spotlight of the avant-garde. At the beginning of the next century the Cubists would further elevate its status.

See: COLOUR, FINISH, NATURE, SENSATION, TOUCH

[1] Delaborde, p. 115

[2] 'Du rang des femmes dans l'art', *Gazette des Beaux-Arts*, 1860, in Parker and Pollock, p. 54

[3] 'Salon de 1865', *Gazette des Beaux-Arts*, 1865, Shennon, p. 63

[4] 6 Feb 1849, in Delacroix, 1971, p. 287

[5] J.E. Blanche, *Propos de peinture: de David à Degas*, 1919, in Mauner, p. 12

[6] T. Thoré, *Les musées de la Hollande*, Paris, 1858-60, in Mauner, pp. 37-8

[7] A. Vollard, *Reminiscences of a Picture Dealer*, 1936, in Mauner, p. 12

[8] See Mauner, pp. 24-5

[9] Letter 1875, in Lucie-Smith, p. 22

[10] In House and Stevens, p. 55

[11] April 1863, in Courbet, p. 220

[12] See Fink, pp. 250-1

[13] In Armitage, p. 177

[14] Late Aug 1888, in Roskill, p. 284

[15] 'Les isolés – Vincent Van Gogh', *Mercure de France*, Jan 1890, in Dorra, p. 223

[16] To A. Aurier, 10 or 11 Feb 1890, in Van Gogh, 1996, p. 480

[17] J.K. Huysmans, in Holt, 1986, p. 488

Sublime

The degree of seriousness of intent and lack of irony which underlay the aesthetic concept of the sublime, locates it firmly within a pre-modernist age. In late antiquity, Longinus had identified the sublime as an overpowering and mysterious form of BEAUTY, a source of aesthetic pleasure which could provide an insight into the divine. Although Boileau had rediscovered Longinus in the seventeenth century, it was to be Edmund Burke's reconsideration that made the concept influential in the late eighteenth and early nineteenth centuries. As a student, the future conservative statesman wrote *A Philosophical Inquiry into the Origin of our Ideas of the Sublime and Beautiful* (1757), which ran into 13 editions before his death in 1799.

Taking a more psychological approach than Longinus, Burke sought to unearth the source of human emotions in relation to aesthetic experience. He identified our most powerful feelings as love and hate, expressed as attraction and repulsion. Spawned by love, attractiveness aroused the sense of beauty, which Burke characterised as roundness, smoothness, tenderness and harmony. Born of hate, it was repulsiveness which aroused a sense of the sublime, which Burke associated with such phenomena as excessive size, gloom, disproportion, the infinitely great, sudden noise, intolerable stenches or bitter tastes. So initially overwhelming were such experiences, that rational thought was momentarily dislocated. When imaginatively relived, or aesthetically mediated, such phenomena became a source of pleasurable terror.

Sublime being initially understood in terms of an aesthetic response to NATURE (a thundering cataract being the most commonly given example), artists such as James Barry, William Blake, Henri Fuseli and Turner had soon encompassed the concept in their works. In paintings such as *Snow Storm: Hannibal and his Army Crossing the Alps* (1812), Turner depicted the uncontrollable and incomprehensible forces of nature. The violent light and weather of a tempest transform the human protagonists, including Hannibal himself, into inconspicuous specks, within the awesome chasms and peaks of the mountains.

The Romantics were suitably repulsed and attracted by Burke's theory. As late as 1857, an ageing Delacroix voiced the attitudes of his youth, focusing on irregularity and lack of proportion as characteristic of the sublime:

> **…the Antin oak looks unimpressive from a distance because its shape is symmetrical and because the mass of foliage is in proportion to the trunk and the spread of branches, but when I stood beneath the branches and could see only portions of the tree unrelated to the whole, I experienced a sensation of the *Sublime*.**[1]

For the American Romantic, Thomas Cole, the unregulated and 'untouched' American wilderness lifted it into the sublime:

> **He who stands on Mont Albano and looks down on ancient Rome, has his mind peopled with the gigantic associations of the storied past; but he who stands on the mounds of the West, the most venerable remains of American antiquity, may experience the emotion of the sublime, but it is the sublimity of a shoreless ocean un-islanded by the recorded deed of man.**[2]

The Romantics' disappointment at the lack of political and social progress, despite recent breakthroughs in the theories of those fields, had led them to question the stress on rational thought, and to view scientific discoveries with such suspicion that Mary Shelley had invented *Frankenstein* (1818). Their preoccupation with the disturbing led to the popularity of such 'sublime' subjects as Milton's *Paradise Lost*. Milton's Satan, Burke's favourite example of the aesthetically mediated sublime, became a symbol of mankind's creative intelligence, soured by self-destructiveness. This subject was chosen by Blake, Barry and Fuseli. Similarly, the fascination with the ruined civilisations of the ancient East embodied the sublime power of mankind over nature but also the ultimate downfall of such grandiose achievements. The popular visionary landscapes of John Martin showed such subjects as the Pyramids, the Ruins of Palmyra and the Caves of Elephanta. In 1827, in the catalogue for his exhibition of *The Fall of Nineveh*, depicting the terror of impending destruction, Martin explained the scene:

> **The mighty cities of Nineveh and Babylon have passed away. The accounts of their great-ness and splendour may have been exaggerated. But, where strict truth is not essential, the mind is content to find delight in the contemplation of the grand and the marvel-lous... Seen through the mist of ages, the great becomes gigantic, the *wonderful* swells into the *sublime*.**[3]

Moreover, the sheer suggestiveness of the sublime attracted the Romantics. In his notes for a dictionary of art Delacroix defined its evocative power: 'The *Sublime*: effect of vagueness in the churches in Dieppe at night, on the sea; the spectacle on a lovely night.'[4] Yet together with other Romantics he was also critical of the concept, linking it to 'the terrible', and warning of the bad taste and even absurdity to which it could give rise: '*The Terrible* is like the *Sublime*, it must never be abused.'[5]

Blake associated Burke's *Treatise on the Sublime* with the dry academic theories of art in Reynolds's *Discourses* (1798) to which he was so passionately opposed. In the annotations to his own copy of this work he recalled having read Burke when young:

> **Burke's treatise on the Sublime & Beautiful is founded on the Opinions of Newton & Locke. on [sic] this Treatise Reynolds has grounded many of his assertions in all his Discourses... I felt the Same Contempt & Abhorrence then; that I do now. They mock Inspiration & Vision Inspiration & Vision was then & now is & I hope will always Remain my Element my Eternal Dwelling place. How can I then hear it Contemnd [sic] without returning Scorn for Scorn.**[6]

For the early Naturalists the concept of the sublime was scoffed at as being mere artifice and fantasy. Constable cited with approval his artist friend, John Jackson's statement:

'The whole object and difficulty of [the] art...is to *unite imagination with nature*.' Adding that they had been discussing John Martin and others he continued, 'art now is filled with *phantasmagoria*.' [7]

Nevertheless, the classical concept of aesthetic stimulation resulting from a single entity of beauty had been challenged and extended; moreover the sublime was soon joined by Gilpin's concept of the PICTURESQUE. Yet both ideas only acted as interim categories of aesthetic experience; they were soon superseded by the French and German Romantics' denial of the idea of universal taste itself. In what was to become a major credo of Romanticism, the Preface to his play *Cromwell* (1827), Victor Hugo extended the concept, associated it with the modern and ultimately challenged its definition:

> **...the modern spirit is born out of this fecund union of the categories of the grotesque and the sublime: a spirit complex, and infinitely varied in its manifestations, inexhaustible in its creativity, totally opposed to the uniform simplicity of the genius of the Ancients.**[8]

To the sober-minded Realists and Naturalists of the mid-century, in their mud-caked boots, the concept was too histrionic, or merely irrelevant, and the term was increasingly used simply to denote the idea of perfection within the broader concept of beauty. Indeed the term had long been used in this more general sense alongside the more specific Burkian concept. Towards the end of the century, Whistler denigrated the Burkian meaning of the term for the cliché which it had become: '...how dutifully the casual in Nature is accepted as sublime, may be gathered from the unlimited admiration daily produced by a very foolish sunset.'[9]

See: BEAUTY, LANDSCAPE, NATURE, PICTURESQUE

[1] 25 Jan 1857, in Delacroix, 1995, p. 369

[2] 'Essay on American Scenery', *American Monthly Magazine*, 1 Jan 1836, in Harrison and Wood, p. 137

[3] In Klingender, p. 105

[4] 25 Jan 1857, in Delacroix, 1995, p. 368

[5] *Ibid*, p. 369

[6] 'Marginalia to Reynolds' *Discourses*', c.1808, in Taylor, p. 152

[7] Letter to Fisher, 4 July 1829, in Leslie, p. 152

[8] In Harrison and Wood, p. 46

[9] '10 O'Clock Lecture', 1885, in Whistler, p. 144

Temperament

When Baudelaire first met Manet and visited his studio, he immediately realised how gifted he was, yet he confided to a friend his anxiety that the painter might lack the strength of character to fight the dominant critical climate:

> **He never will be able to fill completely the certain gaps in his temperament –** *but he has temperament* **– that's the important thing.**[1]

Although Baudelaire's published art criticism had ended in 1863, his acuity of judgement had not. He had identified a characteristic which would become an important aesthetic criterion among the AVANT-GARDE of the 1870s and one which would continue to preoccupy artists until the end of the century.

It was Zola who famously concluded the final article of his 1866 Salon series by defining a work of art as 'a corner of the universe seen through a temperament'.[2] Linked to the individualism of the age, this was an attitude which confronted the academic artist's reliance on absolute, timeless canons of beauty by offering the modern idea of a more objective TRUTH to NATURE mediated through the changeable variety of the individual artist's response. Zola thus identified the beginning of the modernist shift of emphasis away from subject matter towards execution. In the third of his 1866 Salon articles, 'The moment in art', he contrasted his own credo with the taste of the general public, which demanded nothing more of the artist than a subject that 'moves the heart to delight or to horror':

> **To me – and I hope to many – a work of art is, on the contrary a personality, an individual. I don't ask that the artist give me tender visions or horrible nightmares, I ask him to give himself, heart and body, to affirm loudly a powerful and personal spirit, a strong harsh character, who seizes nature in his two hands and sets it down before us as he sees it...**
> **It is no longer a question here, therefore, of pleasing or not pleasing, it is a question of being oneself, of baring one's breast, of energetically forging one's individuality.**[3]

In the final article he praised Monet's *Camille* (1866) on these grounds:

> **Ah yes! here is temperament, here is a man amidst a crowd of eunuchs. Look at the neighbouring canvases, see what a poor showing they make next to this window opened on**

nature. Here there is more than a realist, there is a delicate and strong interpreter.[4]

Forming a central place in his combative art criticism, this was an attitude shared by the Impressionists whom he championed – Pissarro, for example, who referred to the importance of temperament in relating a story about Cézanne's sour, personal attacks on his erstwhile Impressionist colleagues:

> **Pissarro is an old fool, Monet a cunning fellow, they have nothing in them... I am the only one with temperament, I am the only one who can make a red!**

Pissarro excused his old pal on the grounds that he was ill and added:

> **Is it not sad and a pity that a man endowed with such a beautiful temperament should have so little balance?**[5]

While towards the end of his life Cézanne wrote to Emile Bernard:

> **The Louvre is the book in which we learn to read. We must not, however, be satisfied with retaining the beautiful formulas of our illustrious predecessors... let us strive to express ourselves according to our personal temperament.**[6]

Outside the Impressionist circle, Huysmans used the term in 1880 when he granted a critical accolade to the virtuoso naturalist, Alfred-Philippe Roll:

> **This is an artist we should take an interest in, because his works denote a temperament... this year, he gives us a modern canvas full of qualities and faults, but a canvas which is by him and by him alone: which is surely the greatest eulogy I can make.**[7]

The individualism of this stance was echoed in the advice given by William Morris Hunt, the Bostonian disciple of Couture and Millet, to his students:

> **Let Raphael and Titian draw the same nose, and their drawings will be totally unlike. *You* don't see with *my* eyes: *I* don't see with *yours*. Let each see with his own, and let his attempt to render what he sees be respected!**[8]

However, there were also those who challenged such an individualist outlook. By the end of the century a diluted form of Impressionism had become absorbed into academic teaching and informed the palatable offerings in a multitude of official exhibitions. In his challenge to such naturalism the Symbolist Maurice Denis, searching for an art based upon universal values which would transcend singular individualism, attacked Zola's now famous dictum:

> **...does one want to compare the hypothetical and imagined plenitude of the original effect with the mere notation of that effect by such and such a consciousness? Here the great question of temperament presents itself: 'Art is nature seen through a temperament.'**

> **A very just definition because it is very vague, and which leaves uncertain the important point, the criterion of temperaments. The painting of M. Bouguereau is nature seen through a temperament. M. Raffaëlli is an extraordinary observer, but do you think he is sensitive to beautiful forms and colours? Where does the 'painter' temperament begin and end?...**

> **Before exteriorising sensations such as those, it would be necessary to determine their value from the point of view of beauty.**[9]

Yet the concept remained important, for those who no longer linked it to the Impressionists' concern with truth to nature, but associated it with the avant-garde assertion of the right to self-realisation through pure artistic freedom. Hence in the same year as Denis's attack, Oscar Wilde wrote:

> **...a healthy work of art is one the choice of whose subject is conditioned by the temperament of the artist, and comes directly out of it. In fine, a healthy work of art is one that has both perfection and personality... An unhealthy work of art, on the other hand, is a work whose style is obvious, old-fashioned and common, and whose subject is deliberately chosen, not because the artist has any pleasure in it, but because he thinks that the public will pay him for it.**[10]

See: EFFECT, SENSATION, TRUTH

[1] Letter to Mme Paul Meurice, 24 May 1865, in Courthion, p. 52

[2] 'Mon Salon', *L'Evénement*, 1866, in Holt, 1986, p. 388

[3] *Ibid*, p. 380

[4] *Ibid*, p. 386

[5] Letter to Lucien Pissarro, 20 Jan 1896, in Pissarro, p. 280

[6] 1905, in Cézanne, p. 315

[7] 'Le Salon officiel en 1880', in Lemaire, p. 250

[8] In Hunt, pp. 14-15

[9] 'Définition du Néo-traditionisme', *Art et Critique*, 1890, in Chipp, p. 96

[10] *The Soul of Man Under Socialism*, 1890, in Wilde, pp. 1093-4

Tête d'expression

The successful *tête d'expression* aimed to convey specific meaning through the facial expression, PHYSIOGNOMY and posture of its human subject. Charles Le Brun, one of the founders of the Academy in seventeenth-century France, had first evolved his theory of physiognomic expression, in which he established rules for conveying the passions through the *tête d'expression*. Such a skill was vital to a figurative art concerned with the personification of ideas and the imparting of narrative, and Le Brun's theories continued to form part of standard academic teaching throughout the nineteenth century. However, by then they had been enriched and redefined by Lavater, the Swiss theologian and philosopher associated with the German *Sturm und Drang* (Storm and Stress) movement. In the late eighteenth century he had established the relationship between the expression of the individual's character and his or her physiognomy, and his writings proved to be widely influential throughout the following century in Europe and North America. Hence Ingres would note that 'the drooping nostril is a beautiful means of expression, it indicates tranquility.'[1]

The *Prix de la Tête d'Expression* had been founded by the Compte de Caylus in 1760, and students at the ÉCOLE DES BEAUX-ARTS continued to compete eagerly for the prize in the nineteenth century. From 1815 students were asked to execute their works in paint rather than black pencil or pastel, as before. Carried out in three sessions of six hours each, the subject matter would be emotions such as *Fear* (1842 contest) or *Resignation* (1878 contest). In 1835

Manet's future teacher, Thomas Couture, won the prize.

As with all academic practices, the *têtes d'expression* were open to accusations of rigidity and aridity. Edward Armitage, a British history painter who had studied in Paris under Delaroche, barely deigned to mention the perennial problem of how to convey specific emotions through facial expression. In publishing his lectures at London's Royal Academy Schools (1876-82), he dismissed as 'ridiculous and useless' the works of Le Brun and Lavater. There was only one piece of advice that he could provide on this important matter:

Nature is the only book we ought to consult if we wish truly to depict the effects of anger, fear, love and all the other human passions.[2]

However, the innovative Degas continued to find the idea of expressing character through physical attributes a viable challenge. In a notebook written between 1868 and 1872, he expressed his ambitions:

Do portraits of people in familiar and typical attitudes. Above all give to their faces the same choice of expression that one gives to their bodies. Thus if laughter is the hallmark of a person make him laugh. Of course, there are feelings that one can't render, from considerations of propriety; portraits not being just for us, painters.

What fine nuances there are to establish. All this gets revived in this unfortunate *têtes* [sic] *d'expression*. (A prize endlessly contested.) The mystery of the *Belle Feronnière* is not the repose of the figure but her expression.[3]

See: GENRE, HISTORY PAINTING

[1] In Delaborde, p. 131

[2] *Lectures on Painting: Delivered to the Students of the Royal Academy, London*, 1883, in Craig Harrison, p. 7

[3] Notebook 23, in Harrison and Wood, p. 566. The *Belle Feronnière* is a painting in the Louvre once attributed to Leonardo da Vinci.

Tone

It is not possible to define the term tone (*valeur*) in isolation, since it was so closely intertwined with the terms shading, modelling, *ton* (value) and CHIAROSCURO (*clair-obscur*), all of which also described the use of gradations from light to dark. The term really came into its own from around the middle of the nineteenth century. For Corot, for example, tone was paramount:

...colour for me, comes afterwards: because above all I love the overall totality, harmony in the tones; whereas colour can sometimes be jarring, which I don't like. Perhaps it is from an excess of this principle which causes some to say that I often use leaden tones.[1]

Corot's re-evaluation of the function of tone played a major role in the sketch-finish debate.

Nevertheless, the cross-hatching miseries inflicted upon the novice art student testify to the importance of tone within academic theory. Most students would end up working as jobbing illustrators who would need to know how to make their subjects look solid in monochrome drawings for engravings. Engravings remained the dominant reprographic visual language until photographic reproduction processes became widely used during the last decades of the century. Hence a student's move from copying flat prints to DRAWING from casts was a matter of mastering very precisely perceived modulations of tone.

Amaury-Duval related that when he progressed to drawing from the plaster casts (*à la bosse*), his teacher Ingres kept insisting on the *demi-teintes* (half tones):

> **To me, a plaster cast looked white when in the light and dark when in shadow; and it is a curious thing that the unpractised eye does not perceive what we call 'modelling', that is, the transition from light to shade by means of half-tones.**[2]

Moreover, competing with the illusionism of PHOTOGRAPHY from 1839 raised the issue of fine tonal gradation to a higher pitch.

Academic theory viewed tone as a scale of values from light to dark which allowed the artist to create illusions of solidity in individual objects, each of which was understood to have its own value within the tonal scale:

> **For instance, in the chiaroscuro of a picture representing a collection of fruit, an orange would have less 'value' than a lemon because the colour of the latter is the more luminous. In this way, every object of visible nature possesses a degree of lightness or darkness which gives its place in the chiaroscuro scale, together with a value which is also called its tone'.**[3]

In addition, the overall EFFECT of a picture was considered to be dependent on the arbitrary organisation of tonal contrasts. Corot, however, established the overall harmony of his paintings in terms of broad swathes of tonal contrast, which were based upon observations from the motif in his *PLEIN-AIR* studies. He said that he would work in a gradation of about twenty tones. But that was in the finished works. In the studies and sketches (which were also bought and exhibited) he advocated TRUTH to the first impression. This approach encouraged discerning viewers to perceive tonal relationships, which in themselves unified the canvas without too many half tones. Alfred Robaut passed on Corot's advice to a novice:

> **...it lacks emphasis. The tones are indecisive. That must not happen. It is better to exaggerate, and in the opposite way. Take pure black and pure white too, if you want. You will be too harsh. But harshness is better in a beginner than mushiness.**[4]

It is not surprising to discover that Bracquemond credited Corot with the modern notion of *valeur*, which undermined a more traditional concept of chiaroscuro based on an arbitrary arrangement of light and shade. In their *plein-air* studies Corot, Daubigny and others had noticed that many effects in NATURE depended on sharp transitions of tone, with no half tones to unify them, so that what mattered most was the relationship of tones to each other rather than their function as a means of suggesting relief.

Like the academicians Couture also stressed the importance of subtle modelling via the use of many *demi-teintes*:

> **You must establish what I call 'dominants' for light and shade effects...find your strongest and deepest black and use as a guide or tuning fork to establish the values of your other shadows and half-tones.**[5]

Yet his sympathetic respect for the freshness of the first touch depended on a finely tuned sense of tone in terms of COLOUR: 'The most effective colour scheme is perhaps that based on an exact observation of values.'[6]

Such teaching was to prove highly influential. One of Couture's students, William Morris Hunt, would teach a generation of Americans in Boston to be bold and uncompromising:

> **Get a good solid tone! That criss-cross of lines doesn't mean anything, unless it is a snowstorm! If you want black, make it black. If you want white, make it white. Don't be afraid...[7]**

Yet all of the above artists continued to use half tones within their finished works. It was of course Manet, Couture's most famous student, who took the radical step of dismissing the *demi-teintes* in his finished works. They had become for him a finicky irrelevance which distracted from the beauties of ephemeral effects captured in the first fresh moment. Moreover, he realised that colour would sing if it was not attenuated by tonal gradations. Antonin Proust recalled a studio debate, in which Couture complained that Manet refused to represent the intermediate tones beween light and dark. Manet replied:

> **...light appeared to the human eye with a unity such that a single tone was sufficient to render it; moreover it was preferable, crude though it might seem, to pass suddenly from light to darkness rather than accumulate features that the eye does not see and which not only weaken the force of light but attenuate the colouring of shadows which it is important to emphasise. For the colouring of dark areas is not uniform, but extremely varied.[8]**

Manet retained the academic concept of the importance of an intense effect in terms of light and dark, but he divorced this concept from that of *demi-teintes*. In doing so he saw colour in tone. Rather than working to a formula, painting increasingly became an investigation into such relationships, leading to the Impressionists' merging of tone and colour. In 1876 Cézanne wrote to Pissarro from l'Estaque:

> **The sun here is so tremendous that it seems to me as if the objects were silhouetted not only in black and white, but in blue, red, brown and violet. I may be mistaken, but this seems to me to be the opposite of modelling.[9]**

While the avant-garde discovered that the actual facture of a painting can become a source of pleasure and truth in depicting the subject, the closely graduated *demi-teintes* of the academic tradition lived on. Here is Jules Breton, writing at the end of the century on the importance of modelling:

> **It adapts itself to the feelings of every artist, or rather it is the chief carrier of his feelings...** *Modelling, combined with proportion, is the whole of drawing; and, combined with the relationship of values, it forms the whole splendid orchestration of the effect which is improperly called chiaroscuro.*[10]

See: CHIAROSCURO, COMPOSITION, DRAWING, EFFECT, *PLEIN-AIR*

[1] Cailler, I, p. 98

[2] E.-E. Amaury-Duval, *L'atelier d'Ingres*, 1924, in Boime, p. 28

[3] C. Blanc, *Grammaire des arts du dessin*, 1867, in Boime, p. 151

[4] Cailler, I, pp. 91-2

5 T. Couture, *Méthode et entretiens d'atelier*, 1867, in Boime, *op. cit.*, pp. 28-9

6 *Ibid*, p. 151

7 In Hunt, p. 28

8 A. Proust, *Edouard Manet, souvenirs*, 1913, in Boime, p. 30

9 2 July 1876, in Cézanne, p. 146

10 J. Breton, *Un peintre paysan*, 1896, in Boime, p. 29

Touch

The reappraisal of Velasquez by artists such as Cassatt and Manet during the 1860s resulted in part from their questioning of the academic tendency to play down the role of touch. The way in which the artist laid paint on canvas, or handled the surface of clay, was bound up with the sketch-FINISH debate, which in turn raised the crucial question of whether art should appeal to the mind or to the senses. Ingres and his teacher David favoured smooth surfaces. According to the classical stance, which became that of the academies, showing one's brush-work constituted a lapse of professional propriety. The parading of one's virtuosity was vulgar and, more seriously, it interfered with the purity of the cerebral communication of a work's content by titillating the senses. Like colour, touch was distractingly seductive, feminine and untrustworthy. Hence Ingres would tell his students that any comparison between the Dutch and Flemish painters and the divine Raphael was blasphemous: 'there is something of the butcher in Rubens; fresh flesh is foremost in his thoughts.'[1]

Yet in England early in the century, Turner swashbuckled his way across vast canvases with encrustations of pigment and Constable allowed his swirls and dabs of paint to accumulate in his finished pictures. Three of Constable's works, including *The Hay Wain* (1821), would cause a sensation at the 1824 Paris Salon, and the artist won a gold medal. He wrote to his friend, the Rev. Fisher, that his works were much admired by French artists:

> **[They]…acknowledge the richness of texture, and the attention to the surface of things. They are struck with their vivacity and freshness, things unknown in their own pictures.**[2]

But he also noted the adverse French criticism which accused such works of being meaningless, if harmonious, 'warblings of the AEolian [sic] lyre.'[3]

These works made a profound impression on Delacroix who challenged the classical view that touch was non-cerebral. Later in life, when preparing his dictionary of art, he made a note to that effect in his journal: 'Touch is merely one of several means that contribute towards rendering a thought in painting.'[4] He further questioned the classical stance:

> **No doubt it is possible to paint a very beautiful picture in which touch is not apparent, but it is childish to imagine that in so doing you are getting closer to nature: you might as well construct actual reliefs in colour upon the picture… Every art has its accepted methods of execution,… Contour and touch are equally absent in nature. In every art we are always obliged to return to the accepted means of expression.**[5]

In mid-century Baudelaire took the part of the innovators. In his section on the COLOUR /DRAWING debate of his 1846 Salon, he associated touch with colour and celebrated them, precisely for their sensory, and therefore evocative appeal:

The quality of pure draughtsmanship consists above all in precision, and this precision excludes touch; but there are such things as happy touches, and the colourist who undertakes to express nature through colour would often lose more by suppressing his happy touches than by studying a greater austerity of drawing.[6]

From the 1840s onwards, the apparent magic of high illusionism, with its invisible brush strokes and finish like smoothly polished marble, was the most widespread and popular style from Philadelphia to St Petersburg. Yet concurrently, the Independents were claiming looseness of touch as a means of expressing individuality and/or of responding to their sensations. In the 1850s the Barbizon painters, Courbet and the Florentine Macchiaioli, all wielded their palette knives in the battle for modernity. A member of this last group, Adriano Cecioni, explained that the Macchiaioli shared a common purpose:

…their art consisting not in studying form but in studying how to render the impressions they received from nature by means of spots of colour, of lights and darks. For example, a single spot of colour for the face, another for the hair, another, let us say, for the handkerchief…it was not in the nature of the macchia to include detailed study but rather to establish the principles that could serve as a solid base for the development of an entirely new art. These principles are *colour, value,* and *relationship*.[7]

Yet none of the above emphasized liveliness and variety of touch in their finished works as Manet and the Impressionists began to by the mid-1860s. A growing concern with immediacy, TRUTH, MODERNITY and speed of execution caused these artists to cover their canvases with dabs and squiggles and dashes of paint. This, Mallarmé pointed out, was prompted by a desire for truth:

As no artist has on his palette a transparent and neutral colour answering to open air, the desired effect can only be obtained by lightness or heaviness of touch, or by the regulation of tone.[8]

The Impressionist approach to painting drew attention to the process of its creation and the physicality of its presence; in effect, the emphasis shifted from the 'what' to the 'how' in art. As an old man, Monet told Lilla Perry:

When you go out to paint, try to forget what objects you have before you, a tree, a house, a field or whatever. Merely think, here is a little square of blue, here an oblong of pink, here a streak of yellow, and paint it just as it looks to you, the exact colour and shape, until it gives your own naïve impression of the scene before you.[9]

During the closing decades of the century society portraitists such as Singer Sargent were flattering the sophisticated contemporaneity of their sitters' taste by adding bravura flourishes of touch to their portraits. The academies, meanwhile, had absorbed some aspects of *plein-airism* and its concurrent broadness and spontaneity of touch – though perhaps on only a superficial level. The British modernist Walter Sickert dismissed Bastien-Lepage as a mere *Salonnier*:

…[his picture] is born of the exhibition and for the exhibition, [it] wears its air of novelty and interest strictly for the season… The colour is uninteresting, and the execution is the usual mechanically obtrusive square-brush-work of the Parisian schools of art.[10]

The century was to end with artists such as Van Gogh and Munch, whose expressive, emotion-laden swirls and curls of paint (sometimes straight from the tube), took the relationship between means of execution and subject matter in a new direction. Sculpture was subject to similar trends, as suggested in Rodin's statement to the Société des Gens de Lettres, which had rejected the portrait of Balzac commissioned from him:

I sought...to render in sculpture what was not photographic... My principle is to imitate not only form but also life. I search in nature for this life and amplify it by exaggerating the holes and lumps.[11]

After inauspicious beginnings, touch was destined to become one of the major concerns of early Modernism.

See: COLOUR, *ÉBAUCHE, ESQUISSE,* FINISH, *PLEIN-AIR, POCHADE,* SENSATION, TEMPERAMENT, TRUTH

[1] In Delaborde, p. 160

[2] 17 Dec 1825, in Leslie, p. 114

[3] *Ibid,* p. 115

[4] 13 Jan 1857, in Delacroix, 1995, p. 356

[5] *Ibid,* pp. 356-7

[6] C. Baudelaire, *Salon de 1846,* 1846, in Baudelaire, 1965, p. 51

[7] A. Cecioni, 'Telemaco Signorini', *La Domenica letteraria,* 1884, in Taylor, p. 432

[8] S. Mallarmé, 'The Impressionists and Edouard Manet', *The Art Monthly Review and Photographic Portfolio,* 30 Sept 1876, in Harrison and Wood, p. 589

[9] L.C. Perry, 'Reminiscences of Claude Monet from 1889 to 1909', *The American Magazine of Art,* XVIII, March 1927, in Boime, p. 215, n. 13

[10] In Theuriet, pp. 141-2

[11] Elsen, p. 103

Truth

Ingres noted that 'one must find the secret of the beautiful in the true,' while Millet believed that 'the beautiful is the true.'[1] For the Russian painter Ivan Kramskoy the artist's role was to 'serve truth in the form of beauty.'[2] Despite such variations in emphasis, nineteenth-century artists pursued the elusive concept of truth with a faith in its absolute value that may appear either enviable or ridiculous to the twenty-first-century reader. Most often truth was defined in relation to beauty and/or nature, which gives rise to two questions: first, what was meant by the term truth, and second, truth to what?

Jean-Jacques Rousseau's tomb, designed by Hubert Robert, bears the inscription 'Here rests the man of nature and of truth.'[3] In the early years of the nineteenth century, the legacy of the Enlightenment ensured that truth was primarily understood in terms of ethics; art was intended to inspire social and moral improvement by providing elevating and honest subjects with the purest formal means. This was David's message in 1792, when he presented criteria for judging works of art to the National Convention, the government of revolutionary France:

It is for the strong souls, those who have a sense of the true, of the greatness that a study of nature provides, to give new impulse to the arts by returning them to the principles of true beauty.[4]

What became known as Neo-classicism in the later decades of the nineteenth century was known in its own day as the true style. Rejecting the frivolities of the Rococo and the petty vagaries of the particular, and so flawed, aspects of nature, artists studied the ANTIQUE as a way of arriving at its immutable, underlying truths. When Canova first saw the Elgin marbles in 1815, he expressed his admiration: here was 'the truth of nature united with the selection of beautiful forms.'[5]

Yet as Goya realised, the Enlightenment's rationalism brought not only freedom from super-stition and unquestioned dogma, it also liberated the irrational, as he implied in an inscription on the margin of a study for his print series *Caprichos* (c.1799): 'The author's... intention is to banish harmful beliefs commonly held, and with this work of Caprichos to perpetuate the solid testimony of truth.'[6] Yet this very same image, as it appeared in the *Caprichos* (number 43) suggested a more complex message: here the artist sleeps across a table bearing the inscription, 'The sleep of reason produces monsters', while owls, bats and oversized cats plague his dreams. In implying that truth was indeed complex and ungraspable, Goya was expressing the Janus-face of the Enlightenment and pointing the way towards Romanticism.

As the century progressed the values of Neo-classicism stiffened into the aesthetic orthodox-ies of the academies, so becoming severed from their revolutionary, social origins. Moral intent gave way before the imperative need to please a bourgeois market. Of course, Ingres still linked truth to beauty and nature:

> **We are always beautiful when we are true. All the mistakes that you make do not come from your lack of taste or imagination; they arise because you do not put in enough of nature.**[7]

But he also advised that ugliness must be suppressed for the sake of beauty, and that truth must be made pleasing and seductive:

> **Let us try to please so as to better impose the true. It is not with vinegar that you catch flies, it is with honey and sugar... Love the true because it is also beautiful, if you know how to distinguish it and to feel it. Let us make ourselves eyes which see well, which see with wisdom – this is all I ask. If you want to see this leg as ugly, I know that there will be grounds for it, but I would say to you: Take my eyes, and you will find it beautiful.**[8]

For the Romantics, it was not a matter of simple opposition to such ideas. One of the last entries in Delacroix's dairies was 'The Beautiful is truth idealised.'[9] Nevertheless, truth became much more a matter of the personal rather than the universal, and hence of the indi-vidual rather than the social, of the mutable rather than of the absolute. What mattered was that the artist be true to his or her inner response to nature; in turn the quality of this response was an indication of the presence or lack of originality, and so of GENIUS. Goethe simply asserted, 'The first and last thing demanded of genius is: the love of truth.'[10]

Such attitudes percolated far into the century and were held by many conservative and/or aca-demic artists. For example, in her old age Rosa Bonheur advised: 'Always begin with a vision of truth. The eye is the way to the soul, and the crayon or brush must simply and faithfully render what you see.'[11] Yet the Romantics' veneration for NATURE did not prevent them from feeling justified in choosing dramatic motifs, or condensing their responses in order to convey them more powerfully. Stendhal admired the truth that he found in Constable's landscapes, but he still found something lacking:

> **In the pictures of the Old School, the trees do have style, they are elegant, but they lack truth. Constable, by contrast, is as true as a mirror; but I would prefer that the mirror were placed in front of some more spectacular view, like the entry to the valley of the Grande Chartreuse near Grenoble, and not merely in front of a hay cart fording the waters of some sleepy canal.**[12]

The Romantics' questioning of the eternal canons propagated by academic orthodoxy was also born of their desire to engage with contemporary subjects, but only if these were momentous or dramatic. Hence Delacroix was more aghast at the mundane subject-matter of Courbet's *Bathers* (1853) than at the lack of idealisation with which the figures were depicted: '…what a picture! What a subject to choose! The vulgarity of the forms would not signify, the vulgarity and futility of the idea is what is so abominable.'[13]

For the mid-century Realists, truth became a fundamental credo that raised complex social, political and aesthetic issues. Courbet, Daumier, Millet and their followers challenged the subjects favoured by the Romantics, the Classicists and the *juste-milieu* artists on the grounds that they were unverifiable. Truth became associated with honesty, sincerity and empiricism. Eschewing all subjects that they had not personally witnessed, they renounced historical, mythological, literary and religious subjects, and set out to depict only what they observed around them. Having described *The Stonebreakers* (1849) to the critic Champfleury, Courbet wrote:

> **I made up none of it, dear friend. I saw these people every day on my walk… The vine growers and the farmers, who are much taken with this painting, claim that, were I to do a hundred more, none would be more true to life.**[14]

But, as with *The Stonebreakers*, this was also often a matter of not averting the eyes when witnessing the mundanities and harsh realities of contemporary life. Furthermore, the Realists refused to idealise and, in some cases, to dramatise their subjects. This led to the accusations, such as Delacroix's, that they were actively seeking out the ugly or the inconsequential. For example, Delécluze, ex-pupil of David, attacked Courbet's *Burial at Ornans* (1849-50):

> **In that scene, which one might mistake for a faulty daguerreotype, there is the natural coarseness which one always gets in taking nature as it is, and in reproducing it just as it is seen.**[15]

Even the Goncourt brothers, who admired Realism, objected to Courbet's focus on the insalubrious, and ridiculed his so-called belief that 'the beautiful is the ugly.'[16] For some, notably Courbet and Daumier, this understanding of truth stemmed from the conscious political intent of seeking to combat social injustice. In 1851, Courbet wrote a letter to the newspaper, *Messager de l'assemblée*, in which he used the term Realist for the first time in the public realm:

> **I am not only a socialist but a democrat and a Republican as well – in a word, a partisan of all the revolution and above all a Realist… for 'Realist' means a sincere lover of the honest truth.**[17]

During the same period in Britain, the Pre-Raphaelites claimed truth in terms of a scrupulous honesty to the specific and a directness of response to the visible. Unlike the French Realists, they were not averse to recreating imagined worlds, but they refused to idealise their subjects. Keen to create a truthful evocation of *Christ in the House of his Parents* (1849-50), Millais researched the tools and environs of a carpenter's shop in London's Oxford Street, and was careful to choose non-idealised MODELS for the figures. Holman Hunt went so far as to travel to the Holy Land so that he could correctly record the vegetation, animals and human physiognomies that he believed would have existed in Biblical times. Truth was at the root of all his statements as a religious artist. In 1854, he told Augustus Egg: 'Truth, wherever it leads, being above price, must increase the beauty of the story of the Divine Man.'[18]

The Pre-Raphaelites' earnest adherence to the specific answered a chord in Ruskin, the first volume of whose *Modern Painters* (1843) had initially influenced them. The critic, in turn, defended them against hostile criticism. Ruskin was clear that truth in art had a moral dimension. Having already dwelled on this in *Modern Painters*, he returned to it in *The Seven Lamps of Architecture* (1849), with a chapter entitled 'The lamp of truth':

> **I would have the Spirit or Lamp of Truth clear in the hearts of our artists and handicraftsmen, not as if the truthful practice of handicrafts could far advance the cause of truth, but because I would fain see the handicrafts themselves urged by the spurs of chivalry: and it is, indeed, marvelous to see what power and universality there are in this single principle, and how in the consulting or forgetting of it lies half the dignity or decline of every art and act of man.[19]**

By the mid-1850s in Britain, France and elsewhere, conservative artists such as Jules Breton, Rosa Bonheur and Isidore Pils had also turned to humble and mundane aspects of contemporary life for their subject matter. Yet they avoided the accusations of a vulgar and coarse staining of the elevated temple of high art, which were heaped on the Realists and Pre-Raphaelites. It was, of course, as much a matter of formal means as of subject-matter.

The arrival of PHOTOGRAPHY in 1839 had increased the public's expectation of verisimilitude, and the majority of artists answered this demand, despite sometimes rueing such narrowness of taste. Truth became associated above all with the contradictory demands that art provide precise illusions of visible appearances and factual detail while also presenting a refined, elevated interpretation of its subject-matter – as the painter-critic P. G. Hamerton complained:

> **...the truly ignorant person... has but one uniform conception of graphic art when he sees it, and that is the simple copyism of objects. If the picture pleases him, he does not praise it for fine arrangements of colour or light-and-shade, but for imitative fidelity: if he blames it, the blame does not attach to any artistic imprudence or stupidity, but to the neglect of imitative truth.[20]**

Unlike the AVANT-GARDE, academic artists continued to compose and idealise their subjects in a traditional manner. Hence, Hamilton had concluded his essay with a defence of the traditional manipulation of the motif and means of conveying it. This was a commonly held position, also articulated by the academician Henry O'Neil, at the Royal Academy in 1866:

> **... true art consists in seizing the spirit of the scene to be represented, and only imitating so much of the form and colour of its details as shall best satisfy our sensuous perception of the truth of the representation. Every part of the scene should be rendered, as far as possible, with that degree of literal truth (no more, no less) which strikes the eye on looking at the whole... For remember, to the artist every object has two aspects: the one positive, as seen by itself, – the other, relative, as viewed in connection with others; and the**

attempt to depict at the same time and with equal truth, those two distinct distinctive appearances, can only result in total failure.[21]

Such outlooks were anathema to the French avant-garde of the 1860s and 1870s. Late in life, when Cassatt's letters began to dwell on the aesthetic beliefs which had long informed her works, she wrote to a young friend, Theodate Pope:

So you think my models unworthy of their clothes? You find their types coarse... What would you say to the Botticelli Madonna in the Louvre. The peasant girl & her child clothed in beautiful shifts & wrapped in soft veils. Yet as Degas pointed out to me Botticelli stretched his love of truth to the point of painting her hands with the fingernails worn down with field work![22]

Like Courbet, Manet and the Impressionists were committed to conveying their unadulterated observation of contemporary life. In his old age, Monet recalled his teacher Gleyre's critique of a life DRAWING:

'It's not bad,' he said, 'but the breast is heavy, the shoulder too powerful and the foot too big.'
'I can only draw what I see,' I replied timidly.
'Praxiteles borrowed the best parts from a hundred imperfect models, to create a masterpiece,' Gleyre replied dryly. 'When you make something, you must think of the antique!'
That same evening, I took Sisley, Renoir and Bazille to one side: 'Let's get out of here,' I said, 'this place is unhealthy, it is lacking in sincerity.'[23]

Truth had become a matter of scientific objectivity, and this was understood to be as much a matter of *facture* as of subject matter. We see a truth to the materiality of paint on canvas, to evidence of the working process in visible brush marks, to the haphazard, informal organisation of figures or LANDSCAPE motifs, as they really do appear in nature, as well as a truth to the vagaries of proportion, posture, physiology and PHYSIOGNOMY. In 1867 Zola explained Manet to a baffled public, partly in terms of this understanding of truth: '...if I were asked what new language Manet was speaking, I would answer, "He speaks in a language which is composed of simplicity and truth"...'[24] Having warned the public not to search for absolute BEAUTY, historical or literary subjects, or clever compositions, he continued:

Don't expect anything of him except a truthful and literal interpretation. He neither sings nor philosophises. He knows how to paint and that is all... He is a child of our age. I see him as an analyst painter. All problems have been re-examined; science requires solid foundations and this has been achieved by accurate observation of facts... While others break their heads trying to compose a new picture of 'The death of Caesar' or 'Socrates Drinking Hemlock' he quietly places some objects or poses some people in a corner of his studio and begins to paint. I repeat, he is merely an analyst... Art as practised by him leads to ultimate truth. This artist is an interpreter of things as they are.[25]

Yet this truth was one tempered by the subjectivity of the artist's individual TEMPERAMENT. Hence, the ethical dimension was evoked, but now in terms of individualism: the sincerity with which the artist responded to the world around him or her became a matter of personal honour. Truth was equated with integrity, as Manet observed:

We French have an integrity, which, in spite of everything, always leads us back to truth.

> **You've only got to look at the pictures of Le Nain, Watteau, Chardin – or even of David himself. What a feeling for truth there is there![26]**

So highly did Manet value truth that when the Salon jury once again rejected his submission in 1876, he exhibited the works in his studio. On the invitation cards he printed: '*Faire vrai, laisser dire* (make it true, let it speak).'[27]

Yet any possibility of depiction in an entirely objective manner was, of course, a chimera. As Degas was honest enough to point out:

> **Art is the same world as artifice, that is to say, something deceitful. It must succeed in giving the impression of nature by false means, but it has to look true. Draw a straight line askew, as long as it gives the impression of being straight![28]**

By the closing decades of the century the Naturalist search for objective truth had become so hackneyed that the emerging avant-gardes rejected it. Gauguin's critique of Impressionism rested partly on the lack of creative freedom it offered, 'shackled' as it was to verisimilitude:

> **'But you have a technique?' they will demand.**
>
> **No. I have not. Or rather I do have one, but it is very fugitive, very flexible, according to my disposition when I arise in the morning; a technique which I apply in my own manner to express my own thought without any concern for the truth of the common, exterior aspects of Nature.[29]**

The increasing emphasis on artistic freedom was understood by the Symbolists partly as freedom to depart from what they saw as the petty veracity of describing the visible world. Only such departures would allow for the exploration and expression of ideas and feelings. Hence Aurier's article on Gauguin equated such 'truth' with deceitfulness:

> **...certain appropriate laws will have to rule pictorial imitation. The artist will have, necessarily, the task to avoid carefully this antimony of all art: concrete truth, illusionism, trompe l'oeil, in order not to give in any way by his painting that deceitful impression of nature that acts on the onlooker as nature itself, that is, without possible suggestion, that is (if I may be pardoned for the barbarous neologism), not ideistically [sic].**
>
> **It is logical to imagine the artist fleeing from the analysis of the object in order to guard himself against these perils of concrete truth.[30]**

This attitude was also prompted by the Symbolists' vilification of photographic verisimilitude, which was still widely sought by mainstream artists and public. As Redon pointed out:

> **The feverish or unbridled passion for success or fortune has spoiled the artist, to the point of perverting in him the sensitivity to beauty. He uses photographs directly and shamefully to obtain the truth... The photograph transmits only lifelessness. The emotion experienced in the presence of nature itself will always provide a quality of truth which is authentic in quite a different way.[31]**

What the late-century avant-gardes now claimed, above all, was truth to their inner selves. For some, such as Cézanne and Redon (albeit in different ways), this was understood in terms of expressing the emotions elicited by nature. Cézanne returned to this theme many times. To Louis Aurenche he wrote: '...do not entirely give up art; it is the most intimate manifestation of ourselves.'[32] For those Symbolists who were more directly concerned with conveying ideas through formal means, it was vital that they establish a greater distance from the visible world. In one of his rare statements, Munch wrote:

Art is the opposite of nature.

A work of art can come only from the interior of man...

Nature is the unique great realm upon which art feeds.

Nature is not only what is visible to the eye – it also shows the inner images of the soul – the images on the back side of the eyes.[33]

The Realists' and Impressionists' emphasis on integrity of response was now pushed to become the wonder and unworldliness of the childlike. The German painter Hans Thoma, who had moved towards Symbolism from the Realism of his early career, explained:

Fundamentally speaking, the truth of art is nothing but the revelation of the nature of the soul. Art testifies to the perceiving soul, that soul which gives shape and form according to its own laws... In art, too, a natural and childlike attitude is required in order to be genuinely truthful. Children are genuine and honest, and only unconditional honesty is capable of creating great and lasting achievements for humanity.[34]

Similarly, in his praise of Van Gogh, Aurier equated truth with sincerity which he linked to naivety and truth to self:

...it is difficult for anyone impartial and able to use his eyes to deny or disprove the naive truth of his art and the ingenuity of his vision. In fact, independently of that impalpable air of good faith and of the truly observed which is given off by all his paintings, the choice of subject, the constant harmony between even the most extravagant tones, the conscientious study of character, the continuous search for the essential meaning of each object, a thousand significant details affirm beyond all dispute his profound and almost childlike sincerity, his great love of nature and the truth, that is, his own truth.[35]

Yet, well into the early decades of the twentieth century, public taste continued to demand a tempering of harsh factuality coupled with a high degree of veracity in terms of detailed illusionism. Despite their very different understandings of the concept of truth, the naturalists and the younger Symbolist and Expressionist avant-gardes shared a refusal to sweeten their subject matter in the manner indulged in by mainstream artists. As Rodin explained:

When an artist...softens the grimace of pain, the shapelessness of age, the hideousness of perversion, when he arranges nature – veiling, disguising, tempering it to please the ignorant public – then he is creating ugliness because he fears the truth. [36]

See: BEAUTY, IMAGINATION, MODEL, NATURE, PHOTOGRAPHY

[1] Delaborde, p. 117; Scharf, p. 344

[2] Harrison and Wood, p. 523. Kramskoy was the founder-member of the Russian Social Realist Wanderers group, launched in 1870.

[3] Irwin, p. 184

[4] David's report as head of the Committee on Public Education and the Commission of Fine Arts, in Taylor, p. 45

[5] In Honour, p. 23

[6] In Eisenman, p. 78

[7] In Delaborde, p. 117

[8] *Ibid*, pp. 116-7

[9] 15 Jan 1861, Delacroix, 1995, p. 442

[10] *Maxims and Reflections*, 1840, in Harrison and Wood, p. 76

[11] Klumpke, p. 219

[12] 'Salon de 1824', in Harrison and Wood, p. 35

[13] 15 April 1853, in Delacroix, 1995, pp. 181-2

[14] Feb-March 1850, in Courbet, p. 93

[15] *Journal des Débats*, 21 March 1851, in Scharf, p. 128

[16] 'Salon de 1852', in Scharf, p. 129

[17] 19 Nov 1851, in Courbet, p. 103

[18] In Stevens, p. 33

[19] In Ruskin, 1904, p. 57

[20] *Thoughts about Art*, 1873, in Craig Harrison, p. 31

[21] *Lectures on Painting Delivered at the Royal Academy*, 1866, *ibid*, p. 61

[22] 19 Feb 1911, in Mathews, p. 306

[23] Geffroy, pp. 26-7

[24] 'Edouard Manet', *Revue du XIXe Siècle*, 1867, in Courthion, p. 124

[25] *Ibid*, pp. 124-5

[26] In Courthion, p. 6

[27] *Ibid*, p. 167

[28] In Kendall, p. 319

[29] P. Gauguin, *Divers choses*, in Chipp, p. 65

[30] G.-A. Aurier, 'Le Symbolisme en peinture: Paul Gauguin', *Mercure de France*, II, 1891, in Chipp, p. 91

[31] O. Redon, *À soi-même*, in Scharf, p. 250

[32] 3 Feb 1902, in Cézanne, p. 284

[33] Chipp, p. 114

[34] Letter to Emil Hugo, June 1880, in Harrison and Wood, p. 854

[35] G.-A. Aurier, 'Les isolées: Vincent Van Gogh', *Mercure de France*, Jan 1890, in Harrison and Wood, p. 950

[36] *On Art and Artists*, 1957, in Elsen, p. 66

Urban Life

For the academies, depictions of cities mostly meant emulating the idealised Greco-Roman architectural settings of Claude, Poussin and their Renaissance predecessors as backdrops for HISTORY PAINTING. It was during the second half of the nineteenth century that informal observations of contemporary urban life became a major subject. In the 1850s, while still a student in Couture's studio, Manet would goad the models by asking them if they would adopt such declamatory poses when going about their daily life:

'What! Can't you be natural?' Manet would shout. 'Is that the way you would buy a bunch of radishes at the greengrocers?'[1]

Industrialization brought about dramatic changes in the social and geographic conditions of life, above all a rapid growth in city populations. For example, Vienna grew from over 400,000 in 1846 to 700,000 in 1880, Paris from one to 1.9 million between 1851 and 1881, while London grew from 2.5 to 3.9 million in the same period. Peasants poured out of the countryside to work in the cities' factories while the growth of commercial enterprises created a need for an army of clerks, shop assistants, servants etc. Expanding populations as well as new forms of commerce, entertainment and communication led to massive building programmes. By the third quarter of the century many cities were in a constant state of flux: ancient medieval districts became demolition sites, then building sites, from which arose a multitude of modern buildings. The Romantics' earlier commitment to contemporary life had set a precedent; now urban life itself became a major preoccupation for avant-garde artists and writers.

Urban life was central to Baudelaire's definition of modern beauty:

> **But to return to our principal and essential problem, which is to discover whether we possess a specific beauty, intrinsic to our new emotions, I observe that the majority of artists who have attacked modern life have contented themselves with public and official subjects – with our victories and our political heroism… However there are private subjects which are much more heroic than these.**

> **The pageant of fashionable life and the thousands of floating existences – criminals and kept women – which drift about in the underworld of a great city;… we have only to open our eyes to recognise our heroism.**[2]

Baudelaire stressed that it was the artist's task to see and to understand this 'modern beauty.' And they did. In the 1860s and 1870s Manet and the Impressionists answered Baudelaire's call, while by the last quarter of the century official EXHIBITIONS were teeming with GENRE paintings and moralising or social realist works depicting the pleasures and oppressions of urban life.

Some cities such as London grew in an unplanned manner while others, notably Paris, witnessed the planned rebuilding of their centres. In 1853 Napoléon III nominated Baron Haussmann to modernise Paris which was still essentially a medieval/classical city. From 1853 to 1870 one fifth of the residential and commercial streets and boulevards in the centre of the city were built to his regulated plan, as well as a modern sewerage system, bridges, churches, schools, army barracks, markets etc. The modern city brought new kinds of private and public buildings such as office blocks, cafés, restaurants, department stores, exhibition halls and railway stations, as well as the multiplication of older ones such as MUSEUMS, hotels, banks and parks.

To depict the pleasures and dangers of city life in the 1860s was in itself a progressive stance in relation to academic dogma. As a young man, Degas agonised over what were then perceived as opposing polarities: 'Oh Giotto, let me see Paris, and you, Paris, let me see Giotto!'[3] Haussmann's building works transformed the city and provided work – at one stage in the 1860s one fifth of the city's population was working in the building trade. But the new development also displaced vast numbers of people. As 27,500 houses were demolished in the medieval districts where the poor had mostly lived, they were replaced with modern apartments, which were let to the bourgeoisie at high rents. According to Haussmann's own calculations 350,000 people were displaced. The new city embodied the social and economic instabilities of the Capitalist age. Moreover anonymous people of all social classes rubbed shoulders in its public places on a scale hitherto unknown.

Baudelaire had redefined the artist as a *flâneur*, an anonymous observer strolling aimlessly through this changing, evanescent spectacle. In the 1860s, replacing the mud-spattered peasants of Barbizon and Ornans with the fashionable Parisian *flâneurs*, Manet answered Baudelaire's call with paintings such as *Music in the Tuileries Gardens* (1862). Antonin Proust recalled:

> **I have already said what a *flâneur* Manet was. We strolled together, one day, along what was later to be the Boulevard Malesherbes, through the midst of demolitions... At each step Manet stopped me. A cedar standing alone in the middle of a neglected garden caught his attention...**

> **'Look at its bark,' he said to me, 'look at the violet tone of the shadows.'**

> **Farther on, house-breakers stood out white against a wall less white, which was collapsing under their blows, covering them in a cloud of dust. For a long time Manet became absorbed in admiration of this scene.**

> **'There you are,' he exclaimed, 'the Symphony in White Major, which Théophile Gautier speaks about.'**

> **A woman came out of a low tavern holding up her dress and clutching a guitar; Manet went straight up to her and asked her to pose for him.**[4]

The Impressionists followed Manet's example. Commenting on Monet's MODERNITY in a Salon review Zola linked this to the urbanity of his works:

> **Here's an artist weaned in our own age, here's one who has grown up and will continue to grow with an adoration of what surrounds him... he loves the horizons of our cities, the grey and white patches which the houses form against the pale sky... He is a true Parisian, he takes Paris into the countryside, he cannot paint a landscape without putting fashionably dressed men and women in it. Nature seems to lose its appeal for him as soon as she is not stamped with our contemporary mores.**[5]

In 1876 Duranty published a pamphlet in which he summed up the preoccupations of Manet and the Impressionists:

> **The very first idea was to eliminate the partition separating the artist's studio from everyday life, and to introduce the reality of the street... It was necessary to make the painter come out of his sky-lighted cell, his cloister, where his sole communication was with the sky – and to bring him back among men, out into the real world...**

> **Our lives take place in rooms and streets and have their own special laws of light and visual language.**[6]

Such an emphasis on the experience of the modern city's pleasures created a major obstacle to the ambitions of middle-class women art students and artists. Strolling aimlessly about city streets, parks and cafés unaccompanied was considered tantamount to soliciting in the newly expanded cities in which all too many working-class women and girls did survive by prostitution. Respectable women were in danger of being mistaken for prostitutes. The young Marie Bashkirtseff wrote in exasperation:

> **What I long for is the freedom of going about alone, of coming and going, of sitting on the seats in the Tuileries, and especially in the Luxembourg, of stopping and looking at the artistic shops, of entering the churches and museums, of walking about the old streets**

at night; that's what I long for; and that's the freedom without which one can't become a real artist.[7]

A few years late, she partially overcame the problem by working in disguise, yet she still needed an escort:

I go to paint at the Grande Jatte... Luckily Bojidar came with me, for I had not remembered it was a *fête*, and when we got there we found a number of bargees, and Rosalie would perhaps have proved an insufficient chaperon. Moreover, in order to come and go and paint in this aristocratic island, I dress like an old German woman. Two or three woollen petticoats to diguise my figure, a wrap which cost twenty-seven francs, a blacked knitted shawl round the head, and socks on my feet.[8]

In fact artists such as Berthe Morisot and Mary Cassatt did dwell on certain aspects of urban life. They concentrated on the domestic arena, such as taking tea in a modern apartment, or on socially acceptable public sites such as the theatre or the park. By the 1890s it was increasingly acceptable for respectable women to circulate about the city, at least during the day.

Mid-century British artists also tackled modern urban subjects: Ford Madox Brown's *Work* (1852-65) depicted the construction of modern sewers in a London suburb. Using more traditional formal means than the French AVANT-GARDE he was concerned with conveying a social and moral critique of the changing conditions brought about by the modern city. In his painting a wide cross section of social classes mingle without communicating with each other. They include rich and poor, employed and unemployed, the idle and the industrious. The heroes are the navvies and the enlightened 'brain workers', the Christian Socialist F.D. Maurice and the writer Thomas Carlyle, both of whose social critiques influenced Madox Brown. In his long explanation of the painting he pointed to its narrative and symbolic content, its exposure of social inequalities and the lack of communication between social classes. For example, the well-dressed ladies on the left represent the idle rich. One hands an old navvy a religious tract, but he refuses it:

This well-intentioned lady has perhaps never reflected that the excavators may have notions to the effect that ladies might benefit by receiving tracts containing navvies' ideas![9]

At the back is a rich M.P:

...could he only be got to hear what the two sages in the corner have to say, I have no doubt that he would easily be won over. But the road is blocked.[10]

The academic painter William Powell Frith was less concerned with social critique, but equally interested in portraying the co-existence of a wide range of social types and classes that characterised city life. Writing about his large painting *The Railway Station* (1862), he clearly expressed the reservations about urban subject matter which were widely held by conventional artists such as himself:

I don't think that the station at Paddington can be called picturesque, nor can the clothes of the ordinary traveller be said to offer much attraction to the painter – in short, the difficulties of the subject were great and many were the warnings of my friends that I should only be courting failure if I persevered in trying to paint what was in no sense pictorial.[11]

Full of anecdote and physiognomic types, with more than eighty identifiable figures showing all social classes, it provided a panorama of modern British life. Its conventional illusionistic style and complex narrative content, documenting the minutiae of Victorian London, caught the mood of the new art-going public and it was to become one of the most popular works of its age.

The city was often characterised as a tantalising Jezebel, offering the excitements and corruptions of every temptation, in contrast with the healthy calm and wholesomeness of country life. This vision can be traced back to Alexandrian poetry of the third century B.C. While many hailed the modern city's progress, others pointed to its darker effects. London had grown even faster than Paris, but in an unplanned, haphazard manner, and many pointed to its Babylonian character. For example, when Berthe Morisot visited it with her husband she wrote:

> **I am reconciled with London, my dear little mother. I don't know what ill luck during the first days took me into the dreary streets of the city, including my own, which is terribly so. I am tired out. We race about like lost souls. We don't want to take cabs; we board the omnibus, the train, this city is a world in itself – a kind of fantastic Babylon, as one sees it from the Thames on a foggy day.**[12]

In Britain especially, the effects of rapid industrialisation had engendered appalling social and environmental conditions for the new urban workers, and these became the subject-matter of social realist comment, particularly in the work of painter/illustrators working in England from the late 1860s. These included Fildes, Herkomer, Holl and Doré. Van Gogh avidly collected and was inspired by the engravings produced by these artists. Together with the journalist William Blanchard Jerrold, Doré published the illustrated *London, a Pilgrimage* (1872), which was designed to show every aspect of the city:

> **...how the conglomerate millions act and react upon each other... till the ingenious man is lost in wonder over the infinite methods which Competition has invented of earning a leg of mutton...**
> **Waking London is, indeed a wonderful place to study, from the park where the fortunate in the world's battle are gathering roses, to the stone-yard by Shadwell where, at day break... the houseless, who had a crust and a shake-down in the casual ward, turn to the dreary labour by which it is to be paid.**[13]

Prints commissioned by the new illustrated magazines were sometimes used as the bases for paintings. Fildes' *Applicants to a Casual Ward* of 1874 caused a sensation at that year's Royal Academy exhibition and sold for a high price to a cotton manufacturer. Low life was becoming fashionable.

Less contentious depictions of fashionable city life became the staple of anecdotal genre painting in the closing decades of the century, in works by artists such as Tissot, Béraud or Logsdail. Moreover, numerous artists from Montreal to Manchester depicted sentimental genre scenes of urban poverty such as guttersnipes or pretty flower-sellers. Robert Henri and John Sloan in America portrayed unidealised city life, while Rosso in Italy was one of the first sculptors to portray fast-moving street life. In the late 1880s and 1890s artists committed to anarchist beliefs, such as Luce and Signac, depicted the Parisian working-class suburbs and their inhabitants in a non-condescending manner. Signac argued that formal innovation, rather than the choice of subject matter itself, acted as socio-political critique. Significantly he focused on the Impressionists and their urban subject matter to make this point:

> **By their picturesque studies of working-class housing of Saint-Ouen and Montrouge, sor-**

did and overwhelmingly real, by reproducing the broad and strangely vivid gestures of a navvy working by a pile of sand, of a blacksmith in the incandescent light of the forge – or better still by synthetically representing the pleasures of decadence, balls, riotous dances, and circuses, as did the painter Seurat, who had such a strong sense of the debasement of our epoch of transition – they have contributed their witness to the great social process which pits the workers against Capital.[14]

Signac believed that 'revolutionaries by temperament' could produce such works regardless of their politics. In contrast many late-century social commentaries, in which the lives of the oppressed were represented as idealised and melodramatic anecdotes, were essentially reactionary. As Signac pointed out, scenes of factory life and of the Siege of Paris were now painted on public commission 'by people who care not a fig for the Republic or the people.'[15]

Some were energised by the new motifs offered by the spectacle of city life while others were appalled by the misery that it engendered. The aesthetes, however, who congregated around Oscar Wilde and Whistler, saw in the city a poetic BEAUTY that could be extracted by avoiding its particularities:

The sun blares, the wind blows from the east, the sky is bereft of cloud, and without, all is of iron. The windows of the Crystal Palace are seen from all points of London. The holiday-maker rejoices in the glorious day, and the painter turns aside to shut his eyes... And when the evening mist clothes the riverside with poetry, as with a veil, and the poor buildings lose themselves in the dim sky, and the tall chimneys become campanili, and the warehouses are palaces in the night, and the whole city hangs in the heaven, and the fairyland is before us – then the wayfarer hastens home; the working man and the cultured one, the wise man and the one of pleasure, cease to understand, as they have ceased to see, and Nature, who, for once, has sung in tune, sings her exquisite song to the artist alone.[16]

See: GENRE, HISTORY PAINTING, MODERNITY

[1] In Courthion, p. 4

[2] 'Salon de 1846', in Baudelaire, 1965, pp. 118-9

[3] Notebooks nos. 22 and 23, late 1860s, in Kendall, p. 37

[4] Courthion, p. 42

[5] *Les Actualistes, Salon IV*, 1868, in Zola, p. 130

[6] *La nouvelle peinture*, 1876, in Harrison and Wood, p. 582

[7] Journal, 2 Jan 1879, in Bashkirtseff, II, 1890, p. 21

[8] Journal, 1 Nov 1883, *ibid*, p. 389

[9] Treuherz, 1987, p. 32

[10] *Ibid*, p. 33

[11] Frith, p. 104

[12] In Morisot, p. 106

[13] In Klingender, p. 159

[14] 'Impressionists and Revolutionaries', *La Révolte*, 1891, in Harrison and Wood, p. 797

[15] *Ibid*

[16] J.A.M. Whistler, 'Ten O'Clock Lecture', 1885, in Whistler, pp. 143-4

Bibliography

Armitage, Edward, *Lectures on Painting, Delivered to the Students of the Royal Academy*, Trübner & Co., London, 1883

Barasch, Moshe, *Theories of Art*, II: *From Winckelmann to Baudelaire* (1990), Routledge, New York and London, 2000

Bashkirtseff, Marie, *Nouveau Journal Inédit de Marie Bashkirtseff*, Éditions de la Revue, Paris, 1901

Bashkirtseff, Marie, *The Journal of Marie Bashkirtseff*, 2 vols, Cassell & Co., London, 1890

Baudelaire, Charles, *Art in Paris: 1845-1862: Salons and Other Exhibitions*, ed. and trans. Jonathan Mayne, Phaidon, London, 1965

Baudelaire, Charles, *Écrits sur l'art*, I, Le Livre de Poche, Gallimard et Librairie Générale Française, 1971

Baudelaire, Charles, *The Painter of Modern Life and Other Essays*, ed. and trans. Jonathan Mayne (1964), Phaidon, London and New York, 1995

Bazin, Germain, *The Avant-Garde in the History of Painting*, Thames and Hudson, London, 1969

Beardsley, Aubrey, *The Letters of Aubrey Beardsley*, ed. Henry Maas, J.L. Duncan and W.G. Wood, Cassell, London, 1971

Bendiner, Kenneth, *An Introduction to Victorian Painting*, Yale University Press, New Haven and London, 1985

Boime, Albert, *The Academy and French Painting in the Nineteenth Century*, Phaidon, London, 1971

Breton, Jules, *The Life of an Artist: Art and Nature*, Sampson Low, Marston & Co., London, 1891

Brettell, Richard R., *Modern Art, 1851-1929*, Oxford University Press, Oxford, 1999

Brettell, Richard R., *Impression: Painting Quickly in France, 1860-90*, exhibition catalogue, London, National Gallery/Van Gogh Museum, Amsterdam/Sterling and Francine Clark Art Institute, Williamstown, 2000-01

Brown, David Blayney, *Romanticism*, Phaidon, London and New York, 2001

Bryson, Norman, *Looking at the Overlooked: Four Essays on Still Life Painting*, Reaktion Books, London, 1990

Cailler, Pierre, ed., *Corot raconté par lui-même et par ses amis*, 2 vols, Vésenaz-Genève, 1946

Cartwright, Julia, *Jean-Francois Millet, his Life and Letters*, Swan Sonnenschein & Co., London, 1896

Cézanne, Paul, *Letters*, ed. John Rewald (1941), Da Capo Press, New York, 1995

Chadwick, Whitney, *Women, Art and Society*, 2nd edition, Thames and Hudson, London, 1996

Cherry, Deborah, *Painting Women, Victorian Women Artists*, Routledge, London and New York, 1993

Chipp, Herschel B., *Theories of Modern Art, A Source Book by Artists and Critics*, University of California Press, Berkeley, Los Angeles and London, 1968

Clark, Kenneth, *Ruskin Today* (1964) Penguin Books, Harmondsworth, 1967

Clark, Kenneth, *The Nude* (1956), Penguin Books, Harmondsworth, 1964

Clark ,T.J., *The Absolute Bourgeois, Artists and Politics in France,1848-1851* (1973), Thames and Hudson, London, 1982

Clark,T.J., *The Painting of Modern Life, Paris in the Art of Manet and his Followers*, Thames and Hudson, London, 1985

Clark ,T.J., *Image of the People, Gustave Courbet and the 1848 Revolution* (1973), Thames and Hudson, London, 1988

Clemenceau, G, *Claude Monet et les Nymphéas*, Librairie Plon, Paris, 1928

Coke, Van Deren, *The Painter and the Photograph: from Delacroix to Warhol*, University of New Mexico Press, Albuquerque,1972

Courbet, Gustave, *Letters of Gustave Courbet*, ed. and trans. Petra ten-Doesschate Chu, The University of Chicago Press, Chicago and London, 1992

Courthion, Pierre and Pierre Cailler, eds., *Portrait of Manet by Himself and his Contemporaries*, Cassell, London, 1960

Cowling, Mary, *Victorian Figurative Painting, Domestic Life and the Contemporary Social Scene*, Andreas Papadakis, London, 2000

David, Jacques-Louis-Jules, *Le peintre Louis David, 1748-1825: souvenirs et documents inédits*, 2 vols, Victor Havard, Paris, 1880-2

Dawkins, Heather, *The Nude in French Art and Culture, 1870-1910*, Cambridge University Press, Cambridge, 2002

Degas, Edgar, *Lettres de Degas*, ed. Marcel Guérin, Bernard Grasset, Paris, 1945

Delaborde, Henri, *Ingres: sa vie, ses travaux, sa doctrine*, Henri Plon, Paris, 1870

Delacroix, Eugène, *Selected Letters, 1813-1863*, selected and trans. Jean Stewart, Eyre & Spottiswoode, London, 1971

Delacroix, Eugène, *The Journal of Eugène Delacroix*, edited by Hubert Wellington (1951), Phaidon Press, London, 1995

Delécluze, Etienne-Jean, *Louis David, son école et son temps, souvenirs*, Didier et Cie, Paris, 1863

Denis, Rafael Cardoso and Colin Trodd, eds., *Art and the Academy in the Nineteenth Century*, Manchester University Press, Manchester, 2000

Denvir, Bernard, *The Thames and Hudson Encyclopaedia of Impressionism*, Thames and Hudson, London, 1990

Dorra, Henri, ed., *Symbolist Art Theories, A Critical Anthology*, University of California Press, Berkeley, Los Angeles and London, 1994

Duffy, Stephen, *Paul Delaroche, 1797-1856: Paintings in the Wallace Collection*, exhibition catalogue, London, The Trustees of the Wallace Collection, 1997

Eisenman, Stephen and others, *Nineteenth Century Art, a Critical History*, Thames and Hudson, London, 1994

Eitner, Lorenz, *Neoclassicism and Romanticism, 1750-1850: Sources and Documents*, 2 vols, Prentice-Hall International, London, 1970-1

Elsen, Albert E., *Rodin*, Museum of Modern Art, New York, 1963

Escholier, Raymond, *Daumier et son monde*, Éditions Berger-Levrault, Paris, 1965

Fido, Martin, *Oscar Wilde*, Hamlyn, London, 1973

Fink, Lois Marie, *American Art at the Nineteenth Century Paris Salons*, Cambridge University Press, Cambridge, 1990

Frascina, Francis, and Charles Harrison, eds., *Modern Art and Modernism, A Critical Anthology*, Paul Chapman Publishing in association with the Open University, London, 1982

Frascina, Francis and others, *Modernity and Modernism: French Painting in the Nineteenth Century*, Yale University Press in association with the Open University, New Haven and London, 1993

Frey, Julia, *Toulouse-Lautrec, a Life*, Weidenfeld and Nicolson, London, 1994

Frith, William Powell, *A Victorian Canvas, the Memoirs of W.P. Frith, R.A.*, ed. Neville Wallis, Geoffrey Bles, London, 1957

Gasquet, Joachim, *Joachim Gasquet's Cézanne, A Memoir with Conversations*, Thames and Hudson, London, 1991

Gauguin, Paul, *Gauguin's Intimate Journals*, preface Emile Gauguin, Dover Publications, New York, 1997

Gaunt, William, *The Restless Century: Painting in Britain, 1800-1900*, 1972, 2nd edition Phaidon, Oxford, 1978

Geffroy, Gustave, *Claude Monet, sa vie, son temps, son œuvre*, Les éditions G. Crès et Cie, Paris, 1922

Greer, Germaine, *The Obstacle Race: the Fortunes of Women Painters and their Work* (1979), Picador, London, 1981

Groseclose, Barbara, *Nineteenth-Century American Art*, Oxford University Press, Oxford, 2000

Hamber, Anthony J., *A Higher Branch of Art: Photographing the Fine Arts in England, 1839-1880*, Gordon and Breach Publishers, Amsterdam, 1996

Hamerton, Philip Gilbert, *Thoughts about Art*, Macmillan, London, 1873

Harding, James, *Artistes Pompiers, French Academic Art in the 19th Century*, Academy Editions, London, 1979

Harrison, Charles and Paul Wood, with Jason Gaiger, *Primitivism, Cubism, Abstraction*, Yale University Press, New Haven and London, 1993

Harrison, Charles and Paul Wood, with Jason Gaiger, eds., *Art in Theory, 1815-1900: An Anthology of Changing Ideas*, Blackwell, Oxford, 1998

Harrison, Craig, *The Essence of Art: Victorian Advice on the Practice of Painting*, Ashgate Publishing, Aldershot, England and Brookfield, Vermont, USA, 1999

Hauser, Arnold, *The Social History of Art*, IV: Naturalism, Impressionism, the Film Age (1951), Routledge, London and New York, 1962

Herbert, Robert, *Jean-François Millet*, exhibition catalogue, London, Hayward Gallery/ Grand Palais, Paris, 1975-6

Holt, Elizabeth Gilmore, ed., *The Triumph of Art for the Public, the Emerging Role of Exhibitions and Critics*, Anchor, New York, 1979

Holt, Elizabeth Gilmore, ed., *From the Classicists to the Impressionists: Art and Architecture in the 19th Century*, Volume III of *A Documentary History of Art* (1966), Yale University Press, New Haven and London, 1986

Honour, Hugh and others, *The Age of Neo-Classicism*, exhibition catalogue, London, The Royal Academy/Victoria and Albert Museum, 1972

House, John and MaryAnne Stevens, eds., *Post-Impressionism: Cross-Currents in European Painting*, exhibition catalogue, London, Royal Academy of Arts, 1979-80

Howitt-Watts, Anna Mary, *An Art Student in Munich*, 2 vols (1853), Thos. De La Rue & Co, London, 1880

Hunt, William Morris, *On Painting and Drawing* (1896), Dover Publications, New York, 1976

Irwin, David, *Neoclassicism*, Phaidon, London, 1997

Johns, Elizabeth, *American Genre Painting: the Politics of Everyday Life*, Yale University Press, New Haven and London, 1991

Johnston, Sona K., and William R. Johnston, *Ingres to Matisse: the Triumph of French Painting*, Baltimore Museum of Art/Walters Art Gallery, Baltimore/Royal Academy, London, 2000

Jullian, Philippe, *The Symbolists*, Phaidon, London, 1973

Kendall, Richard ed., *Degas by Himself* (1987), Little Brown and Company, Great Britain, 1994

Klingender, Francis D., *Art and the Industrial Revolution* (1947), Paladin, St. Albans, 1972

Klumpke, Anna, *Rosa Bonheur, the Artist's (Auto)biography*, The University of Michigan Press, Ann Arbor, 1997

Kuspit, Donald, *The Cult of the Avant-garde Artist*, Cambridge University Press, Cambridge, 1993

Lacambre, Geneviève, ed., *Gustave Moreau, between Epic and Dream*, exhibition catalogue, Paris, Galeries Nationales du Grand Palais/Art Institute of Chicago, Chicago/Metropolitan Museum of Art, New York, 1998-9

Lemagny, Jean-Claude and André Rouillé, eds., *A History of Photography, Social and Cultural Perspectives*, Cambridge University Press, Cambridge, 1987

Lemaire, Gérard-Georges, *Esquisses en vue d'une histoire du Salon*, Henri Veyrier, Paris, 1986

Leslie, C.R., *Memoirs of the Life of John Constable* (1843, 2nd edition, 1845), Phaidon, London, 1995

Lethève, Jacques, *Daily Life of French Artists in the Nineteenth Century*, George Allen and Unwin, London, 1972

Lübbren, Nina, *Rural Artists' Colonies in Europe, 1870-1910*, Manchester University Press, Manchester, 2001

Lucie-Smith, Edward, *Fantin-Latour*, Phaidon, Oxford, 1977

Mackintosh, Alastair, *Symbolism and Art Nouveau*, Thames and Hudson, London, 1975

Mainardi, Patricia, *Art and Politics of the Second Empire: the Universal Expositions of 1855 and 1867*, Yale University Press, New Haven and London, 1987

Mainardi, Patricia, *The End of the Salon: Art and the State in the Early Third Republic*, Cambridge University Press, Cambridge, 1993

Mallarmé, Stéphane, *Écrits sur l'art*, présentation par Michel Draguet, Flammarion, Paris, 1998

Mathews, Nancy Mowll, ed., *Cassatt and her Circle*, Abbeville Press, New York, 1984

Matisse, Henri, *Écrits et propos sur l'art*, Hermann, Paris, 1972

Mauner, George, *Manet: the Still-Life Paintings*, exhibition catalogue, Paris, Musée d'Orsay/Walters Art Gallery, Baltimore, 2000-1

Meecham, Pam and Julie Sheldon, *Modern Art: a Critical Introduction*, Routledge, London and New York, 2000

Morisot, Berthe, *The Correspondence of Berthe Morisot*, ed. Denis Rouart, Camden Press, London, 1986

Nochlin, Linda, *Realism*, Penguin Books, Harmondsworth, 1971

Nochlin, Linda, *The Politics of Vision: Essays on Nineteenth-Century Art and Society*, Thames and Hudson, London, 1991

Norman, Geraldine, *Nineteenth-Century Painters and Painting: a Dictionary*, Thames and Hudson, London, 1977

Nunn, Pamela Gerrish, *Victorian Women Artists*, The Women's Press, London, 1987

Orr, Clarissa Campbell, ed., *Women in the Victorian Art World*, Manchester University Press, Manchester, 1995

Parker, Rozsika and Griselda Pollock, *Old Mistresses, Women, Art and Ideology*, Routledge & Kegan Paul, London, 1981

Payne, Christiana, *Toil and Plenty: Images of the Agricultural Landscape in England, 1780-90*, Yale University Press, New Haven and London, 1994

Payne, Christiana, *Rustic Simplicity, Scenes of Cottage Life in Nineteenth-Century British Art*, exhibition catalogue, Djanogly Art Gallery/University of Nottingham Arts Centre/Penlee House Gallery and Museum, Penzance, 1998-9

Pevsner, Nikolaus, *Academies of Art, Past and Present*, Cambridge University Press, Cambridge, 1940

Pickvance, Ronald, *English Influences on Vincent Van Gogh*, exhibition catalogue, Nottingham, University of Nottingham, 1974-5

Pissarro, Camille, *Camille Pissarro: Letters to his Son Lucien* (1943), ed. John Rewald, Da Capo Press, New York, 1995

Protter, Eric, ed., *Painters on Painting* (1971), Dover Publications, Mineola, New York, 1997

Renoir, Jean, *Renoir, my Father* (1958), The Reprint Society, London, 1964

Rewald, John, *The History of Impressionism* (1946), 4th revised edition, Secker & Warburg, London, 1973, paperback version, 1980

Rimbaud, Arthur, *Poésies complètes*, édition établie par Pascal Pia, Le Livre de Poche, Gallimard, Paris, 1960

Rosenblum, Robert and H.W. Janson, *Art of the Nineteenth Century*, Thames and Hudson, London, 1984

Rosenblum, Robert, MaryAnne Stevens and Ann Dumas, eds., *1900: Art at the Crossroads*, exhibition catalogue, London, Royal Academy of Arts/Solomon R. Guggenheim Museum, New York, 2000

Rubin, James H., *Courbet*, Phaidon Press, London, 1997

Ruskin, John, *The Seven Lamps of Architecture*, Ruskin reprints, George Allen, London, 1904

Ruskin, John, *The Works of John Ruskin*, 39 volumes, edited by E.T. Cook and Alexander Wedderburn, Library Edition, George Allen, London, 1903-12

Ruskin, John, *Sesame and Lilies: the two Paths and the King of the Golden River*, J.M. Dent & Sons, London & Toronto, E.P. Dutton, New York, 1907

Sauer, Marina, *L'entrée des femmes à l'École des Beaux-Arts, 1880 1923*, École nationale supérieure des Beaux-Arts, Paris, 1990

Scharf, Aaron, *Art and Photography* (1968), Penguin Books, Harmondsworth, 1974

Shennan, Margaret, *Berthe Morisot, the First Lady of Impressionism* (1996), Sutton Publishing Ltd, Stroud, 2000

Smith, Alison ed., *Exposed, the Victorian Nude*, exhibition catalogue, London, Tate Britain/Haus der Kunst, Munich/Brooklyn Museum of Art, New York/Kobe City Museum, Kobe/Geidai Museum, Tokyo, 2001-3

Smith, Lindsay, *Victorian Photography, Painting and Poetry, the Enigma of Visibility in Ruskin, Morris and the Pre-Raphaelites*, Cambridge University Press, Cambridge, 1995

Sterling, Charles, *Still Life Painting, from Antiquity to the Twentieth Century*, Harper & Row, New York, 2nd revised edition, 1981

Stevens, Mary-Anne, ed., *The Orientalists, Delacroix to Matisse: European Painters in North Africa and the Near East*, exhibition catalogue, London, Royal Academy of Arts, 1984

Taylor, Joshua C., *Nineteenth-Century Theories of Art* (1987), University of California Press, Berkeley, 1989

Theuriet, André and others, *Jules Bastien-Lepage and his Art: a Memoir*, T. Fisher, London, 1892

Thomson, Belinda, *Impressionism: Origins, Practice, Reception,* Thames and Hudson, London, 2000

Treuherz, Julian, *Hard Times: Social Realism in Victorian Art*, exhibition catalogue, Manchester, Manchester City Art Galleries/Rijksmuseum Vincent Van Gogh, Amsterdam/Yale Center for British Art, New Haven, 1987-8

Treuherz, Julian, *Victorian Painting*, Thames and Hudson, London, 1993

Van Gogh, Vincent, *The Letters of Van Gogh*, ed. Mark Roskill, Fontana/Collins, London, 1963

Van Gogh, Vincent, *The Letters of Vincent Van Gogh*, ed. Ronald de Leeuw, Penguin Books, London, 1997

Vaughan, William, *Romanticism and Art* (1978), Thames and Hudson, London, 1994

Waterfield, Giles ed., *Palaces of Art: Art Galleries in Britain, 1790-1990*, exhibition catalogue, London, Dulwich Picture Gallery/National Gallery of Scotland, Edinburgh, 1991-2

Whistler, James Abbott McNeill, *The Gentle Art of Making Enemies* (1892), Dover Publications, New York, 1967

White, Harrison C. and Cynthia A White, *Canvases and Careers: Institutional Change in the French Painting World* (1965), University of Chicago Press, Chicago, 1993

Wilde, Oscar, *Complete Works of Oscar Wilde* (1948), Collins, London and Glasgow, 1966

Wilhelm, Hugues, and others, *Berthe Morisot*, exhibition catalogue, Lille, Musée des Beaux-Arts/ Fondation Pierre Gianadda, Martigny, 2002

Yeldham, Charlotte, *Women Artists in Nineteenth-Century France and England*, 2 vols, Garland Publishing Inc., New York and London, 1984

Zola, Émile, *Émile Zola: Salons recueillis*, annotés et présentés par F.W.J. Hemmings et Robert J.Niess, Librairie E. Droz, Geneva and Paris, 1959

Index   Main keywords and their page numbers are in bold type.